# EVALUATION & DEVELOPMENT

**World Bank Series on Evaluation and Development**
**Robert Picciotto, Series Editor**

*Evaluation and Development: The Institutional Dimension,*
edited by Robert Picciotto and Eduardo Wiesner

# EVALUATION & DEVELOPMENT

## The Institutional Dimension

**EDITED BY**
*Robert Picciotto*
*Eduardo Wiesner*

with a foreword by
*James D. Wolfensohn*

Published for The World Bank

Transaction Publishers
New Brunswick (U.S.A.) and London (U.K.)

Library of Congress Catalog Number: 98-9641
ISBN: 1-56000-370-7 (cloth); 0-7658-0423-9 (paper)
Printed in the United States of America

Library of Congress Cataloging-in-Publication Data

Evaluation and development : the institutional dimension / edited by Robert Picciotto
 and Eduardo Wiesner, with a foreword by James D. Wolfensohn.
    p.  cm. — (World Bank series on evaluation and development)
   ISBN 1-56000-370-7 (cloth : alk. paper). — ISBN 0-7658-0423-9 (paper)
   1. Institutional economics. 2. Organization. 3. Economic development projects—
Developing countries—Evaluation. I. Picciotto, Robert. II. Wiesner Durán, Eduardo.
III. Series.
HB99.5.E93   1998
338.9—dc21                                                                                         98-9641
                                                                                                          CIP

# Contents

*In memory of*
*Mancur Olson, 1932–1998*

# Foreword

This volume could not be more timely. More than ever the role of institutions is central to development effectiveness. Efforts to reshape the development assistance business are also putting pressure on evaluators to upgrade their work on capacity building in poor countries. The papers included in this volume address both themes.

For the World Bank, a new approach to evaluation is urgent. On March 31, 1997, our Executive Directors endorsed a Strategic Compact designed to prepare the institution for the challenges of the 21st century and help poor countries adjust their policies and build their institutions to fight poverty.

The bottom line of the Compact is development effectiveness. How will we assess the results of our operations? In the private sector, performance is judged by one basic standard: profitability. The World Bank is, of course, market based and manages its finances on the basis of strict standards of prudence and transparency. But it was not set up for profit. As a result, it needs benchmarks that reflect its fundamental operational mandate—the promotion of equitable development in poor countries. This is where evaluation assumes its crucial role.

To achieve development effectiveness the World Bank faces two major challenges. First, as a fiduciary organization, we must do things right. Through knowledge management, best practice is becoming common practice. And real-time monitoring is reinforcing the results-orientation of Bank activities.

But even more important, as the leading global development agency, the World Bank must show the way by doing the right things: including the poor in the development process; helping to connect developing countries to the global marketplace; providing emergency assistance to reconstruct war-ravaged economies; reshaping our operations so that they contribute directly and visibly to social equity, rural development, and capacity building. Through institutional development, we are also providing leadership in the emerging global fight against the cancer of corruption.

Doing the right things also means taking a systemic approach to development. That means no longer simply financing a project here and a project there, but building country-level management coalitions and global alliances to address the major constraints that stand in the way of broad-based, people-friendly, and environmentally sound development.

Not all the changes that we will support will be successful. As a development agency, we cannot afford not to take risks. But we will manage risks responsibly and judiciously. What development effectiveness management is all about is striking the right balance between ambition and reality, between rewards and risks. And this is where the true potential of evaluation lies.

What then is the role of development evaluators on the eve of a new millennium?

First, they must move away from a near exclusive preoccupation with individual operations and concentrate instead on the impact of the full package of services provided by development assistance agencies. This will mean looking at systemwide impacts rather than simply aggregating the performance ratings of projects. The World Bank and its partners need to know the combined effect of their programs both at country level and at global level. This poses special methodological difficulties, but it is better to be approximately right than precisely wrong.

Second, evaluators will have to learn to work in real time. Without compromising their independence, evaluators have much to offer in translating their findings into operationally useful lessons delivered at the right time and in the right place. Modern technology has enormous potential in facilitating communications and learning and evaluators must be active participants in knowledge management for the benefit of the entire development community.

Third, evaluators must come to terms with the fact that development is not a solo performance. The business of development crucially depends on successful partnerships: partnerships with borrowers, partnerships with the private sector, partnerships with other development agencies. For evaluators too, partnership is a fundamental prerequisite of development effectiveness. This means that the very nature of the evaluation process will have to evolve toward a new understanding of "accountability" that gives greater emphasis to participatory learning processes and less emphasis to assigning blame.

James D. Wolfensohn

# Introduction

Since the 1980s a new development paradigm has emerged. It holds that institutions and economic organizations are the key determinants of economic, social, and political progress. Six Nobel[1] prizes have been awarded to scholars who have made pioneering contributions to "neoinstitutional economics." In parallel, development evaluators have established the crucial role of capacity building in ensuring the sustainability of development programs. Yet, the links between development practice and academics have been loose, and the evaluation profession has been slow in adapting its methods and processes to the new development consensus.

The papers included in this volume illustrate the classic Northian principle that "institutions matter." They explore not only *how* to get the institutions "right" but also how to assess the "fit" between institutions and development challenges through evaluative techniques. Inevitably, the complex web of causalities underlying the process of growth and change requires targeted exploration. The result is a mosaic of issues, ideas, and lessons of experience. The conference participants focused on the determinants (supply and demand) of institutions, the importance of incentives, and the evolving roles of governments, rules, and restraints.

## Neoinstitutional economics builds on the neoclassical model

A common thread runs through the volume: the recognition of the crucial role of institutions, organizations, and political economy restrictions is not tantamount to a rejection of the neoclassical model. Most authors perceive neoinstitutional economics as a broadening of the neoclassical model to deal with situational constraints. The recent ascendance of neoinstitutional economics is traced to its microanalytical orientation and its realistic appreciation of the role of transaction costs, economic incentives, and property rights frameworks.

Yet, the future of neoinstitutional economics is far from assured. Neoinstitutionalists need to test their theories against reality. The budding promise of neoinstitutional economics is that it may revive development economics in situations where the classical paradigms are less complete than in advanced economies and where the institutional constraints are more binding.

## The government as the critical encompassing institution

Several papers converged on the idea that of all institutions, the state is the most critical because of its comparative advantage to promote collective action at least cost to society. The government is seen as the most encompassing of all institutions. Effective governance represents the quintessential public good. If government fails to provide the institutional infrastructure (information, property rights, governance) within which competitive markets can thrive, it becomes extremely difficult to overcome development constraints.

Yet, a benevolent, neutral government is not readily constructed. Just because good government enhances a society's welfare does not mean that good government will materialize. The best insurance against government capture by vested interest is political competition. In turn, such competition implies contestability of ideas, access to information, and a capability to evaluate government actions. Governments can win or lose in this political competition by providing policies that protect competition in private markets while overcoming collective action dilemmas for public goods creation.

### Incentives as the template of theoretical institutionalism

What distinguishes neoinstitutional economics from previous "institutional" or "historical" schools is a resilient theory grounded on two foundations: (1) the recognition that variable admixtures of competition, cooperation, and hierarchy are needed to achieve positive societal outcomes in specific country circumstances, and (2) a belief that getting the incentives right is critical to overcome the restrictions that arise from the neoclassical model.

Indeed, if an algorithm[2] is ever to be found to make institutional causality less intractable, it will be in the area of incentives. Institutions matter because incentives trigger motivation and action in both the public and the private sectors. Incentives, therefore, are the first building block for policy design, implementation, and evaluation of results. Often, the capacity of incentives to improve behavior is questioned. Yet, the impact of negative incentives on organizational outcomes is readily acknowledged. The difficulty lies in aligning the incentives structure with the collective interest.

### The institutional dimension of evaluation

Evaluation itself is an institution. Its importance comes from its capacity to act as an incentive to change behavior. Evaluation rewards *ex post* results or the economizing of efforts to achieve a given result. In institutions where profits are not the bottom line, effective evaluation is crucial to ascertain what results are being achieved and why. Such is the case of the World Bank and most public sector institutions. When budgets are not financed directly by the market, evaluation becomes indispensable for ascertaining performance. Evaluation is an essential surrogate for incentives in public "markets."

### Restrictions as the focus of neoinstitutional economics

Much policy advice becomes esoteric when it focuses mainly on underlining the importance of getting the institutions "right." What matters in effective policymaking is not so much what the objectives are but what stands in the way of their achievement. The restrictions to achievement should be the focus of neoinstitutional analysis, not the desideratum of a given set of objectives. There is not much empty space within the social realm waiting to be filled by the right policy nostrum.

Inefficient economic institutions and dysfunctional collective rules are the norm, not the exception, particularly in developing countries. There is no natural process of evolutionary selection that results in efficient institutions weeding out the inefficient ones. For this reason, the strategy should combine the question of how to get the "right" institutions in with that of how to get the "wrong" institutions out. The normative policy approach should cease to be at the center of the reform process. Instead, a public choice and "contractarian" framework should be used to design feasible strategies for institutional adjustment.

### The research agenda for neoinstitutional economics

Another thread running through the deliberations of the conference is the urgent need to direct empirical research toward specific institutional and organizational factors. Most participants agreed that if the potential of neoinstitutional economics is to be realized, it must concentrate on the problems of collective action and human behavior. The challenge is to focus on microanalytical issues such as transaction costs, property rights, incentives, public sector rent-seeking, informational constraints, and the interplay of governments and markets.

Empirical research in neoinstitutional economics can hardly be separated from evaluation studies. In fact, evaluation is at the heart of almost any research endeavor. Most attempts at understanding economic, social, and political processes involve the evaluation of institutions, initial conditions, causalities, results, and impacts. To improve the yield of research, better evaluation instruments have to be built into policies, projects, and programs. In brief, evaluation has to become more sensitive to institutions.

However, since evaluation itself is an institutional factor, it must also be evaluated and examined. This evaluation of evaluation will most likely be conducted through its capacity to act as an effective incentive to change behaviors and policy outcomes. If evaluation cannot change traditional policy designs and resource allocations, the fault may lie with the design of evaluation strategies.

Empirical research would be most effective if pursued with the following three guiding principles. First, research must be interdisciplinary. Second, it should focus on methodological rigor in order to shed light on causalities and to gradually build a theory with stronger predictive capabilities. Third, the strategy ought to include the relationship between the demand for institutional change and the supply of institutional arrangements.

### Policy implications for evaluation

Private markets tend to be more efficient than public sector ones because evaluation is built into the market system. In business, market failure is quickly identified, evaluated, and resolved. By contrast, government failure is less visible and more difficult to evaluate. Hence, there is a need for formal evaluation processes capable of rectifying public failures.

Within this context, one of the most important policy implications for evaluation is that its effectiveness is determined largely by how quickly and accurately it can link policy, project, and program outcomes to specific public sector characteristics. In fact, evaluation effectiveness can be judged in terms of its efficiency in identifying public sector institutional obstacles and in contributing to the productive mediation between the demand for and supply of the "right" institutional arrangements.

It follows that in order to raise the impact of evaluation, three principles should be followed. First, evaluation should be independent. Second, it should concentrate on strategic areas. And third, it should be connected to institutional learning mechanisms. Thus, the design of evaluation systems is itself a worthy area for neoinstitutional analysis.

Eduardo Wiesner

### Notes

1.   H. Simon, J. Buchanan, R. Coase, R. W. Fogel, D. North, and G. Becker.
2.   Deborah Mayo suggests that in the social sciences, when "an algorithm is unavailable, the matter becomes one of sociology." See Mayo, Deborah G. 1996. *Error and the Growth of Experimental Knowledge.* Chicago: The University of Chicago Press, 60.

# PART 1
## THE ROLE OF INSTITUTIONS
## IN DEVELOPMENT

# 1. Institutions in development: the country, research, and operational challenges

Gautam S. Kaji

*World Bank managing director Gautam Kaji notes that the building of social infrastructure has increasingly eclipsed the building of physical infrastructure and investments in human capital as the central challenge of development. This has thrust institutions and social capital to the fore of the development paradigm, posing new challenges for research and evaluation.*

## Introduction

As development professionals, what do we know and what do we need to know about institutions to do good operational work? My remarks are structured around three themes: country challenges, research challenges, and operational challenges. I will argue that:

- Institutional capital has always been critical to development, and its importance is being increasingly recognized as countries with it have progressed while those without it have stagnated or regressed.

- We do not know how to build institutional capital; nailing down what works and what does not is a major challenge for research.

- Pending better guidance from research, we need to be humble, practical, and yet bold in building capacity in developing countries.

## Country challenges

Fifty years ago, when the Bank was in its infancy, the challenges our clients faced were very different from those our clients face today. Reconstruction in post-World War II Europe was the primary concern. The key challenge was getting sufficient financial and physical capital into European countries. Many of them soon graduated from the Bank: France in 1947, Luxembourg in 1948, the Netherlands in 1957, Belgium in 1958, and so on. Still, infrastructure remains an important sector for the Bank, both operationally and analytically. It continues to constitute one-quarter of our portfolio; it was the subject of a recent World Development Report.

We have learned much about development from early and recent graduates, such as Singapore (1975) and Korea (1995). But we have learned even more from the countries that have *not* graduated. It was from them we learned that—important though bricks and mortar are—development requires much more than physical infrastructure. Looking at these countries taught us that *people* are the key to development.

Reflecting this essential lesson, human resource development has grown from a fringe World Bank activity to one of the largest sectors of lending and policy advice. Human capital is still a major challenge for many of our clients. To a large extent the development community has learned how to build human capital. Many of our clients are doing well on securing the skills needed for economic development. One needs look no further than this week's *Economist* (March 30–April 5) for evidence—nine borrowers and recent graduates did better than the United States on math scores.

These achievements notwithstanding, much remains to be done to accumulate physical and human capital in the developing world. Nevertheless, the development frontier lies elsewhere, in the sphere of social capital—political economy, institutional development, and cultural factors.

The building of "social infrastructure" has increasingly eclipsed the building of physical infrastructure and investments in human capital as *the* central challenge of development. This has thrust institutions and social capital to the fore of the development paradigm. Which brings me to my second theme—the challenge for research.

### Research challenges

As we have gained experience with the financing of projects aimed at enhancing the physical and human infrastructure of our developing member countries, we have come to recognize the importance of social capital—and how little we know about it. Hence, collectively taking stock of what we know in order to set the research agenda is a worthwhile exercise. There's a lot we urgently need to know in this area to be able to help our clients. Let me illustrate this with two examples.

First, consider capacity building in Africa. This is all about building social capital for solving development problems. The need is clearly there. Africa's economic and social program in the 21st century will depend on it. We all agree on this. But how to go about it? Can we build institutions without trained people? Can we train people without institutions? Where should we start? How should we sequence? How can external sources of financing and advice help?

Next, consider corruption. It is costly, but clearly someone benefits or it would not occur with such frequency. A critical question in gauging whether it is amenable to a sustainable solution is whether the gainers (from ending the corruption) can compensate the losers (either the beneficiaries of the corruption that would need to stop voluntarily, or those footing the bill for enforcing the law).

Both examples are amenable to microeconomic analysis using fairly standard tools. Given their dynamic properties, the solution in both cases would need to involve getting incentives right to induce behavior to move in the needed direction. They both have an inherent chicken-and-egg quality to them—a "vicious circle" aspect.

From an operational perspective, the critical research question is how to reverse the vicious circle so that it becomes a virtuous one.

This is the challenge for research:

■ Continue working to understand the dynamic processes that underlie these vicious circles without losing sight of the objective of coming up with ways to reverse them.

■ Evaluate situations in which things have gone from being wrong to being right, and document how it happened. We need the examples, the models, the best-practice cases. Our clients need to see how it can go right. All too often, they know from personal observation how it can go wrong.

### Operational challenges

What can development practitioners do in the meantime—pending best-practice advice from research and evaluation? I believe we need to be bolder than we have been in considering solutions to institutional problems. But we also need to subject our proposed solutions to bread-and-butter evaluation methods to assess the solutions' success and sustainability. And we need to work with researchers to design institutional development operations in such a way that we will also learn from them. What does this entail?

■ Careful analysis of the ultimate financial, economic, and social sustainability of an institutional development proposal. After the dust settles, who will be the gainers? Who will be the losers? Will the gainers be able to compensate the losers? Will the gainers be able to sustain the political dynamics of institutional change? Will the gainers be taxed to compensate the losers?

■ Assuming the proposal is sustainable once equilibrium is reached, can we get there from here? Is the path to equilibrium feasible? Are the risks manageable? Is there a credible value-adding role for external support? Have we subjected the proposal to an on-the-ground "road test" that has authenticated the analysis?

■ Assuming a proposal passes this stringent set of tests, it should be supported. But let's face it; this is a long way from the past donor practice of throwing money at institutional development problems in the name of technical assistance.

### Conclusion

In closing, let me affirm my belief in the central assumption that institutions matter. They matter because they affect incentives and behavior. So the key issue in evaluating institutional impacts and sustainability is to analyze the incentives they entail and engender. This is not rocket science. What is rocket science is the actual design of institutional innovations that embody incentives for behavior that does the job and sustains the innovation. It is for this that we seek the inputs of the research and evaluation community. And given our collective belief that institutions matter, let us not lose sight of why they matter. Not for the continued health of development economics—a trivial pursuit—but rather for the improved circumstances of billions of people living in developing countries—a truly noble task.

# 2. Institutions, markets, and development outcomes

Jeffrey Nugent

*The author takes stock of advances in institutional economics and its relationship to development and identifies methodological difficulties that have to be overcome if new institutional economics is to have a lasting effect on the economics of development.*

Only a little over a decade ago, Nobel prize winner Sir Arthur Lewis complained of his beloved field of specialization: "Development economics will surely die if the [Ph.D.] students come to think, rightly or wrongly, that work on institutions will not count for distinction in Ph.D. exams" (Lewis 1984, 8).

Due to the rapid development of the new institutional economics and the applications to development since 1984, it can no longer be said that development economics is dying, at least not for Sir Arthur's reason. Indeed, almost every year many new converts are added to those who believe that institutions matter to economic performance.

Nevertheless, the distance between where we are now and what would be needed to make valid and reliable policy recommendations in this area is very substantial indeed. To sustain the new interest, we must generate quantitative knowledge about which institutions matter and how changes can be monitored and evaluated. If our experience with research into technological progress is any guide, we could make significant progress in the analysis of institutional change over the next 10–15 years.

The purpose of this paper is threefold:

- To take stock of what we have learned about institutional economics and its relationship to development

- To identify significant methodological difficulties that may hinder empirical study of the determinants and effects of institutional change

- To identify critical missing links in present knowledge and to design a road map for research and evaluation

## The emergence of institutions in development economics

### *Some evidence from the literature*

Using the "rules of the game" definition of institutions, I performed a simple content analysis with three different samples. They include books, journal articles, and chapters in the *Handbook of Development Economics* (HDE) (Behrman and Srinivasan 1995). Each sample supports the hypothesis of a growing recognition of the importance of institutions. I found few books on institutions and development in the decade of the 1970s[1], but a proliferation of such books since 1980. Another indication of this trend comes from comparing the percentage of articles on institutions carried by the *Journal of Development Economics* in the 1970s, 1980s, and 1990s (table 2.1). The chapter content in the four volumes of the HDE is also revealing (table 2.1). In the first two volumes, which came out in 1988, an average of 7.5 percent (12.4 percent and 2.7 percent) of the articles are on institutions, largely accounted for by contributions from Joe Stiglitz, while in volumes 3a and 3b, which came out in 1995, 36 percent of the articles are on institutions.

The dearth of attention to institutional issues in the 1988 volumes of HDE was rather sharply noted in Albert Fishlow's (1991) thoughtful and otherwise very positive review of volumes 1 and 2 for the *Journal of Economic Literature*. Special mention was made by Fishlow on the lack of attention to rent seeking. He also criticized even-handedly contributors from the noninterventionist and interventionist perspectives for not distinguishing between the failure of properly implemented initiatives and the merely inadequate implementation of the interventions. Finally, he criticized them for making unsupported assumptions about institutions and institutional capacity. On these grounds at least, Fishlow should feel much more comfortable with volume 3.

An even more striking indicator of growing attention by economists to institutional issues is the four Nobel prizes that have been awarded to economists for their contributions to institutional issues, one in the 1980s (Buchanan) and three in the 1990s (Coase, Fogel, and North).

TABLE 2.1: INDICATORS OF INSTITUTIONAL CONTENT IN DEVELOPMENT ECONOMICS

| Text | Volume | Period surveyed | Percentage institutional content |
|---|---|---|---|
| *Journal of Development Economics* | | 1970s | 15 |
| | | 1980–present | 27 |
| *Handbook of Development Economics* | 1 | Pre-1985 | 12.40 |
| | 2 | Pre-1985 | 2.68 |
| | 3 | Pre-1995 | 36.01 |

*Source:* Author's compilation.

## *Why interest is rising*

What accounts for the rising interest in institutions? First, a new understanding, through economics and other social sciences, of both the determinants and effects of institutions; second, the realization that development experience and its distinctive and often exotic institutions make it a fertile area for the new institutional economics; third, the crises faced by traditional development economics throughout the 1980s; and fourth, accumulating evidence that institutions matter to economic and social development.

The work of practitioners and economic historians has also provided important sources of knowledge. Historians can offer long-term investigations into the interrelationships between institutions and development.[2] Practitioners have contributed to a growing literature on the effects of specific institutions such as property rights, civil and economic liberties, good governance, and central banks.[3]

If the new institutional economics is to have a more lasting effect on the economics of development than the old institutional economics, systematic empirical analyses will have to be performed. For these to be successful, however, the difficult methodological problems identified in the following section will have to be overcome.

## Methodological problems in empirical analysis and evaluation

Empirical work testing institutional hypotheses has frequently been too weak or ambiguous to narrow the range of alternative explanations. Moreover, since rather exotic institutions in unusual environments often receive the most attention, such knowledge is not easily generalizable. Yet there remains a noticeable failure to integrate the analysis of the determinants of institutions with that of their effects. This failure poses methodological problems. In the discussion that follows, I have identified seven, with a focus on evaluating the effects of institutional innovation on development. There are others besides these.

### *Defining institutions*

Given the existence of so many different institution-like phenomena, it is not surprising that analysts often define institutions in different ways.

A "rules of the game" type of definition, sufficiently broad yet potentially operational, is the one we adopt: *An institution is a set of constraints that governs the behavioral relations among individuals or groups.* By this definition, most organizations are institutions because they provide rules governing the relationships both among members and between members and nonmembers. It is also useful to distinguish between an individual institution (institutional arrangement) and the set of other institutions in which the institutional arrangement is embedded (institutional structure).[4]

Although the definition may be narrowed to make the concept more operational,[5] doing so may rule out interesting and important issues and involve tedious distinctions.[6] Narrow definitions may also exclude institutions that allow productive factors and technology to be used and interact more effectively.

*Identifying the determinants of institutions*

Many difficulties arise in identifying the determinants of institutions. They include the multidimensional nature of a definition based on rules of the game; different theoretical perspectives on how institutions are determined; the differences in scale or level (macro or micro) of different institutions; the variations in sources of influence on institutions, some rising from the bottom and others coming down from the top; and the infrequency of institutional change, which make it difficult to observe the process and collect relevant data. The determinants of many existing institutions may have occurred so long ago that relevant data are difficult or impossible to obtain and relevant questions cannot be defined.[7]

*Identifying the effects of institutions*

The same factors that act as determinants of institutions can also blur institutional effects, particularly since so many different kinds of effects (for example, efficiency and distributional) are relevant to development performance.

The selection bias problem and the nonexogeneity of institutional change are other serious problems. The results of a natural experiment approach that compares the effects of institutional change in one place with the situation in an area where the change did not occur cannot necessarily be taken as conclusive evidence of the value of the change. An area of a country where institutional change was successful may have been chosen because the reform could be expected to work better there than elsewhere, thereby biasing the conclusion.

*Interdependencies and simultaneity problems*

Still another methodological difficulty arises when different institutions are functionally interdependent, making it difficult to separate determinants from effects and identify the direction of causality. To overcome such problems may require not only a complex simultaneous equation framework but also that appropriate identification restrictions be satisfied in order to distinguish between effects going in opposite directions.

*Dynamics and causality*

A way out of the simultaneity problem and uncertain direction of causality may be to introduce time lags and test for directions of causality. Yet doing so raises the issues of dynamics and how to specify changes, especially given the nonincremental and noncontinuous character of institutional change. Considering the slow pace and infrequency of institutional change, the introduction of time lags compounds the difficulty of satisfying the data requirements.

*Complexity of the growth process*

The link between institutions and development is not necessarily a simple and direct one. Even with respect to narrowly defined growth, the potential links between institutions and growth are numerous. The literature to date has focused rather exclusively on property rights and hence the link to capital formation. But equally, if not more important, are the links between institutions and growth that can arise through human capital (Campos and Nugent 1997).

Furthermore, development is broader and more multifaceted than mere economic growth and necessarily includes distribution, equity, and considerations of basic needs. However, as North (1995, 20) points out, "it is the polity that defines and enforces property rights." Therefore, political economy considerations should be allowed to play a role in explaining both the determinants and effects of macrolevel institutions[8] (Lin and Nugent 1995).

### *Heterogeneity of theoretical tools*

All the above factors mean that quite different theories and models are relevant to institutional analysis and may be needed at the same time. These very different models are far from synergistic and thus often have to be used together. A common framework may therefore become impractical for analysis, making an interdisciplinary approach necessary.[9]

### The basis for hope: simple ingredients of the analysis of institutions and institutional change

Although methodological difficulties are daunting, the analyst is by no means powerless to overcome them. Two basic strategies are suggested. The first involves simplifying the analysis as much as possible and taking advantage of complementary theoretical approaches. The second requires organizing a systematic research program around common themes.

The complexity of the issues can be reduced by using analytical tools available for tackling two basic and easily understood issues: transaction costs and collective action. The former relates to the demand side of institutions and the latter to the supply side. The explanation for the emergence of any institutional arrangement is likely to have both a demand side and a supply side, just as in the familiar analysis of the supply and demand for a commodity or factor.

The supply of an institutional arrangement is often provided by an individual or group at a higher level in the institutional structure—for example, at the community, state, or international agency level. The mechanisms through which the agent can increase the supply of the institution might include providing access to the knowledge of the institution, case studies of the international or historical experience with it, technical assistance or advice on how to design or implement it, and subsidizing the costs of its introduction, including the costs of compensating those deemed to lose from the change. There is also a demand side for the institutional arrangement, typically from the members of a particular group who demand a change in rules for the benefits that members expect to derive from such a change (that is, for distributional as well as efficiency reasons).

### *The demand for institutional change*

Institutions provide valuable services but are costly to establish and operate. The costs, broadly defined as transaction costs, include those of organizing, maintaining, and enforcing the rules of an institutional arrangement. Economic rationality predicts that, *ceteris paribus*, a more efficient institution should be preferred over less efficient alternatives, though this need not be the case.

Transaction costs of a new institutional arrangement include the direct costs of providing information about rules, benefits, and costs; the costs of negotiating agreements among the affected parties; and the costs of communicating its provisions to all relevant agents. As important, transaction costs include the indirect costs of opportunistic behavior, which include monitoring and enforcing the terms of agreements and output lost to contractual default. In transaction cost analysis, generally only the total of component costs is relevant to a particular institutional arrangement. Therefore, the analysis can be in terms of aggregate transaction costs.

Changes in institutional arrangements that occur relatively smoothly as a result of transaction cost savings are identified as induced institutional changes, just like induced technological change (Hayami and Ruttan 1985). Prominent among the conditions giving rise to induced institutional change are increases in the price of a particular factor of production. Prominent among the effects of such conditions is the creation or strengthening of property rights in ownership of that factor.[10]

A sufficiently strong demand for institutional change by those positively affected by it may be sufficient to bring about change. This is especially likely at lower levels—for example, between an individual farmer and an employee—or with larger numbers of relatively homogeneous individuals or groups who are potential winners. Where the institutional arrangement is either not well known or not well understood, or where large numbers and different kinds of interests are involved, the supply side of institutional change is more important.

### The supply of institutional change

For a given institutional change, there may be losses or at least uncertainties for some of those affected, so that opposition may emerge. In such cases, the relative propensities of the winners and losers to engage in successful collective action become relevant. If losers are likely to be more successful than gainers, change is unlikely to occur. Even without effective opposition, successful collective action may not occur and institutional change may be aborted because of its transaction costs. Groups weak in the propensity for effective collective action may therefore fail to implement desirable institutional changes, even if they represent a majority.

Determinants of collective action are political entrepreneurship that can help weak groups overcome their unfavorable group characteristics, the actions or threatened actions of other groups, the relative prospects for "exit" and "voice" by group members, organizational ability, leadership, and the use of selective incentives. What makes these principles relevant and potentially important is that most of them are amenable to practical application.

Given the importance of organizations in general and of the state in particular (because of its coercive powers in reducing the cost of collective action), the ability of directly affected groups to gain access to the state is also relevant. Yet the same principles of collective action are generally believed relevant in determining such access. Only an entirely autonomous state is immune from such pressure.

Since the structure of organizations and the rules by which they function (governance structures) may well be determined by transaction costs, indirectly the transaction cost advantages of certain governance procedures can be decisive for institutional change. Hence, the state is an especially influential organization as far as institutional change is concerned. One way the state influences change is by prohibiting or encouraging a given group's practice of selective incentives. Other means at the state's disposal are changing the level, breadth of distribution, and composition of the benefits it provides free to the public; and regulating the rules that the group can use in making its decisions and in monitoring or enforcing collective adherence to them.

If the state is not a hostage to narrow special interests advocating the "wrong institutions," it will have a natural interest in demonstrating its responsiveness to the desires of its constituents. Hence the barriers to indirect collective action by way of the state may well be considerably weaker than those to direct collective action without the involvement of the state. Another important advantage of collective action by way of the state is the stamp of legitimacy that state acceptance or tacit authorization can give to such action for states whose legitimacy is generally accepted (Baumol 1952). Yet, if the state is a hostage to narrow interest groups favoring institutions unfavorable to the welfare of society as a whole, institutional change will prove that much more difficult to achieve. Solutions, if any, will have to be sought step by step and often only quite indirectly.

### The road ahead: some questions for the research agenda

The difficulties noted will have to be overcome if institutional analysis is to become an effective component of development economics and a reliable and flexible tool for evaluating policy.

As mentioned, there are numerous parallels between the analysis of technological and institutional change. In both cases, measurement is difficult yet fundamental to success; the patterns of change may be abrupt, discontinuous, and uneven; determinants and effects must both be analyzed; and the effects on the different factors of production may well be nonneutral.

In both technological and institutional change, externalities may be very important, suggesting a possible justification for policy interventions. We now know a great deal about these issues in the case of technological change but are only beginning to scratch the surface in the case of institutional change. While the road ahead is long, the payoff in terms of human welfare is likely to be substantial.

Figure 2.1 provides a crude skeletal framework for viewing the relationships between institutions and development and therefore for identifying the many different points at which external intervention might be useful in changing institutional direction. The top of the diagram is the institutional structure, showing different institutional arrangements. Immediately below are the economic, political, and social spheres of the country, which interact with each other, feed up into the institutional realm, and help determine its structure. Below comes development performance, whose effect on the political, economic, and social spheres will vary. Note that through the policies that affect all three spheres, economic development perfor-

FIGURE 2.1: THE ROLE OF INSTITUTIONS IN POLITICAL ECONOMY AND DEVELOPMENT
PERFORMANCE — INSTITUTIONAL STRUCTURE

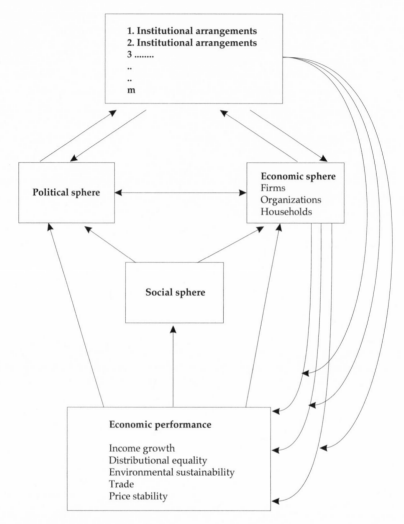

*Source:* Author's compilation.

mance is being affected, largely indirectly, by influences coming down from institutions. Note also that the links between the economic sphere and economic development performance are multidimensional.

The following questions identify, more or less in logical order, key tasks that must form part of the research agenda for the next 10–15 years.

*Which institutions matter for development and why?*

Answers to this question must be sought at different levels. Because of the slow pace of institutional change, we need to look at history as one of the sources of answers.

But we need to look beyond what we have inherited from existing economic historians to seek new links that may have been overlooked in the literature to date. And then the "why" question is crucial if we are to get inside the so-called black box of institutions to identify items that may have changed over time. Policies are likely to be more effective when they target items and issues that are known to be changeable.

*Can the institutions that matter be changed? If so, how?*

Given the importance that has been attached to path dependence in the literature on institutions and development to date, researchers and policymakers may be inclined to be pessimistic about the prospects for change.[11] Development practitioners may also have had reason to be pessimistic because social norms and other informal institutions may be especially resistant to change.

But this pessimism may be exaggerated. First, some rules of a particular game (institution) are likely to be more changeable than others. Even change in a single rule (out of many) can trigger a significant institutional change and bring about fundamental changes in performance. Second, once change comes, it may become cumulative and occur swiftly, frequently surprising even those who expected it—or worked toward it. Kuran (1995) describes many interesting and important examples, ranging from the French Revolution to the Iranian Revolution of the late 1970s to the crumbling of the Iron Curtain in the late 1980s. This work also identifies some useful conceptual tools for explaining such "surprises." Third, since the perspective is long term, even institutional changes that are very slow can still be relevant and important. Fourth, the interdependencies among different individual institutional arrangements imply that an institutional arrangement that may not be susceptible to change directly may be subject to indirect change. Fifth, since there are two different margins to work with—the demand for institutional change and the supply of institutional change—what might not be accomplished on one margin might well be accomplished on the other margin. Finally, there remains ample room for leadership, good intuition about the use of selective incentives, and political entrepreneurship for overcoming many of the barriers to institutional change.

*How can institutional change or development be measured?*

The development of appropriate ways of measuring the important variables is crucial. I will just say the measures we have are seldom optimal. However, since none of the individual measures available is likely to be sufficiently comprehensive, it is often desirable to combine them into an aggregate measure. Yet considerable care needs to be given to how it is done. By varying the weights and choice of indicators slightly, numerous different hypotheses can be generated and tested at a very low marginal cost. Once again, Campos and Nugent (1997) provide a demonstration of how this might be done.

*How and how much do environmental conditions affect institutions and their effectiveness?*

Over the long run, there may be few constants or purely exogenous forces in the system, and sources will differ. One such source may be international conditions; others may be climate or endowments of natural resources.

For example, some years ago Binswanger and Rosenzweig (1984) and others (Binswanger, McIntire, and Udry 1989) provided fairly convincing explanations and evidence showing why agrarian institutions, at least, might be expected to vary in fundamental ways with differences in environmental, especially climatic, conditions. Recently, various authors have argued that differences in environmental conditions may be sufficiently important to explain the difference in performance among East Asia and other regions. Yet existing "tests" for hypotheses such as these consist of two or three observations. Clearly, larger data sets will be necessary to provide convincing test outcomes of such hypotheses, especially considering the methodological problems raised in this paper.[12]

### How can the direction of causality be established?

Because the determinants and effects of institutions have seldom been studied simultaneously, the direction of the causality issue has not been squarely confronted. Moreover, since most of the studies are of the international cross-section variety, causality could not have been established even if the authors of the various studies had wanted to establish it. To identify the direction of causation, therefore, will require the use of panel data. It will also require the estimation of models with lags on one side (for example, that institutional change in period $t$ is affected by performance in period $t-1$), and then again with the lags on the other side (for example, when performance in period $t$ is affected by institutional change in period $t-1$).[13] Yet the vast majority of even the best-designed micro data sets for getting at various kinds of institutional issues are one-shot affairs, done for a specific purpose and study and then abandoned. Updating such studies and maintaining the panel can be costly. Hence appropriate judgments will have to be made on the relative benefits of, on the one hand, fewer studies with panels and, on the other, larger numbers of simple cross-sections.

### How and when should the international community intervene in institutional change?

Since some institutions are important for performance, a case can easily be made for international intervention. So how, where, and when should it occur?

The discussion in earlier sections has indicated that principles of collective action could be used to identify optimum conditions for some form of intervention. For example, suppose there are ten different types of policy reform that would generate the same level of social benefits (that is, the social cost of maintaining the status quo is the same in each case). Assume also that the benefits to the group of losers would vary by the type of reform, so that the position and possibly also the slope of the pressure against reform would vary from one such reform to another. Assume also that in each case there are some transaction costs of change that have to be supported for the reform to be carried out. Among the ten cases, the one in which the pressure for reform outweighs the pressure against reform at the lowest transaction costs would seem a reasonable candidate for the start of the reforms and the focusing of external support and research energy.[14] Certainly, such considerations should not be the only ones taken into account. For example, given the interdependencies among institutions, and following the dynamic externalities logic of Hirschman (1958), the pressures exerted by one reform on the likelihood of others should also be considered. Such dynamic considerations are crucial to the success or failure of institutional reforms.

## Conclusion

The methodological problems identified in this paper are many and difficult, and there is a relative dearth of solid and generalizable knowledge on the links between micro and macro institutions, on the one hand, and between institutions and development, on the other. Each of these problems complicates the job of evaluation. Yet in view of the strategies identified above that deal with these problems, they are not insurmountable. The most fundamental problem is how to conduct a genuine counterfactual analysis—that is, to simulate the time trajectory of all relevant performance indicators with and without the institutional change or intervention under consideration. Also difficult is how to do it in a timely manner. [15]

Obtaining the answers to such questions will take time. But if we could reconvene ten years from now, we could find ourselves already well down the road laid out above if we join forces now in a systematic effort, engage in true interdisciplinary research, and are candid about its limitations.

## Notes

1.  I know of no books that are general treatments of the subject, but more specialized ones include Buchanan 1975; Hirschman 1970; Libecap 1978; Lipton 1977; Olson 1965; and Williamson 1975.
2.  See, for example, Barzel 1989; Easterlin 1996; North 1986, 1990; Putnam 1993; Reynolds 1983; and the review of many other earlier contributions by Eggertsson 1990 and Alston, Eggertsson, and North 1996.
3.  Only a few of these studies (and very recent ones at that) are on the macro level (for example, Sachs and Warner 1996; Easterly and Levine 1996). Among some of the important contributions of this sort at the sectoral, micro, or project level have been Klitgaard 1991, 1995; Morawetz 1981; Picciotto 1995; and Wiesner D. 1993.
4.  For a more complete discussion of these issues, see Lin and Nugent 1995.
5.  North (1990) defines institutions as society's rules of the game, which cannot be seen, felt, or even measured, and organizations as the players, that is, "groups of individuals bound by a common purpose to achieve objectives" (North 1995, 23).
6.  Harris, Hunter, and Lewis (1995) argue that the interaction between institutions and organizations is what makes the neoinstitutional economics approach of special relevance to the study of long-run development in developing countries. Also, in the light of the important time delays and rent-seeking behavior that arise from conflict-prone reforms, organizations that serve to reduce these conflicts may well be a crucial ingredient in institutional change and development.
7.  Some examples include the origin of the caste system in India and of the *qanat* in Oman.
8.  As Bates (1995, 44) suggests: "Taking political factors into account thus provides an explanation for the direction and magnitude of the departures from the status quo that economic institutions make possible and yields insights into the source of variability in their performance. The new institutionalism originates in economics. To fulfill its agenda, however, it must move into the study of politics. It needs to take into account the allocation of power in society and the impact of the political system on the structure and performance of economic institutions."
9.  One visible indicator of the strength of this problem is that the three books that perhaps come closest to carrying out such a program—namely, Nabli and Nugent 1989; Harris, Hunter, and Lewis 1995; and Alston, Eggertsson, and North 1996—are essentially books of relatively loosely connected case studies. Each case illustrates the use of a different theoretical tool and empirical approach but never integrates them within a single case.

10. See, for example, Feeny 1989 and Libecap 1979, 1989.

11. As a result of all the constraints including those attributable to path dependence, Eggertsson (1996) characterizes the institutional approach to policy determinism as implying that the scope for policy reform is far more constrained than in any of the alternative approaches.

12. Other factors frequently brought in as environmental conditions in explaining economic development performance are various indicators of social and political instability (SPI). Nevertheless, as the rapidly growing literature on the subject illustrates, the SPI can also be traced back to income inequality (an important dimension of economic development performance) and numerous institutional and structural aspects of the political, social, and economic spheres. A useful avenue for research would be the relationship between the SPI and the evolution of development-enhancing institutions.

13. A striking example of this analytic schizophrenia is the fact that two literatures exist side by side, one on economic development performance, in which the SPI is an explanatory variable, and the other on the SPI in which income inequality and various other measures of economic growth performance are treated as the explanatory variables.

14. Instead of ten different industries, the ten alternatives could be different countries. This would allow the country with the best prospects for reform to be selected.

15. An implication of this is that the data for such an evaluation must be generated automatically as part of the program.

## References

Adelman, I. 1995a. *Africa's Management in the 1990s and Beyond: Reconciling Indigenous and Transplanted Institutions.* Washington, D.C.: World Bank.

———. 1995b. *Institutions and Development: The Selected Essays of Irma Adelman*, Vol. 1. Brookfield, Vt.: Ashgate.

Akerlof, G. 1980. "A Theory of Social Custom, of which Unemployment May be One Consequence." *Quarterly Journal of Economics* 94:749–75.

——— and W. Dickens. 1982. "Economic Consequences of Cognitive Dissonance." *American Economics Review* 72(3):307–19.

Alston, L. J., T. Eggertsson, and D. C. North, eds. 1996. *Empirical Studies in Institutional Change.* Cambridge: Cambridge University Press.

Arthur, W. 1994. *Increasing Returns and Path Dependence in the Economy.* Ann Arbor: University of Michigan Press.

Baland, J., and J. Platteau, eds. 1995. *Halting Degradation of Natural Resources: Is There a Role for Rural Communities?* Belgium: Facultés Universitaires Notre-Dame de la Paix.

Bardhan, P. 1989. *Conversations Between Economists and Anthropologists: Methodological Issues in Measuring Economic Change in Rural India.* Oxford: Oxford University Press.

———, ed. 1988. "Alternative Approaches to Development Economics: An Evaluation." *Handbook of Development Economics.* Amsterdam: North Holland.

———. 1989. *The Economic Theory of Agrarian Institutions.* Oxford: Oxford University Press.

Barzel, Y. 1989. *Economic Analysis of Property Rights.* Cambridge: Cambridge University Press.

Bates, R. M. 1981. *Markets and States in Tropical Africa: The Political Basis of Agricultural Policies.* Berkeley: University of California Press.

———. 1989. *Beyond the Miracle of the Market: The Political Economy of Agrarian Development in Kenya.* Cambridge: Cambridge University Press.

———. 1995. "Social Dilemmas and Rational Individuals: An Assessment of the New Institutionalism." In J. Harris, J. Hunter, and C. Lewis, eds., *The New Institutional Economics and Third World Development.* London: Routledge.

Baumol, W. 1952. *Welfare Economics and the Theory of the State.* Cambridge, Mass.: Harvard University Press.

Becker, G. 1995. *Accounting for Tastes.* Cambridge, Mass.: Harvard University Press.

Behrman, J., and T. N. Srinivasan, eds. 1995. *Handbook of Development Economics*, Vols. 3a and 3b. Amsterdam: North Holland.

Bernheim, B. D. 1994. "A Theory of Conformity." *Journal of Political Economy* 102:841–77.

Binswanger, H., and M. Rosenzweig, eds. 1984. *Contractual Arrangements, Employment, and Wages in Rural Labor Markets in Asia.* New Haven: Yale University Press.

Binswanger, H., J. McIntire, and C. Udry. 1989. "Production Relations in Semi-Arid African Agriculture." In P. Bardhan, ed., *The Economic Theory of Agrarian Institutions.* Oxford: Oxford University Press.

Bromley, D., ed. 1992. *Making the Commons Work: Theory, Practice and Policy.* San Francisco: ICS Press.

Buchanan, J. 1975. *The Limits of Liberty: Between Anarchy and Leviathan.* Chicago: University of Chicago Press.

———, R. Tollison, and G. Tullock. 1980. *Theory of the Rent-Seeking Society.* College Station: Texas A&M University Press.

Campos, N., and J. B. Nugent. 1997. "Institutions and Economic Growth: Can Human Capital Be a Link?" Economic Working Paper No. 9703. University of Southern California, Los Angeles.

Chenery, H., and T. N. Srinivasan, eds. 1988. *Handbook of Development Economics*, Vols. 1 and 2. Amsterdam: North Holland.

Coleman, J. 1990. *Foundations of Social Theory.* Cambridge, Mass.: Harvard University Press.

de Janvry, A., S. Radwan, E. Sadoulet, and E. Thorbecke, eds. 1995. *State, Market and Civil Organizations: New Theories, New Practices and their Implications for Rural Development.* London: The MacMillan series of ILO studies.

de Soto, H. 1989. *The Other Path—The Invisible Revolution in the Third World.* New York: Harper and Row.

Dia, M. 1996. *Africa's Management in the 1990s and Beyond: Reconciling Indigenous and Transplanted Institutions.* Washington, D.C.: World Bank.

Easterlin, R. 1996. *Growth Triumphant: The Twenty-First Century in Historical Perspective*. Ann Arbor: University of Michigan Press.

Easterly, W., and R. Levine. 1996. *Policies and Ethnic Divisions*. Washington D.C.: World Bank.

Eggertsson, T. 1990. *Economic Behavior and Institutions*. Cambridge: Cambridge University Press.

———. 1996. "A Note on the Economics of Institutions." In L. J. Alston, T. Eggertsson, and D. C. North, eds., *Empirical Studies in Institutional Change*. Cambridge: Cambridge University Press.

Elster, J. 1989. *The Cement of Society*. Cambridge: Cambridge University Press.

Feeny, D. 1989. "The Decline of Property Rights in Man in Thailand, 1800–1913." *Journal of Economic History* 49:285–96.

Fishlow, A. 1991. "Review of Handbook of Development Economics." *Journal of Economic Literature* 29(4):1728–37.

Gershenkron, A. 1962. *Economic Backwardness in Historical Perspective*. Cambridge: Belknap Press.

Gibbon, P. 1995. *Liberalized Development in Tanzania: Studies on Accumulation Processes and Local Institutions*. Stockholm: Almqvist and Wiksell.

Granovetter, M. 1978. "Threshold Models of Collective Behavior." *American Journal of Sociology* 83:1420–43.

Harris, J., J. Hunter, and C. Lewis, eds. 1995. *The New Institutional Economics and Third World Development*. London: Routledge.

Hayami, Y., and M. Kikuchi. 1982. *Asian Village Economy at the Crossroads*. Baltimore: Johns Hopkins University Press.

Hayami, Y., and V. W. Ruttan. 1985. *Agricultural Development: An International Perspective*. Baltimore: Johns Hopkins University Press.

Hirschman, A. 1958. *The Stategy of Economic Development*. New Haven: Yale University Press.

———.1970. *Exit, Voice and Loyalty: Responses to Decline in Firms, Organizations and States*. Cambridge, Mass.: Harvard University Press.

———. 1981. *Essays in Trespassing*. Cambridge: Cambridge University Press.

———. 1982. *Shifting Involvement: Private Interest and Public Action*. Oxford: Blackwell.

———. 1984. *Getting Ahead Collectively: Grassroots Experience in Latin America*. New York: Pergamon Press.

Klitgaard, R. 1991. *Controlling Corruption*. California: University of California Press.

———. 1995. *Institutional Adjustment and Adjusting to Institutions*. World Bank Discussion Paper No. 303. Washington, D.C.: World Bank.

Krugman, P. 1992. *Toward a Counter-Counterrevolution in Development Theory.* Washington, D.C.: World Bank.

———. 1994. "The Fall and Rise of Development Economics." In L. Rodwin and D. A. Schön, eds., *Rethinking the Development Experience: Essays Provoked by the Work of Albert O. Hirschman.* Washington, D.C.: Brookings/Lincoln.

Kuran, T. 1995. *Private Truths, Public Lies: The Social Consequences of Falsification.* Cambridge, Mass.: Harvard University Press.

Landa, J. T. 1994. *Trust, Ethnicity, and Identity: Beyond the New Institutional Economics of Ethnic Trading Networks, Contract Law, and Gift Exchange.* Ann Arbor: University of Michigan Press.

Lewis, W. A. 1984. "The State of Development Theory." *American Economic Review* 74(1):8.

Libecap, G. D. 1978. *The Evolution of Private Mineral Rights: Nevada's Comstock Lode.* New York: Arno Press.

———. 1979. "Government Support of Private Claims to Public Minerals: Western Mineral Rights." *Business History Review* 53:362–85.

———. 1989. *Contracting for Property Rights.* Cambridge: Cambridge University Press.

Lin, J., and J. B. Nugent. 1995. "Institutions and Economic Development." In J. Behrman and T. N. Srinivasan, eds., *Handbook of Development Economics*, Vol. 3a. Amsterdam: North Holland.

Lipton, M. 1977. *Why Poor People Stay Poor: A Study of Urban Bias in World Development.* London: Temple Smith.

McCormick, R. E., and R. D. Tollison. 1981. *Politicians, Legislation, and the Economy: An Inquiry into the Interest-Group Theory of Government.* Boston: Martinus Niijhof.

MacLeod, B. 1993. "The Role of Exit Costs in the Theory of Cooperative Teams." *Journal of Comparative Economics* 23:234–46.

Ménard, C. 1995. "Markets as Institutions Versus Organizations as Markets? Disentangling Some Fundamental Concepts." *Journal of Economic Behavior and Organization* 28(2):161–82.

Morawetz. D. 1981. *Why the Emperor's New Clothes Are Not Made in Colombia.* Oxford: Oxford University Press for the World Bank.

Morrisson, C., H-B. S. Lecomte, and X. Oudin. 1994. *Microenterprises and the Institutional Framework in Developing Countries.* Paris: Organization for Economic Cooperation and Development.

Nabli, M. 1996. "Institutional Analysis of State-owned Enterprises Reform and the MENA Region." World Bank, Washington, D.C.

———, and J. B. Nugent, eds. 1989. *The New Institutional Economics and Development.* Amsterdam: North Holland.

North, D. 1986. *Institutions and Economic Growth: An Historical Introduction.* Ithaca: Cornell University, Conference on Institutions and Development.

———. 1990. *Institutions, Institutional Change and Economic Performance.* Cambridge: Cambridge University Press.

———. 1995. "The New Institutional Economics and Third World Development." In J. Harris, J. Hunter, and C. Lewis, eds., *The New Institutional Economics and Third World Development*. London: Routledge.

Olson, M. 1965. *The Logic of Collective Action: Public Goods and the Theory of Groups*. Cambridge, Mass.: Harvard University Press.

Ostrom, E. 1990. *Governing the Commons: The Evolution of Institutions for Collective Action*. Cambridge: Cambridge University Press.

Ostrom, V., D. Feeny, and H. Picht, eds. 1988. *Rethinking Institutional Analysis and Development: Issues, Alternatives and Choices*. San Francisco: Institute for Contemporary Studies Press for the International Center for Economic Growth.

Picciotto, R. 1995. *Putting Institutional Economics to Work: From Participation to Governance*. World Bank Discussion Paper No. 304. Washington, D.C.: World Bank.

Putnam, R. D. 1993. *Making Democracy Work—Civic Traditions in Modern Italy*. Princeton: Princeton University Press.

Putterman, L., and D. Rueschemeyer, eds. 1992. *State and Market in Development, Synergy or Rivalry?* Boulder: Lynne Rienner Publishers.

Reynolds, L. 1983. "The Spread of Economic Growth to the Third World: 1850–1980." *Journal of Economic Literature* 21:2134–50.

Rodrik, D. 1996. *Institutions and Economic Performance in East and Southeast Asia*. Cambridge, Mass.: Harvard University Press.

Rutherford, M. 1996. *Institutions in Economics: The Old and the New Institutionalism*. Cambridge: Cambridge University Press.

Sachs, J., and A. Warner. 1996. "Economic Convergence and Economic Policies." Working Paper No. 5039. National Bureau of Economic Research, Washington, D.C.

Scully, G. 1992. Constitutional Environments and Economic Growth. Princeton: Princeton University Press.

Sen, A. 1981. *Poverty and Famines: An Essay on Entitlement and Deprivation*. Oxford: Clarendon Press.

Stiglitz, J. E. 1989. "On the Economic Role of the State." In A. Heertje, ed., *The Economic Role of the State*. Oxford: Blackwell.

———. 1992. Comment on "Toward a Counter-Counterrevolution in Development Theory" by Krugman. World Bank, Washington, D.C.

Taylor, L. 1994. "Hirschman's Strategy at Thirty-Five." In L. Rodwin and D. A. Schön, eds., *Rethinking the Development Experience*. Washington, D.C.: Brookings Institution.

Taylor, M. 1987. *The Possibility of Cooperation*. Cambridge: Cambridge University Press.

Uphoff, N. 1986. *Local Institutional Development*. West Hartford: Kumarian Press.

Wiesner D., E. 1993. *From Macroeconomic Correction to Public Sector Reform: The Critical Role of Evaluation.* World Bank Discussion Paper No. 214. Washington, D.C.: World Bank.

Williamson, O. E. 1975. *Markets and Hierarchies: Analysis and Antitrust Implications.* New York: MacMillan.

————. 1985. *The Economic Institutions of Capitalism: Firms, Markets, Relational Contracting.* New York: Free Press.

World Bank. 1993a. *Governance: The World Bank's Experience.* Washington, D.C.

————. 1993b. *The East Asian Miracle: Economic Growth and Public Policy.* Washington, D.C.

Young, H. P. 1990. "The Economics of Convention." *The Journal of Economic Perspectives* 10(2):105–12.

## Comments on "Institutions, markets, and development outcomes," by Nugent

*Thráinn Eggertsson*

Jeffrey Nugent's essay provides an excellent analysis of the links and complex inter-actions between institutions and economic development. Few people are better acquainted than he is with both the theory and practice of economic development and the new institutionalism. In particular, the paper is valuable for explaining where our knowledge of these links is relatively weak and for suggesting a research agenda.

### Definitions

I concur with the paper's definition of institutions as rules of the game or as social constraints on behavior, but I would make a clear distinction between institutions, on the one hand, and organizations or economic systems, on the other. Organiza-tions can be perceived as actors that process or produce information and make deci-sions in ways that transcend the capacity of individual members. Organizations also generate new institutions, and they are qualitatively different from rules and social constraints. Similarly, markets are not institutions; they are organizations or systems constrained by specific institutional arrangements and environments.

### Which institutions matter for economic development, and why?

Nugent gives a good account of how difficult it can be to verify empirically the effect of institutions on outcomes. I would like to add to his excellent discussion a new complexity, which I call *imperfect policy models* (Eggertsson 1997, forthcoming [a]). The notion is elementary: actors who operate in a social system or try to manipulate it must model the structure of the system. But knowledge is scarce, and policy mod-els tend to be incomplete or even outright misleading. When errors are detected, public and private policy models are updated by trial and error with the help of new insights. Policy models matter because their content affects both the evolution of institutions and economic outcomes.

To illustrate the point, let me use an example from macropolitical economy that econ-omists should find easy to understand. Imagine that a national employment act—a new institution—is introduced in a country. The act requires the government to main-tain full employment. A few years later, unemployment increases rapidly. What is the content of the new institution, and how does it influence government behavior?

As figure 2.2 shows, the answer depends in part on how the authorities model vari-ous aspects of their environment. Before acting, the government must use formal and informal policy models to answer various questions:

Is the new constraint (the full employment law) a hard or a soft constraint? For instance, how does the judiciary interpret the law?

FIGURE 2.2: THE ROLE OF POLICY MODELS IN MEDIATING THE INFLUENCE OF
INSTITUTIONS ON BEHAVIOR—AN EASY EXAMPLE FOR ECONOMISTS

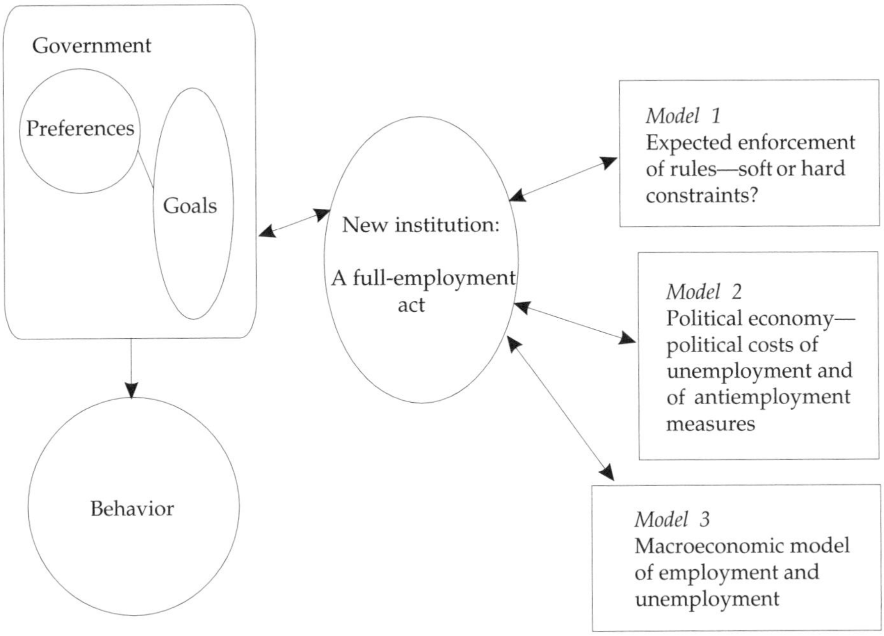

A government's response to a new rule (institution), a full-employment act, in part depends on what model of the macroeconomy it favors.

*Source:* Author's compilation.

- What are the political and electoral consequences of high rates of unemployment? What are the political and electoral consequences of harsh anti-inflation measures?

- And, equally important, how can a government influence the level of unemployment? What is the appropriate model of the macroeconomy?

Clearly the effect of a new constraint—a new institution—depends not only on preferences and goals, but also on the way in which actors model various aspects of their social systems. In our example, it matters whether the authorities rely on a Keynesian or rational expectations model of the macroeconomy. In sum, incomplete modeling affects behavior at all levels of social action and involves not only simple modeling of strategic interaction but also attempts to understand the structure of social systems. Incomplete modeling, therefore, influences the design of rules and social constraints and the effects of these institutions on behavior.

### Dynamics of institutional change

At various points the paper considers the dynamics of institutional change, emphasizing that institutional change is nonincremental and noncontinuous. This is not always true. The notions of bounded rationality and incomplete public and private policy models suggest that institutional change can be incremental and continuous (Sargent 1993).

Figure 2.3 shows a representative actor and a government interacting with each other and with a social system such as the market for rental housing in Hong Kong (Cheung 1975) or the Scandinavian welfare state (Lindbeck 1995). Both parties

FIGURE 2.3: REVISION OF POLICY MODELS AND EVOLUTION OVER TIME OF SOCIAL SYSTEMS AND THEIR OUTCOMES

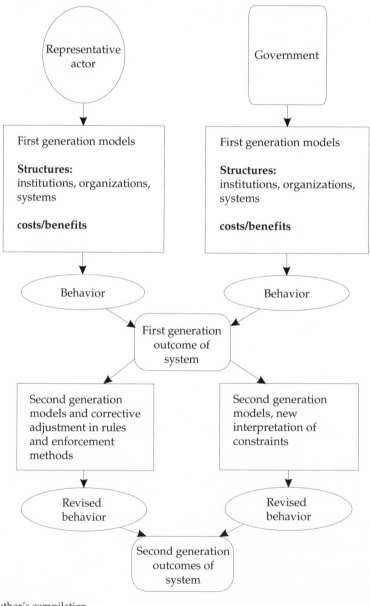

*Source:* Author's compilation.

attempt to estimate the interrelationships and relevant properties of the systems. Private actors search for new margins of operation to soften their constraints, and the polity attempts to better constrain the actors by improving its understanding of the relationship between instruments and targets. Both sides sequentially update their models and reinterpret the implications of rules and constraints.

Through these interactions, institutions and social systems evolve over time. The direction of change can be toward collectively rational outcomes or toward collectively irrational outcomes, and the direction may not be fully understood until relatively late in the game.

### Supply and demand analysis of institutional change

The paper advocates a supply and demand approach to institutional change that I find quite useful, but the discussion in the paper does not emphasize enough the role of the state as an independent actor or entity with its own objective function or functions. Political economy sometimes pictures the state as a passive organization, a mere playing field for lobbyists who find it convenient to obtain legitimacy by operating through the public sector. But, as Bates (1990) and others have emphasized, the state is also an actor with interests and initiatives of its own. For instance, the state may actively forge coalitions of supporters by handing out privileges rather than waiting for coalitions of rent-seekers to emerge. Of course, the state is not a homogeneous entity, and its various branches often have their own agenda. The study by Riker and Sened (1991) of the origins of property rights in airport slots in the United States is a good example of the independent role of government agencies in institutional change.

### Can institutions that matter be changed? Should the international community intervene?

My first point here is that we must distinguish change that is driven by endogenous shifts in institutional supply and demand from attempts by exogenous actors to move the system against the tide.

The new institutionalism, which endogenizes political action as well as the behavior of economic actors, does not appear to leave much room for independent policy actions, social scientists, and international civil servants. If a social system, under its own steam, is heading in a direction that is deemed desirable, outside actors may be able to facilitate the prevailing trend. When outsiders try to introduce and enforce institutional change that goes against endogenous political and economic forces in the system, there seem to be few degrees of freedom. Still, I see at least four solutions to this dilemma, four possible escapes from policy determinism. Consider the following situations:

■  The outside actor has substantial power of compulsion—for instance, by threatening to withhold loans or trade.

■  Within limits, the power elite is relatively indifferent to the direction the system takes, or different political interests are equally balanced, and it is relatively easy for outsiders to tilt the system in the desired direction.

- Fundamental uncertainty prevails in the community about the correct structure of relevant policy models. When social policy relies on incomplete models, the system often evolves in an undesirable direction. After attempts at marginal reforms have failed, key players may write off institutional arrangements they previously supported. When players reject their own models, institutions, and systems, fundamental uncertainty prevails, and the vacuum often creates demand for alternative arrangements (Eggertsson forthcoming [b]). Rejections may involve particular organizational forms, institutional arrangements in a specific market or industry, or even the institutional framework of the entire economy. Such system "crashes" can create opportunities for outside reformers who claim to know what they are doing.

- Finally, people in power who rely on incomplete models can sometimes be tricked into accepting measures they don't fully understand. The new institutions eventually may result in outcomes that leaders or voters don't want, but at the moment of truth it may be too late for them to turn back. Some proponents of a big bang approach to institutional change in the former Soviet world have used this argument (Åslund 1995).

Obviously the idea of incomplete models has important implications for institutional design. The topic is too big for a short comment, but institutional design coming from the top down should avoid micromanagement and aim at creating favorable institutional environments for learning. The prevalence of incomplete models also indicates that reformers should emphasize flexibility and avoid large-scale experiments that can be reversed only at great cost.

## References

Åslund, Anders. 1995. *How Russia Became a Market Economy.* Washington, D.C.: Brookings Institution.

Bates, Robert. 1990. "Macropolitical Economy in the Field of Development." In J. Alt and K. Shepsle, eds., *Perspectives on Political Economy.* Cambridge: Cambridge University Press.

Cheung, Steven N. S. 1975. "Roofs and Stars: The Stated Intents and Actual Effects of Rent Ordinance." *Economic Inquiry* 13:1–21.

Eggertsson, Thraínn. Forthcoming (a). "Limits to Institutional Change." *Scandanavian Journal of Economics*.

———. Forthcoming (b). "When the State Changes its Mind: The Puzzle of Discontinuity in Government Control of Economic Activity." In Herbert Giersch, ed., *Privatization at the Turn of the Century.* Berlin: Springer Verlag.

———. 1997. "The Old Theory of Economic Policy and the New Institutionalism." *World Development* 25:1187-1203.

Lindbeck, Assar. 1995. "Welfare State Disincentives with Endogenous Habits and Norms." *Scandinavian Journal of Economics* 97:477–94.

Riker, William H., and Itai Sened. 1991. "A Political Theory of the Origin of Property Rights: Airport Slots." *American Journal of Political Science* 35:951–69.

Sargent, Thomas J. 1993. *Bounded Rationality in Macroeconomics.* Oxford: Oxford University Press.

**Comments on "Institutions, markets, and development outcomes," by Nugent**

*Ishrat Husain*

I agree that institutions do matter and that there is a growing recognition of the importance of institutions in development economics. Jeffrey Nugent has done a superb job of outlining the kinds of methodological problems faced by institutional analysts. His research agenda is also on target. But I am less sanguine than he on whether there are insights from institutional economics that can guide a practicing development economist to do a better job.

First of all, we do not have an analytical framework that can help us incorporate institutional issues in our tool kit. Of course, there is a theory of path dependence, but a theory should be able to explain how earlier practices actually developed and give us some postulates of future outcomes under a given set of assumptions. I don't think that the theory of path dependence really provides that insight to us.

As a practicing mainstream economist, I would like to see the integration of the apparatus of mainstream economics and institutional economics carried out consistently. I would like to see it done in a way that can help me explain how economies evolve over time, why some economies outperform others, and why so little evidence exists of persistence in growth rates among countries over time.

We can apply such questions first to the second theorem of welfare economics—the Arrow-Debreu theorem—and ask whether institutions will necessarily emerge to compensate or offset deficiencies in a theory based on transaction cost, incomplete markets, imperfect information, and imperfect competition.

Let us assume actual conditions are less than optimal for the allocation of resources through markets. Can we conclude that new institutional arrangements will set in motion forces to reduce transaction costs, supply information, promote competition, create missing markets—all the things required to attain the Pareto optimality? Can institutional economics define the circumstances in which such dynamics will take place?

A second set of questions relates to the growth accounting framework: when and how will institutions affect the rate of accumulation of physical capital and human capital? Is the rate and speed of assimilation on diffusion of technology affected by institutions? Or is it the production technology that is transforming these factor inputs into outputs that the institutions are trying to modify? We have to be very clear as to the particular set of variables institutions are affecting.

If you don't believe in neoclassical economics and in the validity of Pareto optimality conditions, and if you are a structuralist, then you know that developing countries have well-known rigidities and factor immobilities. There are scale economies that are quite significant. Capital markets are likely to be segmented and imperfect, and financial systems do not perform intermediation to any significant extent. How is the interplay between policies and institutions going to take place in the presence of these rigidities? The responses to market movements and price signals under these constraints are likely to be muted and not as pronounced as they should be. Are institutions then trying to modify and relax these constraints to alter the structure of the economy so that it becomes more responsive?

Unfortunately, institutional economics has little to say on such central issues. Mostly it is preoccupied with the rules of the game—the norms of behavior—and the way these rules are enforced.

This brings another set of questions to mind: why is it that in some countries the incentives or rewards for promoting technological change, higher savings or investment, or education and skills are either weak or missing? Why is it that in some other countries the formal organizations and the rules may all be in place, but the enforcement of these rules is highly selective and varied? Why is it that in some countries rent-seeking and speculative activities have displaced productive activities? If institutional economics can shed light on these questions, then it would indeed advance our understanding of development economics.

I see a fundamental tension between the norms of conventional economic analysis and the conditions needed for institutions to work effectively. Under a given set of assumptions, the former can predict outcomes that are universally valid, generalizable, and applicable under different economic circumstances. The latter will require not only such formal rules of the game but a wide variety of norms of behavior, conventions, and codes of conduct that can alter the formal rules.

The enforcement of these rules may vary widely, and the transaction costs themselves may have a frequency that we cannot predict. Such uncertainties, and the degree of asset specificity, are the important dimensions. Then, besides the transaction costs, each generic mode of organization (such as the market, hybrid structures, and public and private delivery systems) is defined by a distinctive form of contract law. Each mode also differs with respect to incentives and controls, and each mode also implements a mix of autonomous and cooperative adaptations differently.

Such a variety and heterogeneity of transactions and organizational modes makes me doubt whether institutional economics can provide us, as economists, with solutions or the insights we can apply in different situations. And that to me is the major source of concern. Because unless it can, we will find ourselves having to make a specific contextual analysis in every mode, for every transaction, and in every way of doing business, and that to me is a fundamental shortcoming.

Therefore, I question the analogy that Nugent makes with technological change. The latter is very strongly enshrined in a body of theoretical and empirical literature that has been highly validated over time. I don't feel that the analogy is very appropriate, at least for now.

Those are my reactions, but they have little to do with the paper. It is excellent, but the whole discipline of institutional economics needs to be examined with a harder set of questions and far more demanding expectations.

**Floor discussion on "Institutions, markets, and development outcomes"**

In response to Ishrat Husain's remarks, Jeffrey Nugent noted that the comparative advantage of institutional economics lies in extending the scope of ordinary economics, which in its standard form "assumes away" many important and realistic problems. Institutional economics is an attempt to get at more realistic issues and move closer to the real world. Rewards and incentives in relation to rent-seeking issues are at the heart of institutional economic analysis. It can also usefully address such questions as how one party may try to take advantage of another.

On the issue of where institutional economics is going to fit into growth accounting, Nugent observed that it can affect the factors of production, the technology, or the way in which the factors go together. The scheme is not exclusive. Because it recognizes that institutions can play a role in matters that affect economic and social outcomes at either the micro or macro levels, its approach is quite flexible and the scope of its analysis broad.

Nugent also stated that the principles of analysis are very general, involving simple ideas about transaction costs or collective action. Thus, the tendency toward generalization presents a challenge, since the appropriate response to institutional change may be quite different for individual countries or even for sectors, regions, or particular ethnic groups within a country. It remains to be seen how "generalizable" a particular solution may be, although research thus far has revealed considerable commonalities.

Nugent questioned the suggestion that the analogy between institutional change and technological change is false. He observed that 40 or 50 years of research has gone into analyzing technological change. Only after a similar period of time will we know if it is possible to say, as it is about technological change, that institutional change has become part of the mainstream.

In his response, Husain said he was trying to show that there is a body of knowledge in mainstream economics that attempts to come to grips with some of the deficiencies or weaknesses of the assumptions on which the standard economic theory is based. He wanted to know what institutional economics can contribute to inform our judgment on development economics. He agreed that 40 years from now there may be a body of knowledge that can inform us, but it is not available yet. He therefore uses the tools he has.

One participant thought such concerns were overstated and provided an example from monetary policy. A "generalizable" lesson from this field is that central bank independence is critical to monetary management. Another participant observed that part of the difference between Husain's position and his was simply a matter of definition. Institutional economists consider the economics of information part of the institutional approach, not part of standard economics. Yet Husain seems to consider it part of standard economics, showing that institutional analysis is becoming mainstream. What institutional economics is saying is that we need to pay attention to why people obey the rules. What are the incentives? It is not just a matter of hard economic incentives but of mental models and fair play. By applying the tools of economics with due attention to the problems of information, we can make some headway.

A participant asked about the evaluation side of the discussion as opposed to the institutional side. He observed that Nugent's paper is largely silent about evaluation and the linkages between evaluation and institutional change and development. He cited the question the speaker had brought up: can the institutions that matter be changed, and if so, how? It may be a matter of organizational learning and the capacity of institutions to change themselves through reflective forces from within. In particular, what role might evaluation play in enhancing organizational learning through its focus on internalities rather than externalities?

Addressing the question of external versus internal sources of change, Nugent noted that organizations have dynamics and rules that change over time. Thráinn Eggertsson's presentation of policy models adds to the question of how different people's models and rules are adjusting over time. Nugent also cited the examples that Joe Stiglitz gave of setting up the right kind of incentives in evaluations. Such incentives can keep people from setting their goals too low. Further, good counterfactual analysis of the institutions provides a basis for evaluating performance vis-à-vis those goals. Examples already exist, including in the work of Operations Evaluation Department of the World Bank.

Eggertsson was asked to comment on his point that change can be long, slow, and incremental. When change actually happens, a participant noted, it is normally in a crisis situation. People then need to know how to get out of the crisis and manage the change. In effect, the most important thing to know is the time frame in which change takes place.

In response, Eggertsson commented that probably nobody really knows how to design organizations and institutions in detail and that political forces often inhibit substantial change. When periods of fundamental uncertainty do emerge, it is good to know exactly what to do. One problem is that we really do not know how different arrangements work against different environmental or institutional backgrounds. Some things that work well in one country may not work so well in a different situation. Producing institutions that work well and give us strong economic systems throughout the world will depend on political and, to some extent, cultural practices.

# 3. Institutions, policies, and development outcomes[1]

Ajay Chhibber

*The results of three survey studies developed for the 1997 World Development Report shows that the quality of institutions, particularly the institutional capability of the state, is important for efficient markets, productive investments, and equitable access to development opportunity. The author discusses a framework for improving the effectiveness of the state and its impact on the institutional environment.*

*Men are powerless to secure the future; institutions alone fix the destinies of nations.*
—Napoleon I, Imperial séance, June 7, 1813

Fifty years ago, World War II had ended, and reconstruction was underway in much of Europe, the Soviet Union, and Japan. Many developing countries had just emerged from colonialism, and the future seemed full of promise. The difficulties of economic development were not yet haunting us. Economic development—and with it an improvement in people's lives—seemed so easily possible through ideas, technical expertise, and resources. In some cases things did work out well. But in others they did not. Despite five decades of enormous human progress, we still see huge disparities in the quality of life of people around the world. Indeed, some even argue that the disparities have increased.

Explanations of differences in living standards across countries have changed over the years. For a long time, access to natural resources, such as land and minerals, was considered the prerequisite to development. Countries went to war over resources, and many parts of Africa, Asia, and the Americas were colonized to acquire them. Gradually thinking shifted, and physical capital—machines and equipment, for instance—came to be identified as the key to development. "Industrialized" was synonymous with "developed." But about the middle of this century, it was recognized that this explanation was too simplistic (Solow 1956). Embodied in machines and equipment was physical capital as well as technology—knowledge and ideas. And no straightforward explanation offered itself for the fact that technology developed better and faster in some parts of the world. A large residual in unexplained growth remained.

Since then other factors, such as human capital, have commanded much attention in explaining differences both in income and in the ability of poorer countries to catch up with the richer ones. Human capital leads to new knowledge and ideas, and it increases the speed with which they are absorbed, disseminated, and used in a country (Becker, Murphy, and Tamura 1990). Since the 1980s, attention has begun to focus on policies that hinder the accumulation of human and physical capital and on the reasons countries accumulate human and physical capital at different rates. This in turn has led to a further, more recent shift in attention to the quality of a country's institutions (North 1990, 1993; Olson 1996). These shifts in thinking reflect a search for deeper sources of differences in development outcomes. New, more complex questions have emerged. What institutional arrangements best allow markets to flourish? What is the role of the state both as a direct agent (mostly in the provision of services) and as a shaper of the institutional context in which markets function? How do policies and institutions interact in the development process?

The answers to these questions are central to our understanding of the deeper sources of differences in development outcomes—and of why the response to economic reforms often varies so widely from one country to another. They help explain, for example, why investment and economic activity have revived more strongly in Poland than in Russia (Shleifer 1996). They also help explain why many countries in Africa and Latin America still do not see the investment, growth, and improvement in the quality of life that was expected when they began economic reforms a decade or so ago.

In all these arrangements, the institution of the state plays a critical role—because the state is not only the arbiter of rules but, through its behavior, can also affect the overall environment for business and economic activity. The second part of this paper explores the relationships among the state, the institutional environment, and development outcomes.

Attempts have been made to include policy variables in explanations of development outcomes (Easterly and others 1993; Fischer 1993). Efforts to include the impact of uncertainty have been made in two separate directions—first, by measuring the variance of economic variables (Serven and Solimano 1994), and second, by measuring the direct impact of political variability (Alesina and others 1996). But these results have remained unsatisfactory because they do not try to measure the quality of the underlying institutions that bring about these outcomes. Very few attempts have been made to try to quantify systematically the impact of the quality of a country's institutions (and of the behavior of the state) on economic outcomes.

In this paper, we report three results that were developed for the *World Development Report* (WDR) (World Bank 1997) to try and make a strong empirical case for a refocus on the institutional capability of the state—to bring institutions into the mainstream of our thinking on development outcomes.

■　The first uses a panel data set for 30 years for 94 countries—developed and developing—to show that policies and the quality of institutions matter for economic growth and other indicators of the quality of life, such as infant mortality (Commander, Davoodi, and Lee 1996). The variable used in this particular set is similar to that used by Knack and Keefer (1995). These results are reported in the third section of the paper.

■　The measurement of the quality of institutions is taken a step further in the fourth section. Here we report on a survey of over 3,600 local firms in 69 countries. We show that the variable reflecting the quality of institutions that emerges from this survey affects both growth and investment (see Brunetti, Kisunko, and Weder 1997).

- In the fifth section, we turn to the ways the quality of institutions affects not just the business environment but also the overall environment for effective development. We take the results from the survey on the quality of institutions in the fourth section and show that they explain the rate of return to development projects financed by the World Bank.

In the sixth section, we turn very briefly to some concluding comments and discuss a framework for improving the effectiveness of the state and its impact on the institutional environment.

### Institutions, the state, and economic outcomes

Institutions are the formal and informal rules that affect human behavior. Organizations (firms, nongovernmental organizations, companies, central banks) produce goods and services that are used by society. Through most societies and much of history, a well-functioning state has played a central role in establishing the institutional framework for the creation of wealth. However, economic prosperity and the creation of wealth do not necessarily need a strong state. Informal rules can in some situations be enough. Against the backdrop of states with good policies, the overseas Chinese community now generates the third-highest GDP in the world and transacts business and contracts largely through informal rules. But such cases are an exception.

The state produces goods and services in singular or joint production, but at the same time it produces the formal rules that are part and parcel of an institutional environment (figure 3.1). These formal rules, along with the informal rules, make up the institutional environment. The state is therefore a unique organization, because it must establish the formal rules (institutions) through a social and political process. It must also play by these rules as an organization.

In what way can state action influence performance? First, it establishes the formal rules by which economic agents—households, firms, labor—must play the game. But the state and its agencies must also abide and play by these rules. They cannot be above the law.

History also teaches us that the state can do enormous harm, as follows:

- First, it may establish inadequate rules for the creation of wealth. The former Soviet Union and India provide examples of these types of states.

- Second, the state can do damage not through the impact it has on the institutional environment, but through the manner in which its organizations apply them. It can apply a heavy tax on private wealth through misaligned prices, overvalued exchange rates, or agricultural marketing boards that tax agriculture. It can also impose huge transaction costs on the setting up of new and the restructuring of old businesses, as well as by the requiring of bribes.

FIGURE 3.1: STATE, INSTITUTIONS, AND ECONOMIC OUTCOMES

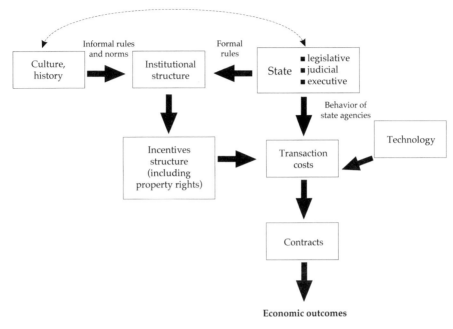

*Source:* Author's compilation.

■  Third, the state can impose an even heavier cost on society through the uncertainty its actions can create. If it often changes or does not clarify the rules by which the state itself will behave, then uncertainty occurs, and businesses and common citizens must adopt costly strategies to try and protect themselves against such behavior by, for instance, going underground, hiding wealth, and sending capital abroad (capital flight).

Empirical work on institutions and institutional change has been scanty (Alston, Eggertsson, and North 1996). It has also typically involved historical case studies (Alston 1996). This paper tries to go beyond case studies and bring together some recent cross-country evidence to address the impact of the quality of a country's institutions on development outcomes. We hope to show that the study of the quality of the institutional environment and, more specifically, the role and behavior of the state in it deserve more careful attention.

### Economic growth and the state[2]

The state can affect development outcomes in a number of ways:

■  By providing a macroeconomic and microeconomic incentive environment conducive to efficient economic activity.

■  By providing the institutional infrastructure—property rights, peace, law and order, and rules—that encourages efficient long-term investment.

■ By ensuring the delivery of basic education, health care, and infrastructure required for economic activity.

But the state must constantly try to provide these collective goods at the lowest cost to society. If it does not, it taxes society too heavily. The desire to get the state to provide collective goods must be constantly weighed against the costs of providing them. We turn to this trade-off between what the state does and how well it does it in this section by reporting on the impact of policies, size (government consumption), and the quality of state institutions.

Figure 3.2 takes all these factors into account and shows their impact on income growth over the last three decades across 94 developed and developing countries. In countries with weak institutions and poor policies, per capita income grew only at about 0.4 percent per annum. In contrast, in countries with strong institutions and good policies, per capita income grew at an average of 3 percent per annum. Over a 30-year period, these differences in income growth would make a huge difference to the quality of people's lives. A country with an average per capita income of $300 in 1965, with distorted policies and weak institutional capability, would over 30 years reach an income level of only about $338 at 1965 prices. On the other hand, a country with strong institutional capability and good policies would more than double its average income to $728 at 1965 prices. Many countries in East Asia have done even better than that.

Good policies by themselves also produce beneficial outcomes, but these benefits are magnified in a country where the institutional quality is also high—where the poli-

FIGURE 3.2: INSTITUTIONAL CAPABILITY OF THE STATE IMPROVES ECONOMIC GROWTH IN 94 COUNTRIES, 1964–93

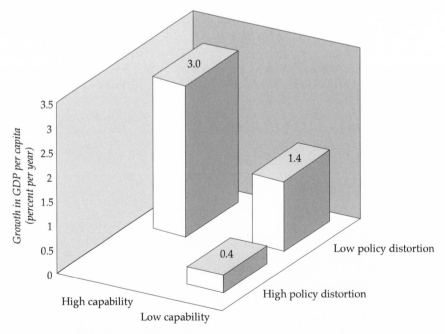

*Source:* Commandor, Davoodi, and Lee 1996.

cies and programs are well implemented and where there is greater reliance in the minds of citizens and investors on government actions. Good policies alone—such as those now being pursued by many countries in Latin America and Africa—would increase the growth of per capita income by about 1.4 percent per annum. That means that citizens in a country with an average income of $300 in 1965 would have an average income of about $450 after 30 years—an increase, but not as much as in a country with strong institutions. Reforms should therefore focus both on improvements in policies and on institutional strengthening.

## Institutional capability: the local investors' view[3]

But what constitutes institutional capability? The surest way to get an idea of the private sector's perception of the institutional environment is to ask private entrepreneurs directly. So, in preparation for the WDR, a large-scale private sector survey questioned over 3,600 firms in 69 countries. The survey sought to capture the full array of uncertainties that entrepreneurs can face.

Sometimes the source of uncertainty is in the stability of the rules to which firms are subject. Two key indicators are:

- *The predictability of rule making,* or the extent to which entrepreneurs have to cope with unexpected changes in rules and policies: whether they expect their government to stick to announced major policies, whether they are usually informed about important changes in rules, and whether they can voice concerns when planned changes affect their business.

- *Perception of political stability:* whether changes in government (constitutional and unconstitutional) are usually accompanied by far-reaching policy surprises that could have serious effects on the private sector.

At other times, uncertainty relates to the extent to which entrepreneurs can rely on the enforcement of rules and, more broadly, on protection property rights. Relevant indicators here include:

- *Crime against persons and property*: whether entrepreneurs feel confident that the authorities will protect them and their property from criminal actions, and whether theft and crime represent serious problems for business operations.

- *Reliability of judicial enforcement*: whether the judiciary enforces rules arbitrarily, and whether such unpredictability presents a problem for doing business.

- *Freedom from corruption*: whether it is common for private entrepreneurs to have to make some irregular additional payments to get things done.

Firms ranked each indicator on a scale ranging from 1 (extreme problem) to 6 (no problem), and the answers were averaged to give an overall indicator of how reliable private entrepreneurs in each region perceived the institutional framework to be. The answers were averaged for each of the individual components of the institutional capability (IC) indicator by regions and normalized on a scale on which the

institutional capability for the countries of the Organization for Economic Cooperation and Development (OECD) is equal to one (figure 3.3). Bearing in mind the usual
caveats about regional averages, consider these regional patterns:

- As a region, the Commonwealth of Independent States (CIS, the countries of the
former Soviet Union, excluding the Baltics) has the worst overall IC rating.
Entrepreneurs particularly fear crime and theft, but they also have little faith in
the judiciary or in the predictability of the rule-making process, and they com-
plain about corruption and disruptive political instability.

- On most indicators, average ratings are similar for Central and Eastern Europe
and Africa. Entrepreneurs in both regions are troubled by basic problems of probity—corruption, the unpredictability of the judiciary, crime, and theft—though
not to the same extent as their counterparts in the CIS. They are similarly concerned about the unpredictability of rule making. African entrepreneurs, however, are much more concerned about political instability, and many entrepreneurs appear to lack even the most basic guarantees of property, security, and
personal safety.

- Latin America's entrepreneurs found problems of probity—crime and theft,
judicial unpredictability, and corruption—to be somewhat greater than did
entrepreneurs in Africa and Central and Eastern Europe.

FIGURE 3.3: CREDIBILITY RATING OF COUNTRIES: INSTITUTIONAL CAPABILITY VARIES
ACROSS REGIONS

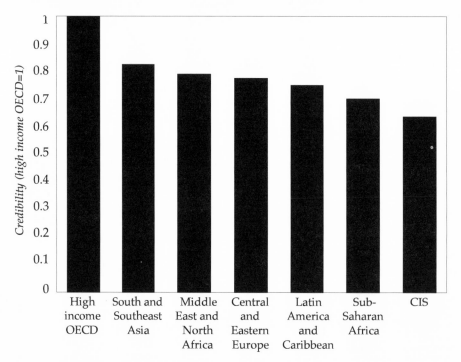

*Source:* Brunetti, Kisunko, and Weder 1997.

■   Corruption is a serious problems for the conduct of business and, in South Asia, for the security of property. In the Middle East and North Africa, a weak judicial system and political stability are considered serious problems.

More revealing than these regional variations in IC indicators are the relations between countries' IC ratings and their growth and investment performance. Even controlling for other variables, there is a strong positive association between IC and investment (figure 3.4), a finding consistent with expectations. Investments usually require some up-front commitment of resources that can be lost if the business environment turns unfavorable. These sunk costs make entrepreneurs wary of investing in environments with high uncertainty and more likely to adopt a wait-and-see strategy. Higher IC affects economic growth as well (figure 3.4), both through its impact on investment and on the return to that investment.

FIGURE 3.4: CREDIBILITY RATING OF COUNTRIES: INSTITUTIONAL CAPABILITY AND ECONOMIC PERFORMANCE GO HAND IN HAND

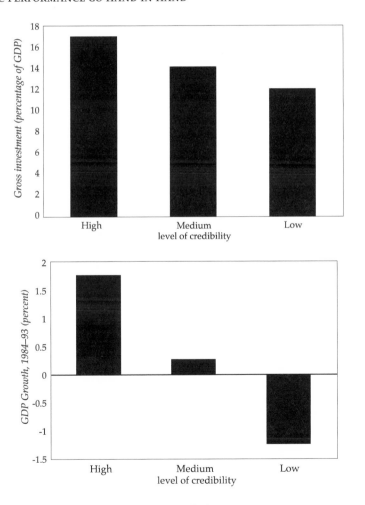

*Note:* Findings are controlled for income, policies, and education.
*Source*: Brunetti, Kisunko, and Weder 1997.

### Institutional capability and project rates of return

We turn in the last section to how the quality of institutions affects not only the business environment but also the environment for the implementation of development projects. The same factors—crime, theft, corruption, and uncertainty about the policy regime and the judiciary—affect the outcome for all development projects. One reason why this happens is that these factors are part and parcel of any contractual environment and of human behavior. If corruption affects the private sector, it is likely to be equally prevalent in determining the outcome on development projects.

A second reason is that many public projects are implemented by private contractors who are subject to the same behavioral problems implicit in an environment of weak institutions. The contractor gets a project, pays off corrupt officials, and gets more projects even if the first are not effectively implemented. Pilferage, theft, and the problems of enforcement are even more prevalent in many public projects than in the private sector. Many projects are delayed because of poor coordination and subject to cost overruns.

Figure 3.5 shows the impact of institutional capability on project rates of return for 293 projects in 28 countries. A shift from a weak IC environment to a strong IC environment makes, on average, a difference of about 8 percentage points in the economic rate of return of World Bank-funded projects. These results control for economic policies and other project and country variables and show how strongly institutions matter in determining project outcomes.

### Refocusing on the state's institutional capability

This brief review of international evidence on the relationship between institutions and income and growth has emphasized the importance of refocusing attention on the ingre-

FIGURE 3.5: ECONOMIC RATES OF RETURN AND QUALITY OF INSTITUTIONS

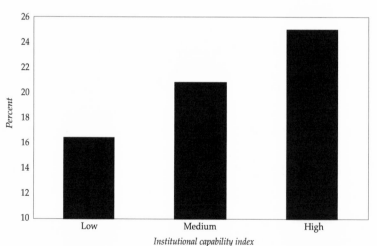

*Note:* Findings are controlled for income, policies, and education.
*Source:* Brunetti, Kisunko, and Weder 1997.

dients of institutional capability. It shows that the emphasis over the last decade on policies is appropriate. But it is not enough. Institutions matter—and matter a great deal. In many developing countries, weak and arbitrary governments can intensify the climate of uncertainty that comes from weak and underdeveloped markets. In many parts of the world, an institutional vacuum now threatens economic and social development.

The state and its actions are central in determining the institutional environment. The state's capability—defined as its ability to provide collective goods at the lowest cost to society—is key to the provision of a viable institutional framework that allows development to occur. But the state's effectiveness in providing the right institutional infrastructure can be improved over time by matching the state's role to its capabilities and rebuilding its capabilities by focusing on incentives.

### Matching role to capability

Where state capability is weak, how the state intervenes—and where—should be carefully assessed. Many states try to do too much with few resources and little capability and often do more harm than good. A sharper focus on the fundamentals would improve effectiveness. The state may then take on more as its capability grows and as society chooses (figure 3.6). But where capability is weak, the solution is not a simple matter of getting the state to do less. It is also a matter of choosing how to intervene. Getting states to regulate and assist market development in a manner that fits their capability is critical. [4]

### Reinvigorating capability

Matching role to capability is a key first step only. Over time, the state's capability must be built up. Three central incentive mechanisms can be used in different set-

FIGURE 3.6: MATCHING ROLES AND CAPABILITIES TO IMPROVE THE STATE'S EFFECTIVENESS

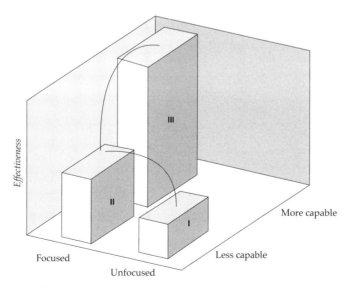

*Source*: Author's compilation

tings and with different emphasis to improve the state's ability to provide a better institutional framework (figure 3.7):

*Rules and restraints.* A state that plays by the rules and the rule of law will have more credibility to make others do the same.

*Competitive pressure.* This can come from a variety of sources: from outside the state, such as through the scrutiny of economic policies provided by financial markets; or from inside, through contracts. This pressure leads to more effective and responsive government.

*Voice and partnership.* Governments must listen to be effective partners—to business councils, consumer groups, and any number of other groupings. Institutional working arrangements with community groups may also be needed. Voice and partnership help achieve more open and accountable government.

### Lessons for evaluation

Based on the findings of this paper, three clear lessons emerge for the way we assess development and the development effectiveness of interventions.

*Lesson 1: Institutions matter.* Countries' development strategies and their likely success must be evaluated not just by economic policies but also by the quality of institutions. It's not just economic fundamentals but also institutional fundamentals—rules and laws—that matter for explaining development outcomes. Therefore, outcomes must be assessed not just on the basis of economic fundamentals.

FIGURE 3.7: MECHANISMS TO ENHANCE STATE CAPABILITY

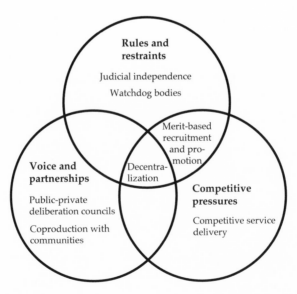

*Source*: Author's compilation

*Lessons 2: Rules and laws matter—but how they are applied matters as much, if not more.* Arbitrary behavior by the state and its agencies creates a climate of uncertainty, raises transaction costs, and reduces investment and growth. Designing rules and restraints that reduce arbitrariness is critical.

*Lesson 3: Use institution—light interventions—when capabilities are weak.* Interventions can be tailored to suit capabilities and can be evaluated using other than the first-best approaches used by high-income countries.

This paper has attempted to show that the state's actions are central to the quality of a country's institutions. Institutional change is difficult, because it involves changes in the formal rules. Informal norms change even more slowly. Typically, the groups in society that benefit from the existing rules and control the power of the state are likely to resist changes in the formal rules. Hence institutional change is a slow, deliberate process—or it occurs in discrete jumps through war, revolution, or upheaval. But even when institutional change occurs, it does so on the debris of the older institutions and is always path dependent. What is needed is an emphasis on the incentive mechanisms (Pradhan 1997) rather than on the importance of technical systems and training that is the focus of much of the technical assistance in this area. What is also needed is much better and interactive use of internal and external evaluation and feedback mechanisms of the type used in this paper—the private sector survey—to help identify the quality of institutions and institutional arrangements.

These are not academic issues. Citizens, households, and firms try to improve their outcomes by investing in economic activity within a given set of institutions. But they also try to change institutions through a political process to alter the behavior of the state. Voting out government, social protest, capital flight, and migration are responses to dissatisfaction with the state. Dissatisfaction with state and the institutional environment can result in political and social instability, which also affects the environment for the creation of wealth. The stakes are much higher now. Whereas in the past, lack of economic development meant postponed benefits, it now involves more: it includes the possibility of state collapse if the dissatisfaction with existing institutions is not addressed.

## Notes

1.   The paper draws on the work of my colleagues, Commander, Davoodi, and Lee (1996), that of Brunetti, Kisunko, and Weder (1996), and other background work prepared for the 1997 *World Development Report* (World Bank 1997).
2.   This section is based on the results reported in Commander, Davoodi, and Lee (1996).
3.   This section relies on Brunetti, Kisunko, and Weder (1997).
4.   My colleague, Brian Levy, expands on this point later in the volume.

## References

Alesina, Alberto, Sule Oezler, Nourel Roubini, and Philip Swagel. 1996. "Political Instability and Economic Growth." *Journal of Economic Growth* 1:189–211.

Alston, Lee. 1996. "Empirical Work in Institutional Economics: an Overview." In Lee Alston, Thraínn Eggertsson, and Douglass North, eds., *Empirical Studies in Institutional Change*. Cambridge: Cambridge University Press.

Alston, Lee, Thraínn Eggertsson, and Douglass North. 1996. *Empirical Studies in Institutional Change*. Cambridge: Cambridge University Press.

Becker, Gary S., Kevin M. Murphy, and Robert Tamura. 1990. "Human Capital, Fertility, and Economic Growth." *Journal of Political Economy* 98(5):12–37.

Brunetti, Aymo, Gregory Kisunko, and Beatrice Weder. 1997. "Economic Growth with 'Incredible' Rules: Evidence from a World Wide Private Sector Survey." Background paper for *World Development Report*. World Bank, Washington, D.C.

Commander, Simon, Hamid Davoodi, and Une J. Lee. 1996. "The Causes and Consequences of Government for Growth and Well-being." Background paper for *World Development Report*. World Bank, Washington, D.C.

Easterly, William, Michael Kremer, Lant Pritchett, and Lawrence Summers. 1993. "Good Policy or Good Luck? Country Growth Performance and Temporary Shocks." Presented at World Bank conference, *How do National Policies Affect Long Run Growth?* Washington, D.C., February 1993.

Fischer, Stanley. 1993. "Macroeconomic Factors in Growth." Presented at World Bank conference, *How do National Policies Affect Long Run Growth?* Washington, D.C., February 1993.

Knack, Stephen, and Philip Keefer. 1995. "Institutions and Economic Performance: Cross-Country Tests Using Alternative Institutional Measures." *Economics and Politics* 7(3):207–27.

Levy, Brian. 1997. "Credible Regulatory Policy: Options and Evaluation." World Bank, Washington, D.C.

North, Douglass. 1990. *Institutions, Institutional Change, and Economic Performance*. Cambridge: Cambridge University Press.

———. 1993. Presentation for the Prize Lecture in Economic Science in Memory of Alfred Nobel, Nobel Foundation.

Olson, Mancur, Jr. 1996. "Distinguished Lecture on Economics in Government. Big Bills Left on the Sidewalk: Why Some Nations Are Rich, and Others Poor." *Journal of Economic Perspectives* 10(2):3–24.

Pradhan, Sanjay. 1997. "Reinvigorating State Institutions." Paper presented at World Bank conference, *Evaluation and Development: The Institutional Dimension*, Washington, D.C., April 1–2, 1997.

Serven, Luis, and Andres Solimano, eds. 1994. *Striving for Growth after Adjustment: The Role of Capital Formation*. Washington, D.C.: World Bank.

Shleifer, Andre. 1996. "Government in Transition." Discussion Paper No. 1783. Harvard Institution of Economic Research, Cambridge, Mass.

Solow, Robert. 1956. "A Contribution to the Theory of Economic Growth." *Quarterly Journal of Economics* 70 (February):65–94.

World Bank. 1997. *World Development Report*. Oxford and New York: Oxford University Press for the World Bank..

## Comments on "Institutions, policies, and development outcomes," by Chhibber

*Lee J. Alston*

There is much to praise in this paper and relatively little to criticize. Ajay Chhibber's underlying premise is that institutions are the ultimate source of economic development. The paper makes both conceptual and empirical contributions to our understanding of institutions. The conceptual contribution, to which he devotes relatively little space, includes discussions of two issues: first, the relationship between a "given" institutional capability and the role of the state; and second, methods of changing a country's institutional capability. The empirical contribution is a summary of a number of World Bank studies.

Chhibber argues convincingly that states need to match their roles in society to their institutional capabilities. If the institutional infrastructure of the state is weak, the role of the state should be narrow. I suspect that there is little disagreement over this static argument, yet its wisdom is often not heeded in countries around the globe. Chhibber also discusses how societies might go about building institutional capabilities. He suggests a three-pronged approach: adopt transparent rules, promote competitive pressure, and allow voice and partnerships. Transparent rules allow all actors to see that the state is "playing by the rules." This transparency can have a positive feedback effect on society's norms regarding honesty and corruption. Competitive pressure should give us government services at lower costs. The benefits from competition may be secured through decentralization, privatization, or contracting services to the private sector. Allowing voice—for example, a free press—and fostering partnerships with informed parties—for example, nongovernmental organizations—gives governments the information necessary to institute correct policies. Furthermore, voice provides a check on government abuses by bringing them to the attention of the public.

The empirical studies that Chhibber discusses are background papers for the *World Development Report* (World Bank 1997). The results from Commander, Davoodi, and Lee (1996) indicate that institutional capability and the degree of policy distortion affect economic growth, though institutional capability is more important than policy distortion. This main result is not surprising, but quantifying the impacts is. But why is policy distortion less important than overall institutional capability? One answer may be that we can view policies as defining property rights and institutional capability as the enforcement of property rights. Without an institutional commitment to property rights (that is, enforcement of property rights), actors in the economy will not invest for the long run.

Chhibber next turns to a study by Brunetti, Kisunko, and Weder (1997). The authors drew five measures from a survey of local investors to construct a cross-country index of institutional capability: predictability of rule making, perception of political stability, crime against persons and property, reliability of judicial enforcement, and freedom from corruption. They found considerable variation across regions and a higher index of institutional capability associated with greater investment and higher economic growth. These are important results, because the authors have quantified the impact of institutional capability. Even if there are some problems with the estimates, the overall result still stands: institutions matter for economic growth.

My comments for the authors of this study consist of suggestions on how to get more information out of the collected data. By analyzing the impacts within regions, the authors may be able to shed some light on the relative importance of formal rules (as opposed to informal norms) for economic growth. For example, assuming that informal norms vary less within a region than across regions, the authors may be able to assess the role of formal rules by analyzing the impact of their index on economic growth and investment across countries within a region.

I also advise the authors to decompose their index. The first two measures—predictability of rule making and perception of political stability—relate to formal rules. The last three measures in their index—crime against persons and property, reliability of judicial enforcement, and freedom from corruption—capture a large component of informal norms. With this decomposition, the authors could not only assess whether formal rules or informal norms matter more for investment and growth but also gauge the empirical relationship between the first two and last three measures of institutional capability. Insights into the empirical relationship may help us in assessing which way causation runs. In turn, this understanding may eventually help us in designing policies.

The final research discussed is that of Chhibber and Kisunko, who use the index of institutional capability constructed by Brunetti, Kisunko, and Weder (1997) and correlate it with rates of return on World Bank projects in 28 countries. Chhibber and Kisunko find that moving from a weak to a strong institutional environment raises the economic rate of return by 8 percent on World Bank-funded projects. This figure is large. My suggestion is similar to the one I made for Brunetti, Kisunko, and Weder. Decompose the index of institutional capability into my notion of formal rules and informal norms to see which components matter the most. For Bank projects, I would expect that the informal norms of corruption and respect for property matter more than the stability of formal rules.

All in all, the studies reported by Chhibber are impressive pieces of empirical work concerning the importance of institutions to macroeconomic performance—that is, rates of return, investment, and economic growth. But where do we go from here? Following are my recommendations for research on the empirical importance of institutions:

- We need more studies of the interaction between formal rules and informal norms. Because of the seemingly similar cultural backgrounds across some countries in Eastern Europe, the region may be a good laboratory for such a study.

- We need more studies on the role of informal norms. One approach would be to analyze countries with similar formal laws and compare economic performances. A starting point would be to pick countries with similar scores on the first two institutional measures constructed by Brunetti, Kisunko, and Weder (1997) and to assess cross-country performances in investment and growth.

■ We need more micro studies over time at the country or regional level. Such studies would allow us to better control for the role of informal norms and thereby to isolate the importance of formal rules. Using the analytical lenses provided by the new institutional economics to reevaluate existing studies in economic history may be a fruitful exercise.

■ We need more micro studies of specific institutions—both their causes and effects. This issue is especially important for policymakers, because countries' macroinstitutional capability environments are less amenable to change than specific laws and policies. I will briefly report on some collaborative work of mine in this vein.

Alston, Libecap, and Schneider (1996) analyzed the determinants and impact of land titles in the Brazilian Amazon, using data from surveys of households and municipal-level census data. From the household survey data, we found that secure titles raised land-specific investment across our sites from 150 to 300 percent. We also found that the primary determinants of property rights are the potential increases in land value from secure property (a function of distance from market) and political factors (state governments assigned titles more quickly than the national government).

Alston, Libecap, and Mueller (forthcoming) analyzed the sources of violent conflicts over land in the Brazilian Amazon. We found that the ultimate sources of violence are an inconsistency in the property rights that titled holders receive from statutory law and constitutional property rights. Statistically, conflicts are likely in areas where land values increase, on large holdings of uncleared land, and in close proximity to land reform agencies. The violence generated by conflicts over land also affects economic behavior across municipalities. We found that violence reduces land-specific investment by about 20 percent and land values by 8 percent.

## References

Alston, Lee J., Gary Libecap, and Robert Schneider. 1996. "The Determinants and Impact of Property Rights: Census Data and Survey Results for Land Titles on the Brazilian Frontier." *Journal of Law, Economics, and Organization* 12(1):25–61.

Alston, Lee J., Gary D. Libecap, and Bernardo Mueller. Forthcoming. *Titles and Land Use: The Development of Property Rights on the Brazilian Amazon Frontier.* Ann Arbor: University of Michigan Press.

Brunetti, Aymo, Gregory Kisunko, and Beatrice Weder. 1997. "Economic Growth with 'Incredible' Rules: Evidence from a World Wide Private Sector Survey." Background paper for *World Development Report*. World Bank, Washington, D.C.

Commander, Simon, Hamid Davoodi, and Une J. Lee. 1996. "The Causes and Consequences of Government for Growth and Well-being." Background paper for *World Development Report*. World Bank, Washington, D.C.

World Bank. 1997. *World Development Report*. Oxford and New York: Oxford University Press for the World Bank.

## Comments on "Institutions, policies, and development outcomes," by Chhibber

*Mustapha K. Nabli*

The paper presents a number of macroanalysis results quantifying the impact of a country's institutions—and more accurately, of the state—on development outcomes. It is concerned only with the state, presumably because the state is more prone to change and improvement in design, at least in the medium term, than other institutions embedded in customs and culture. The paper gives a brief summary of results from studies conducted at the World Bank for the *1997 World Development Report*. Since I do not have the original studies, my remarks will be based only on the summaries given in the paper, and they may not do justice to the original work.

The general approach is part of an increasing stream of studies and results that take institutions as exogenous and attempt to measure, by cross-section regression analysis, their impact on development performance. The results presented are impressive in showing the existence of a strong impact on outcomes using different measures of the quality of institutions and outcomes. I would like, however, to raise a few issues about these results.

### Institutions and policies

The first issue is the distinction between institutions and policies used in the studies, which has significant implications. The distinction between institutions and policies is often obscured by the fact that the same analytical approaches—for example, transaction costs—are applied to both institutional and policy change. However, whether one uses a restrictive definition of institutions, such as "formal and informal rules that constrain individual behavior," or a more extensive one, such as that argued by Jeffrey Nugent, the distinction has to be clearly kept in mind.

In the empirical analysis discussed in the paper, both institutions and policies are used as variables for explaining outcomes. This suggests an *implicit assumption of their independence* that may be questioned. There may be arguments for the existence of substitution as well as complementarity between them. This possibility is also suggested by the diagram presented in Jeffrey Nugent's paper.

Let us take the case of a very restrictive foreign trade policy favoring import substitution. Political economy problems constrain the liberalization of trade, but it is possible to develop a parallel institutional arrangement, such as free trade zones, that exempts exporters from the restrictive rules and regulations governing imports. A bad policy is partially corrected by the development of new institutions. Some also argue that in East Asia, the effects of bad policies that create financial repression have been mitigated by good institutional capacity. It can also be argued, and this is a well-recognized and general theme in many papers in this volume, that good institutions are conducive to good policies. This argument suggests complementarities between them.

50

The preceding remarks are important to the interpretation of the empirical results presented in the paper and their policy implications. Let's refer to figure 3.2 in the author's paper. The author concludes that good policies and good government capability are conducive to better performance. This notion cannot be disputed, but don't the figures also mean that *institutions are more important than policies*? The gain from better capability, using this dichotomous classification, is much greater than that from better policies: 1.6 percentage points of growth or more, compared with 1 point or less. We notice that the same order of magnitude for the effect of better institutional capacity is inferred from figure 3.4 using the local investor's view, and the gain from high capability is about 1.5 percentage of growth. These results would mean that developing a better capability to implement policies, even in the presence of bad policies, is more important than changing bad policies.

This analysis may well be interpreted, as noted earlier, as suggesting that good institutional capacity is a very good substitute for good policies, since it allows the costs of bad policies to be mitigated. However, if institutions and policies are viewed as independent, as presumed in the regression, good implementation of bad policies is preferable to bad implementation of good policies. In such a case, how do we reconcile this idea with results showing that various mechanisms that develop to counter bad polices (such as smuggling, in the case of trade controls) improve welfare?

## Institutional capability and the state

The second issue is the concept of "institutional capability" used in the analysis. The paper does not address the issue of institutions in general and their impact on performance. Rather, it deals with one dimension of the state as an institution and terms this dimension institutional capability. IC is the central concept of the paper and is defined as "the state's ability to provide collective goods at the lowest cost to society."

Institutions, like policies, have many characteristics or dimensions. One basic dimension is the quality of the incentives institutions support. Another one is the *predictability and enforceability* of the rules or policies. The concept of IC measures the quality of the state by reference only to this last dimension, which is important but may not capture the full content of an institution. The state's institutions may be good at producing predictable policies and enforcing them. But at the same time, they may have a number of negative features. Among these might be a political system that tends predictably to favor less dynamic groups or to maintain the status quo and fails to adapt policies to a changing environment.

By focusing on the efficient provision of collective goods, the concept tends to ignore the question of how good the institutions are at determining the appropriate levels of these goods and making changes when required. The state may provide a very good and efficient educational system but emphasize higher education at the expense of primary and secondary education for the larger segment of the population.

Further, the focus on efficiency makes institutional capability closer to an *outcome* than to a determining factor. When we measure institutional capability through the response of entrepreneurs to the stability of rules and their enforceability, the result is closer to an outcome than to a characteristic of an institution. The fact that "rule making is not predictable" clearly has a negative impact on performance. But why it does, and the features of the institutional arrangements that make it so, remain unknown.

## Aggregation and causality

The third issue is aggregation in this type of work. While I am not quite sure how the aggregation was done in the reported analysis, the IC index is an aggregate of many indicators. And it is not clear what the best approach is. Campos and Nugent (1996) argue for using principal components. But a more important question is whether it is desirable, in this type of analysis, to disaggregate and use various institutional variables. With reference to the state, such variables might include the extent of checks and balances and of enforcement of property rights, bureaucratic capability, and openness and accountability of government. These variables are probably highly correlated, and while it may be difficult to determine their specific effects, the task should be attempted. The issue of causality between institutional development and performance is well known and has to be kept in mind for the interpretation of the results.

## Policy implications

The paper draws several policy implications from the results discussed. In addition to my remarks about the relative importance of institutions and policies, I would like to add the following.

The aggregation of institutions into a single index transforms it into a kind of a black box, making it difficult to draw policy implications. From the principle of "matching the state's role to its capabilities" one can argue that there is a need for prioritization in changing and improving institutions in developing countries. Institutions are not a free good; developing and implementing them requires the allocation of already limited human and financial resources. A developing country has to prioritize. Is it more important—at a given stage of development—to invest in improving the systems for defining and protecting property rights or in improving the general bureaucracy? How about the educational system? And how important are government openness and democratic processes compared with the proper enforcement of property rights?

For institutional analysis to have an impact on policy, these difficult issues have to be addressed and institutions unbundled in the study of their impact on development performance.[1]

## Note

The study of the impact of policies on performance progressed when various specific policies—such as macroeconomic, trade, financial, and fiscal—were analyzed separately. A similar approach is needed for institutions.

## Reference

Campos, Nauro, and Jeffrey Nugent. 1996. *Institutions and Economic Growth: An Economic Study.* Los Angeles: University of Southern California.

**Floor discussion on "Institutions, policies, and development outcomes"**

The discussion centered around three questions from participants. The first participant confirmed the correlation between institutional capabilities and policy based on his experience with the United Nations Development Programme. Looking at this selection of samples, he asked whether similar methodologies can be used to assess institutional capability in terms of social and human development.

The second participant noted that one of the two indexes in the paper is about individual rights, the second about the state. In an ideal situation, he said, both individual and state would act only for the common good. But that kind of behavior is rare and is in fact the reason economists try to understand how institutions are created. He asked how, given this situation, the two indexes interact and what we can learn from them.

The third participant commented on the situation of East Asia in the late 1950s. If the question of institutional capabilities had been asked then, would the answer have been the same as it is today?

Ajay Chhibber said that the Bank's 1997 *World Development Report* answers these questions. Specifically, he noted that part of making good policies goes back to institutions. Moses Naim has noted that first- and second-generation reform need different approaches. The first requires a quick fix, while the second involves more institutional solutions. The WDR team learned that economists tend to think mostly in terms of policies. But as the Bank emphasizes to "hard-core" economists, if policies are held constant, outcomes are not necessarily the same. Policy is not the only thing that matters.

Chhibber went on to say that he is not a great believer in the idea that cultural factors play a role in economic development. He mentioned that the WDR team found enormous variations in outcomes based on such variables. A particularly relevant example is lawmaking and the application of laws, since crime and theft can occur through laws and state agencies. But political regimes do not matter once institutional variables are brought into the picture.

On the question of participation, perceptions are important for the kind of issues under discussion here. Private investors' perceptions of the effects of institutional capabilities affect growth. The WDR team tried to compare more objective measures of capability, such as how long it takes ships to get through ports and goods to clear customs.

On the relationship between liberalization and institutional capability, Chhibber noted that liberalization is close to a policy index. The bottom line is that all the issues that have been raised are relevant. The WDR team has been able to push the envelope a little further, if not far enough, and it is important to add some data in a generalizable form.

In a quick postscript, Lee Alston commented that development economics should take history more seriously, first because it offers abundant data, and second because it is a laboratory.

# 4. Reinvigorating state institutions[1]

## Sanjay Pradhan

*The author illustrates how three interrelated set of institutional mechanisms—effective rules and restraints; competitive pressures from markets, civil society, and other state organs; and voice and partnerships—can improve the credibility, accountability, and responsiveness of governments.*

An effective state is vital to the provision of goods and services—and rules and institutions—that promote sustainable development. But there is no guarantee that state intervention will benefit society. The state's monopoly on coercion, which gives it the power to intervene effectively in economic activity, also gives it the power to intervene arbitrarily. Combined with the problems of asymmetric information that permeate the state apparatus, this power creates considerable opportunities for public officials to engage in actions—rent-seeking and corruption—that promote their own welfare, or those of friends and allies, at the expense of the general interest. Therefore, while restraining arbitrary action and corruption, countries must work to establish and nurture mechanisms that give state agencies the flexibility and incentive to act in the public interest.

Unfortunately, governments in many developing countries have exhibited behavior that suggests a clear imbalance between flexibility and restraint. Consequently, their actions have not been viewed as credible, and investment and growth have suffered. Three interrelated sets of institutional mechanisms can improve the credibility, accountability, and responsiveness of such governments: effective rules and restraints, competitive pressures, and voice and partnerships.

- *Rules and restraints.* Many countries need to strengthen formal instruments of restraint—judicial independence and effective separation of powers, for instance—to enhance the credibility and accountability of the state. Within the executive branch as well, credibility of rules—for instance hard budgets, financial accountability, and restraints on political patronage in personnel policies—provides an enabling environment for effective public sector performance.

- *Voice and partnerships.* Mechanisms that foster voice and partnerships for businesses and civil society in state activities provide opportunities for input and oversight by external stakeholders. For instance, public-private deliberation councils can promote well-informed and credible policymaking, while client surveys can make transparent the quality of service delivery and generate external pressures for improved performance.

- *Competitive pressures.* Competitive pressures—from markets and civil society and other state organs—check the potential abuse of the state's monopoly in policymaking and service delivery. Competition in civil service recruitment and promotion can help build a motivated and meritocratic bureaucracy that is crucial to an effective state.

This paper illustrates how a combination of these mechanisms can improve the state's institutional capability to undertake collective actions at the lowest cost to society. The first section discusses formal checks and balances, including judicial independence and the separation of powers. The subsequent three sections examine institutional mechanisms to build a more capable public sector in three core areas: policymaking, service delivery, and fostering motivated, capable staff. The last section shows that corruption is a symptom of underlying incentive problems, which can be addressed using the same mechanisms that enhance state capability more broadly.

## Formal checks and balances

Arbitrary and capricious state actions can undermine credibility and the rule of law. Sustainable development generally calls for formal instruments of restraint that hold the state and its officials accountable for their actions. To be enduring and credible, these mechanisms must be anchored in core state institutions. If these institutions are too weak, international mechanisms can substitute temporarily. The two key formal mechanisms of restraint are a strong, independent judiciary and the separation of powers.

Societies have devised a broad array of formal and informal mechanisms for resolving disputes and enforcing compliance with rules, none more important than the formal judiciary. Yet for judiciaries to be effective, they must be independent and have resources and instruments for enforcement. India provides a striking recent example of the exercise of judicial authority relative to other organs of the state. In many countries, however, judicial independence and enforcement have repeatedly been compromised. In Malta, for instance, judges of the superior court had their duties suspended one hour before a case challenging executive action was to be heard. In Poland, bailiffs are not under the control of judges, and their offices are understaffed (Webb 1996).

Developing relationships among the judiciary, legislature, and executive that ensure judicial independence and enforcement is a gradual process. Studies show that private sector confidence in the rule of law increases with each year a stable regime remains in place (Clague and others 1996). More broadly, the success of third-party enforcement depends largely on citizens viewing the mechanisms as legitimate. In Peru during the late 1980s, for instance, popular participation and community norms helped institute effective property rights and dispute resolution mechanisms in urban areas. In countries where judicial institutions are weak, it may be at least as important to demonstrate to citizens and firms the potential benefits of a well-functioning judiciary and to win support for good laws and impartial enforcement as to proceed with wholly technocratic programs of judicial reforms.

Even where judiciaries are capable of enforcing rules, the state's credibility can be limited if the public has little reason to believe that the rules will be reasonably stable over time. One classic constitutional mechanism for restraining untrammeled legislative change is to divide power horizontally (among the judiciary, legislature, and executive) or vertically (among different levels of government). In countries with multiple political parties, patterns of party organization can also determine the extent to which political power is concentrated or diffused.

The broader the separation of powers, the greater will be the number of veto points that must be navigated to change any rule-based commitments. The separation of powers adds to the public's confidence that rules will be sustained over time or adapted only after considerable negotiation. However, the presence of multiple veto points can be a double-edged sword, making it hard to change not only beneficial rules but also harmful ones. And it can create gridlock among the branches of government. In many developing countries, however, there are few effective checks and balances, even where there is formal separation of powers. In some countries, legislative oversight is weak because of poor capacity and inadequate information. In others, the executive dominates a compliant legislature.

To some extent, external restraints can substitute for limitations on the ability of national institutions to enforce rules or to credibly signal that rules will remain reasonably stable over time. One option is to use extraterritorial adjudication to underpin—or to compensate for weaknesses in—the domestic judicial system. Confidence in the Jamaican judicial system is buttressed by the fact that the United Kingdom's Privy Council serves as its appellate court of last resort. Cross-border agreements are a second mechanism for strengthening commitments. Examples include the European Union, the North American Free Trade Agreement, and the West African franc zone.

## Strengthening institutions for policymaking

Instruments of restraint provide a vital foundation for sustainable development. However, they need to be balanced by institutional arrangements that provide the executive with sufficient flexibility to formulate and implement policies and adapt to new information and changing circumstances. Although the precise institutional arrangements vary, effective public sectors in industrial countries and much of East Asia have generally been characterized by a strong central capacity for macroeconomic and strategic policy formulation; mechanisms to delegate, discipline, and contest policies among government agencies; and transparent links to external stakeholders for feedback and accountability. By contrast, policymaking capacity in many developing and transition economies is weak and fragmented, with few institutionalized arrangements for input or oversight from key stakeholders.

Among industrial countries, Australia provides an example of reforms aimed explicitly at creating a more transparent, competitive, and results-oriented policymaking process. Of particular relevance to other countries is the emphasis on publishing the medium-term costs of competing policies, facilitating debate and consultation on policy priorities in the cabinet and among government agencies (within hard budget constraints), and focusing attention on results through ex post evaluation and reporting on outcomes. These reforms helped turn the fiscal deficit into a surplus during the 1980s (Campos and Pradhan 1996).

The United States and some continental European countries have instituted other mechanisms for consultation and oversight in policymaking. U.S. executive agencies, for instance, are governed by the Administrative Procedures Act (APA) of 1946, which imposes certain procedural requirements, enforceable in the courts, such as public announcements of new policy. This procedures-oriented approach to policy formulation allows legislators to shift substantive policymaking to specialist agencies, plus other interested parties closer to the problem. And it creates a decentralized mechanism that uses citizen voice and the judiciary for ensuring accountability.

The successful East Asian countries have adopted an approach that shares some key aspects with the approaches used in industrial countries. In Japan, Malaysia, Singapore, Thailand, and the Republic of Korea, policymaking has been delegated to elite central agencies. These agencies are nevertheless embedded in processes—public-private deliberation councils—that provide input and oversight from private firms. The central agencies are staffed by professional and capable employees recruited on the basis of merit, often through highly competitive examinations. Transparent and institutionalized mechanisms of consultation with nongovernment actors constrain the pursuit of costly programs, while providing the flexibility to adapt policy to changing circumstances (Campos and Root 1996).

Many developing countries in Africa, Central America, and the Caribbean lack the critical mass of effective capacity to formulate strategic policies. Poor pay at senior levels and the absence of meritocracy are factors contributing to weak central capacity. The problem of weak central capacity is compounded by poor discipline and an absence of competitive pressures in decisionmaking. For instance, budgets are unrealistic, and decisions are made in an ad hoc manner during implementation. In recent years, the variation between budgeted and actual recurrent expenditures has averaged more than 50 percent in Tanzania and 30 percent in Uganda. Further, there are long lags in the production of financial accounts and audits and often no system of costing or of contesting competing policies. In Guinea, for instance, an exercise to cost out policies to meet the government's stated priorities revealed that the three priority programs were grossly underfunded and that their share would need to triple over four years (figure 4.1).

In aid-dependent countries, donors sometimes alleviate, but too often worsen, the problem of weak central capacity. To the extent that donors provide policy advice that supplements weak capacity, they help the short-term problem at hand, but the long-term problem remains. Donors also splinter central capacity for policy formulation through the fragmentation in decisionmaking introduced by individual projects. Ministries and donors enter into bilateral deals on multiple projects without determining whether their cumulative effects are collectively sustainable or mutually consistent. In many countries, public investment programs have become passive repositories of donor-driven projects, and the future recurrent costs of projects have become unsustainable (figure 4.1). The lack of coordination between ministries of planning and ministries of finance further impedes the integration of capital and recurrent expenditures. The result of similar problems in many developing countries is that newly built roads fall into disrepair, schools find themselves without textbooks, and health centers lack drugs.

Several initiatives have been launched to address these problems. The Africa Capacity-Building Foundation, established by donors and African governments, seeks to

FIGURE 4.1: GUINEA'S POLICY GOALS AND SPENDING ALLOCATIONS DO NOT ADD UP

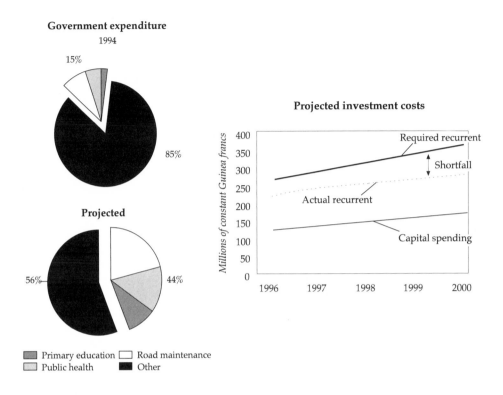

Primary education  Road maintenance
Public health  Other

*Source:* World Bank 1996.

strengthen indigenous African policymaking capacity. But its focus is not on reforming the incentive framework that governs decisionmaking in the public sector. Governments and donors have also launched sectoral investment programs that coordinate donor assistance, such as the Agricultural Sector Investment Program in Zambia, which aims to replace 180 individual donor projects. Countries like Malawi and Uganda are moving beyond coordinating donor policies within a given sector to developing a systematic process for strategic prioritization across sectors, working within aggregate spending constraints. A few countries, such as Colombia, are undertaking efforts to institute an ex post evaluation system to assess whether policies are achieving intended outcomes.

In the transition countries of Central and Eastern Europe and the former Soviet republics, the shortage of administrative expertise is not as much of a problem. Their experience shows the equal importance of mechanisms able to channel that competence into coherent policy. When the communist regimes in these countries collapsed, so did the centralized decisionmaking apparatus for coordinating the activities of ministries and departments. As a result, these countries developed confused, overlapping responsibilities and multiple rather than collective accountability—a sure-fire formula for disastrous policy formulation. Ukraine exemplifies a particularly egregious set of such problems. But countries like Poland and Hungary have introduced reforms to streamline multiple and conflicting responsibilities and speed decisionmaking (Nunberg forthcoming). In Georgia, streamlining has removed overlapping and conflicting positions, and draft laws are decided in the presence of all members of the president's economic council. Such reforms have aided coordination and consultation in central government decisionmaking.

## Reforming institutions for delivery

Even well-designed policies can experience major implementation problems. In many countries, services simply are not delivered or are delivered badly. Poor quality, high costs, waste, fraud, and corruption have marred delivery in many developing countries. Politicians often intervene in the day-to-day operations of public agencies, and managers have limited flexibility. There is limited accountability for the use of inputs, and virtually none for the achievement of results. And in many countries, the public sector has assumed a monopoly in delivery, eliminating pressures for better performance.

To improve delivery, governments are experimenting with a range of institutional mechanisms. Greater use of markets is creating competitive pressure and providing users with more exit options or a choice of alternative suppliers. Exit options are also being enhanced by competitive contracting out to the private sector and nongovernmental organizations (NGOs). Some governments are setting up performance-based agencies in the broader public sector and entering into contracts with these agencies, providing them with greater managerial flexibility while holding them accountable for results. Many other governments are relying on more traditional bureaucratic forms in the core public sector or the civil service, with much more limited managerial flexibility. These governments rely on accountability in the use of inputs, meritocracy, and an esprit de corps to build loyalty for effective performance. Finally, voice mechanisms—such as user participation, client surveys, and published benchmarks—are providing external pressures for improving delivery.

The so-called new public management reforms in the industrial countries have sought to improve delivery primarily by using market-type mechanisms and formal contracting. New Zealand provides the most dramatic example. Commercial and contestable activities were hived off, corporatized, and often privatized. All remaining conglomerate ministries were broken into focused business units headed by chief executive officers on fixed-term, output-based contracts with considerable managerial autonomy, including the right to hire and fire. These reforms helped turn the budget deficit of 9 percent into a surplus during the 1980s; unit costs of delivery declined by more than 20 percent for some agencies (Campos and Pradhan 1996).

The new public management reforms have attracted considerable attention and are now being emulated in several developing countries. But what is feasible in New Zealand may be beyond the realm of possibility in many developing countries. It takes considerable capacity and commitment to write and enforce contracts, especially for outputs that are difficult to specify, as they are in the social sectors. The appropriate mechanism to improve performance depends on the characteristics of the service and the capability of the state to enforce internal and external contracts (table 4.1).

Table 4.1: Mechanisms to improve service delivery

| Mechanism | Delivery characteristics and enforcement capability | | |
| --- | --- | --- | --- |
| | Contestable | Easy to specify and enforce | Difficult to specify and enforce |
| Markets and the private sector | Strengthen markets: credible regulation Create markets: vouchers | Contract out to for-profit or nonprofit agencies | |
| Broader public sector | Enhance internal competition Create hard budgets and divest state firms | Set up performance-based agencies Corporatize and establish enforceable performance contracts Strengthen voice mechanisms | |
| Core public sector | | | Clarity of task and purpose Improved rule compliance Increased loyalty Strengthened voice mechanisms |

*Source:* Author's compilation.

For services that are contestable (that is, where there is scope for actual or potential competition), such as commercial products and, more recently, telecommunications and power generation, market-type mechanisms can generate powerful competitive pressures for improved delivery. The deregulation of telecommunications and power generation has led to significantly lower unit costs and a rapid expansion in services in many countries throughout the Americas, Europe, and Asia. But greater use of market mechanisms nonetheless requires an effective regulatory capacity, which is not always easy to achieve.

For services whose outputs the state can specify and enforce at low transaction costs, contracting out to private firms and NGOs is an attractive option. In industrial countries, the contracting out of services to the private sector has become a prominent phenomenon. The case of Victoria State in Australia provides a dramatic example. Each local council is required to contract at least half of its annual budget through competitive tender, including complex community care services. In developing countries, contracting out easily specified services competitively can potentially lead to efficiency gains. For instance, contracting out road maintenance to private contractors in Brazil led to savings of 25 percent. Leases have increased the efficiency of water supply in Guinea and the operation of Port Kelang in Malaysia (World Bank 1994).

Some governments are also contracting out the delivery of services that are difficult to specify, especially social services, to NGOs. For instance, governments in Bolivia and Uganda have subcontracted to NGOs perceived to be committed to high quality or able to serve certain groups better because of their religious or ideological orientation (van der Gaag 1995). In general, however, contracting out activities that are complex or nonroutinized will inevitably incur high transaction costs. Further, such contracting is prone to corruption and mismanagement, much like internal contracting within the public sector.

For activities that remain in the public sector, industrial countries undertaking public management reforms are setting up performance-based agencies and entering into formal contracts even for complex activities (for example, defense, education, and health care). But countries with limited capacity to enforce complex contracts and weak bureaucratic controls to restrain arbitrariness need to proceed with caution. The industrial countries that have now relaxed their detailed control over inputs developed credible restraints over a long period of time. Many developing countries have often been unsuccessful in enforcing contracts with public enterprises that produce commercial and easily specified outputs. A recent study of public enterprises found the overall record of performance contracts in developing countries quite disappointing (World Bank 1995).

Although performance contracts have not been successful, developing countries have sought to create performance-based agencies for easily specified and high-priority tasks such as road maintenance or tax collection. Generally, these agencies have been enclaves within the civil service with greater managerial flexibility, better pay, and greater accountability for results. In Sub-Saharan Africa, such agencies have been created to achieve tax collection targets in Ghana, Uganda, and Zambia, and some other countries appear poised to follow suit (Dia 1996). The results have been impressive, but the approach is not without problems. While tax revenues have increased (for instance, from 6 percent of GDP to over 12 percent of GDP in Ghana between 1984 and 1988), the rest of the civil service has chafed at the benefits provided to the tax collectors.

More troublesome has been the establishment in several aid-dependent countries of project enclaves, each with its own system of remuneration and accountability. Often donors have created these enclaves with little if any systematic consideration of the nature of services provided or of the optimal sequencing of institutional reforms. And in doing so, they have created disparities.

Enclaves have often been designed as quick fixes. And though they sometimes accomplish short-term goals, they can create obstacles for deeper institutional reform. Where the outputs are easily specified—tax collection, for example—enclaves can be useful as an experimental stage of reforms to be progressively extended and as a demonstration that reforms can be effective. But enclaves cannot substitute for the long-term institutional reforms needed to create a professional, rule-based bureaucracy.

Many developing countries need first to strengthen rule-based compliance and financial accountability, provide greater clarity of purpose and task, and introduce performance measurement. In this regard, countries are undertaking an array of reforms to improve the quality and credibility of their financial accounting and auditing systems. Modern computer-based information systems, such as those in Argentina and Bolivia, are helping to improve transparency and strengthen aggregate controls, reducing the need for transaction-specific controls. Countries as diverse as China, Indonesia, and Moldova are setting into law the principles of accounting practices, backed by strong professional associations within and outside government. As input controls are strengthened, countries such as Colombia, Mexico, and Uganda are also introducing performance measurement to orient managers to achieve desired results. As output measurement and ex post controls on inputs are strengthened, agencies can be allowed more flexibility in exchange for greater accountability for results.

Alongside better systems of financial accountability, mechanisms to enhance the loyalty, motivation, and competence of the civil service are also needed. Loyalty is essential in the core public sector, where activities are not easily specifiable or monitorable and exit has no meaning. As discussed in the next section, the experience of successful countries suggests that developing such a staff requires meritocratic recruitment and promotion, long-term career rewards, adequate pay, and mechanisms to instill an esprit de corps.

Instituting a professional, rule-based bureaucracy will take time. Where internal monitoring and enforcement capacity is weak, pressures from clients can improve performance through participation, client surveys, and publicly disseminated standards or charters. Feedback mechanisms such as client surveys can provide valuable information about an agency's performance. Experience with client surveys in India, Nicaragua, and Tanzania suggests that they increase transparency and improve accountability. Several countries, including Malaysia, Portugal, and the United Kingdom, are setting and publicizing minimum service standards. With clear and specific service standards, clients and staff know what is expected—in some cases for the first time. Combined with client surveys, charters can encourage lower-cost, third-party enforcement.

## Motivated, capable staff

Whether making policy, delivering services, or administering contracts, capable and motivated staff constitute the life blood of an effective state. Efforts to build a motivated, competent civil service usually focus almost exclusively on pay. Adequate pay is thus essential to an effective civil service. But other elements are also vital, including merit-based recruitment and promotion and creating an esprit de corps. A recent cross-country study created an index representing meritocratic recruitment and promotion and adequacy of pay based on a study of 30 countries (Evans and Rauch 1996). As shown in figure 4.2, this index is correlated with economic growth and with investors' perception of bureaucratic capability, even after controlling for income and education. Meritocracy can therefore yield high payoffs.

### Merit-based recruitment and promotion

Building a competent bureaucracy requires, among other things, establishing a merit-based recruitment system. Such a system injects high-quality staff into the civil service, creates prestige for civil service positions, and thus makes it attractive to talented individuals. The opposite is true of a recruitment system based on favoritism, which in the long run leads to a poor-quality personnel pool. In many industrial and successful developing countries, the basic merit system is a national civil service entrance exam with tough enough standards to separate out the top

FIGURE 4.2: MERITOCRACY PROMOTES BUREAUCRATIC CAPABILITY AND ECONOMIC GROWTH

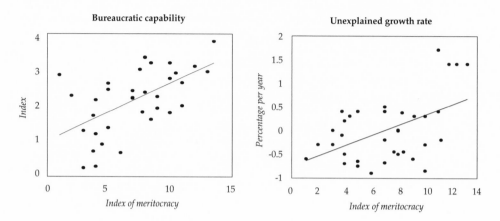

*Note:* Controlling for income and education.
*Source:* Evans and Rauch 1996.

applicants (for example, Japan and Korea). In some countries, school performance is the primary filter. In Singapore, for example, recruitment is based on high standards of academic performance and rigorous personal interviews (Campos and Pradhan forthcoming).

Introducing a merit-based promotion system is also essential. To motivate workers, the civil service must establish objective, meritorious criteria for upward mobility and offer long-term career rewards. If promotions are personalized or, worse, politicized, civil servants will focus on doing favors for influential politicians. Korea avoids this problem by basing promotion on a formula that combines seniority with merit.

Many countries have had trouble instituting meritocratic recruitment and promotion except in isolated enclaves, partly because political appointees tend to be granted extensive powers. As a result, the state has become a massive source of jobs for people recruited on the basis of connections rather than merit. In East Asia, political appointments are more common in the Philippines than in Korea (figure 4.3).

*Adequate compensation*

Building prestige through merit-based recruitment and promotion makes employment in the civil service attractive. But if public sector compensation substantially lags behind the private sector pay, then prestige alone will not make up for the difference. Comparisons between public and private salaries are complex; in general, though, civil servants nearly everywhere are paid less than their private sector counterparts. In the Philippines and Somalia, public pay averages just 25 and 11 percent, respectively, of private wages. In many countries, the difference in public-private pay has widened over time. For example, in Kenya public wages relative to private wages declined by 3 percent a year during 1982–92.

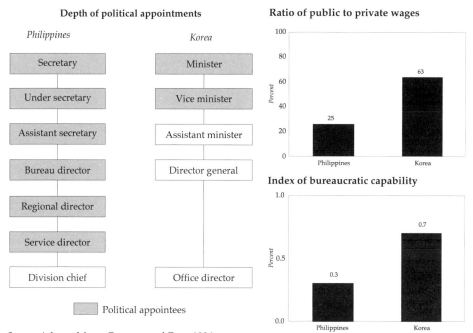

FIGURE 4.3: KOREA HAS RELIED ON MERIT-BASED APPOINTMENTS AND BETTER PAY TO MAKE ITS BUREAUCRACY MORE CAPABLE THAN THAT OF THE PHILIPPINES

*Source:* Adapted from Campos and Root 1996.

Despite the overall wage erosion and declines relative to the private sector, the central problem in many developing countries is the low level of remuneration for higher cadres. This limitation is the one that most constrains the ability of government to attract and retain quality skills. Wage compression, which allows the highest-level civil servants' wages to erode more than those of lower-level workers, often for political reasons, is thus a key problem in many countries. In a study of ten African countries, the ratio of salaries of the highest- to lowest-grade civil servant declined from 13:1 to 9:1 (Lindauer and Nunberg 1994). Across-the-board increases do not solve this problem. In many developing countries, such as in Africa, expanding employment, especially at lower skill levels, has been an important contributing factor in compressing wage rates within a constrained overall wage bill.

In response to these problems, countries have embarked on civil service reforms geared toward reducing employment, decompressing the wage structure, and raising average pay. These efforts have met with only limited success. In a study of a sample of civil service reform efforts between 1981 and 1991, fewer than half the countries succeeded in reducing wage bills and decompressing salaries (World Bank 1991). More than half achieved employment reductions, but some later reported that these gains had been reversed.

The mixed and often disappointing experiences nevertheless provide some lessons for future efforts at civil service reform. First, strategies for civil service reforms have focused unduly on pay and employment issues. Other elements of a reform strategy—

greater accountability for results, merit-based recruitment and promotion, and mechanisms to instill an esprit de corps—are often not emphasized. Second, a more careful sequencing of reforms is called for that emphasizes decompression of wages—even within a constrained wage bill—to attract high-quality people and concentrate scarce skills in strategic areas. Third, in countries that are considerably overstaffed, reforms so far have been too modest to really downsize governments to sustainable proportions or to be self-financing. Inevitably, pay and employment reforms will face political obstacles, although expectations of political backlash have often been overstated.

### Building an esprit de corps

Effective and capable bureaucracies are characterized by an esprit de corps, or shared commitment to organization objectives. An esprit de corps creates internal partnerships or a high degree of coherence among group members and gives them a strong sense of purpose and belonging. King Arthur's Knights of the Round Table, the samurai in Japan, and even the mafioso of past generations all embodied some form of esprit de corps. A few of today's civil services are said to do so as well, including those in Chile, France, Germany, Japan, South Korea, and the United Kingdom. Most bureaucracies, however, do not have this feature.

It is possible to develop an esprit de corps among civil servants. Singapore's civil service is well known for its coherence and sense of purpose, but in the early 1960s it barely existed. In just two decades, the country's civil service evolved into one of the world's most reputable. Prospective recruits were taken from the top 200 (less than 5 percent) of the graduating class at the National University of Singapore and put through the same one-year training program. Their education and training gave the recruits a common understanding of what was expected of them and helped build trust among them. The meritocratic promotion system helped generate among officials a stake in the goals or mission of the agency. The single-mindedness of leadership and its efforts to imbue the service with its desired values helped strengthen the bond among civil servants (Campos and Pradhan forthcoming).

Worker dedication and commitment are not confined to industrial countries or to East Asia. In Brazil's poor northeast region of Ceará, worker commitment dramatically improved the quality of public services delivered (Tendler 1997). This outcome was made possible by the sense of calling felt by workers and the prestige of the tasks created by the state government. Such experiences underscore the importance of nonmonetary rewards—such as recognition, prestige, and awards—in motivating staff, beyond pay and meritocratic recruitment, and promotion.

### Corruption: a symptom of underlying incentive problems

Even if flexible bureaucracies are embedded in processes of policy formulation and service delivery that provide ample opportunity for oversight and competition, the risk remains that individual officials will pursue goals other than those mandated. Self-seeking behavior by officials can degenerate into corruption when private interests wield their influence illegally and circumvent legal requirements meant to apply across the board. Corruption represents the abuse of public power for private gain. It is symptomatic of the more general problem of perverse underlying incentives. Corruption flourishes where distortions in the policy and regulatory regime provide scope for it and where institutions for restraint are weak.

Some corruption stems from opportunities generated by the policy environment. Countries with highly distorted policies, as measured by variables such as the black market premium, provide more control rights to politicians and bureaucrats and are more corrupt (figure 4.4). A second cause is the relative riskiness of corrupt deals to the person paying a bribe and the official receiving it (Rose-Ackerman 1996). Law-breakers may believe that they stand little chance of being caught if the system of justice can be corrupted. Indeed, there is a negative correlation between reported levels of corruption and the predictability of the judiciary (figure 4.4).

Finally, the consequences of being caught and disciplined may be low relative to the benefits. Corruption is often positively associated with the extent of public-private pay differentials, or what may be termed the "rate of temptation." But simply raising civil service salaries may do little to reduce corruption. Merit-based mechanisms that restrain political patronage and create a more impartial public service are also associated with lower corruption (figure 4.4).

These results show that corruption cannot be attacked effectively in isolation. It needs to be combated with a multipronged strategy. One thrust of this strategy is to institute a professional, rule-based bureaucracy with a pay structure that rewards

FIGURE 4.4: CAUSES OF CORRUPTION, VARIOUS COUNTRIES

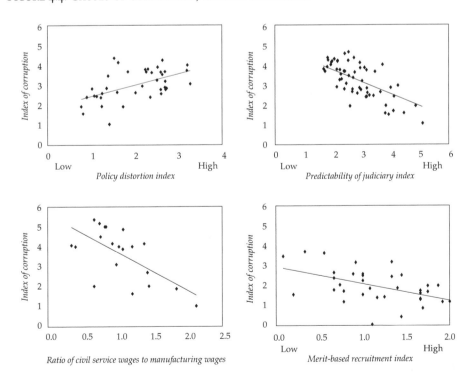

*Source:* Van Rijckeghem and Weder 1996; Evans and Rauch 1996.

civil servants for honest efforts, a merit-based system to shield the civil service from political patronage, and credible financial controls to prevent the arbitrary use of public resources. A second thrust aims to reduce opportunities for officials to act corruptly by cutting back on the discretionary authority of individual officials and by increasing competition. A third thrust aims to enhance accountability through greater transparency and the strengthening of the mechanisms of monitoring and punishment using not only criminal law, but also oversight by formal institutions (such as statutory watchdogs in Hong Kong) and ordinary citizens.

### Reducing regulations and increasing competition

In general, any reform that increases the competitiveness of the economy will help reduce corrupt incentives. Thus policies that lower controls on foreign trade, remove entry barriers for private industry, and privatize state firms in a way that ensures competition will contribute to the fight against corruption. If the state has no authority to restrict exports or license businesses, no one will pay bribes in those areas. If price controls are lifted, market prices will express scarcity values, not bribes.

A variety of measures can help reduce official discretion in ongoing programs. These include clarifying and streamlining laws (as in the reform of Mexico's customs service), introducing market-based schemes that limit discretion (such as user charges), making rules transparent, and introducing competitive pressures (such as open, competitive bids for public procurement).

### Statutory watchdogs

Independent oversight institutions that are part of the government structure can help limit corruption. Countries have experimented with a variety of approaches. Some countries (such as Botswana, Singapore, and Uganda) have independent anti-corruption commissions or inspector generals that can carry out investigations and bring cases to trial. The most famous is the Hong Kong Independent Commission Against Corruption, which reports exclusively to the governor general and has extensive powers. Ombudsmen, who hear citizen complaints of all kinds, can help increase the accountability of government agencies, as they have in South Africa since the passing of the Ombudsman Act of 1991.

### Transparency and citizen voice

Citizens can be an important check on the arbitrary abuse of power by government. To facilitate the development of a well-informed public, governments should publish budgets, revenues, statutes and rules, and proceedings of legislative bodies. Financial data should be audited by independent authorities similar to the U.S. General Accounting Office. Freedom of information acts in the United States and many European countries are an important precondition to effective public oversight. The European Union recently promulgated a directive requiring member states to pass such laws with respect to environmental information. These laws permit citizens to obtain government information without having to show how their lives are affected by it.

Information is of little value, however, unless there are mechanisms through which people can influence government behavior. In countries with democratic electoral systems, citizens can vote against officials believed to be corrupt. If independent courts exist and citizens can sue the government, another route is opened up to control government malfeasance. Public exposure of corruption through the media is another option.

Yet even if both information and the means of sanctioning corrupt practices are available, individual citizens are unlikely to act alone. Laws that make it easy to establish associations and nonprofits can help resolve this collective action problem. Such groups might not only seek information *from* the government but also supply information *to* the government about citizens' opinions of the quality of public services. One promising experiment by an NGO to publicize the performance of public agencies is under way in Bangalore, India. The international nonprofit organization Transparency International aims to mobilize citizens in developed and developing countries to fight corruption and to publicize the track record of individual nations. Yet precisely because transparent information can be so potent in promoting government reform, many countries limit such groups or make it costly for them to organize.

## Conclusion: integrating institutions with the reform agenda

States in many developing countries have exhibited behavior that suggests a clear imbalance between flexibility and restraint. These countries need to strengthen formal instruments of restraint—judicial independence, effective separation of powers—to enhance credibility and accountability. Within the executive, several countries lack the most basic underpinnings of rule-based bureaucracy. Even reform-minded leaders cannot translate their goals into reality because the machinery linking policy statements to action has ceased to function. As a result, a vast gap has opened up between what the state says and what it does, between the formal rules and the real ones, as manifested in large deviations between budgets and actual spending, long lags in the production of financial accounts, and rampant political patronage in personnel policies.

The first step toward building a more effective public sector must be to close these gaps and to reestablish the credibility of the government's policies and the rules it claims to live by, making sure they operate in practice. This step includes setting hard budget limits, making the flow of resources predictable, ensuring accountability for the use of financial resources, and instituting meritocracy in civil service recruitment and promotion.

Where these preconditions are absent, public management reforms must be introduced cautiously. If informal norms have long deviated significantly from formal ones (in personnel practices, for example), simply introducing new formal rules will not change much. Where countries have been unable to establish credible controls over inputs, giving managers much greater flexibility will only encourage arbitrariness and corruption. Nevertheless, countries can begin by providing greater clarity of purpose and task and introducing performance measurement and ex post evaluation on a selective basis (to be extended over time). As output measurement and input controls are strengthened, managers can be granted more operational flexibility in exchange for greater accountability for results.

Instituting a professional, rule-based bureaucracy will take time. In the meantime, some measures can be instituted more quickly to yield early payoffs. Well-functioning policymaking mechanisms can make the costs of competing policies transparent, focus attention on results by reporting requirements for performance and evaluation, and encourage debate and consultation among internal and external stakeholders. Using the market to deliver contestable services can lower costs and improve service quality. Likewise, contracting out easily specified activities can reduce the burden on overstretched capacity and build partnerships with markets and NGOs to improve efficiency. As internal mechanisms of monitoring and enforcement are being built up, voice and participation—for instance, through client surveys—can generate powerful external pressures for improved performance.

These mechanisms will also help combat corruption. A multipronged strategy to combat entrenched corruption requires introducing formal instruments of restraint (such as an independent judiciary), reforming the civil service (by raising pay and restraining political patronage in personnel practices), reducing opportunities to act corruptly (by increasing competition and reducing official discretion), and enhancing accountability through transparency and citizen voice.

### Note

1. This paper summarizes some work done for the World Bank's *1997 World Development Report*. I am grateful to Ed Campos, Hamid Davoodi, Gregory Kisunko, Brian Levy, Nick Manning, Gary Reid, and Susan Rose-Ackerman for many useful contributions.

### References

Campos, José Edgardo, and Sanjay Pradhan. Forthcoming. "Building Institutions for a More Effective Public Sector." Background paper for 1997 *World Development Report*. World Bank, Washington, D.C.

———. 1996. "Budgetary Institutions and Expenditure Outcomes: Binding Governments to Fiscal Performance." Policy Research Working Paper No. 1646. World Bank, Washington, D.C.

Campos, José Edgardo, and Hilton L. Root. 1996. *The Key to the Asian Miracle: Making Shared Growth Credible*. Washington, D.C.: Brookings Institution.

Clague, Christopher, Philip Keefer, Stephen Knack, and Mancur Olson. 1996. "Property and Contract Rights Under Democracy and Dictatorship." *Journal of Economic Growth* 1(2):243–76.

Dia, Mamadou. 1996. *Africa's Management in the 1990s and Beyond: Reconciling Indigenous and Transplanted Institutions*. Directions in Development Series. Washington, D.C.: World Bank.

Evans, Peter B., and James Rauch. 1996. "Bureaucratic Structure and Economic Growth: Some Preliminary Analysis of Data on 35 Developing Countries." Working Paper, University of California, Berkeley.

Lindauer, David, and Barbara Nunberg, eds. 1994. *Rehabilitating Government: Pay and Employment Reform in Africa*. Washington, D.C.: World Bank.

Nunberg, Barbara. Forthcoming. *The State After Communism: Administrative Transitions in Central and Eastern Europe.* Washington, D.C.: World Bank.

Rose-Ackerman, Susan. 1996. "When Is Corruption Harmful?" Background paper for 1997 *World Development Report.* World Bank, Washington, D.C.

Ul Hauq, Nadeem, and Ratna Sahay. 1996. "Do Government Wage Cuts Close Budget Deficits? Costs of Corruption?" IMF Staff paper, December 43:4.

Tendler, Judith. 1997. *Good Government in the Tropics.* Baltimore, Md.: Johns Hopkins University Press.

van der Gaag, Jacques. 1995. *Private and Public Initiatives: Working Together for Health and Education.* Washington, D.C.: World Bank.

Van Rijckeghem, Caroline, and Beatrice Weder. 1996. "Corruption and Rate of Temptation: Do Low Wages in the Civil Service Cause Corruption?" Background paper for 1997 *World Development Report.* World Bank, Washington, D.C.

Webb, Douglas. 1996. "The Judiciary: The Arbiter of Rules and Resolver of Disputes." Background paper for 1997 *World Development Report.* World Bank, Washington, D.C.

World Bank. 1991. *The Reform of Public Sector Management: Lessons of Experience.* Policy Research Series No. 18. Washington, D.C.: World Bank.

———. 1994. *World Development Report 1994: Infrastructure for Development.* New York: Oxford University Press.

———. 1995. *Bureaucrats in Business: The Economics and Politics of Government Ownership.* A World Bank Policy Research Report. New York: Oxford University Press.

———. 1996. "Republic of Guinea: Public Expenditure Review." Report No. 15147-GUI. Western Africa Department, World Bank, Washington, D.C.

## Comments on "Reinvigorating state institutions," by Pradhan

*Robert Klitgaard*

The examples in Sanjay Pradhan's encyclopedic paper whet my appetite. For example, I would like to know more about how Brazil saved 25 percent by contracting out road maintenance, how NGOs have been used to provide some social services (perhaps sometimes fostering a kind of competition with the state's own provision of those services), how citizens' charters and minimum service standards function in countries such as Malaysia and Portugal, and how countries that have been successful in performance contracting solve the problem of what Pradhan calls "instituting credible controls over the use of inputs." We need Pradhan with hyperlinks. The examples remind us of one of the World Bank's great, and perhaps underexploited, comparative advantages: experience from around the world.

But this volume concerns evaluation, and what I'm missing is the link. Perhaps in our discussion we can consider how that link can be established.

### Implications of institutions for evaluation

A spate of recent studies attempts to estimate the importance of institutions to growth and to project performance. Pradhan provides a few interesting examples. Evidently, part of his mission (and Ajay Chhibber's, in his paper) is to establish, especially to economists, that institutions and governance make a difference that can be quantified and that this difference makes sense in qualitative economic terms.

They succeed to a degree. An unfortunate feature of the research reported by Pradhan and Chhibber is that many of the data remain confidential and the operational definitions of many variables are not supplied. Moreover, full statistical results are not included. Some of the graphs show that outliers or groups of countries (East Asian sometimes, African other times) drive the regression lines. As a result, proper scientific appraisal of the findings is difficult.

What do these results mean for evaluation? Pradhan's paper, as well as other pieces of the puzzle provided in Chhibber's, works at the country level. But for evaluation purposes, much of the interest is in projects. An interesting fact not reported in their papers is that comparatively little of the variance in project outcomes is statistically explained by institutional, economic, or other included variables. In the Bank's own evaluations of its projects, economic rates of return (ERRs) vary greatly, even among projects in the same sector and in the same country. Suppose ERRs on more than 1,800 projects are regressed against such predictors as government spending as a percentage of GDP, the black market premium on the country's currency, the budget deficit, the GDP growth rate, levels of civil liberties and political rights, levels of corruption, and pay levels of civil servants compared with those in the manufacturing sector. Any of these together or separately will explain less than 10 percent of the variance (Klitgaard forthcoming). In other words, a lot depends on the project itself (and perhaps some of the variance is random noise introduced by the process of estimating ERRs). I deduce that, among other things, project evaluation is important and that project design and management are also important. Everything isn't determined by the country and the sector.

But notice also a radical implication of Pradhan's paper—an argument that is made explicitly by Robert Picciotto (1994). Apart from their effects on growth or project success, institutions are dependent variables as well. Picciotto notes a sea change in the evaluation of development activities. From an overwhelming preoccupation with the evaluation of public investment, through cost-benefit analysis and estimates of ERRs, development evaluation has shifted to the analysis of policies and institutions and the design of flexible enabling environments for private enterprise, local initiative, and social action.

Today Picciotto points out that only about a third of World Bank project appraisals include rate-of-return calculations. One reason is that projects have many incommensurate objectives, such as economic growth, poverty reduction, and environmental sustainability. Another may be that institutional benefits and costs lie at the heart of development activity. Therefore, evaluation is being increasingly pressed to consider the processes out of which development projects emerge and through which they are executed. These include the legal and regulatory environments in which projects operate and especially the growing role that local authorities, NGOs, and other elements of the civil society play in development.

### Models and measures: the issues

If institutional variables are important, then the evaluators' task becomes knowing how to take account of them—as intervening variables and as outcomes in their own right. The impact of the Bank's work, Pradhan correctly implies, cannot be assessed adequately without a model and measures that include both.

Do we have the models and measures? We don't find them in Pradhan's paper—and this is not necessarily his fault, because they do not exist yet in the literature (see Jeffrey Nugent's paper in this volume). Pradhan's broad coverage is a strength, but it also requires him to move quickly, to use shorthand and generalizations. And these often obscure more than clarify.

- Consider, for example, Pradhan's emphasis on *commitment*. Two problems emerge. First, how do we know if commitment is present or absent? Can commitment become a "weasel word" such as the infamous "political will?" Second, how much commitment is needed and where? Some experts, including Mary Shirley and Brian Levy, emphasize commitment's importance; others note the need for flexibility. Pradhan points out that the task is balancing commitment and flexibility. But stating this generally, it does not advance us far in modeling or measuring, nor does it help practicing evaluators do better.

- What about the *separation of powers in government*? As Pradhan tells us, the separation of powers adds to confidence that rules will be sustained over time or adapted only after considerable negotiation. However, as he notes, the presence of multiple veto points can be a double-edged sword—making it hard to change not only beneficial rules, but also harmful ones. They can create gridlock among the branches of government. Again, a balancing act is needed; again, Pradhan does not provide much help in modeling or measuring these difficult concepts.

- To what degree should policymaking be separated from implementation? Separating them avoids capture by special interests, but it is not without its risks. Having an independent, elite civil service bound together by an esprit de corps and shared external influences (such as the Chicago Boys and Berkeley mafia) is a good thing, Pradhan says—or it seems to be until we consider some other examples, such as the old Indian civil service, or the London School of Economics mafia.

- There are many other examples in Pradhan's paper. *Contestability* is a nice word, but what is contestable and how contests are won also matter. *Consultation* and *participation* also sound pleasant and have measurable results, but they also create transaction costs, and therefore trade-offs enter. Thus, saying that these things may be helpful, while perhaps news to some economists, does not help evaluators figure out how to take them into account in theory or in practice.

Pradhan's fascinating overview gives economic meaning to good governance and suggests that easy answers are not in the cards. How might we apply these insights in evaluation? Do we have a good model for including them and taking account of the trade-offs? Do we have good measures? The answers are not supplied, but the reader may be forgiven for taking away the impression that the answers are "not yet."

## Implications for evaluation

How, then, might we make progress in taking institutions into account in evaluation?

First, my sense is that it is time to move beyond cross-country regressions. In cross-sectional studies, institutional variables are statistically significant predictors of economic growth and project success. But interpreting the coefficients is much less straightforward than Pradhan's paper would perhaps lead the unwary reader to believe. Johannes Fedderke and I have reviewed econometric estimates of the effects of institutional, social, political, and other variables on growth and carried out new work of our own (Fedderke and Klitgaard forthcoming). We take away from this body of research some skepticism about the power of cross-country statistical studies to differentiate among the many explanatory hypotheses available. Problems of poor data, no clearly accepted model, badly behaved data (outliers, skewness, and so forth), and possibly heterogeneity among countries all mean that we face tremendous difficulties of identification and inference. (I say this as a believer in the crucial importance of institutions to development.)

When many variables may matter—and when it is difficult to use regression-like techniques to "control" for them statistically—we may attempt to control for them experimentally. This is a metaphor, as strict social experiments are usually infeasible. But as we design development projects, to the extent that we can introduce experimental design features, we may help our partners and ourselves understand better what happens and why. For example, when institutional variation can be introduced into projects (some sites work with indigenous organizations, others don't; some sites use performance-based incentives, others don't), we may learn more than we can from regression-based studies of thousands of existing projects. To evaluate institutional factors in development, we may need to rely more on the metaphor "experiment" than on the metaphor "regression analysis."

Second, as elsewhere in social research, we may be spending too little time analyzing exceptional performers and estimating average effects across all projects or countries. The Operations Evaluation Department's 1995 *Evaluation Results* (Morra and Thumm 1997) devotes only a few pages to projects that were "performance outliers"—the 16 projects (or 5 percent) that were "outstanding"—and 8 projects that were awful. Interestingly, two of the former and one of the latter were in Argentina (although six of the latter and only one of the former were in African countries). The discussion is thin. It says that exceptionally good projects had excellent appraisals, were "owned" by the recipients, and were well supervised, but it does not help us see what these concepts mean. If these case studies could be carried forward in the style of the Harvard Business School, they could be a valuable source of learning for the Bank's partners and staff.

Third, we might usefully apply Pradhan's ideas in considering the World Bank's comparative advantage in development work. He mentions cross-border mechanisms and international restraints that help states credibly commit themselves to rules of the game. An interesting if possibly politically incorrect question is how the Bank might help its partners even more by employing more fully its comparative advantage in making commitments credible.

Consider performance-based incentives in governance, a topic that evokes considerable skepticism from Pradhan and Shirley, perhaps because they worry that such issues may distract governments from a more urgent need: state devolution. (This became clear in the discussion following Shirley's paper.) Pradhan worries that flexible management schemes driven by performance may be fine for New Zealand but not for countries with less capacity and commitment. He notes that many countries have not succeeded in instituting credible controls over the use of inputs. He adds that in such circumstances, providing greater managerial flexibility will only increase arbitrariness and corruption without commensurate improvements in performance.

Might this conclusion not seem overdrawn? Does it not bear an unfortunate resemblance to what is hopefully the discredited argument of those who opposed free-market reforms as fine for countries with lots of capacity and commitment but not for countries at lower stages of economic development? The problems with instituting performance-based pay, Pradhan and Shirley observe, include scarce capacity to enforce complex contracts and weak bureaucratic controls to restrain arbitrariness. The constraints are capacity and commitment: couldn't those be areas where cooperation with an organization such as the World Bank could pay off? Could the Bank not rework its civil service reforms and institutional development projects to help make credible the commitment to performance-based incentives? Could the Bank not provide technical assistance to design, with local officials themselves, the performance measures and a transparent process for evaluating *experiments* with incentive schemes? Couldn't the "complex contracts" be simplified, second-best versions, subject to review by stakeholders every two years?

And these questions lead to a final point. Might one usefully apply Pradhan's principles to the World Bank itself? For example:

- Does the Bank have a strong central capacity for strategic policy formulation? In the last years of the tenure of the Bank's previous president, an elaborate effort was made to derive four strategic objectives for the Bank—one of which, by the way, was governance. Did those directions make a dent in the Bank's work? If not, what does this failure say about the governance of the institution?

- How effective are its mechanisms to delegate, discipline, and contest policies among agencies (parts of the Bank)? Does the Bank practice what Pradhan praises in Malawi, where four ministries are costing out policies within a hard budget constraint and, for the first time, are focusing on what competing policies are designed to achieve and how much they cost?

- Does the World Bank have effective, transparent links to external stakeholders for feedback and accountability? Or is policymaking fragmented, with few institutionalized inputs and little oversight from stakeholders?

## References

Fedderke, Johannes, and Robert Klitgaard. Forthcoming. "Economic Growth and Social Indicators: An Exploratory Analysis." *Economic Development and Cultural Change.*

Klitgaard, Robert. Forthcoming. "Cleaning Up and Invigorating the Civil Service." *Public Administration and Development* 17:4.

Morra, Linda, and Ulrich Thumm. 1997. *1995 Evaluation Results*, Vols. 1 and 2. Operations Evaluation Department. Washington, D.C.: World Bank.

Picciotto, Robert. 1994. "Visibility and Disappointment: The New Role of Development Evaluation." In Lloyd Rodwin and Donald A. Schön, eds., *Rethinking the Development Experience.* Washington, D.C.: The Brookings Institution and Cambridge, Mass.: The Lincoln Institute of Land Policy.

**Comments on "Reinvigorating state institutions," by Pradhan**

*Christopher Clague*

This is an excellent paper. I kept agreeing with the judgments and emphasis that the author put on different points. So I shall merely try to extend what the paper says, starting with comments on where we are in the new institutional economics and how this relates to the work of the World Bank in general and the Operations Evaluation Department in particular.

We have come a long way in the last 10 or 15 years in restoring institutions to a central place in our understanding of the process of development. There is no longer much dissent from the proposition that institutions differ across countries and that these differences matter a lot for development. We also have a good idea of what constitutes an appropriate set of institutions for development. There is not a single set that is right for all countries, but the number of sets that works well is much smaller than the number that works badly. We have some idea about how the different institutions in the business sphere interact with those in the government sphere to produce good or bad outcomes. So we have fairly solid foundations of knowledge about the *effects* of different institutional arrangements on economic outcomes. Publicizing this knowledge and trying to persuade the elites in poor countries to make use of it in their thinking is surely very useful.

But when we come to the determinants of institutional arrangements, we are on much weaker ground. Establishing the determinants is inherently a much more difficult task, as Jeffrey Nugent explained in his paper.

World Bank staff are basically in the business of trying to promote institutional change. In this endeavor, it certainly helps to have a good knowledge of the institutional arrangements that work well. But that is not enough. We also need to know how interventions in the existing institutional structure can foster the right sort of change. Foreign assistance officials have long been criticized for going to less-developed countries and telling them, "You ought to do it the way we do it in our country, because we have a system that works." We all recognize the inadequacy of this approach, but going beyond it requires a level of sophistication in the social sciences that is hard to achieve.

A politician or high-level civil servant can use his or her power to push or nudge the existing institutional structure in a desired direction. Knowledge of the success and failure of past reform efforts is very useful for such a reformer, and here the new institutional economics can play a role, assuming the reformer has enough political power to influence the scope and sequence of change.

But think how much more difficult is the task for the Bank official who is drafting a plan for reform in a particular sector. The Bank doesn't have political clout; it mainly has money to offer. The Bank staff, with their worldwide information network, have a good knowledge of what has been tried in other countries and of how well it has worked. But the fact that a particular organizational innovation has worked in some countries doesn't mean that putting a certain organizational change into a specific Bank project is going to have a beneficial effect. That requires a very difficult judgment regarding the intentions and political clout of the people who are supposed to implement the project, and of their various opponents in the political and bureaucratic arenas.

I would suggest that it is even very difficult to tell, after the project is completed, whether it has had much of an effect or not, especially when we are looking for institutional and organizational change. The domestic environment in the country is changing all the time. How can we tell whether the project made any difference? There is no standard methodology for assessing the institutional impact of a project or a particular variant of a project.

The World Bank has considerable expertise in designing reforms in policies, institutions, and organizations. But whether the reforms take hold or not depends far more on the political clout of the reformers than on the expertise that has gone into the design. This point is illustrated by the following observations. As we look at the strengths and deficiencies of different organizational forms where there are varying degrees of difficulty in measuring the outputs of organizations, it is often quite obvious that the least inefficient form of organization is some variant of the market. Yet privatizations aren't carried through, and political resistance cannot be overcome.

Another example: tax collection is organizationally one of the simpler areas to reform, because its outputs are relatively easy to measure. Of course even here, measurement is not simple, since we are concerned with the effects of the tax collection system on the economy, not just the revenue collected. But tax collection is surely easier to measure than the outputs of most other public services. Much thought has gone into the design of a good tax reform program. Yet tax reform programs typically fail.

Many of the success stories of institutional reform mentioned have depended on political arrangements that are not transferable to other countries. In general, I don't think that Pradhan's paper is guilty of overlooking this point, for at numerous points in the paper Pradhan provides very insightful judgments about the feasibility of particular types of organizations. For example, Pradhan observes that deliberation councils have not been successful in Africa, notes the retreat from civil service reforms, and expresses caution about attempting to introduce complex performance contracts into countries with weak bureaucratic controls. Perhaps one place where the political background to the organizational forms might have received more emphasis is in the discussion of elite central agencies in East Asia (and in Chile). Most of the countries involved have had strong authoritarian governments and unusual political traditions; even the democracies have had a high degree of deference to political authority.

There is a recurrent theme in the paper that reforms take time, that we can't expect too much too quickly. See, for example, the paper's discussion on the gradual development of the judicial system and systems of checks and balances, as well as the development of the relatively new public sectors in Africa. It takes time to develop institutions, Pradhan emphasizes.

There is an alternative view that reforms and institution building are path dependent. Countries and organizations can go down a wrong path and get stuck there. The passage of time is not going to help. Patterns of behavior reinforce attitudes and expectations, which in turn reinforce the patterns of behavior. Politicians and bureaucrats become corrupt, and the public becomes cynical and apathetic. There may be no escape until there is a drastic change in the political system. But there are cases of rapid improvement in institutions; examples are Singapore (given in the paper), Korea after Park came into power, Botswana after independence, and Poland after the fall of communism. But in the case of some African countries, bureaucratic performance has deteriorated over time.

Finally, I want to consider the implications for Bank assistance and for the evaluation of Bank projects of the idea that reform depends mainly on the political clout of reformers rather than on expertise or the detailed design of reforms. I suggest that external assistance is most usefully channeled to those countries and sectors where genuine reformers are in charge. I suspect that external donors are rarely able to bribe politicians into becoming reformers, but they may be able to increase the leverage and durability of reforming politicians. The major task of evaluation, then, is the identification of genuine and false reformers.

## Floor discussion on "Reinvigorating state institutions"

The discussion opened with the comment that the Bank has participated in institutional change and is planning to use the *World Development Report* to step up its participatory strategy. This area is one in which bilateral agencies can provide the benefit of their experiences and perspectives from inside the countries. However, the participant noted that the discussion throughout the conference has been based on the assumption that the Bank can be an exogenous actor. But there is no such thing as an exogenous actor, since change cannot be imposed from the outside.

Sanjay Pradhan responded from the point of view of the state. He noted that the "double-edged sword" of the separation of powers can cause a tension between flexibility and restraint. This tension can be at the root of the problems that emerge when countries are trying to effect change. The Bank's role is to advise governments on which actions to take first in the interests of sustainable development. This role creates a dilemma that must be met differently, depending on the context. For example, where elite policymaking bodies exist, countries will adopt measures designed either to influence the people or to affect the policy body itself. The model in industrial countries will differ from that in, say, East Africa, and each model will be embedded in a different set of assumptions. Pradhan emphasized that this fact says nothing about whether institutions are good or bad. If transaction costs can be lowered, that is a positive development for the state. And if the state can provide collective action, it can lend balance to an incentive structure—and the incentive structure, another participant noted, is at the heart of any movement toward change.

# PART 2: INSTITUTIONS AND GOVERNANCE STRUCTURES

# 5. Fostering fiscally responsive and accountable governance: lessons from decentralization

Anwar Shah

*Decentralized fiscal structures are more suitable in the institutional environments of developing countries provided careful attention is paid to the design of institutions vital to the decentralization process, including institutional capacity for evaluation at all levels.*

During the past half century, most developing countries have followed a path of centralization by subscribing to various paradigms of development based on central planning. As a result, they are more centralized today than industrial countries were in their early stages of development (Boadway, Roberts, and Shah 1994). A number of recent developments are prompting most developing countries to reexamine the roles of governments, the private sector, and civil society as partners in development. This rethinking has caused much heated controversy and debate in development policy fora. Regrettably, the debate has focused on the straw men of "centralization" and "decentralization," ignoring the federalist precept that institutions matter for governance  (Prud'homme 1995; Sewell 1996; Tanzi 1996).

This paper examines the reasons for this rekindling of an interest in fiscal rearrangements in both industrial and nonindustrial countries. It furthers the debate on decentralization by providing empirical evidence on the decentralization experience. It draws general and institutional lessons to enhance understanding of the effectiveness of decentralization in fostering an environment of listening, learning, and evaluation for responsive and accountable governance. An overall conclusion of the paper is that decentralized fiscal structures are more suitable in the institutional environment of developing countries provided careful attention is paid to the design of institutions vital to the success of decentralization policies. These institutions include, especially, the rule of law, conflict resolution and coordination, the charter of rights, effective limitations on the authority of governments beyond their designated spheres of influence, accountability, and institutional capacity for evaluation at all levels.

## The quest for the right balance

The reasons for rethinking fiscal arrangements are manifold, and the importance of each factor is country specific. Nevertheless, there are some generic catalysts for change. They include the demise of communism, the desire to break away from the vestiges of colonialism (as in Africa, for example), national government failures, subnational government failures, the assertion of basic rights by the courts, the globalization of economic activities, and the demonstration effects of the European Union and Latin America (see Picciotto 1995; Shah 1996a). The demise of communism prompted a major change in government organization and geographical boundaries in some countries, especially in Eastern Europe and the former Soviet Union. These countries sought guidance from the principles and practices pursued in industrial countries where federal systems of decisionmaking have evolved over a long time. In Africa, both former French and English colonies inherited highly centralized systems of governance geared toward command and control and away from responsiveness to the public. In most countries, national governments have failed to ensure regional equity, economic union, central bank independence, a stable macroeconomic environment, or local autonomy. The record of subnational governments is also not very commendable. Subnational governments have often followed beggar-thy-neighbour policies, sought free ridership with no accountability, and, in pursuit of narrow self-interest, often undermined national unity.

The judicial systems in some countries are also providing stimuli for change by providing a broader interpretation of basic rights and requiring that national and subnational legislation conform to the basic rights of citizens. The emergence of a new "borderless" world economy and the revolution in information/knowledge complicates this picture by bringing new challenges to constitutional federalism (Courchene fortcoming). These challenges arise from the diminished control national government exerts on the flow of goods and services, ideas, and cultural products. With globalization, it is becoming increasingly apparent that nation-states are too small to tackle large things and too large to address small things. The European Union's policies and principles regarding subsidiarity, fiscal harmonization, and stabilization checks are also having demonstrable effects on country policies. Similarly, the success of decentralization in improving the efficiency and equity of public provision and public sector accountability in some Latin American countries, especially Colombia and Chile, has encouraged other countries to review their own fiscal arrangements (Wiesner 1994a). Finally, the resurgence of interest in federalist principles and best practices has served as a powerful basis for restructuring and reorienting the public sector in various parts of the world.

The overall impact of these influences is to force a rethinking on assignment issues and a jurisdictional realignment in many countries around the globe. At the conceptual level, the new thinking is that some functions need to be passed upward (centralized) beyond nation-states, for example, the regulation of financial transactions, international trade, global environment, and international migration. Some subnational functions should have greater central government inputs (centralization)—for example, training. Local functions should be completely decentralized and should involve greater participation by the civil society and the private sector. In a small but growing number of developing countries, rethinking these arrangements has led to the gradual and piecemeal decentralization of responsibilities for local public services to lower levels. The development and strengthening of institutional arrangements to foster decentralized policies has significantly lagged behind decentralization itself. It is remarkable that, with the exception of Colombia, no developing country has paid any attention to developing the institutional capacity for evaluation. Even the strengthening of the central- and intermediate-level functions required for the success of their realignment has not always materialized. In fact, in some countries decentralization is motivated by the opportunity it provides to shift the budget deficit and associated debt burdens to subnational governments. The following section looks at important factors that are at play in impeding the progress of realigning functions in developing countries.

### Why the road to reform remains a field of dreams

Fiscal systems in most developing countries require significant restructuring. Progress to date on such reforms has been uneven. A number of factors impede the progress of reform.

*Political factors*

Political ownership is critical to the success of any fiscal rearrangements. In Latin America and former centrally planned economies, the emergence of democratic governance and political freedoms has led to a heightened interest in improving public sector performance. The decentralization of local public services is seen as an important element in this reform. In Latin America, disenchantment with military rule and dictatorships has led to the creation of a political culture that places a premium on decentralized decisionmaking. In China, decentralization has been seen as a means of creating social cohesion, speeding economic growth, and preserving communist party rule.

In recent years, therefore, social development, economic prosperity, and concerns for improving the delivery of public services have created a degree of accommodation for decentralized institutions. But politics blocks reform in a number of countries. In Pakistan, for example, political instability and feudal interests have contributed to the setting aside of constitutional dictums and the introduction of a system of centralized governance. In Indonesia, forefathers of the constitution clearly intended the country to be centralized and unitary and dictated against establishing "states within the state." These concerns for political unity have dominated the design of institutions. Military and civil services with well-entrenched roles in political affairs and a strong belief in command and control from the center have sustained the centralization of responsibility. The power of appointment from the center for governors and mayors also strengthens centralization and limits local autonomy.

*Bureaucratic factors*

Many countries in Africa and Asia share a common colonial heritage. To achieve the colonial objectives with maximum efficiency, the British, Dutch, and French colonial rulers each instituted a system of bureaucratic control that created a highly educated core of civil service elite who were dedicated to serving the colonizers. Their loyalty to the colonial rulers and detachment from the common man were duly rewarded with preferential access to all public service employment through elite institutions and guaranteed financial security through a system of cash rewards and land grants. Thus colonized countries such as India, Indonesia, Kenya, and Pakistan inherited civil service structures that were highly centralized, efficient, accountable, professional, and completely detached from the local population. These structures have remained resistant to change.

*Institutional factors*

Institutional factors also impede effective decentralization. Traditional institutions and mechanisms of governance and accountability have withered away over time but have not been replaced by newer institutions. Instead, the all-pervasive role of the state has retarded critical scrutiny of public policies and institutions. In many countries, the government has an almost complete monopoly of the institutions of critical thought and the media. Any critical review of government policies and programs invites a government backlash. In Pakistan, rural self-government worked well in the early days of its independence. But this system was abandoned in favor of a more centralized system that has resulted in rural populations being denied access to basic services. Lack of institutional capacity was cited as a reason for disbanding the participatory system, but the newer arrangements have left a majority of citizens with no voice and no access to basic public services. Indonesia, by contrast, is now nurturing self-government in rural areas through its village development and poor villages grant programs (Shah 1996b).

Another important aspect of institutional factors is the philosophy of citizens toward government. Do people in general—politicians, bureaucrats, public employees, voters—view the public sector as a place where one does service for fair compensation or rather as a position for personal gain? Various surveys suggest that prevailing public perceptions about the public sector, especially in South Asia and Africa, tend to support the latter view and that citizens tend to associate the public sector with a predatory role.

Contrary to common misconceptions, a strong, responsive, and accountable government at the national level is critical to the success of decentralization policies. Similarly, centralized governance depends on responsive, accountable, and competent field offices. This is the least understood "paradox of decentralization" (rearrangements). This suggests that centralization requires a higher degree of local (field office) institutional capacity and competence and greater sophistication and integrity of public information monitoring, finance, accounts, and audit systems than required under a decentralized system. Although the success of decentralized structures depends less on local institutional capacity and information networks—at least at the outset—citizen participation fostered by an enabling environment at the center is crucial. This notion is confirmed by the Colombian experience (World Bank 1995). Local institutional capacity and information networks can be supplied by borrowing such capacity from internal and external sources, at least during the earlier phases of decentralization, provided a supportive higher-level enabling environment prevails.

*External participants*

Some external participants may also unwittingly impede public sector decentralization in developing countries. A multitude of factors contribute to this problem. First, a centralized system enlarges the comfort zone for external participants by making it easier for them to monitor how their funds are used and thereby lowering their transaction costs. Second, some external participants are concerned about the revenue performance ("resource mobilization") of developing countries. This concern may lead to larger centralized bureaucracies that pay little attention to the efficient delivery of public services. For example, in Pakistan, the improved revenue performance of governments has been accompanied by deterioration in quality and quantity of public services (Shah 1995). Third, a lack of citizen participation tends to make a centralized system less likely to have an internal policy agenda and more dependent on external advice on policy reform. This tendency typically leads to quick policy fixes with little sustained reform.

## Making dreams come true: getting institutions right

Adherence to federalist principles, "getting prices right," or even "getting the rules of the game right" is, as discussed earlier, a necessary but not sufficient condition for success in decentralized decisionmaking. Complementary formal and informal institutions are needed to ensure that all players in the game adhere to agreed ground rules and that deviant behavior is dealt with properly. These considerations are discussed below.

### Coordinating different levels of government

Federal countries require both formal and informal institutions to coordinate different levels of government. In some federal countries, potential conflict among different levels of government is minimized through clear separation of national and subnational responsibilities (the so-called layer-cake model of federalism practiced in Australia, Canada, India, and Pakistan). The two levels interact through meetings of officials and ministers (executive federalism), and in Australia, India, and Pakistan, through federal unilateralism, with the federal government acting as final arbiter. Some countries, such as Germany (a federal country) and the Republic of South Africa (a pseudo-federal country), place a greater premium on a common response through shared or joint tasks. In these countries, in addition to executive federalism, the upper houses of parliament (the Bundesrat and Council of Provinces) play a key role in coordinating different levels of government. In countries with overlapping responsibilities (the so-called marble cake model of federalism), such as Brazil and the United States, state lobbying of the congress and interstate relations serve coordinating roles. In China, where growth concerns have imposed a federalist structure on a unitary country, regional communist party bosses-governors exercise a moderating influence on an otherwise monolithic state council at the federal level.

Constitutional provisions per se can also provide coordinating influences. For example, in some federal countries, constitutional provisions require that all legislation recognize that ultimate power rests with the people. For example, all legislation in Canada must conform to the Canadian Charter of Rights. In Switzerland (a confederation by law but a federal country in practice), major legislative changes require approval by referenda. In Switzerland, there is also a strong tradition of coordination through consensus initiatives by cantons.

### Institutional arrangements for fiscal relations

The structure of fiscal relations among levels of government, especially the system of grants, must be determined by some body. There are four main alternatives:

■ The federal government alone decides the structure. This alternative negates federalism and would not be acceptable in many countries.

- As practiced in Australia, India, and the Republic of South Africa, a quasi-independent body, such as a grants commission, designs and reforms the system. This alternative is better adapted to ideal solutions than to pragmatic approaches and therefore risks presenting complex solutions and recommendations that may not be politically palatable.

- Federal-state committees negotiate the terms of the system, as in Canada.

- A joint intragovernmental commission, such as the Finance Commission in Pakistan, or an intragovernmental legislative body, such as the upper house of the German parliament (Bundesrat), acts as an intralegislative commission.

The last two options allow for explicit political inputs from the jurisdictions involved and are therefore likely to opt for simple and feasible but less than ideal (compromise) solutions.

### Institutions of accountability

Institutions of accountability are key to the success of decentralized decisionmaking. They include institutions and mechanisms for citizen voice and exit; norms and networks of civic engagement ("social capital," according to Putnam 1994); social consensus (Williamson 1994; Weingast 1993 ); the self-preservation instinct of a "stationary bandit" who monopolizes and rationalizes theft in the form of taxes; judicial accountability; and vertical and horizontal accountability (Olson 1993). Citizen voice and exit require institutions of democratic participation and accountability provisions for elected officials. The origins and success of decentralization programs in Latin America are traceable to the democratic traditions that emerged there in late 1980s. In the Philippines, recently enacted local government legislation (Republic of Philippines Act No. 7160, the Local Government Code, 1991), while empowering these governments, has provided for regular elections and recall of elected officials for breach of public trust.

Norms and networks of civic engagement were reasonably well developed in the precolonial traditionalist societies found in many developing countries—for example, the Panchayat Raj in pre-British India. But these institutions withered away, either under colonial rule or the subsequent undercentralized bureaucratic governance structures. The net result, when formal and informal institutions of governance have failed, has been a rise of opportunism and social distrust culminating in dysfunctional societies. The African and the South Asian development fiascoes share this common underpinning.

Societal consensus on economic and political rights is also conducive to accountability at all levels. According to Weingast (1993), this consensus need not take any formal expression; it will work so long as a majority of people share a common belief in the limits of governmental intervention and are willing to police those limits by withdrawing their support from a government that fails to abide by them. The preservation instincts of taxing authorities also respect accountability, because the strength of their influence depends on economic performance that allows citizens to see their well-being improved (Olson 1993). This scenario partly explains the success of the Asian Tigers and the failure of some South/Southeast Asian regimes. The latter regimes were controlled by "roving bandits," such as Ferdinand Marcos of the Philippines and Mobutu Sese Seko of Zaire (Republic of Congo), whose main aims were to take the loot to pad their Swiss bank accounts and then disappear in a foreign haven.

Judicial accountability strengthens the credibility of public commitments. It is particularly important for transition economies, where framework laws on property rights, corporate legal ownership and control, bankruptcy, and financial accounting and control are not fully developed. Judicial accountability is much more difficult to enforce in a parliamentary democracy than in the type of democratic system that observes the separation of the legislative and executive functions. Under a parliamentary democracy, the executive branch can override judicial accountability by amending legislation—a game played ad infinitum in Pakistan to undermine a decentralized federal constitution. Judicial accountability is further compromised under British-style civil service organizations such as those in India and Pakistan, where divisional and district commissioners simultaneously hold executive, legislative, and judicial powers. As noted by Montesquieu (1970), such a situation is ripe for the abuse of powers: "When the legislative and executive powers are united in the same body of magistrates, there can be no liberty . . . Again, there is no liberty, if the judiciary power be not separated from the legislative and executive" (397).

### Evaluation capacity

We noted earlier that there is a broad consensus on the principles that should guide the division of powers and partnerships among different governmental and nongovernmental agents (Shah 1994). How to adapt these principles to the existing institutional and cultural contexts to improve public sector performance should be an ongoing concern. Such improvements will automatically evolve over time and will obviate the need for major, painful realignments if learning by doing, evaluation, and accountability for results are embedded in the organizational culture of the public sector. Such a cultural change can be induced by building the institutional capacity for evaluation, which is vital for citizen participation and higher-level oversight—the two important ingredients in the success of any decentralization program. To build such a capacity, it is important to adopt a simple and reasonably objective evaluation methodology and to have in place mechanisms for self-, higher-level, and independent evaluation.

Independent evaluations of government programs may be encouraged by formal institutions, such as fiscal commissions or associations of local governments (as in South Africa), by think tanks, press, and the informal sector. The methodology adopted by the Operations Evaluation Department (OED) of the World Bank provides a good starting point for such evaluation. In determining how well a program is performing, OED asks some simple yet powerful questions, as follows:

### Is the public manager doing the right things?

- *Relevance*: Are the objectives the manager seeks responsive to the needs of the community he or she is expected to serve?

- *Institutional development*: Will the initiative being undertaken result in improvements in local capacity so that things are done better in future?

*Is the public manager doing things right?*

- *Efficacy*: Are the programs achieving agreed-upon objectives?

- *Efficiency*: Are resources being used economically to forge appropriate partnerships within and without the public sector?

*Will the benefits of interventions be sustained?*

- *Social consensus:* Is there social consensus on sustaining the reforms?

- *Government commitment and resources:* Does the government have the will and means to sustain reforms?

Linking evaluation to performance incentives and budgeting nurtures a culture of responsive and accountable governance (see Wiesner 1994b). Thus, building institutional capacity for evaluation should rank high on the list of priorities for those interested in creating governments that work and strive for excellence in serving their citizens.

In spite of the benefits associated with building evaluation capacity, attention to the development of such capacity is unlikely to materialize without changes in the existing incentive structures. Rationalizing fiscal transfers to include conditionality on standards of services and access to such services provides positive stimulus for evaluation at all levels. Educating citizens about their rights and obligations and the role of the public sector and developing independent institutions of critical thought will strengthen the demand for such evaluations. Horizontal information exchanges, developed through groups such as voluntary associations of local governments, would also enhance demand for evaluations. Municipalities would also be interested in learning from experiences of member municipalities.

### Traditional channels of accountability

The audit, inspection, and control functions tend to be weak in transition and developing economies and should be strengthened. Auditor-generals should be given greater authority and autonomy in exercising their mandate. At the same time, a case can be made for loosening the constraints of the central planning process in developing countries. Central plans lead to a centralization of authority, reduced flexibility, innovation, and autonomy at the local level, and delays in private sector activity. On a more specific point, as fiscal responsibility is decentralized to the state and local levels, it would be beneficial to create the institutional capacity for local borrowing so that local authorities rely on borrowing and less on capital grants to finance capital projects. Examples include loan councils or municipal finance corporations (see Shah 1997 for further details).

### Oversight of local governments: freedom and responsibilities within boundaries

An important area of concern in both federal and unitary countries is monitoring and oversight of local governments. For example, the Republic of South Africa Constitution Act of 1996 (Section 139[1] [b]) provides for the disbanding of a local government if it fails to "maintain national standards or meet minimum standards of service"; "prevent actions prejudicial to the interests of another municipality or the nation as a whole"; and "maintain economic unity." The act further provides for withholding tax shares and transfers for noncompliance with tax efforts (section 227[2]). The fulfillment of constitutional obligations regarding these provisions requires a significant and superior evaluation capacity at provincial and national levels. Certain evaluative measures can assist in this oversight. They include the requirement that local governments be subject to annual commercial corporate audit; fiscal capacity measurement using a common yardstick, such as the equalization of municipal assessments; greater emphasis on formula grants over project grants in provincial-local transfers; greater emphasis on public and private civil society partnerships in public provision; opinion polls on service standards and citizen satisfaction; and performance ratings of local governments based on outputs, outcomes, and citizen satisfaction.

In industrial countries, audits of local governments at the most fundamental level pay attention to three elements: adherence to the principle of ultra vires and the procedural bylaw, and the fulfillment of funded mandates. The principle of ultra vires states that a local government should do only those things the statutes say it can do; it may not do anything for which it has no express authority.

The procedural bylaw requires that all policies of local councils be embodied in bylaws and that an auditor look at council operations for conformity with policies (beyond the system of internal control). Thus, a local government audit would involve the following:

- *Revenues*: bylaws for tax collection and administration, established procedures for assessments and appeals, budget reports incorporating all revenues, financial reports with necessary information, and observance of legal requirements of statutes.

- *Expenditures*: Bylaw for policies; established procedure for purchasing, tendering, payments, inventories, and so forth; establishment of expenditure limits; financial regulations; observance of statutes; and fulfillment of funded mandates.

- *Others*: legal requirements for borrowing, insurance coverage, unfunded mandates, debt, deficit, long-term budget commitment, contingent commitments, cost controls, resource use, and staffing.

- *Services*: quality, quantity, and distribution.

### Decentralization—fine in theory, but what about in practice?

Empirical evidence on the relationship between quality of governance and decentralization is scant. A recent study by Huther and Shah (1996) approaches this issue from an institutional perspective. The study examines evidence for 80 countries to determine whether centralized or decentralized fiscal systems provide better institutional settings in improving quality of life for an average citizen. They find that the record of decentralized fiscal systems—in providing for citizen participation, ensuring that the government is committed to serving its citizens, fostering social equity and development, and creating institutions for improved economic management—is far superior to the records of centralized countries. (See table 5.1 for a correlation of the decentralization index with the quality of governance.)

## Some lessons for developing countries

The following important lessons for reforming fiscal systems in developing countries can be distilled from a review of past experiences.

*Any serious reform of fiscal systems must provide an enabling environment for decentralization—that is, institutions of citizen participation and accountability.* Even in older societies, such as pre-British India, systems of local governance worked effectively to deliver local services and collect local charges because the mechanisms of citizen participation and accountability were well understood. Some modern systems of local governance, such as those run by elite Pakistani bureaucrats with training in management (including financial management), have failed due to a lack of citizen voice and accountability checks. The reform effort must embody appropriate provisions to recall elected officials for negligence or misconduct. Fostering institutions of critical thought and evaluation, judiciary independence, and a free media can play an important part in political and bureaucratic accountability. These elements have not been sufficiently addressed in most reform efforts.

TABLE 5.1: CORRELATION OF THE DECENTRALIZATION INDEX WITH GOVERNANCE QUALITY INDICATORS
(*sample size: 80 countries*)

| Indicator | Pearson correlation coefficients |
|---|:---:|
| *Citizen participation* | |
| Political freedom | 0.599[a] |
| Political stability | 0.604[a] |
| *Government orientation* | |
| Judicial efficiency | 0.544[a] |
| Bureaucratic efficiency | 0.540[a] |
| Absence of corruption | 0.532[a] |
| *Social development* | |
| Human development index | 0.369[b] |
| Egalitarianism in income distribution | |
| (inverse of gini coefficient) | 0.373[b] |
| *Economic management* | |
| Central bank independence | 0.327[b] |
| Debt management discipline | 0.263[b] |
| Outward orientation | 0.523[a] |
| *Aggregate* | |
| Governance quality index | 0.617[a] |

a. Significant at 0.01 percent level (2-tailed test).
b. Significant at the 0.05 percent level (2-tailed test).
*Source:* Huther and Shah 1996.

*Societal norms and consensus on the roles of various levels of governments and the limits to their authority are vital to the success of decentralized decisionmaking.* In the absence of such norms and consensus, intergovernmental gaming—or strategic behavior by various levels of government to serve their own political ends—leads to dysfunctional constitutions.

*Civil service reform is critical to the success of a decentralization program.* Bureaucratic ownership of a reform program is critical, but such ownership will not be forthcoming in most developing countries, which see decentralization as an attempt to weaken the powers of central bureaucracy. To overcome this problem, the reform of fiscal systems must embody a reform of central bureaucracies. Such a reform must ensure that the center has no direct say in the recruitment and promotions of civil servants, other than ensuring that standards of transparency and fairness are met at the subnational levels and that remuneration for subnational services is competitive with the central government. Further, the civil service incentive structure should reward a service orientation and performance and discourage "command and control" and rent-seeking. Performance contracts, recognition of specialized skills, and the development of a "stick-with-it" culture and evaluation systems linking performance, rewards, and budgeting will help accomplish these ends.

*Developing evaluation capacity is of fundamental importance in public sector reform in developing countries.* Formal ex post evaluation nurtures a climate of listening, learning, and accountability in the public sector. Such evaluation is of particular importance in developing countries where government failures are apt to be spectacular. However, as institutions for accountability in these countries are weak or nonexistent, there has been little afterthought on the appropriateness of development objectives and strategies. In such an environment, evaluation can nurture a "bottom-line" or "development effectiveness culture" as Picciotto (1993) argues. He notes that "evaluation is to the public sector what accounting is to the private sector." The 1996 constitution of the Republic of South Africa, for example, has imposed stringent monitoring and evaluation requirements on the central government to ensure the proper monitoring and oversight of local governments.

*Traditional administrative capacity matters, but it should not be considered an impediment to decentralization.* The administrative capacity to develop and maintain modern organizational practices such as budgeting, auditing, and accounting systems is no doubt important. But its absence should not be considered a barrier to decentralization, provided citizen participation and transparency in decisionmaking are ensured. Technical capacity can be borrowed from supportive central governments and elsewhere.

*Asymmetric decentralization, like that provided for under the Indonesian decentralization program and provincial local government ordinances in Pakistan, offers a thoughtful approach to decentralization.* Regardless of the availability of help from central governments, a lack of institutional capacity should never be considered an excuse not to decentralize. Instead, an objective program of decentralization that recognizes the natures and types of local governments, their clientele, and their fiscal capacity can be developed. Various local governments can be assigned differential powers, taking into account the factors just mentioned, as has been done in Pakistan and is more systematically accomplished in Indonesia, which rates each local government.

*A major separation of spending and taxing decisions leads to a lack of accountability in the public sector.* In Mexico, Pakistan, and South Africa, federal revenue-sharing transfers finance up to 99 percent of expenditures in some provinces. This delinking of taxing and spending responsibilities has led to accountability problems at provincial levels. In the event of such delinking, the role of conditional block transfers (on standards of services and access to such services, not on expenditures) and evaluation is worth examining to enhance accountability.

*The sharing of revenues on a tax-by-tax basis distorts incentives for efficient tax collection.* In Pakistan, tax-by-tax sharing of income and sales taxes have impeded the reform of trade taxes that are not shared with the provinces.

*Successful decentralization cannot be achieved in the absence of a well-designed fiscal transfers program.* The design of these transfers must be simple, transparent, and consistent with their objectives (Shah 1994). Properly structured transfers can enhance the accountability of the fiscal system, just as general revenue sharing has the potential to undermine it. The experiences of Indonesia and Pakistan offer important insights for grant design. Indonesia's education and health grants are examples of thoughtful design. They use simple and objectively quantifiable indicators in the allocation of funds, and conditions for continued eligibility for these grants emphasize objective standards. Indonesian grants for public sector wages, however, are examples of a less thoughtful design that introduces incentives for public employment at subnational levels. Pakistan's matching grant for resource mobilization similarly rewards relatively rich provinces for collecting additional tax. It also calls into question the commitment of the federal government, which has not been able to meet the obligations arising from this program.

*The role of fiscal transfers in enhancing competition for the supply of public goods should not be overlooked.* For example, transfers for basic health and primary education can be made available to both public and not-for-profit private organizations on an equal basis. Eligibility criteria can include the demographics of the population served, school age population, student enrollments, and so forth. Such a program would promote not only competition but also innovation. Chile permits Catholic schools access to public education financing. Canadian provinces allow individual residents to apply their property taxes to either public or private schools, introducing strong incentives to improve performance and become competitive. Such financing options are especially attractive in rural areas which largely remain unserved by the public sector.

*Finally, contrary to a common misconception, a developing country's institutional environment calls for a greater degree of decentralization than an industrial country.* In order to be effective, a centralized bureaucracy needs advanced information gathering and transmittal networks, an efficient and dedicated civil service, and well-developed institutions of citizen participation and accountability. Such an environment is possible in an industrial country. But a more primitive public sector environment is better suited to a decentralized form of governance, because moving the decisionmaking closer to the people it affects minimizes information requirements and transaction costs. Closeness also serves to increase participation, preference matching for public services, transparency, and accountability. Pakistan's experience demonstrates that decentralized decisionmaking significantly improves public sector performance, even when the enabling environment is weak.

# References

Boadway, Robin, Sandra Roberts, and Anwar Shah. 1994. "The Reform of Fiscal Systems in Developing and Emerging Market Economies: A Federalism Perspective." Policy Research Working Paper Series, No. 1259. Washington, D.C.: World Bank.

Courchene, Thomas. Forthcoming. "Macrofederalism." In Anwar Shah, ed., *Macrofederalism*. Washington, D.C.: World Bank.

Huther, Jeff, and Anwar Shah. 1996. "A Simple Measure of Good Governance and Its Application to the Debate on the Appropriate Level of Fiscal Decentralization." World Bank, Washington, D.C.

Montesquieu, M. 1970. "The Spirit of the Laws." In M. Curtis, ed., *The Great Political Theories*. New York: Disus/Avon Books.

Olson, Mancur. 1993. "Dictatorship, Democracy, and Development." *American Political Science Review* 87(3):568–76.

Picciotto, Robert. 1993. "Visibility and Disappointment: The Evolving Role of Development Evaluation." World Bank, Washington, D.C.

———. 1995. *Putting Institutional Economics to Work: From Participation to Governance.* World Bank Discussion Paper No. 304. Washington, D.C.: World Bank.

Prud'homme, Remy. 1995. "On the Dangers of Decentralization." *The World Bank Research Observer*, August 1995, 201–10.

Putnam, Robert. 1994. *Making Democracy Work: Civic Traditions in Modern Italy.* Princeton: Princeton University Press.

Sewell, David. 1996. "The Dangers of Decentralization According to Prud'homme: Some Further Aspects." *The World Bank Research Observer* 11(1):143–50.

Shah, Anwar. 1994. *The Reform of Intergovernmental Fiscal Relations in Developing and Emerging Market Economies.* Washington, D.C.: World Bank.

———. 1995. "Fiscal Federalism in Pakistan: Challenges and Opportunities." World Bank, Washington, D.C.

———. 1996a. "Design of Economic Constitutions." *Canadian Economic Journal* XXIX (special issue: April 1976):S614–S618.

———. 1996b. "Fiscal Decentralization—an Elusive Goal? A Case Study of Indonesia and Pakistan Experience." Presented at the International Conference on Fiscal Decentralization in Developing Countries, Montreal, Canada, September 19–20, 1996. Forthcoming in Richard Bird and François Vaillencourt, eds., *Fiscal Decentralization in Developing Countries.* New York and London: Cambridge University Press.

———. 1997. "Fiscal Federalism and Macroeconomic Governance: For Better or for Worse?" Presented at the International Conference on Decentralization, Intergovernmental Fiscal Relations and Macroeconomic Performance, Brasilia, Government of Brazil and OECD, June 16–17, 1997.

Tanzi, Vito. 1996. "Fiscal Federalism and Decentralization: A Review of Some Efficiency and Macroeconomic Aspects." *Annual World Bank Conference on Development Economics, 1995.* Washington, D.C.: World Bank.

Weingast, Barry. 1993. "Constitutions as Governance Structures: The Political Foundations of Secure Markets." *Journal of Institutional and Theoretical Economics* 149:286–311.

Wiesner, Eduardo. 1994a. "Fiscal Decentralization and Social Spending in Latin America: The Search for Efficiency and Equity." Working Paper Series No. 199. Inter-American Development Bank, Washington, D.C.

———. 1994b. *From Macroeconomic Correction to Public Sector Reform: The Critical Role of Evaluation.* Discussion Paper No. 214. Washington, D.C.: World Bank.

Williamson, Oliver. 1994. "The Institutions and Governance of Economic Development and Reform." *Proceedings of the World Bank Annual Conference on Development Economics.* Washington, D.C.: World Bank.

World Bank. 1995. "Decentralization Can Work: Experience from Colombia." Dissemination Note No. 3. Agriculture and Natural Resources Department. World Bank, Washington, D.C.

## Comments on "Fostering fiscally responsive and accountable governance: lessons from decentralization," by Shah

*Wallace E. Oates*

In his opening paragraph, Anwar Shah refers to the "straw men" that have characterized much of the recent debate over the role of fiscal decentralization in economic development. In recent years, in the wake of much dissatisfaction with the results of centralized economic planning, critics have turned to the idea of fiscal decentralization as a reform that would break the grip of central management. Such an approach, it is argued, will both improve economic performance and induce broader participation in democratic governance. But the case has generally been made in a very broad and uncritical way with little in the way of systematic empirical support. Predictably, the argument has provoked some response from observers like Remy Prud'homme (1995), who maintains that the case for fiscal decentralization is being much overstated.

The issue here, of course, is not really one of centralization versus decentralization. In the jargon of public finance, the problem is one of "optimal fiscal federalism." Central and decentralized levels of government both have important roles to play, and the issue is one of structuring the public sector properly, so it can carry out its functions in the most effective way. In the public finance literature on fiscal federalism, the issue has been addressed in terms of the "allocation of functions" among levels of government (Oates 1972, 1994).

But as Shah stresses in his paper, there is more at stake here than simply assigning the tasks of the public sector to the appropriate level of government. It is also of crucial importance to get the institutions right. In addition to a rational assignment of functions, the different levels of government must have the appropriate fiscal instruments and sets of incentives to carry out their functions efficiently. In Shah's paper, this means "accountability."

In the recent literature, this theme has taken the form (in part) of a prescription for "hard," as opposed to "soft," budget constraints (Weingast 1995; McKinnon 1997). The central principle here is that decisionmakers in the public sector must be positioned so that the costs of their choices are as fully visible to the electorate as the benefits of the public programs they adopt. Public officials, in short, must not be able to shift the costs of programs somewhere else in order to make the expansion of the public budget a relatively costless process.

### On the design of decentralized fiscal institutions

This section discusses three facets of hard budget constraints: intergovernmental transfers, debt finance, and fiscal equalization.

Nearly all systems of fiscal federalism use various forms of intergovernmental grants. The central government transfers funds, sometimes for specific purposes and other times unconditionally, to lower levels of government. While such grants, properly designed and employed, can play a useful role in a federal system of finance (Oates 1972), they can also be a major source of fiscal inefficiencies and instability. Two principles of intergovernmental grant systems are fundamental to Shah's criterion of accountability:

- First, such grants must not be too large. I do not have any magic number to offer here, but it seems clear that decentralized governments should, in general, be required to raise most of their revenues from their own sources—largely taxes, fees, and other levies on their own constituencies. They should not be able to rely on financing from above to cover their expenditures. This is especially critical at the margin. Decisions to expand or contract existing programs must be made in full light of their costs.

- Second, intergovernmental grants must not be expansible. Provincial, state, and local officials must not have access to expanded grant moneys to cover any emerging fiscal distress.[1] The grant system must not serve to bail out public authorities in time of fiscal difficulty if we are to expect these authorities to make the requisite, tough fiscal decisions.

In sum, decentralized governments need to have well-developed revenue systems of their own to finance the bulk of their spending. Intergovernmental grants may supplement these revenues, but provincial, state, and local governments must rely primarily on their own systems of taxation.

### Debt finance

Governments at all levels typically rely on debt issues to finance some part of the budget. In this respect, the importance of a central bank that is independent of the central treasury is now widely acknowledged. Public debt issues must not be easily monetized as an alternative to taxation for financing the public budget. What is not so widely discussed is the relevance of this proposition to decentralized levels of government. Yet provincial or state governments sometimes have ready access to state-owned banks to absorb their bond issues, notably in developing countries. This access obviously serves to create a soft budget constraint that provides perverse incentives for decentralized fiscal choices.

As McKinnon (1997) observes, state and local governments in the United States have traditionally used debt finance to fund capital projects. This system makes economic sense because it spreads costs over the useful life of the infrastructure. However, these governments have no recourse to public sources for funding their debt issues; they operate in private credit markets just like private borrowers. And these markets themselves, through the determination of credit ratings and other forms of monitoring of fiscal performance, create an environment in which fiscal authorities must perform responsibly. These markets, in short, have imposed a very useful fiscal discipline on decentralized governments.

### Fiscal equalization

This issue is the most complicated and contentious. In many systems of federal finance, central governments perform a fiscal-equalization function. They effectively transfer funds from relatively wealthy jurisdictions to poorer ones. Such transfers are often based on an equalization formula that measures the "fiscal need" and "fiscal capacity" of each province, state, or locality. Funds are then disproportionately channeled to those jurisdictions with the greatest needs and the least fiscal capacity.

Such programs are by no means a necessary feature of federal fiscal systems. Relief is often handled through programs that redistribute income from wealthy individuals to poorer ones. But the determination (based on social values) may be made that, in addition to income transfers to poor individuals, it is desirable for various reasons to transfer income from wealthy jurisdictions to the governments of more fiscally hard-pressed ones. Such equalizing grants play an important role in the fiscal systems of Canada, Australia, and Germany. In contrast, they are not a prominent feature of the intergovernmental transfer system in the United States; intergovernmental grants in the United States provide support for specific functions or programs, but typically do not accomplish much in the way of fiscal equalization.

More relevant to the discussion here are the implications of fiscal equalization measures for economic development and performance more generally. And here there is real disagreement. Some observers see equalizing grants as playing an important role in allowing poorer jurisdictions to compete effectively with fiscally stronger ones. This view holds that fiscally favored jurisdictions can exploit their position by encouraging continued economic growth, sometimes at the expense of poorer jurisdictions. Fiscal equalization, in brief, can create a more level playing field for the process of economic development.

But this argument is not fully compelling. Others contend that equalizing transfers can actually impede needed regional adjustments. For example, McKinnon (1997) argues that in the United States, the economic resurgence of the South after the Civil War resulted from the generally low level of wages and other costs. These low costs eventually induced industry and other economic activity to move to the South, bringing with it new prosperity. Equalizing transfers, from this perspective, may hinder needed regional adjustments by discouraging the interregional movement of resources.

Which view is the correct one is by no means clear; moreover, the impact of fiscal equalization on economic performance may vary by time and place. But the issue continues to occupy a central place on the political stage. In some cases, like the Canadian federation, fiscal equalization programs may be politically necessary to hold the federation together. In other cases, however, such measures may become a real source of political division. In Italy, for example, there have been recent, serious proposals to break the country into two separate nations. These proposals have their source in intense discontent in the North with the long-standing and sizable transfers of wealth to provinces in the South. Fiscal equalization is a complex economic and political issue.

### Empirical studies of the impact of fiscal decentralization on economic and political performance

As Shah points out, one of the serious shortcomings in the debate over fiscal decentralization has been the dearth of hard evidence on how decentralization affects economic performance. Shah provides a valuable contribution in his paper by summarizing the existing evidence and presenting some new findings stemming from his work with Jeff Huther.

Huther and Shah (1996) have assembled from diverse sources a set of indexes for some 80 nations. These indexes cover a wide variety of measures of economic and political structure and performance: quality of governance, political freedom, political stability, debt-to-GDP ratios, measures of income, the degree of equality of the distribution of income, and many more. The initial efforts of the research have involved looking at the statistical association between each of these indexes and an index of decentralization. And they find in nearly every case a statistically significant association (correlation) between increased decentralization and improved performance (in either political or economic terms).

Such results are surely intriguing and suggestive, but (as the authors are well aware) they must be interpreted with care. Statistical association does not prove causation: it cannot be concluded from these findings that decentralization causes better economic and political performance. Indeed, it seems clear that the degree of fiscal decentralization is itself an endogenous variable; it is in some sense an outcome of various political and economic forces. The interaction among decentralization and other characteristics of the political and economic system is obviously a very complicated one that involves a whole set of interacting institutions.

These findings may be generated largely by a feature that I have found in my own econometric work using international comparative data. In this work, countries tend to fall into two distinct groups:

- The relatively high-income industrial nations with generally good governance and relatively decentralized systems of government.

- The developing nations who typically score less well on measures of economic performance and effective governance and have relatively centralized government sectors.

These particular constellations of characteristics specific to the two groups of countries may be producing the results that Huther and Shah obtain. My suggestion is that they break their sample down into subsamples of the industrial countries and the developing nations and see if the results hold up in the subsamples. There is clearly some interesting further work to be done here (as the authors are well aware).

Shah's paper, in summarizing both the Huther-Shah work and a variety of other research, marshals an impressive body of evidence supporting the potential effectiveness of decentralization in improving the quality of both governance and economic performance in developing countries. I might add to their summary the findings of a recent (and as yet unpublished) dissertation at the University of Maryland. Sang-Loh Kim (1995), in an intriguing econometric study of economic growth with an international panel data set, estimated a Barro-type growth model. In addition to the usual explanatory variables, he included a measure of fiscal decentralization that, in most of his estimated equations, has a significant partial association with the rate of economic growth. Kim's results, in short, provide further support for Shah's contention that decentralization enhances economic performance—in this case, more rapid economic growth.[2]

In conclusion, Shah's paper is valuable in several respects. First, it emphasizes that decentralization in itself is not enough—we must get the institutions right. Second, he makes the important point that this issue is a broad one. It is not just a matter of the proper design of fiscal institutions. Fiscal decisionmaking obviously does not take place in a political vacuum, and, as Shah argues, for decentralization to work, it is essential that the supporting political institutions and processes provide a framework of good governance. And he has a number of constructive proposals to offer on these matters, including, for example, civil service reform and citizen participation. And, third, Shah gives us a valuable survey of the existing empirical work bearing on these matters (including his own recent work with Huther). His paper provides some real illumination on the role and form of fiscal decentralization in economic development.

### Notes

1.   This is subject to the qualification that certain matching grant programs should encourage spending on programs with benefits that spill over into other jurisdictions (Oates 1972). But for such programs, the formulas (notably the matching shares) should be clearly established, not subject to discretionary manipulation.
2.   Kim's work needs some further extensions, but the existing results are certainly suggestive.

### References

Huther, Jeff, and Anwar Shah. 1996. "A Simple Measure of Good Governance and its Application to the Debate on the Appropriate Level of Fiscal Decentralization." World Bank, Washington, D.C.

Kim, Sang-Loh. 1995. "Fiscal Decentralization, Fiscal Structure, and Economic Performance: Three Empirical Studies." University of Maryland, unpublished dissertation.

McKinnon, Ronald I. 1997. "Market-Preserving Fiscal Federalism in the American Monetary Union." In Mario I. Blejer and Teresa Ter-Minassian, eds. *Macroeconomic Dimensions of Public Finance: Essays in Honour of Vito Tanzi*, pp. 73–93. London: Routledge.

Oates, Wallace E. 1972. *Fiscal Federalism.* New York: Harcourt Brace Jovanovich.

———. 1994. "Federalism and Government Finance." In J. Quigley and E. Smolensky, eds., *Modern Public Finance*, pp. 126–151. Cambridge, Mass.: Harvard University Press.

Prud'homme, Remy. 1995. "On the Dangers of Decentralization." *The World Bank Research Observer* (August):201–10.

Weingast, Barry. 1995. "The Economic Role of Political Institutions: Market-Preserving Federalism and Economic Development." *Journal of Law, Economics, and Organization* 11(April):1–31.

## Comments on "Fostering fiscally responsive and accountable governance: lessons from decentralization," by Shah

*Laura Kullenberg*

Of particular interest to me in Anwar Shah's paper were his comments on institutional arrangements and settings and the relationship between evaluation and accountability. My comments will focus on national decentralization programs in developing countries—programs that promote the devolution of both development budgets and authority to locally elected governments. The United Nations Capital Development Fund (UNCDF) supports these efforts with local development funds (LDFs), which are essentially small-scale models of a system of intergovernmental fiscal transfers. These transfers move capital grant money to district and subdistrict authorities for the planning and management of public sector investments in rural infrastructure.

LDFs are similar to social funds or municipal development funds, but with several important differences. First, investment planning and allocation are carried out within, not parallel to, the existing public sector planning process. Local authorities receive set allocations for planning, and investments are made according to the principles of bottom-up participatory planning, using techniques that are often introduced and technically supported by UNCDF. The LDF programs emphasize not only the government's role in providing public services but the private sector's in producing them, and they encourage high levels of community participation.

I will address two questions. First, how do we evaluate these kinds of programs in a meaningful way? Second, which institutional issues are of the most concern in assessing performance? The answers to these questions depend on the context and goals of specific programs, but two assertions in Shah's paper serve as a point of departure.

Presenting lessons for reforming fiscal systems in developing countries, Shah states first that any serious reform of fiscal systems must address institutions of citizen participation and accountability. Second, evaluation capacity development is of fundamental importance to public sector reform in developing countries. The paper also raises the question of whether and under what conditions evaluation can be to the public sector what accountability is to the private sector. For LDF programs, accountability is a powerful issue, for a number of reasons. First, we often transfer capital budgets to newly formed or elected governments that have no prior experience managing this level of direct capital funding. In such environments, systems of financial control and sanctions are often embryonic and/or uncertain, and the risk of financial impropriety and mismanagement is high.

Concern with accountability is a strong preoccupation in almost all of the countries where UNCDF has launched LDF programs. Even in countries like Uganda, which have strong decentralization policies, our field consultations have documented deep mistrust within each level of government. This mistrust can be about the layer above (and sometimes below) and concerns primarily the capacity for financial steward-ship and effective use of resources. Further, if newly elected officials misappropriate LDF funds or fail to honor investment choices agreed to during the local planning process, the success of the individual projects is endangered. Even more important, however, the wider policy agenda of such projects is compromised. This agenda aims to demonstrate that, given conditions of democratic decentralization and favorable institutional arrangements, local governments can successfully manage capital transfers for local development and service delivery. If such programs con-tinuously fall victim to misappropriation and fiscal mismanagement at the local level, donors and central governments are likely to return to more centralized sec-toral funding through central line ministries.

## Accountability and risks

It is important to distinguish among the various types of accountability and risk associated with decentralization programs. For example, *institutional accountability* refers to the responsibility of political authorities to communities and of civil ser-vants to elected authorities. We have learned how important it is in designing LDF projects to work with certain institutions at each level. There is no set formula, as the choices play out differently in different contexts. In the context of a small commune in francophone West Africa, elected authorities are generally closer and more accountable to local communities than civil servants. Conversely, in larger rural dis-tricts in East Africa, politicians tend to be distant from the electorate, and civil ser-vants are accountable to them.

The underlying goal of UNCDF's LDF projects is the maximum feasible devolution of authority for planning, allocation, and control of funds to local governments. A level of risk is associated with giving local governments planning and allocation authority—the last word in their investment preferences. But another part of the strategy, which carries different risks, is to entrust local governments with control of funds, allowing them to contract with line ministries and private sector producers, thereby ensuring accountability of implementation.

Tension between technical and political authorities often arises very quickly in these programs, generally around the issues of power and accountability. In one LDF project currently under design in Uganda, district council members complained that central development funds provided travel and supervision costs only for technical staff, not counselors. As the district chairman put it, "This LDF project means an enhanced level of political activity, and we are concerned about the participation of policymakers. I am not happy with technical people dominating these discussions. Even our sectoral coun-cil meetings are superficial—we need allowances for policymakers to meet seriously!"

*Capacity building is one solution to risk*

One common response of donors to these risks, especially those associated with entrusting local governments with authority over funds, has been to tie the provi-sion of capital budgets to technical assistance (TA) for capacity building. The point is to provide local officials with a training package that will enable them to exercise their new responsibilities. The training typically covers some combination of accounting, financial management, local development planning, responsibilities and administrative functions of elected officials, and so forth. One problem with these packages is that they are usually supply driven. Typically, they are designed by outsiders—donors or central or regional governments—based on the outsiders' perceptions of the kind of training local governments need to perform well. In many cases, significant benefits also accrue to suppliers through allowances, contracts, and jobs for civil servants and international consultants and/or increases in bureaucratic territory or control.

One interesting alternative, which we have been exploring in-house, is to create a demand-driven capacity-building fund that is more in keeping with principles of decentralized control and decisionmaking. Local officials and communities could access this fund for TA. But this type of system could significantly reduce the incentives of current suppliers of TA (donors, central/regional governments, and contractors), eroding support that is crucial to the project. I will address the issue of central/ regional government buy-in later.

A second problem with these "good governance" capacity-building packages is that they are often directed only to local government officials and not to communities. This type of single-target training is often helpful but not sufficient, and it can sometimes be harmful. One bilateral district development program in Tanzania invested heavily in training for local councils in project accounting and management but failed to strengthen lower-level community organizations. After four years of training, the local officials were simply better equipped to manipulate financial accounts and misappropriate public funds, which they did to such an extent that the project had to be suspended.

It is thus important to train beneficiary populations in capacity building so that they can better generate demand for services and accountability from their local authorities. This capability is necessary if communities are to participate effectively in the political process or in decisionmaking related to development budgets. In short, capacity-building efforts should be composed of mirrored investments that both help citizens to make reasonable demands on their local governments and increase the capacity of those governments to respond effectively.

### Information and evaluation programs are important

Given the above considerations, we have had to think quite a bit about simple and effective ways to encourage accountability. Transparent and well-publicized monitoring and evaluation activities can provide demand as well as incentives for financial accountability and good performance of local officials, especially when tied to additional allocation of funds. How information about projects is communicated, through whom, and when are also key to establishing pressure for accountability. Communities receive most of their information about projects through local political leaders (mayors, counselors, and sometimes even contractors), who can easily impose their preferences. Disseminating clear, timely information about projects directly to beneficiary communities through independent sources can be a powerful accountability check on local officials, contractors, and project managers (Serrano Berthet 1996).

UNCDF's field experiences have also shown that information should be provided in accessible locations, using understandable languages and images, both before and during project implementation. It should include details about project objectives and rules of access, entitlements and project budgets, the level of local government commitment, timelines, investment options, project coverage, design standards, and unit costs. The downside of a successful information campaign is that it can create the kind of tremendous demand local officials fear for legitimate reasons. They may not have the capacity to respond, but failing to respond can have serious political consequences for newly elected councilors. It is important to develop robust and defensible allocation formulas that local politicians can use to deal with unanticipated and overwhelming demand for services.

Information about design standards, unit costs, and construction requirements is particularly useful both at the project prioritization stage and during microproject construction. In a project village in the Palestinian Territories, we learned that providing project committees with basic information about school construction standards leads to spontaneous but effective ad hoc supervision of contractors. The result is significant cost and time savings in school construction.

However, even with effective information campaigns, community-driven programs are still taken over and local preferences overridden in subtle ways. Even with an open menu of qualifying investments, certain types of projects tend to be processed more quickly than others during the appraisal process. Soon the projects that are easiest to approve become community priorities, regardless of the "openness" of the menu. Serrano Berthet's 1996 study in Brazil found that the projects approved most easily tended to be those from which local officials could gain politically, such as "showcase" infrastructure, productive (rather than social) projects, and projects for which resident technical staff had appropriate experience (sectoral bias). Technical staff can influence investment decisions in other ways. In one LDF in rural Laos, communities showed a high preference for kindergarten construction to the exclusion of other, more pressing needs. An evaluation showed that this preference was the result of advocacy by a popular education extension worker—the only technical staff member who visited the area regularly.

Biases are also built into the consensual community planning process, generally toward investments with equitable benefit spread, so that no one member of the community gains or loses more than the others. Thus LDFs tend to invest in schools, which are relatively easy to manage and offer widespread benefits, rather than in irrigation schemes, even though irrigation may meet a more pressing production need in the community. Such preferences are even embodied in language. In Malawi, our counterparts told us that the word for self-help in Chichewa means "making bricks." Heavily demand-driven programs can also risk distorting patterns of infrastructure services by favoring small, local investments and neglecting larger public infrastructure. For these reasons, it is important to establish workable relationships and fora where balanced technical and political judgments can be made.

Programs that emphasize demand-driven projects to the exclusion of government preferences are also unlikely to succeed politically for very long. Most often, in projects generated through the political process and based on principles of local choice and nonsubordination, investment choices may conflict with national standards or sectoral plans. Technocrats and local politicians may also fail to see the desirability of demand-driven projects, raising contradictions that can erode both crucial support for projects and decentralization policies. This last point is particularly important, because if LDF communities succeed in preserving their preferences over the strong views of technical staff or counselors, they may lose the element of local ownership or "buy-in" essential to the project's success. If technical people are marginalized during the appraisal process or disagree strongly with the outcome, they will not be motivated to provide the project with technical support. Nor will officials be inclined to provide what is sometimes crucial political support and cover.

## Evaluating LDFs and decentralization programs

To conclude, I would like to make three points about evaluation. First, there are obvious methodological problems (such as the counterfactual and "what if" scenarios) in evaluating the impact of supporting local governments and governance. These problems are difficult to solve. One admittedly imperfect approach is to compare project districts retroactively with the performance of neighboring districts without projects.

Currently, the emphasis is on developing standard indicators for measuring governance goals. However, it is important to avoid the rush to indicators. While agencies must develop a standard set of indicators for comparability and analysis, locally developed and contextual indicators are also necessary for understanding performance, especially for measuring broad goals such as increased accountability or more inclusive public decisionmaking. A number of techniques can be used to register local perceptions or indicators about what progress in these areas means. These data not only provide useful guidance for project monitoring but inform project design in surprising ways, providing checks on initial design assumptions.

Second, similar groups are often good at coming up with performance measures for others. It may not be feasible for local councils to evaluate each other, for when these peer evaluations are tied to the allocation of further funds, they can quickly become exercises in collusion and mutual praising. However, I have found that council members can provide excellent advice about how to measure or assess the performance of an "abstract" local council. The same holds true for other groupings, such as project committees and technical staff.

Last, external advisors have warned us not to be blinded by our project model and objectives when evaluating the LDF projects. Rather, we should attempt to make meaningful contributions to research and learning about decentralization and the types of transfer systems, rules, and institutional arraignments that work on the ground. In doing so, we are better served by looking at where these types of LDF programs are working, finding out why local governments are performing well, and then seeing what our project interventions, among other factors, have to do with their success.

## Reference

Serrano Berthet, Rodriguez. 1996. "Who Knows What's Best for the Poor: Demand-Driven Policies and Rural Poverty in Northeast Brazil." Master's Thesis, Massachusetts Institute of Technology.

**Floor discussion on "Fostering fiscally responsive and accountable governance: lessons from decentralization"**

The first participant, Nabli of the International Economic Association, noted that the speakers had made a distinction between choosing projects and implementing them. Either way, political constraints and rent-seeking are involved at the local level, a situation that compares unfavorably with centralized decisionmaking. Nabli suggested that asking people to select and screen at the central level provides a check, since screening at the regional level tends to be inefficient.

Jeffrey Nugent noted that an important new feature of the decentralization process is that people can "vote with their feet." Rural-to-urban migration can be interpreted in this light as a form of "exiting" unpopular policies. Has evaluation taken internal population mobility into consideration in looking at the effects of decentralization?

Another speaker asked if mobility undermines the rationale for fiscal equalization transfers. Further he inquired as to how one judges the success of decentralization.

Responding to Nabli's question, Anwar Shah argued that a central planning approach to project selection may not yield outcomes consistent with local preferences. Instead, if the central government uses conditional block transfers with conditions on standards and access to basic services to be achieved, then it can ensure that local selection process will pick up the best projects to achieve agreed upon outputs. Thus local autonomy will be preserved while ensuring accountability and safeguarding national interests.

In reply to Nugent's question about mobility and a related question on fiscal equalization transfers, Shah remarked that indeed mobility questions are at the heart of evaluation discussion of alternate policies. For example, in the absence of full capitalization, fiscal equalization transfers have been advocated to reduce fiscally induced migration. With full capitalization of public sector benefits and burdens, fiscal equalization may work against factor mobility in response to economic stimuli. In such a situation, the rationale for fiscal equalization transfers in a federal system is a political one to give a sense of participation to all members of the union.

Shah suggested that the ultimate question is how to address economic trade-offs within the political system. Some countries, such as Germany, are better at addressing trade-offs than others, such as Canada and Australia. Political compromises become more explicit in the process of agreeing to trade-offs, and large transfer payments can be a serious threat to a federation. Such payments may have been a factor in the separation of the Czech Republic and Slovakia.

In determining the success of decentralization policies, Shah suggested that the governance quality indices that he developed with the help of a colleague for eight countries offer a useful framework.

# 6. Transaction cost economics and public sector rent-seeking in developing countries: toward a theory of government failure

### Eduardo Wiesner

---

*Public sector rent-seekers raise the transaction costs of public goods, services, and "contracts" with which the public and private sector try to create an efficient market for public goods. The high transaction costs lead to a special type of market failure—the market failure of externalities. These constitute the main obstacle to development.*

---

*In almost every policy area, those who stand the most to gain are the men who earn their incomes there.*

—A. Downs (1957)

On October 10, 1932, Ronald Coase (1937) said in a letter to his friend R. Fowler that he had "succeeded in linking up organization with cost." Coase's ebullience was understandable. He had just provided the analytics of why firms arise and had planted the seeds of a research program that led him to the Nobel prize. According to Coase, firms come about to economize on transaction costs. Since this explanation, "transaction cost economics"[1] has become the basic unit of analysis of the firm, organizations, and even governance structures.[2] By economizing on costly market transactions, firms lower transaction costs within and outside themselves. Lower transaction costs enhance the functioning of markets and lead to more efficient societal outcomes.

In the hope of following Coase's felicitous relationship, this paper seeks to link organization with cost, but in the market for externalities rather than in private markets. More specifically, the paper tries to link transaction costs with externalities and with rent-seeking in developing countries.[3] The organizing hypothesis is that in many of these countries, the transaction costs of key public goods—such as education, health, information, public services, and democratic governance—are extremely high because public sector rent-seeking institutions have been able to monopolize those markets and the inputs of those markets. In terms of neoinstitutional economics, these institutions have become the "wrong institutions." The end result is what Stiglitz (1991) calls public government failure. This is the specific failure that development theory and practice need to address.

This paper suggests that public sector rent-seeking and the institutional arrangements that arise from it should become the unit of analysis of development theory and practice. Sharing North's (1990) dictum that "institutions matter" and Olson's insights (1965) into "collective logic," the paper seeks to add specificity to the normative nostrums that countries should get the institutions "right."

Within this approach, the challenge for development is to find ways in which, first, the influence of public sector rent-seekers can be mitigated and, second, the markets in externalities can function more efficiently.[4] In sum, the challenge is to find ways to economize on the transaction costs of the externalities markets.

### Externalities, development theory, and transaction costs

The "new growth" economic literature (Lucas 1988; Romer 1986) (new growth is sometimes called "Neo-Schumpeterian growth"; see Romer 1994), has reinforced the view that the externalities of social overhead capital are critical elements for economic growth and for the alleviation of poverty. Given the characteristics of public goods—such as education, health, justice, and public services—governments have a major role to play in financing and supplying social overhead. In adopting this new view of development, many developing countries have increased their social spending and embarked on privatization drives to expand and improve their physical infrastructure. They want to correct for the classical market failure associated with public goods.

However, classical market failure is no longer the key issue. The real emerging need is to explain—and it is hoped to predict—public government failure. This paper submits that such failure is explained largely by public sector rent-seeking institutions and by the consequences of the peculiar institutional arrangements that emerge from them.

In Colombia and several other Latin American countries, public sector labor unions in the social and infrastructure sectors, and even in the judicial and security sectors, have captured a major portion of the additional social spending and have thwarted privatization drives. The additional budget resources end up raising the factor costs of the public goods, with little effect on the actual results of the expenditure. And privatization ends up creating additional entry barriers to future competition.

These public sector rent-seekers raise the transaction costs of public goods, services, and "contracts" with which the public and private sectors try to create an efficient market for public goods.[5] The high transaction costs lead to a special modality of market failure—that is, the market failure of externalities. These market failures constitute the main obstacle to growth and social development.

### Public sector rent-seeking: toward a theory of externality failure

Stanley Fischer (1977) put Coase's transaction cost theory to a severe test. He said that "transaction costs have a well-deserved bad name as a theoretical device . . . because almost anything can be rationalized by invoking suitable specified transaction costs." The issue he raised was that of the tautological nature of explaining phenomena through ex post rationalization. If there was a theory behind transaction costs, it had to have a modicum of predictive power.

Applying a similar question to this paper would mean that the special characteristics of public sector rent-seeking would need to be specified. Whether they have a predictive power is an empirical question to which this paper cannot give a definitive answer. The answer will come about as a research agenda on public sector rent-seeking in the externalities markets is developed.[6] In the case of Colombia, the explicative power of this "infant theory" seems persuasive.

Public sector rent-seekers have three major distinctive characteristics. First (and most generally), they operate in the realm of the public sector, where they find a propitious climate in which to grow, evolve, and learn. They emerge basically out of government interventions seeking redistributive objectives in areas where public choices are particularly politicized and the price system has been considered inadequate to deal with externalities. In this protected environment, public sector rent-seeking institutions can easily camouflage their real interests and thrive on the naiveté of the public, which normally is unaware of the risks of government failure.

Second (and this characteristic gives public sector rent-seeking institutions their special advantage), they are able to shape the institutional and even constitutional governance structure within which they operate.[7] Neoinstitutional economics distinguishes among institutions, interinstitutional structures, rules, and norms, on the one hand, and players, actors, and organizations within those rules, on the other. The latter "play the game" within the rules emanating from the former. Those rules can lead to more or less efficient outcomes. As Schiavo-Campo (1994) has emphasized, the dynamics of the interplay between the rules and the players—the causality—is the critical factor in a society's capacity to develop the "right" or the "wrong" institutions.[8]

An example occurs in Latin America when organized public sector rent-seekers influence legislation to ensure national and earmarked financing for education, child care, health, or the environment. Another example emerges when labor unions in key public sector entities are able to obtain legislation that gives them de facto veto power to prevent real competition.

Third, public sector rent-seeking institutions are able to organize themselves as special hybrid firms, not fully private nor really public, whose main purpose is not to maximize profits but to appropriate quasi-rents. Profits are not, at least explicitly, their major concern, because labor unions are not, after all, supposed to be profit maximizers. Shirking, and rapidly changing forms of public sector shirking, is their business. To enhance this potential, they create environments in which information is diffuse, ambiguous, inconclusive, and linked to policy objectives that in turn lead to more quasi-rents.

The hybrid firm, located within the public sector (but whose interests are not the same as the government's or the public's and with a ready disposition to collude with private sector rent-seekers), is a largely underestimated "wrong institution."[9] It explains the precarious results of the efforts of many countries to reform[10] and to modernize.

One of the most ingenious schemes public sector rent-seekers use to enhance their influence involves becoming "agents" to multiple "principals." A sort of common agency problem evolves when no single principal has full authority, allowing the agents to play the principals against each other. One of the more costly consequences of this situation is that "the power of incentives in the equilibrium among several principals is weakened" (Dixit 1996).

In brief, public sector rent-seekers appear to have a comparative advantage over private sector rent-seekers. Their superior competitiveness comes basically from the fact that they operate in an environment where competition is the exception, where information is asymmetrical, and where they can control evaluations. Public sector rent-seekers find it easy to collude with private and public agents to politicize processes and to restrict real competition, since, after all, the private sector's main interest is not to preserve competition but to capture it.

In the last analysis, public sector rent-seekers restrict the capacity of the executive power—indeed of all powers in government—to deliver the political platform on which they were elected. This is a serious political problem. To McCubbins, Noll, and Weingast (1987), it gives rise to the question of whether elected political officials can effectively assure that their policy intentions will be carried out.

### Public sector rent-seeking in Colombia

This section provides three examples of rent-seeking capture in the externalities markets in Colombia (Wiesner 1997b). The aim is to show the underlying common characteristics that can sustain an infant theory of failure in the externalities market.

#### *The capture of the primary and secondary educational market*

Colombia's new 1991 constitution and decentralization drive enabled the central government and territorial entities to adopt specific revenue-sharing targets. This meant assured financing, by constitution and by law, of national resources to cover such costs as the salaries of public sector teachers at the state and municipal levels. This financing, which in 1997 amounted to $3 billion, or nearly 4 percent of GDP, is supposed to grow each year in real terms at a much faster pace than GDP. By the year 2000, total public expenditures for primary and secondary education will probably have tripled as a percentage of GDP from a 1993 base—a major budgetary achievement, indeed.

But the results of this enormous effort do not correspond to the size of the investment. The microanalytics of the process suggests that qualitative improvements are negligible and difficult to measure, that teachers' strikes are just as frequent as before, that whenever a local authority tries to hire new independent teachers, it faces serious legal and financial problems. In brief, real educational opportunities for the poor have not increased significantly.

Several factors explain the poor outcomes: there is no real competition in the market of primary and secondary education. The teachers' union has a de facto monopoly on the supply of inputs. By law, it is virtually impossible to have independent evaluations. The private sector cannot compete with the public sector. In brief, the consumer does not buy the product. Rather, the product is bought by the national government and distributed by a political process controlled by the teachers' union.[11]

*The capture of the telecommunications market*

In Colombia, a decentralized public sector institution has for decades had the monopoly of long-distance telephone service. Parallel to this national monopoly, there are several "local" monopolies for municipal service. In theory, the local monopolies are independent institutions. In reality, however, labor unions have managed them as one large corporation. Although Colombia has a Ministry of Communications and even a new regulatory authority charged with fostering competition and creating the conditions for privatization, in reality the "integrated" national labor union dictates policy. And within this policy there is no room for competition or for privatization.

Through a process of strikes (or the threat of strikes) the directorate of the sector's labor unions has been able to force governments over the last ten or more years to accept its policy as the de facto official policy. Significantly, the directorate has been able to induce a financial process according to which about 80 percent of the assets of the National Telephone Company (TELECOM) are owed to the labor union. The exact amounts of those liabilities are impossible to ascertain.

Why is this so? The explanation lies in the monopoly power of the unions and in the earmarking of financing that accrues through tariffs to monopolies governed by a "directorate" of labor unions. The little privatization that has taken place has been "negotiated" with the directorate. As long as a national directorate remains in place with powers that are stronger than the political will of the government to confront it, significant competition cannot occur.

*The capture of the environmental market*

Following the principles of decentralization, the 1993 law on the environment established that local and decentralized institutions would be the main instrument for managing environmental problems (Wiesner 1995). This approach was the right one (Oates 1991), but it lost its effectiveness the moment political actors and local rent-seekers were able to ensure that within virtually all of the country's previous state boundaries there would be one—and sometimes even more than one— "environmental corporation." With this approach, established rent-seekers were able to ensure against any new way of distributing additional financing for the environment.

The need for efficiency should have suggested giving jurisdiction over the main river basins or the most critical environmental basins to the environmental corporations. But this logical solution would have disrupted established political interests. What is disheartening is that with these manipulations, little incentive was left in the law to encourage the Coaseian bargaining of interjurisdictional externalities.

In sum, the outcomes of these and other empirical studies indicate that if there is a national de facto labor union with monopoly power, no competition either from the private sector or from within the public sector, and no incentive structure for the efficient use of public resources, the externalities markets cannot develop. In such conditions, public government failure can be anticipated. Here lie the specifics of an infant theory of public government failure.

### Public sector rent-seeking and morality

The success of public sector rent-seeking institutions is explained less by their dexterity in restricting competition than by the unwitting complicity of those who believe in the neoclassical market model. Walrasian economic theory and the presumption that people tend to maximize have such a strong intellectual appeal that they quickly become largely unquestioned paradigms—to the point that the situational restrictions of the neoclassical model are often neglected. But markets do not always clear. According to Stiglitz (1995):

> The fundamental problem with the neoclassical model and the corresponding model underlying market socialism is that they fail to take into account a variety of problems that arise from the absence of perfect information and the costs of acquiring information, as well as the absence of or imperfections in certain key risk and capital markets. The absence or imperfections of these markets can, in turn, to a large extent be explained by problems of information.

When policymakers start out from the neoclassical assumption of competition, as they should, they tend to underestimate what Williamson (1993, 1995) calls the "microanalytics" of processes, behavior, and incentives. They tend to assume that competition will prevail and that all that is needed is to enunciate it, decree it, or convince somebody of its logic. In the meantime, the organized rent-seekers stay focused on their immediate and tangible interests, which are to build monopoly power and to prevent competition. Walras is their unwitting partner. Without him, the Austrians[12] might have had the upper hand. After all, rent-seekers do not begin with an abstract general equilibrium model but with the specific case at hand. They begin with the individual institution.

Morals as individual and collective rules enter the realm of public sector rent-seeking in developing countries through a curious paradox. On the one hand, rent-seeking thrives because the public at large naively believes that morality—"a general disposition to follow moral rules" (Vanberg 1994)—will restrict abuses, shirking, and plain skullduggery. On the other hand, the specific interest groups will behave with different "morals" if the conditions under which they perform (that is, the real incentive structure) allow them to do so.

What matters for policymaking is that the problem of rent-seeking is taken out of the realm of morals and normativity and placed in the perspective of positive political economy and rational choice. When the public sector labor unions in Colombia monopolize the supply of primary education, restrict competition, and capture special rents, they are not being immoral, censurable, or poor citizens. They are only taking advantage of conditions that reward their behavior. Changing that behavior requires more than moral rules. It requires a different incentive structure and a more positive strategy.

### The realm of neoinstitutional economics

Following the methodology suggested by Lakatos (1970) for science in general (but now followed by a number of economists), we can say that neoinstitutional economics is part of the evolutionary protective belt of the hard-core neoclassical model. Neoinstitutional economics does not reject competition or rational choice assumptions. Rather, it builds on them, emphasizing the need to satisfy restrictions related to information, incentive structures, property rights, transaction costs, and rent-seeking in the political and economic markets. In brief, and as Eggertsson (1990) puts it, neoinstitutional economics seeks "a new synthesis of neoclassical and institutional economics."[13]

What distinguishes neoinstitutional economics from previous "institutional" or "historical" schools is that the former has more of a theory behind it.[14] That particular theory has two interdependent components: first, a reliance on competition as the condition that induces efficiency, and second, the belief that the right incentive structure is the best answer to the restrictions that arise from the neoclassical model.

The success or strength of neoinstitutional economics is largely attributable to its microanalytical orientation.[15] In essence, this means devoting less attention to the traditional aggregate questions of resource allocation, equilibrium, and scarcity and more to incentives, contracts, transaction costs, organization, information, process, rent-seeking, rules of choice, and asset specificity. [16]

According to Nugent and Lin (1995), although essentially microeconomics in perspective, neoinstitutional economics has two broad interdependent approaches—transaction costs and collective action. The first is useful in analyzing the demand for institutional arrangements. The second is useful in the study of the supply of institutional arrangements (Feeney 1993). Within the context of this paper, the political economy question that arises asks how the collective political process will supply the right institutional arrangements to restrict exuberant public sector rent-seeking. After all, as Olson (1965) demonstrated, there is little collective logic.

What does the future hold for neoinstitutional economics? Will it be absorbed by neoclassicists? According to Richter (1996), neoinstitutional economics will not disappear "provided that neoinstitutionalists continue to develop, test, and improve new institutional economic theories, and keep themselves at a safe distance from the assumptions of perfect rationality, perfect foresight, and zero transaction costs." The demise of neoinstitutional economics, if it were to come, would be particularly costly for developing countries, where the classical paradigms are more incomplete than in more developed ones. Should that happen, developing countries would run the risk of again being seduced by the standard neoclassical prescriptions.

### Policy implications

Three major policy implications follow from the previous analysis. First, the starting point in designing policy should be the restrictions that will most likely be faced instead of the intrinsic merit of what is being sought. For example, in terms of investment in primary education, the question to be answered is how to deal with the labor unions, with shirking, and with the inelasticities of supply. The restriction will seldom be insufficient resources. Rather, it will be the difficulty of bringing competition into the process. The challenge is to look at the problem from the perspective of the rational choice of the rent-seekers associated with the public good in question. An alternative approach is needed that asks the "right" questions about how the rent-seekers will try to restrict competition instead of assuming that normativity alone will do the job. This approach will also show policymakers where to focus their attention.

Second, before a policy design is finalized, an agreement must be formalized with the potential rent-seekers for specific evaluations of performance and of results. The conclusions of these evaluations would then be built into the process as conditions for financing. In other words, the effective feedback of the conclusions of the evaluations must be assured beforehand. Needless to say, these evaluations must be independent and must focus on results, not on process compliance.

It is indeed curious that neoinstitutional economics, with all its emphasis on microanalytics and situational constraints, has not focused more on the potential of independent evaluations to enhance public sector reforms (Wiesner 1993) and to ensure a more efficient use of resources.

Third, an incentive structure has to be built into the access to public resources. In other words, a results-oriented budget allocation has to be built into the financing of public goods. Often, a complex institutional framework accompanies primary education financing and delivery, but if no real reward is given to schools that show better results, very little is accomplished in real terms. To Picciotto (1996), "The logic . . . is to link budget allocations and teachers' salaries to student achievements."

Often, the capacity of incentives to change behavior and outcomes is questioned. This view neglects the fact that negative incentives seem always to work and to explain many reform failures. In sum, incentives are there. The difficulty is orienting the incentives toward the collective interest.

The overall policy implication is that the normative policy approach should cease to be at the center of the reform process and that a more public choice and "contractarian" (Buchanan 1988; Rawls 1971, 1993) framework should be utilized. Picciotto (1995) has summed it well by saying, "Policy is useless without an institutional machinery capable of implementing it."

### The strategy to deal with public sector rent-seeking

The strategy for dealing with public sector rent-seeking should begin at the macroinstitutional and policy levels. This means having an environment propitious to competition, to incentives, and to the development of effective rules for actors and organizations, as outlined above (Wiesner 1997a). Two specific types of actions can be used to create this environment: decentralization and global rules "behind a veil of ignorance," as defined by Rawls (1971).[17]

*Decentralization strategy*

The decentralization strategy should have three interdependent operational paths. The first requires rewarding local fiscal efforts to complement national transfers in financing the transactions of externalities (Wiesner 1997b). Coopting local public actors and decentralizing public choices is likely to restrict the influence of rent-seekers. At worst, it will be shared. In either case, overall efficiency will be enhanced.

The second involves finding ways to decentralize or denationalize national public sector labor unions to reduce the disruptive impact of national strikes and mitigate the political pressures for national governments to compromise. Moving toward this objective requires that a significant portion of national resources be appropriated on the basis of results and performance.

Third, political power in the legislature needs to be decentralized. Specifically, this means having senators elected not for regions but for the country as a whole. The senators would act according to their political interests according to what Olson (in progress) calls "encompassing interests."[18] Establishing fixed terms for all elected officials or legislators is also a mode of temporal decentralization that should be given a chance.

In brief, the strategy should begin not with the question of how to get the "right" institutions in but how to get the "wrong" institutions out. This apparent game of words has immense significance. Once the problem is viewed from the perspective of the restriction that needs to be overcome, instead of from the desirability of the objectives to be achieved, the entire strategy changes completely. Not to view the challenge in this way is to assume, wrongly, that there are some empty spaces out there in the social realm waiting to be filled with the right policy nostrum.

*Collective rules for encompassing interests*

While it is not feasible to adopt all rules behind a Rawlsian "veil of ignorance," a lot can still be accomplished if some constitutional contracts and enforcement mechanisms are negotiated before policy is settled (Greif 1993). The establishment of strategic evaluations of results, of "sunset clauses," of cofinancing, of incentives, and so forth are not politically impossible.[19] Constitutional frameworks that restrict negative games among players, or what Diamond (1994) calls "subgame perfectness," have considerable capacity to induce cooperation and more efficient outcomes.

## Summary and conclusions

- While it is clear that institutions matter and that information and incentives are essential for markets to work, such postulates are incomplete if we fail to note the restrictions that limit operationalizing those principles. Failing to specify restrictions is like saying that domestic savings matter or that social capital is critical without specifying why and how some societies do, in fact, raise the relative importance of domestic savings or find better collective rules. By focusing on public sector rent-seeking institutions and arrangements, this paper has sought to add specificity to the neoinstitutional tenet that "institutions matter."

- One of the most harmful consequences of public sector rent-seeking is higher transaction costs in the externalities markets. Public goods with great significance for the formation of social capital—primary and secondary education, health, and governance—can hardly be transacted between the public and private sectors because of high transaction costs and a variety of restrictions arising from organized public sector rent-seeking institutions. The end result is public government failure.

■ From the perspective of developing countries, what really matters is resolving public government failure and understanding the dynamics of the relationships between governments and markets. Public government failure can be anticipated if public sector rent-seeking is able to monopolize the markets of public goods, capture public and legislative choices, and enjoy the political support of public opinion. Colombia has had this experience.

■ Public sector rent-seeking institutions cannot be wished away. They are very resilient, and they are part of the culture and of the political institutions at play. They simply and inexorably emerge out of the incentive structure that is in place. To change behavior, the "normative policy approach" has to be replaced by a more positive strategy with a greater role for contractarian incentives.

■ Inefficient economic institutions and collective rules are the norm and not the exception, particularly in developing countries. There is no process of evolutionary selection that results in efficient institutions weeding out the inefficient ones. It is rather the contrary in most cases. For this reason, the strategy should begin not with the question of how to get the "right" institutions in but how to get the "wrong" institutions out.

■ The strategy to mitigate the effects of public sector rent-seeking institutions is as follows: decentralize the structure of government, denationalize the financing of public goods, and bring competition into the economic and political processes. This strategy is what Mäki (1993) calls "theoretical institutionalism."

### The heuristics of a research agenda

In developing countries, it is not easy to formulate a research agenda that will effectively induce more work in neoinstitutional economics in general and in public sector rent-seeking in particular. The primary reason for this difficulty is that most of the best-trained scholars find it more attractive to test their talent against elegant and abstract models than to go into the seemingly intractable problems of institutions and politics. Fortunately, the situation is changing. Scholars and policymakers are paying more attention to the restrictions of political economy and to issues of methodology.[20] They are beginning to ask questions that place relevance above elegance. Following are some examples:

■ Why is there so little convergence among nations and often within nations?

■ Why do reforms fail?

■ Why do some countries have the wrong "collective rules?"

Following Lakatos's (1970) suggestion that the primary unit of appraisal in science is the research program rather than the scientific theory, I suggest the following positive heuristic research agenda:[21]

- Evaluate the determinants of institutions in general and of public sector rent-seeking institutions in particular. What are the macroinstitutional arrangements and the microanalytical factors that determine a given institutional outcome and evolution?

- Undertake strategic evaluations of specific reform experiences under different institutional arrangements—that is, the characteristics of property rights, information markets, centralized or decentralized governance structures, incentives, and rules of choice.

- Do specific studies on the relationships among public sector rent-seeking, transaction costs, and public government failure.

All these studies should be empirical and focused on the specific institutional restrictions that influence the effectiveness of public policies.

Two negative heuristic programs should be avoided: insisting on the "normative" policymaking approach, and blaming everything on politics, concluding that reform in developing countries is an intractable political problem.[22] It may be, but only if tackled without understanding the underlying etiology and without what Blaug (1992) calls a "falsifiable theory."

## Notes

1. According to Noorderhaven (1996), "transaction cost economics, as developed by Williamson (1979, 1985, 1991), focuses on the relationship between attributes of transactions and characteristics of the governance structures used to accommodate these transactions. Transactions vary in many dimensions, the most important of which is the degree of asset specificity. A party incurring relation-specific investments will demand safeguards to prevent its counterpart from attempting to appropriate the quasi-rents associated with these assets. Safeguards can take the form of formal, legally enforceable contracts, or of extra-legal private ordering arrangements."

2. According to Williamson (1996), "Viewing the firm as a governance structure, rather than as a production function, has had numerous ramifications. For one thing, the boundary of the firm is no longer defined by technology but is something to be derived from comparative transaction cost considerations. For another, marginal analysis gives way to discrete structural analysis. Also, attention is focused on much more microanalytic features of transactions and organization. The roles of power and authority come under renewed scrutiny in the process."

3. Rent-seeking is, of course, a universal phenomena that cannot be ascribed exclusively to developing countries. The concept itself was coined by scholars (Tullock 1967; Krueger 1974) from industrial countries. However, rent-seeking can be more pervasive and pernicious in developing countries trying to reform their public sectors. These countries have a propensity to respond with direct government intervention to all sorts of alleged market failures. They thus provide the opportunity for rent-seekers to extract nonmarket rents. Often the rent-seekers themselves are the sponsors of particular modalities of governmental interventions.

4. According to Coase (1993), what the classical market model needs is to be enhanced and strengthened. Particular restrictions should be dealt with by furthering the markets rather than by intervention.

5. Public sector rent-seeking institutions will try to impede Coaseian negotiations of externalities or will ask for high bribes to allow them. Their individual rationality will prevail over social rationality. They will not voluntarily concede their monopoly power. On the conditions

under which Coaseian bargaining may lower transaction costs, see the forthcoming article by Dixit and Olson.

6.  For an analysis of rent-seeking in the private markets, see Beck and Connelly (1996).

7.  See Montenegro (1995) for an interesting discussion on the impact of constitutional design on transaction costs. See also Sutter (1995) for an analysis of the relationships between rent-seeking and constitutional politics.

8.  Schiavo-Campo (1994) puts it well by saying that "organizations can be improved—sometimes even created *ab nihilo*—but economic, social and political behavior will not change unless the rules and procedures change as well. However, the reverse is also true: rule modification is unlikely to produce results in an operationally meaningful time frame unless organizational improvements proceed apace. And, in the absence of results, institutional reforms are more likely to be reversed. Furthermore, neglect of the organizational requirements of a policy reform is usually lethal for the implementation of the reform. Clearly, then, the massive challenge of institutional transformation in transition economies comprises both institutional (regulatory and procedural) reform and organizational development. Consequently, while the distinction between institution and organization is essential, it must not be overinterpreted to imply that if institutional change occurs organizational development will follow spontaneously. Furthermore, institutional change does not occur by osmosis: organizations are themselves the agent of institutional changes."

9.  This type of firm is an example of a negative hybrid institutional arrangement. But, as Ostrom (1996) and Tendler (1993) have shown, it is quite possible for positive forms of hybrid coproduction to develop, where the actors make synergistic contributions toward a common goal. For an analysis of the choice of the institutional mix (between hierarchy and participation) according to the particular nature of public goods, see Picciotto and Grover (1996).

10.  For a rigorous examination of why reforms fail, see Nugent and Lin Yifu (1995), Vol. 3a, chapter 38.

11.  This is one case in which the actual outcome of this particular modality of government intervention is not positive. For a rigorous analysis of whether government interventions in the markets for education and health are actually successful or not, see Poterba 1996.

12.  On the characteristics between the different Austrian Schools, see Foss 1995.

13.  According to Gustafsson (1993), "neoinstitutional economics is still in its infancy, and it is far too early to hope for a synthesis between general equilibrium theory and neoinstitutional theory. Terms have to be clearly defined, theorems in delimited areas of investigation should be elaborated, and relations between various entities must be established before consistent and meaningful general theories could be established. If neoinstitutional economics applies the method of isolation and goes into depth in selected areas of economic behavior, and if it succeeds in attracting the best brains of the profession, we could expect interesting new results in the decades ahead."

14.  For a contrast between the older institutional economics and the new institutional economics, see Arrow (1987).

15.  A rigorous, "positive" analysis of the new institutional economics was conducted by Frey (1993).

16.  Dixit (1996) emphasizes the importance of asset specificity: "In asset specificity, opportunism arises in a particular way, combining dynamic inconsistency with moral hazard, when, in a contract between two parties to exploit a mutually profitable opportunity, at least one party must generally make an irreversible investment. Once it has done so, it will become vulnerable to demands of the other party to renegotiate the contract and get for itself a greater share of profit, made under the threat of dissolving the whole relationship. This makes even ex ante competitive relationships ex post bilateral. If unresolved, this problem would lead to severe underinvestment because the party contemplating its investment decision would look ahead and recognize that its return on the investment is going to be expropriated by the other."

17.  Rawls coined the concept of the "veil of ignorance" in his widely read *A Theory of Justice* (1971), in which he sets out to develop a set of principles to apply to the basic structure of society. For a more recent discussion of the "veil of ignorance," see his *Political Liberalism* (1993), which introduces the distinction between a thick and a thin veil.

18  This is a sort of "second invisible hand" that "guides encompassing interests to use their power, at least to some degree, in accord with the social interest, even when serving the public good was not part of the intention. This second invisible hand is as unfamiliar and perhaps counterintuitive as the first hidden hand was in Adam Smith's time, but that does not mean it is less important" (Olson, in progress).

19. Colombia has been conducting strategic evaluations of key sectors and policies. These evaluations are part of a larger effort by the National Planning Department to enhance the role of evaluation in public policymaking and the effectiveness of policies in general.

20. Recent years have witnessed an increased interest in economic methodology, as evidenced by the copious literature on the subject. A cursory review of the relevant section in the *Journal of Economic Literature* confirms that notion. This development reflects the incompleteness of the rational choice or competition models for explaining and predicting. The research proposals made in this paper do not aim at resolving theoretical issues. Rather, the suggestion is that for many reforming countries, more attention to microanalytics and methodology would be very useful.

21. According to Hands (1993), "positive and negative heuristics provide instructions about what should and should not be pursued in the development of the program. The positive heuristic guides the research toward the right questions and to the best tools to use in answering those questions; the negative heuristic indicates what questions should not be pursued and what tools are inappropriate."

22. For a useful discussion on whether neoinstitutional economics is apolitical or takes politics into consideration, see Bates (1995). To Bates, new institutionalism "stands as an important addition to the development literature. However, it will achieve its full promise only when it becomes a part of a broader field, the field of political economy." This statement, however, begs the question, How can it be argued that neoinstitutional economics has neglected considerations of political economy?

# References

Arrow, Kenneth. 1987. "Reflections on the Essays." In George Feiwell, ed., *Arrow and the Foundations of the Theory of Economic Policy.* New York: New York University Press.

Bates, Robert. 1995. "Social Dilemmas and Rational Individuals: An Assessment of the New Institutionalism." In John Harris, Janet Hunter, and Colin Lewis, eds., *The New Institutional Economics and Third World Development.* London and New York: Routledge.

Beck, R. L., and J. M. Connelly. 1996. "Some Empirical Evidence on Rent-seeking." *Public Choice* 87 (April):18–33.

Blaug, Mark. 1992. *The Methodology of Economics.* Cambridge: Cambridge University Press.

Buchanan, James. 1988. "Contractarian Political Economy and Constitutional Interpretation." *American Economic Review* 78(2).

Coase, Ronald. 1937. "The Nature of the Firm." *Economica n.s.* 4:386–405.

_____. 1993. "Coase on Posner on Coase." *Journal of Institutional and Theoretical Economics* 149 (March).

Diamond, Peter. 1994. "Theory and Policy." Paper presented at the World Bank Social Safety Net Seminar. Washington D.C., Nov. 7, 1994.

Dixit, Avinash. 1996. *The Making of Economic Policy.* Cambridge, Mass.: The MIT Press.

_____, and Mancur Olson. Forthcoming. "The Coase Theorem is False: Coase's Insight is Nonetheless Mainly Right." World Bank, Washington, D.C.

Downs, Anthony. 1957. *An Economic Theory of Democracy.* New York: Harper and Row.

Eggertsson, Thraínn. 1990. *Economic Behavior and Institutions.* Cambridge: Cambridge University Press.

Feeney, David. 1993. "The Demand and Supply of Institutional Arrangements." In Vincent Ostrom, ed., *Rethinking Institutional Analysis and Development.* San Francisco: ICS Press.

Fischer, Stanley. 1977. "Long-term Contracting, Sticky Prices and Monetary Policy: Comment." *Journal of Monetary Economics* 3:317–24.

Foss, Nicolai. 1995. *The Austrian School and Modern Economics: Essays in Reassessment.* Copenhagen: Munkogaard International Publishers.

Frey, Bruno. 1993. "An Economics Analysis of New Institutional Economics." *Journal of Institutional and Theoretical Economic* 149 (March):351–60.

Greif, Avner. 1993. "Contract Enforceability and Economic Institutions in Early Trade: The Maghribi Traders' Coalition." *American Economic Review* 83(3):525–48.

Gustafsson, Bo. 1993. "Preface." *Rationality, Institutions and Economic Methodology.* London and New York: Routledge.

Hands, Wade O. 1993. "Popper and Lakatos in Economic Methodology." In Uskali Mäki, Bo Gustafsson, and Christian Knudsen, eds., *Rationality, Institutions and Economic Methodology.* London and New York: Routledge.

Krueger, A. 1974. "The Political Economy of the Rent-Seeking Society." *American Economic Review* (June):291–303.

Lakatos, Imre. 1970. "Falsification and the Methodology of Scientific Research Programmes." In I. Lakatos and A. Musgrave, eds., *Criticism and the Growth of Knowledge.* Cambridge: Cambridge University Press.

Lucas, Robert. 1988. "On the Mechanics of Economic Development." *Journal of Monetary Economics* 22:3–42.

Mäki, Uskali. 1993. "Economics with Institutions: Agenda for Methodological Enquiry." In Uskali Mäki, Bo Gustafsson, and Christian Knudsen, eds., *Rationality, Institutions, and Economic Methodology.* London and New York: Routledge.

McCubbins, M., Roger Noll, and Barry Weingast. 1987. "Administrative Procedures as Instruments of Political Control." *Journal of Law, Economics, and Organization* 3(2):243–78.

Montenegro, Alvaro. 1995. "Constitutional Design and Economic Performance." *Constitutional Political Economy* 6(2):160–69.

Noorderhaven, G. Niels. 1996. "Opportunism and Trust in Transaction Cost Economics." In John Groenewegen, ed., *Transaction Cost Economics and Beyond.* Boston, Dordrecht, and London: Kluwer Academic Publishers.

North, Douglass. 1990. *Institutions, Institutional Change and Economic Performance.* Cambridge: Cambridge University Press.

Nugent, Jeffrey, and Justin Lin Yifu. 1995. "Institutions and Economic Development." In J. Behrman and T. N. Srinivasan, eds., *Handbook of Development Economics,* Vol. 3a, Chapter 38. Amsterdam: North Holland.

Oates, Wallace. 1991. "Decentralization of the Public Sector: An Overview." *Studies in Fiscal Federalism.* Great Britain: Edward Elgar Publishing Limited.

Olson, Mancur. 1965. *The Logic of Collective Action.* Cambridge, Mass.: Harvard University Press.

Ostrom, Elinor. 1996. "Crossing the Great Divide: Coproduction, Synergy and Development." *World Development* 24(6).

Picciotto, Robert. 1995. *Putting Institutional Economics to Work: From Participation to Governance.* Discussion Paper No. 304. Washington, D.C.: World Bank.

_____. 1996. "What Is Education Worth? From Production Function to Institutional Capital." Working Paper No. 75. World Bank, Washington, D.C.

_____, and Neelima Grover. 1996. "Rural Development: Hierarchy or Participation?" Paper presented at the Sixty-Sixth Annual Conference of the Southern Economic Association. Washington D.C.

Poterba, James. 1996. "Government Intervention in the Markets for Education and Health Care: How and Why?" In Victor Fuchs, ed., *Individual and Social Responsibility.* Chicago: University of Chicago Press.

Rawls, John. 1971. *A Theory of Justice.* Cambridge, Mass.: Harvard University Press.

_____. 1993. *Political Liberalism.* New York: Columbia University Press.

Richter, Rudolf. 1996. "Bridging Old and New Institutional Economics: Gustav Schmoller, the Leader of the Younger German Historical School, Seen With Neoinstitutionalists' Eyes." *Journal of Institutional and Theoretical Economics* 152(4):567–92.

Romer, P. M. 1986. "Increasing Returns and Long-run Growth." *Journal of Political Economy* 94:1002–37.

_____. 1994. "The Origins of Endogenous Growth." *The Journal of Economic Perspectives* 8(1):3–22.

Shiavo-Campo, Salvatore. 1994. *Institutional Change and the Public Sector in Transitional Economics.* Discussion Paper No. 24. Washington, D.C.: World Bank.

Stiglitz, J. E. 1991. "Economic Organization." In Holis Chenery and T. N. Srinivasan, eds., *Handbook of Development Economics,* Vol. 1. Amsterdam: North Holland.

_____. 1995. *Whither Socialism?* Cambridge, Mass.: The MIT Press.

Sutter, Daniel. 1995. "Constitutional Politics Within the Interest-Group Model." *Constitutional Political Economy* 6(2):127–38.

Tendler, Judith. 1993. *New Lessons from Old Projects: The Workings of Rural Development in Northeast Brazil.* A World Bank Operations Evaluation Study. Washington D.C.: World Bank.

Tullock, G. 1967. "The Welfare Costs of Tariffs, Monopolies, and Theft." *Western Economic Journal* 5 (June):224–32.

Vanberg, Viktor. 1994. *Rules and Choice in Economics.* London and New York: Routledge.

Wiesner, Eduardo. 1993. *From Macroeconomic Correction to Public Sector Reform: The Critical Role of Evaluation.* World Bank Discussion Paper No. 214. Washington, D.C.: World Bank.

_____. 1994. "Fiscal Decentralization and Social Spending in Latin America: The Search for Efficiency and Equity." Working Paper Series. Inter-American Development Bank, Washington, D.C.

_____. 1995. "The Political Economy of the Environment in Developing Countries: Market Failure and Institutional Response." In Lans Boverberg and S. Cnosseen, eds., *Public Economics and the Environment in an Imperfect World.* Boston, Dordrecht, and London: Kluwer Academic Press.

_____. 1997a. "Evaluation, Markets, and Institutions in the Reform Agenda of Developing Countries." In E. Chelimsky and Shadish William, Jr., eds., *Evaluation for the 21st Century.* San Francisco: SAGE Publications, Inc.

_____. 1997b. *"La Efectividad de las Políticas Públicas en Colombia: Un Análisis Neoinstitucional."* Tercer Mundo Publishers.

Williamson, Oliver E. 1979. "Transaction-Cost Economics: The Governance of Contractual Relations." *Journal of Law & Economics* 22:3–61.

_____. 1985. *The Economic Institutions of Capitalism: Firms, Markets, Relational Contracting.* New York: Free Press.

_____. 1991. "Comparative Economic Organization: The Analysis of Discrete Structural Alternatives." *Administrative Science Quarterly* 36:269–96.

_____. 1993. "The Logic of Economic Organization." In Oliver E. Williamson and Sidney G. Winter, eds., *The Nature of the Firm.* New York: Oxford University Press.

_____. 1995. "Introduction." In *Organization Theory: From Chester Barnard to the Present and Beyond.* New York: Oxford University Press.

_____. 1996. "Efficiency, Power, Authority and Economic Organization." In John Groenewegen, ed., *Transaction Cost Economics and Beyond.* Boston, Dordrecht, and London: Kluwer Academic Publishers.

## Comments on "Transaction cost economics and public sector rent-seeking in developing countries: toward a theory of government failure," by Wiesner

*Mancur Olson, Jr.*

Though I am by no means an expert on Colombia, I am nonetheless reasonably sure that what Eduardo Wiesner says about the situation in that country is right. What he says is entirely consistent with such information as I do have about Colombia. It also is what I would expect on the basis of observation of other countries and from what I know of the logic of collective action.

I also share Eduardo Wiesner's enthusiasm for the great insight in Ronald Coase's famous 1937 article on "The Nature of the Firm." To the best of my knowledge, before that article no one had understood that the existence of the hierarchical firm in a competitive market could be explained in terms of a market failure, and, at the same time, appreciated how profoundly important markets are as a source of efficiency for societies. If the resources that the firm allocates through its hierarchy were not coordinated more efficiently by the firm hierarchy than by the market, then the firm hierarchy would shrink or disappear. As Coase and others have shown, this insight is indispensable and leads to many other important insights into the nature of the firm and industrial organization.

Ronald Coase apparently thought that a single metaphor or concept was sufficient to cover all of the market failures that accounted for the hierarchical firm, and this metaphor was, of course, "transaction costs." As I see it, this expression was used by Coase to cover all of the disadvantages or costs of using the market. Many others would rather say that there is only one cost or disadvantage of using the market and that is the cost of making transactions. Coase's notion of transaction costs has, of course, come to be widely used.

When we are looking at the advantages and disadvantages of vertical integration for a firm—whether it will make something within the firm or buy it from others—the transaction costs metaphor is superb. The advantage of "make" is that the firm saves those costs of making deals with suppliers and also is protected against a "bad deal" with a supplier. The costs of the salesmen of supplier firms, of the firm's own buyers of the pertinent input, and the losses from bad deals with the relevant suppliers disappear when the firm chooses "make." On the other hand, the market incentive for efficiency is, within a restricted domain, lost or attenuated: the competitive market is not operating, at least fully, inside the hierarchical firm, so it sometimes is better to "buy." As Oliver Williamson has shown, when one party has had to invest in relationship-specific assets, then it can be the victim of a "hold up" by the opportunism of the other party, so the cost of using market transactions is then higher and the case for vertical integration greater. Here transaction costs is an illuminating concept. As Coase showed in his famous 1960 article, it can also give us some insight when there is an externality from one party to another: if a rancher's cattle trample a farmer's grain, the farmer and the rancher will have an incentive to bargain with one another until they achieve efficiency, unless the costs of bargaining or transacting are too high.

Eduardo Wiesner uses the concept of transaction costs not so much for analysis of the firm and for two-party interaction over an externality, as for a general explanatory concept to account for rent-seeking and the failures of government and politics. In extending the concept of transaction costs to cover government and politics in general, Wiesner is in distinguished company—there is at least one substantial and distinguished school of economists for whom the concept of transaction cost is the central tool for analyzing government and politics. Though obviously there are some costs of bargaining in government and politics and these transaction costs are sometimes important, I do not share the view of Wiesner and many others that transaction costs are the key to understanding failures in this sphere.

One problem is that the metaphor of the transaction is not apt for most of what happens in government and politics. The deals in the market are *voluntary* transactions, but the essence of government and politics is that it is about how government's power of coercion is to be exercised—about how much is to be taken in compulsory taxation and for what or for whom the proceeds will be spent and about what rules and regulations the government will enforce with its police power. The problems that arise when coercive power is misused do not have much in common with the costs of using the market.

Moreover, most of the transactions in the market are two-party or bilateral transactions between firms or individuals, but government and politics is about policies that normally affect all of the people in some industry or locality and often all of the millions of people in a country. Occasionally there are externalities involving only two parties, one of whom generates the externality whereas another is impacted (the notable examples in Coase's 1960 article are mainly of this kind), but with government and politics this is the exception and large numbers is the norm. Large-number public good or collective action problems have very little in common with bilateral interaction or with voluntary transactions in the marketplace.

Some economists suppose that, no matter how many individuals are involved or whether public or private goods are at issue, transaction costs are the only thing that can keep rational parties from achieving Pareto-efficiency through voluntary bargaining. They have claimed that there is a "Coase Theorem" that states exactly this and that it is valid. Ronald Coase never claimed any such theorem. This is very much to his credit, for the "Coase Theorem" claim that transaction costs are the only thing that can keep rational individuals, no matter how numerous, from achieving Pareto efficiency through voluntary interaction, is most unsatisfactory.

It would take much more space than is available here to show why, but one aspect of the matter can be stated quickly. Eliminating transaction cost does not eliminate conflicts of interest. Whenever collective action is required to obtain some common objective or public good, there is the question of who will contribute to the costs of this collective action and of how any contributors will share the costs. In other words, public goods are costly and there is a conflict of interest over who will bear how much of the costs. In the absence of transaction costs, bargaining about this is costless, and in one respect this favors voluntary agreement on a Pareto-efficient outcome. But in another respect, the absence of transaction costs makes it easier—indeed costless—for each individual to hold out for a lower share of the costs and even to try to avoid them altogether by free riding on the provision of others. Thus, even in the absence of transaction costs, there can be no assurance whatever that voluntary mechanisms will achieve efficiency when collective action is necessary.

So compulsory methods, such as taxation, are required to finance public goods. And there is nothing, even in the absence of transaction costs, to ensure that the coercive power needed to collect the taxes will be used in ways that bring Pareto-efficiency. Indeed, there is not even any reason to be confident that coercive power will not be used for predatory purposes. There are some governments in the world today that are best described as kleptocracies. And in practically all societies there are special-interest groups that use their influence on the government to induce it to use its coercive power in ways that implicitly redistribute income to these special-interest groups.

In short, there is often exactly the sort of special-interest predation that Eduardo Wiesner has found in Colombia. Though this problem does not mainly arise because of transaction costs (or Coaseian logic, which always works in the direction of efficiency), it is nonetheless a very serious problem. Unfortunately, this is true not only in the Colombia that Eduardo Wiesner describes, but in most other societies as well.

## Comments on "Transaction cost economics and public sector rent-seeking in developing countries: toward a theory of government failure," by Wiesner

*Peter Eigen*

My perspective is that of an anticorruption activist and practitioner, half lawyer and half economist. I want to draw some useful lessons for a practical strategy to protect economic policies and institutions against the corruption that seems to have infested us all like a cancer, as President Wolfensohn has put it. I will relate these lessons to some of the approaches Transparency International (TI) has adopted in its operations and will appeal to economists and the evaluation community to help us sharpen our tools.

### Empirical evidence from Colombia

Eduardo Wiesner presents three interesting case studies of public sector rent-seeking institutions in Colombia. He describes how labor unions have taken policymaking in education and telecommunications hostage and how the geographical misfit of environmental corporations frustrates environmental competition. In these circumstances, "externality market failure can be anticipated." But is this corruption? Or is it the most significant example of corruption to be addressed in Colombia?

The experience of the development community shows that there are more typical, more drastic, more common scenarios all over the world—and I would suggest also in Colombia. It would be helpful to discuss both the empirical evidence and ways to protect policies and institutions against corruption. For example:

- Investment in a large public sector infrastructure project, say in the energy sector, is being planned. To promote the project, a supplier from Europe offers to pay, through a middleman, millions of dollars into the Swiss bank account of the minister or another high official in charge of the sector.

- It can be anticipated that project selection will be suboptimal and that the project will be overdesigned, premature, unnecessary, or even harmful not only to the economy but to the people and the environment.

- It can also be anticipated that the wrong supplier will be selected during the procurement process, that the quality and price of the project will be distorted, and that the benefits will not justify the costs, including the debt burden for the economy.

This scenario is familiar to many of us. It has shown its ugly face in economic, sector, and project work on all continents. This crude form of grand corruption has become so widespread that many business leaders and officials in developed countries consider it the norm in most international markets. Wiesner's paper offers useful advice relevant to this practical reality.

## Policy implications of "neoinstitutional economics"

Wiesner attributes the success, or strength, of neoinstitutional economics to its microanalytical orientation. This means "less attention to the traditional aggregate questions of resource allocation, equilibrium, and scarcity and more to incentives, contracts, transaction costs, organization, information, process, rent-seeking, rules of choice, and asset specificity." He lists three policy implications that relate well to some basic tenets of TI's approach. He suggests the following for project design: looking at the problem from the perspective of the rational choice of rent-seekers, concluding a contractual agreement with the other side for specific evaluations of performance and results, and building an incentive structure. For the latter, he provides examples of results-oriented budget allocations for financing public goods.

There are parallels in TI's work, dictated by common sense. Our basic approach is based on building awareness and consensus, creating areas of common interest, building coalitions for joint action, and strengthening incentive systems for transparency and accountability.

## Building coalitions

Two basic tenets are essential to TI's approach: first, TI clearly addresses the source of international corruption, which to a large extent fuels grand corruption in the developing world. This source of corruption lies in the north, where most governments openly permit their firms to offer bribes in order to promote exports. Many governments even support these practices by permitting businesses to deduct foreign bribes from their taxes as if the bribes were legitimate business expenses. TI spends a significant part of its time and resources working for changes in the laws, institutions, and policies of countries from the Organization for Economic Cooperation and Development (OECD) that permit this double standard. This approach opens the way to the formation of a truly global coalition to tackle corruption that includes north, south, east, and west.

The key is the realistic appreciation of the other side's predicament—the "prisoner's dilemma" of firms that have fallen into the habit of active corruption. They do not dare stop offering bribes unless they can be assured that their competitors will also stop. The answer is a strategy to coordinate anticorruption efforts internationally. It would hardly be the rational choice for an exporter to engage heroically in a unilateral halt to bribery. A way must be found to minimize the risk of penalizing, through contracts lost to competitors in the international market place, firms or exporting nations that unilaterally end corrupt practices.

The OECD has initiated an important coordinated effort that can be seen as a breakthrough in the international arena. Since May 1995, it has worked on developing concrete recommendations for its members on ending corrupt practices. This effort has led to significant progress and has now reached a critical stage. The OECD recommendations were confirmed at the meeting of the Council of Ministers in April 1996 and were reaffirmed by the heads of state of the G7 meeting in France. TI is pleased to have been involved in this effort and will work toward promoting the implementation of these recommendations through credible follow-up activities in 1997.

## Islands of integrity

In the meantime, TI has developed a mechanism that can harness the common interests of the most important actors in the international arena. TI feels it has defined a promising concept that may be an escape route for those trapped in the vicious circle of corruption. It relies largely on building coalitions against corruption by promoting antibribery pacts in well-defined markets, thus fostering what we call "islands of integrity." TI is promoting this concept in a number of countries.

In 1994, we saw the first successful implementation of this mechanism in Ecuador's energy sector. The government decreed that all firms wishing to do business with the public sector would have to pledge not to engage in any corrupt practices to win contracts. This mandate would apply to all firms, local and international, and to all types of government contracts, although initially it was intended to focus on large public development projects. Most major corporations were briefed and asked to sign the integrity pact. The government made its pledge in the form of a letter signed in June 1993. Procurement in cases where this pledge was signed has been successful. The technical complaints that were raised about the evaluation process were settled. However, efforts to make this pact a binding requirement for all Ecuadorian public procurement did not succeed, because political events in connection with the 1995 elections disrupted the cooperative process TI had started in the country.

The basic principle of the TI integrity pact (TI-IP) has been further developed. With the support of our strong Argentine chapter, it was recently introduced by the provincial government of Mendoza. The key is to create credible assurance for all firms that their competitors will not bribe. The TI-IP does not rely merely on legal commitments—legal prohibitions against bribery already exist in most countries—but seeks to establish an effective attitude of transparency, a sense of mutual trust and confidence between the public and private sectors and among the competitors themselves.

It can be expected that in addition to the de facto impact, there will be significant legal sanctions connected with the pact. These could involve, among other things, invalidating the contract or providing damages for the state and competitors if the pledge is violated. These sanctions should give this instrument credibility competitors can rely on when they refuse to offer bribes. The credibility of this approach will be enhanced through the active participation of civil society in enforcing the mechanism—for instance, in the form of observation and monitoring by an NGO.

## Incentive system against corruption

Of course, the use of integrity pacts is only one element in the spectrum of instruments that must be addressed in a coherent way in order for the system of incentives against corruption as a whole to work. To facilitate this approach, TI has developed an analytical framework that addresses what we call a "national integrity system." The framework was published last year, with the support of the Ford Foundation and assistance from the Bank's Economic Development Institute, as *The TI Source Book*. It will serve both as a reference document for governments and policymakers and as a source of action plans for national chapters. The source book will be developed and refined further in appropriate areas as funding permits and will tabulate evolving best practices in salient areas of government and private sector activity.

*The TI Source Book* has been translated into a number of languages. The Spanish version served as the basis for an adaptation workshop that resulted in a Latin American version, which has just been completed. It will appear, along with the English version and more than 1,000 pages of models and samples of best practice, on the TI homepage on the Internet in 1997.

These examples from our practical work validate somewhat the essence of the policy implications enumerated by Wiesner. The most powerful impetus for the coalition against corruption comes, of course, from the strength of civil society. It drives the definition of the public interest, the creation of proper incentive systems, and the convergence of interests for an effective coalition against corruption.

## Conclusion

Today's discussion is part of the increasing global awareness that corruption destroys economic institutions and policies. Since this volume concerns evaluation and development, I will admit that we have to build more important tools for evaluation into our strategies. We are revisiting projects periodically; for instance, we had repeat integrity workshops in Tanzania to review progress. We also take stock of project impact through periodic surveys, but we aim for more systematic instruments in this area. I would like to appeal for your help in building tools for monitoring and evaluating the impact of our approaches.

Our current evaluation efforts, which use surveys and periodic reviews to verify the impact of our approaches, are only rudimentary. Common sense tells us that we are on a useful track. Wiesner's paper gives us some reassurance that we are not alone with our approach, that something has to be done against corruption—and that something can be done.

**Floor discussion on "Transaction cost economics and public sector rent-seeking in developing countries: toward a theory of government failure"**

The questions were addressed primarily to Mancur Olson. The first participant asked if the practice of bargaining to compensate for disincentives had developed because transaction costs were too high. A second participant suggested that in order to move away from the present dilemma, we need to think more seriously about political property rights. If they were made explicit, political property rights would be something people could bargain with. Ultimately, they would become similar to economic rights. A third participant asked why a single phenomenon—the presence of a state-enforced monopoly—produces unlike outcomes in different countries. What is it that causes these unique outcomes? A fourth participant asked whether "hybrid" institutions could provide the vigor needed to solve the "hybrid" problems involved in decentralization. And a fifth wanted to know, in terms of the incentive structure, how best to encourage local governments to serve rural constituents.

In response, Olson noted that the absence of compensation for disincentives may be the result of high transaction costs, but this possibility is much rarer than is generally understood. The insight that organization can be linked to costs is nonetheless mainly right. Even when transaction costs are zero, different responses will emerge and the incentive to be a "free rider" still exist. Different outcomes across countries are not explained simply by natural resources or transaction costs, however. The question seems to come down to understanding that societies organize themselves differently and that some have better arrangements than others for dealing with such issues.

# 7. Performance contracts: a tool for improving public services?[1]

Mary M. Shirley

*Performance contracts often fail to improve the performance of state-owned enterprises because of information asymmetry, insufficient commitment, and poor incentives. The author suggests that such contracts be used sparingly, and only when a government's commitment to the exercise is strong, and in conjunction with supportive reforms.*

Performance contracts have been suggested as a way to improve the performance of public agencies at all levels of government. These contracts between the government and the managers of its various agencies or enterprises spell out in writing the obligations of both parties over a defined period and set targets for performance that are then assessed at the end of the period.

The experience with performance contracts has implications for far more than written contracts in government. This paper focuses on written contracts because it is methodologically more convenient to analyze explicit agreements. However, we view performance contracts as one of a class of interactions between a government and other actors that are governed by contracts, whether explicit or implicit (Buchanan 1975, 1988). Thus, we can expect the advantages and disadvantages of performance contracts to be mirrored in less explicit arrangements, so that the findings of this paper may have wide applicability for government reforms.

The intuition for performance contracts is straightforward and follows the principal/agent literature (for reviews of principal/agent theories, see Ross 1991; Sappington 1991). The problem, according to this literature, is that the principal can observe only outcomes and cannot accurately measure the effort expended by the agent or sort it out from other factors affecting performance. As a result, even though managers have the most information about how to operate their agencies or enterprises to achieve the best results for the least cost, governments are unwilling to give them the freedom to use their superior information to maximize efficiency. This problem is compounded in the public sector because agents serve multiple principals, such as politicians with many points of view and bureaucrats with different agendas, and thus face multiple, conflicting objectives. Under such circumstances, it is hard to judge performance and to motivate the managers and hold them accountable for results. Moreover, many public principals (in contrast to private owners) do not benefit from better performance and hence try to make the agent serve objectives that conflict with efficiency, such as rewarding political supporters with jobs or subsidies.

A contract between the government and state-owned enterprise (SOE) management is expected to reduce this agency problem by several means. These include specifying and assigning clear priorities for each of the multiple objectives by spelling out the obligations for which managers will be held accountable. They also include detailing how performance on those obligations will be measured and (sometimes) specifying rewards or penalties for good or bad performance. Agents are expected to be given more freedom, since they can be held accountable under the contract. However, they may still lack the freedom to make the decisions that a private manager can usually make without board or shareholder approval—for example, to hire or fire, to select among competitive suppliers, to change prices in a competitive market, or to make other operational decisions. In such cases, the degrees of freedom public agents have can be explicitly taken into account in the contract. Thus, targets can be set to encourage managers to maximize performance in areas where they have enough control to affect outcomes.

Such contracts have been used for many types of public agents, but the focus in this paper is on performance contracts for SOEs. SOE performance contracts are widespread in developing countries; a World Bank survey found over 550 such contracts in use in 32 developing countries, plus over 100,000 in China (table 7.1). These contracts go by various names (contract plan in francophone Africa, signaling system in the Republic of Korea and in Pakistan, memorandum of understanding in India) and vary in duration from one to five years. They also vary in comprehensiveness: some include investment, others focus only on current operating performance, and some specify the obligations of the government as well as the company. Their common feature is that they set forth in writing specific, measurable targets that, at the end of an agreed period, can be compared with actual performance.

Since SOEs have clearly defined products and standardized accounts, their performance contracts should be easier to write and monitor than contracts with public

TABLE 7.1: NUMBER OF PERFORMANCE CONTRACTS IN DEVELOPING COUNTRIES, BY SECTOR

| Sector | Africa | Asia | Latin America | Middle East and North Africa | Central Europe[a] | Total |
|---|---|---|---|---|---|---|
| Transport | 26 | 8 | 4 | 6 | 2 | 46 |
| Telecom and post | 15 | 2 | 1 | 1 | 0 | 19 |
| Extractive industries | 6 | 26 | 2 | 2 | 3 | 39 |
| Agriculture | 13 | 3 | 2 | 0 | 0 | 18 |
| Water | 4 | 4 | 0 | 1 | 0 | 9 |
| Electricity | 11 | 8 | 6 | 1 | 1 | 27 |
| Other | 61 | 160 | 1 | 1 | 4 | 227 |
| Total | 136 | 211 | 16 | 12 | 10 | 385[b] |

a. Data for Romania only. Contracts are also being used in Bulgaria, but no details are available.
b. Total figures cover 31 countries. In addition, Indonesia reports 180 firms, and China 103,000; no breakdown by industry was available. Data reflect the situation as of June 1994, based on a worldwide search using World Bank and other sources. In some countries, additional contracts may have been awarded.
*Source:* Survey of World Bank reports and staff.

agencies in less market-like circumstances (such as regulatory bodies, courts, schools, licensing agencies, and so forth). Thus, while success with SOE performance contracts may not imply that the contracts necessarily succeed in improving the performance of public agencies operating in nonmarket activities, the failure of contracts with SOEs would suggest that they are not likely to work in the less favorable contracting circumstances of nonmarket agencies.[2]

The next section of this paper presents a theoretical framework for analyzing contracts and discusses the sample studied here. The third section analyzes the impact of performance contracts on the sample SOEs and assesses why the contracts performed as they did. The fourth section provides some conclusions.

## Analyzing performance contracts

To understand why performance contracts succeed or fail, this paper uses a framework based on contracting literature (see especially Sappington 1991; Laffont and Tirole 1986; Williamson 1976, 1985). This literature suggests that three factors are crucial in determining the outcome of contracts: information, incentives, and commitment. *Information* problems arise because contracting agents have different sets of information; thus, each side can use the information it holds exclusively to improve its position at the expense of the other. In particular, information asymmetries and the imperfect observability of performance give company managers the leeway to pursue interests that are at odds with the principals'—in this case, the government's—interests. At the same time, there is always information unknown to both parties, such as what the future holds, so it is impossible to design a contract that will cover all eventualities. To alleviate these information problems, contracts usually include promises of *incentives* to induce the contracting parties to reveal information and comply with contract provisions. But promises of rewards and penalties alone are not enough. Each party needs to be convinced of the *commitment* of the other to adhere to its side of the contract, even as circumstances change and unforeseen events occur. This point is especially important in the case of contracts with governments, since there are no neutral third parties with the power to compel the government to act. If SOE managers do not believe that the government will actually monitor their performance carefully, provide them the freedom to achieve their targets, or deliver the promised rewards or penalties, they will have an incentive to try to use their information advantage to make it look as though they are achieving the contractual goals without actually increasing their efforts.

The rest of this paper measures how well performance contracts improved performance in a sample of 12 SOEs in 6 countries and explains the successes and failures in terms of the three factors (information, incentives, and commitment). The first question the sample addresses is whether enterprise performance changed in ways that can be attributed to the contract (or, more weakly, whether enterprise performance changed in ways that mean the contract cannot be ruled out as an explanatory factor). The sample—shown in table 7.2—is small, so care must be used in generalizing from the results. (For ease of reading, we have used the simplified enterprise names shown in caps in table 7.2.) There are also weaknesses in the data. We relied on the firm's own audited accounts, which are poor in Ghana and Senegal. In some cases, our precontract period was short and the length of the postcontract period varied, making it hard to measure trends.[3] Even so, the sample does include countries at very different levels of income that employed varying approaches to performance contracting. An improvement in postcontract performance across such differing country and contract experiences would suggest that contracts can work (unless some other factor was at work, something we also investigated).[4]

The companies' economic performance is assessed by comparing trends in profitability (return on assets, or ROA), labor productivity, and total factor productivity (TFP) before and after the introduction of the contract.[5] A contract is deemed to have had an impact when there is a noticeable kink in the company's performance trend (either a turnaround in direction or a more than doubling of pace in the same direc-

TABLE 7.2: CASE STUDY ENTERPRISES

| Country (contract type) | Enterprise name (name used in text) | Contract duration | First contract year |
|---|---|---|---|
| Ghana (performance contract) | Electricity Corporation of Ghana (ECG): GHANA ELECTRICITY | Yearly | 1989 |
| | Ghana Water and Sewerage Corporation (GWSC): GHANA WATER | | 1989 |
| | Ghana Posts and Telecommunications (GP&T): GHANA TELECOM | | 1990 |
| India (memorandum of understanding) | National Thermal Power Corporation (NTPC): INDIA ELECTRICITY | Yearly (published) | 1987 |
| | Oil and Natural Gas Commission (ONGC): INDIA OIL | | |
| Korea, Rep. of (performance evaluation and measurement system) | Korea Electric Power Corporation (KEPCO): KOREA ELECTRICITY | List of yearly targets | 1984 |
| | Korea Telecommunications Authority (KTA): KOREA TELECOMS | | |
| Mexico (*convenio de rehabilitación financiero*) | Comisión Federal de Electricidad (CFE): MEXICO ELECTRICITY | 3 years | 1986 |
| Philippines (performance monitoring and evaluation system) | Metropolitan Water and Sewerage System (MWSS): PHILIPPINES | List of yearly targets | 1989 |
| | National Power Corporation (NPC): PHILIPPINES ELECTRICITY | | |
| Senegal (The French *contrat plan*) | Société Nationale d'Electricité (SENELEC): SENEGAL ELECTRICITY | 3 years | 1987 |
| | Société Nationale des Télécommunications du Sénégal (SONATEL): SENEGAL TELECOMMUNICATIONS | | 1986 |

tion) in the period after its introduction. The presence of any exogenous factors that could have determined the outcome was ascertained by checking for major changes in markets and prices, natural or manmade disasters, and the like during the period under investigation. For example, each company's TFP trends were compared with trends in GDP growth to see if an acceleration or deceleration in growth (and thus demand) could explain changes in the firm's performance. Any exceptional developments in the companies' markets and major work stoppages were explored to determine if they could fully account for the results. In no case did exogenous factors rule out the contracts as a possible source of performance changes.[6]

Some readers may ask, "Why not simply judge each firm's performance by its attainment of the economic targets specified in the contract, especially since these presumably indicate what the firm is striving to achieve?" It is true that all of the sample SOEs achieved at least satisfactory ratings when some sort of score was assigned (Senegal has no such scoring), and all of the contracts assigned a high weight to economic goals (two-thirds, on average). The problem is that many of the targets are soft or flawed measures of economic performance. Thus, the fact that a firm successfully attained its contracted economic targets does not necessarily mean that it is operating more profitably or productively. For example, 30 percent of India Electricity's total score in 1991–92 depended on the volume of electricity generated. The company achieved its target and received a score of excellent under its contract, yet its TFP actually fell below precontract levels. Output did go up, but the company's use of material inputs rose even faster. The target was flawed, but it could be achieved by increasing inputs without an increase—even with a decrease—in the firm's efficiency. The economic targets exhibit many such flaws, for reasons that are explored below.

Another comment might be that since many SOEs were created to serve social goals rather than to earn profits, they should be judged accordingly. The three indicators used here implicitly allow for social goals, since the indicators compare a firm's performance to its own past performance rather than to an absolute standard. For example, even if prices in a firm are deliberately kept low to benefit consumers, this would affect the return on assets but not trends in labor productivity or TFP. Similarly, even a firm that is not allowed to lay off redundant workers may still be able to improve on all three indicators by stopping the waste of raw materials or using its capital to full capacity. Indeed, one of the important arguments made in favor of performance contracts is that they provide managers who face constraints because of their social objectives with incentives to improve company performance within those constraints. Furthermore, the fact that all of the contracts assign a high weight to economic goals suggests that improved economic performance was an important objective of the exercise.

## The impact of contracts on performance

Contracts had little positive impact on performance trends for most of our sample on any of the three indicators (see figure 7.1). None of the firms improved their trends in ROA; three showed worse trends after the contracts than before. Since profitability trends in SOEs reflect government behavior (in setting prices, for example) more than managerial behavior, this finding suggests that the contracts had little impact on government.

FIGURE 7.1: PERFORMANCE CHANGES AFTER THE INTRODUCTION OF PERFORMANCE
CONTRACTS

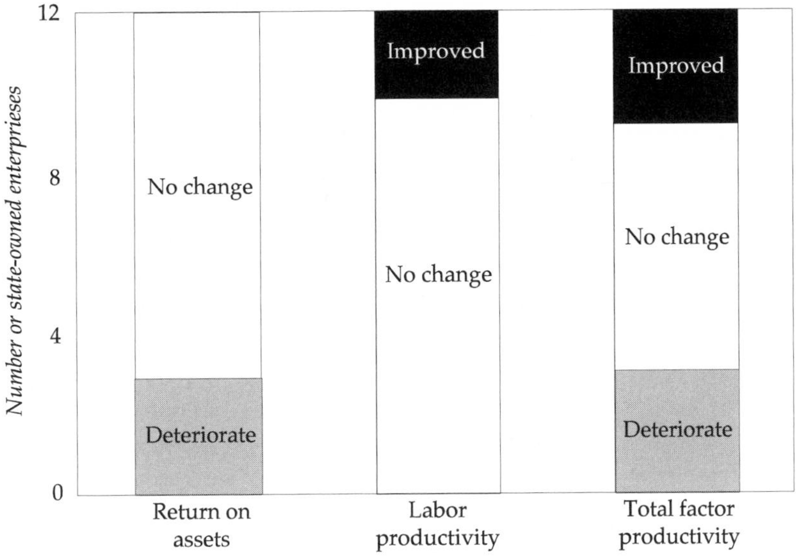

*Source:* Company data and World Bank estimates.

Labor productivity growth was positive in all 12 cases, but again the data suggest
that the contracts had little impact on this trend. Only two companies showed a kink
in their labor productivity trends after the contracts were signed (declines in labor
productivity accelerated in Senegal Telecoms, and the rate of increase in labor productivity more than quadrupled in Ghana Water after the contract). The rest continued their precontract trends. Partial measures such as labor productivity can be misleading, however, since labor productivity might increase because the company is
using more inputs or capital per worker, not because the overall efficiency of the
firm has improved.

TFP measures the efficiency with which all inputs are used and is thus the most reliable of the three indicators as a measure of the impact of the contracts on managerial
performance. Performance on TFP is mixed: in three companies, declining TFP
began to increase after the contracts were introduced; in six, the precontract trend in
TFP continued unchanged; and in three, improving TFP deteriorated.

A decline in an SOE's TFP trend after it signs a contract is especially worrisome,
since it raises the possibility that the contract contributed to a deterioration in performance. This could happen if targets are so soft that managers slack off to the point
where performance worsens. It could also happen if the targets themselves are at
odds with improved performance. There is also some evidence of targets with perverse effects, and of problems with multiple targets. For example, even though Philippines Electricity badly needed to upgrade its infrastructure, it was able to achieve
two 1991 targets by cutting capital expenditures by over one-fifth. By cutting capital
spending, the firm was able to exceed its targets for self-financing and debt service,

because the combined scores on these two criteria exactly canceled out its poor score on its capital project target. While each target made sense in isolation, together they had unintended consequences. Another example of a target with the potential to have perverse effects is India Oil's target for meters drilled. Since it can be achieved regardless of whether the company strikes oil or not, this target could encourage riskier drilling.[7] Although the contracts contain many similar examples of potentially perverse targets, the evidence for a negative effect is weaker than the evidence showing the contracts had no measurable impact on managerial performance.

A closer analysis of the three contracting factors—information, incentives, and commitment—reveals several reasons why the performance contracts failed to improve performance.

### Information

The manager of a company, public or private, always has more information about its operations than the monitoring party, the government or owner. Performance contracts suffer from more than the usual information problems. The negotiating parties must agree on the general set of targets to be achieved, the way achievement against the target will be measured, and the value that constitutes an "A," "B," or "C" grade. This task is tougher when, as in our sample, the targets are a mix of different social and economic objectives.

Competition is one way for the monitor to get more information (since performance among competing firms can be compared), but performance contracts have been used principally for monopoly SOEs (the exceptions are China and Pakistan). All of the SOEs analyzed for this study operated in monopoly markets. Conceivably, governments could increase their information by allowing competing managers to bid for contracts to operate the SOEs. However, few governments have done so (China is again an exception), and none of the sample contracts was bid. As a result, the agents responsible for negotiating and monitoring the contract from the government side had less information than parties to a contract in a competitive market.

The government agents faced other disadvantages as well. All of the governments in the sample set up special units to monitor the contracts. These units were usually staffed by middle-level civil servants with lower pay and status than the powerful SOE managers they were dealing with. The government agents were further weakened by frequent changes in responsibility and authority. For example, the agency responsible for negotiating, monitoring, and evaluating contracts in Senegal has moved twice since the contracts began (from the president's office to the prime minister's office to the ministry of finance). Similar changes have undermined the authority of government agents in the Philippines and Ghana.[8] Poor or late data from the SOEs further disadvantaged the government actors in Ghana and Senegal, where the evaluations were done largely by the firms themselves.

Three characteristics of the targets are evidence that the managers' information advantage was not overcome in the contracts. First, half the firms have more than 20 targets; large numbers of targets are hard to translate into overall objectives against which performance can be judged. Numerous targets also make it harder for the monitors to learn what the company can achieve and thus to measure and evaluate achievement.

Field interviews suggested that the managers negotiated for the addition of more targets, especially more engineering (as opposed to financial) targets. Second, many of the targets fluctuated frequently, making it even harder for the monitors to learn what constituted good and bad performance on each criterion. For example, over one-third of the targets for Ghana Water and Ghana Electricity fluctuated every year. In most of the contracts, weights were assigned to the targets so that scores on each criterion could be added up to an overall score, a feature that helped signal managers about the relative priorities of numerous goals. However, the weights also fluctuated, adding another layer of complexity and uncertainty. India Oil's financial targets went from 20 percent of its total score in 1989 to 12 percent in 1990 and 40 percent by 1992. All the firms in the sample had either many targets (more than 20), highly fluctuating targets (on average, more than 18 percent of the targets changed every year), or both.

Finally, the evidence suggests that targets were soft in some cases. For example, Senegal Telecom's call completion rate target was lower in the 1986 contract than it had been in the business plan of ten years earlier, and the company's achievement by 1992 was about half the international industry standard (55 percent in Dakar and less than 40 percent in interurban calls). According to field interviews, negotiations in India sometimes dragged on so long that targets were set to be the same as the actual performance. In Ghana, where targets are set by the companies themselves, the monitoring agency (the State Enterprise Commission) considers many targets too low and has set a penalty for undertargeting (State Enterprise Commission 1991). In the Korean contracts, the share of public profitability—an indicator that follows a trend very close to TFP and is hence hard to achieve without additional effort—had fallen from 20 percent of the total score to 12 percent by 1992. Similarly, Philippines Electricity's reliability indicator (the percentage of electricity its customers contracted for but which the company never supplied) fell from 30 percent of total targets in 1990 to 10 percent in 1991 and 15 percent in 1992. This decline did not occur because the firm became more reliable; on the contrary, by 1991–92, outages of seven hours per day were common in many parts of the country.

The flaws in the contract targets suggest that one reason the contracts failed to improve performance is that they failed to solve the information asymmetry problem. Managers were able to use their information advantage to negotiate targets that were hard to evaluate or easy to achieve. Government actors may also have unwittingly assigned targets that had perverse effects on performance, as in the example of Philippines Electricity's multiple targets.

## *Incentives*

One reason managers used their information advantage to negotiate targets that were hard to monitor or easy to achieve was that the incentives provided for in the contracts did not motivate them to reveal information and improve performance. Managers could get a monetary reward (a bonus) in only 5 of the 12 sample companies, and in 3 of those (Ghana Electricity, Water, and Telecoms) the promised bonus was not paid. Only Korea Electricity and Korea Telecoms paid a bonus for good performance (up to three months' salary for an "A" grade was paid to all employees, not just managers). Since all the bonuses were based on flawed targets, it is not certain that bonuses would have motivated performance gains even if they had been paid. Indeed, bonuses were not associated with improvements in TFP, although

TABLE 7.3: COMPARISON OF CONTRACT INCENTIVES AND GOVERNMENT COMMITMENT
*(companies ranked by TFP performance)*

| Company | Bonus/award | Contract has government promises | Government reneging? |
|---|---|---|---|
| *Improving* | | | |
| Ghana Water | Bonus/award | Yes | Some |
| Mexico Electricity | None | Yes | Little |
| Senegal Telecoms | None | Yes | Much |
| | | | |
| *Unchanged* | | | |
| Ghana Electricity | Bonus/award | Yes | Some |
| Ghana Telecoms | Bonus/award | Yes | Some |
| India Oil | Award | Yes | Much |
| Korea Electricity | Bonus/award | No | None[a] |
| Korea Telecoms | Bonus/award | No | None[a] |
| Philippines Electricity | None | No | Implicit[a] |
| | | | |
| *Deteriorated* | | | |
| India Electricity | Award | Yes | Much |
| Philippines Water | None | No | Implicit[a] |
| Senegal Electricity | None | Yes | Much |

a. Although government actions are not specified in the contracts in Korea and the Philippines, the fact that targets were not achieved because of government action is taken as a form of implicit reneging. The opposite situation is treated as no reneging.
*Source:* World Bank data and company reports.

none of the firms that achieved a bonus had a deteriorating performance (table 7.3). Seven of the contracts included a nonmonetary award with a public ceremony; this also was not associated with TFP improvements.

Penalties for poor performance under the contract were also not applied, except in Korea. Instances of Korean managers being demoted for poor performance on the contract and promoted for good results were reported in field interviews (Shirley 1991). According to survey respondents, managers' job assignments in all the other sample cases were largely politically determined, and managers were not fired or demoted for poor performance under the contract.

The incentives of the government negotiators and monitors may have contributed to the contracts' lack of success. The civil servants representing the government did not receive any explicit rewards or penalties associated with the contracts; unlike private owners, they did not benefit directly from improvements in the company's returns. As low-level civil servants facing high-level presidential appointees, they had little incentive to take a tough negotiating position or give a low score to an underperforming SOE.

In the case of Korea Electricity and Telecoms, the participation of private parties (accountants, lawyers, academics) and a prestigious think tank (the Korean Development Institute, which is public but operates autonomously) may have changed incentives. Field interviews suggest that the prominent position of these outsiders in the community motivated managers to treat the performance contracts seriously. Public opinion was also cited by Korean SOE managers as an important incentive, since performance ratings are widely reported in the press (Shirley 1991).

## Commitment

Probably the most serious failing of the contracts stems from the fact that government commitment to the contracts was not credible. None of the contracts specified an enforcement mechanism that could compel both parties to comply. Indeed, the absence of credible enforcement mechanisms is an inherent problem in contracting with governments.

In Ghana, Mexico, and Senegal, obligations under the contract might have been enforced by the World Bank, since the government's contractual obligations were part of loan covenants (which meant that disbursements of loan funds could be suspended if the government failed to live up to its side of the bargain). The loan covenants were included for project or sector needs and not necessarily because they were part of the performance contract. This outside involvement may have helped in Ghana and Mexico, where there was relatively less reneging by government than in other cases, but it may have reduced the contracts' credibility in Senegal. Survey respondents and other observers agree that the contracts in Senegal were viewed as donor driven and were not an obligation the government took seriously. A 1989 report from Senegal Telecoms explicitly stated, "It must be remembered that the contract plan was never considered a binding contract by the public powers." The suspension of disbursement of a World Bank loan to Senegal Electricity after the government reneged on its promise to settle arrears did not change this behavior and penalized the company as much, if not more, than the government.

The participation of outsiders in the case of Korea Electricity and Telecoms may have helped credibility as well as incentives. Knowledgeable outsiders may informally supervise the government monitors and act as a check on government actions that violate the contracts. Yet even in the Korean cases, some of those interviewed cited waning government commitment to performance contracting after ten years of their contracting system.

The low credibility of most of the contracts was born out by widespread government reneging on its own promises (table 7.3). Government obligations were specified in all but four of the companies' contracts (the Korean and Philippine contracts did not spell out actions promised by the government). In only one of the eight cases where government obligations were specified did the government keep most of its promises (Mexico Electricity, see table 7.4). Governments reneged in areas critical to the ability of the managers to improve performance, such as prompt payment of bills, timely approval of tariffs, and increases in autonomy. Reneging was most pronounced in the contracts in India and Senegal.

Every year the contract for India Electricity promised government help in enforcing prompt payment from its customers, the State Electricity Boards, yet circumstances did not improve. (Accounts receivable went from 149 days in 1986, the year before the contract was introduced, to 207 in 1990; in 1991 they fell to 150 days when a

TABLE 7.4: INSTANCES OF GOVERNMENT RENEGING IN WHOLE OR IN PART

| Company | Promises where government reneged |
|---|---|
| Ghana Electricity | Support collection revenues and arrears, timely approval of tariffs |
| Ghana Telecoms | Timely approval of tariffs |
| Ghana Water | Prompt payment of water bills by government and state-owned enterprises |
| | Release investment funds on schedule |
| | Reimburse for noncommercial |
| India Electricity | Support collection of arrears, increase autonomy to invest |
| | Streamline red tape, prompt approvals, increase tariffs |
| India Oil | Increase autonomy to invest, streamline red tape, prompt approvals |
| Mexico Electricity | Delay in some promised support |
| Senegal Electricity | Prompt payment of bills by government and state-owned enterprises |
| | Contribute to investment program, increase |
| Senegal Telecoms | Prompt payment of bills by government and state-owned enterprises |
| | Increase tariffs, abolish subsidy to post by 1989 |
| | Limit investment in rural areas |

Source: World Bank data and company reports.

power plant was turned over to the SOE in partial payment of arrears.) The government of Ghana reneged on some, not all, of its obligations; it also suspended the bonus awards ceremony because of the 1992 elections and failed to pay the promised bonuses. However, reneging on the Ghana contracts may not have been as damaging to credibility as in some of the other cases, since the contracts provided for recalculation of the company's targets if the government failed to deliver on its contractual obligations. Although this stipulation betrays a disconcerting expectation that the government will renege, it did mean that the companies were not penalized for government misbehavior.

Even though the government's obligations were not spelled out in the two Philippines cases, there were implicit promises, since some of the targets (such as returns on assets) were directly dependent on government actions (such as timely approval of tariffs). Again, the government reneged on these implicit promises. Although in theory a contract can be written to motivate managers in isolation from government behavior, in only the two Korean companies were targets written to exclude the impact of government behavior. This was possible partly because, when performance contracts were introduced in Korea (1983–84), the two Korean SOEs in the sample (along with all the so-called government-invested enterprises, or GIEs) were given major increases in their autonomy.[9]

Judging from table 7.3, reneging was associated with poorer performance. All of the contracts for firms that had deteriorating TFP were cases where the government reneged extensively on its written promises, sometimes every year. Since the annual or triennial evaluation and negotiation exercises drew attention to the government's consistent noncompliance, such repeated government reneging may well have increased managers' incentives to use their information advantage to negotiate targets they could easily achieve. The low credibility of government commitment to these contracts was one major reason for their failure to improve performance.

## The implications of the performance contract findings

The evidence from this small but diverse sample of performance contracts gives little support to the premise that explicit contracts can help improve the performance of public agencies. Precontract trends in profitability remained the same or deteriorated; 2 contracts improved the labor productivity trend, but in the remaining 12 cases, it stayed the same. Most contracts showed no impact on TFP and, where there was a change in the trend, as many deteriorated as improved.

As noted, the contracts failed to overcome the problem of information asymmetry. Both rewards and penalties were weak to nonexistent. And the credibility of the government was in serious doubt in almost all the contracts. Gains in productivity occurred only when the governments offered managers credible incentives and signaled their own commitment by following through on at least some promises.

The lack of association between performance contracts and improvements in SOE productivity and efficiency makes it hard to justify the investment of time and effort the contracts required. While other observers point to the fact that most firms achieved the targets set under the contracts as a sign of success, this evidence could just as well be considered indicative of failure. The fact that the SOEs were judged to be performing well against contract targets (which, it will be recalled, were largely economic) when in fact they showed no improvement in their trends in efficiency means that the performance-contracting exercise was a hollow one. If a company achieves a contract target of doubling its production by trebling inputs, then the cost of such inefficiency must be assessed against the contracts. Some survey respondents said that the contracts helped improve the dialogue with government or the corporate culture in the firm, but again, if these qualitative judgments are not supported by performance improvements, it is hard to use them to support contracting.

The idea that SOE performance can be improved without any change in government behavior by designing a contract that provides targets and incentives directed at managers alone proved ephemeral. Managers' incentives depended on government actions, whether or not these actions were specified in a performance contract. Contract outcomes also depended on the incentives of government negotiators, as well as on their power and the quality of information they commanded. Large differences in status, income, and influence between government and SOE negotiators contributed to weak and incoherent targets. Frequent shifts in locale, staff, and responsibilities further weakened the position of government actors.

Although the involvement of informed individuals outside of government and politics may have helped prevent reneging and improved the caliber of monitoring in Korea, the involvement of donors as enforcement agents had mixed results in other sample countries and led some of the contracts to be viewed as purely donor-driven exercises. The role of outside pressure in performance contracts is necessarily a limited one, since outsiders are not party to the contract and have, at best, only an indirect stake in the outcome.

Can performance contracts improve the performance of public agencies? The evidence of this small but diverse sample does not offer much encouragement. And the fact that contracts were not successful in improving the performance of the more easily measured SOEs raises doubts as to their utility for other kinds of government units. An underlying problem in any government contract with a public manager is the absence of a residual claimant—that is, the agent who can claim whatever benefits remain after other claims are met and hence has the greatest incentive to improve performance. While providing incentives linked to performance can alleviate the incentive problem, such rewards are unlikely to approximate those of private managers with a clearer stake in performance when sunk costs and reputation are at stake. Moreover, private managers start from a different negotiating position. Since they can refuse to sign the contract, they can insist on credible signals of government commitment or demand a bond or risk premium.

Ultimately, the success of performance contracts depends on the government's willingness to make the exercise a meaningful one. It requires politically difficult actions, such as allowing SOE managers to cut costs through layoffs, raising tariffs to allow cost recovery, or firing managers who fail to perform. The governments in our sample were not politically able to take actions such as these. Absent the willingness to enact such reforms, performance contracts become a cosmetic exercise, with the government signing a contract and then reneging.

If a government is prepared to enact politically difficult reforms, then performance contracts might be a useful tool to help clarify the goals of government agencies and hold managers accountable for results. This analysis suggests that performance contracts might stand a better chance of success if:

- Managers compete for the contract.

- Both rewards and penalties are clearly specified.

- Targets are few, weighted, and infrequently changed. Jones (1981) provides excellent guidance on how to avoid perverse effects from double counting or sending conflicting signals.

- The status of the actors responsible for negotiating and monitoring the contract is similar to that of the SOE managers. (The involvement of knowledgeable individuals outside government and politics may also make the exercise more credible.)

- The government signals its commitment to the contract by specifying a neutral enforcement mechanism and adhering to its decisions.

These recommendations are speculative, however, since there are no successful cases in this sample from which to draw lessons. Rather, this analysis suggests that performance contracts should be used either sparingly or not at all, and only when a government's commitment to the exercise is strong and in parallel, supportive reforms (such as the increases in SOE autonomy in Korea) can be enacted.

### Notes

1.  The paper draws heavily on analysis done for World Bank (1995).

2.   There may be other factors that make performance contracts easier to write in less market-oriented government services, however. SOE income is harder to predict than the income of a service agency whose revenues are entirely appropriated by government. Moreover, since SOEs generate revenues, there may be more principals with a stronger stake in the SOE's operations than there are for an agency issuing drivers' licenses, for instance, making it harder to reach agreement on goals.

3.   Korea Telecoms was created as a separate company only two years before its contract started. Senegal Telecoms was separated from the post office in the same year that it signed its first contract; the precontract period was estimated by extrapolating backwards two years, using data from prereorganization telecom units. Senegal Electricity's second contract (starting in 1990) was included, even though it was never signed. The conclusions would not change if that period were omitted. The start date for India Oil's contracts was taken as 1987, even though the company signed a pilot contract in 1986 (based on the multiyear French *contrat plan*). The government later switched to a very different sort of contract (closer to the Korean model, using yearly weighted targets). The conclusions would not change if the earlier contract period were included.

4.   Performance improvement should not be confused with good performance in some absolute sense. For example, Ghana Water and Sewerage increased total factor probability (TFP) by an average of 12.5 percent a year during the three years of contracts for which data exist (1990, 1991, and 1992). Yet almost 50 percent of this company's water is still unaccounted for, and only about two-thirds of the population is served with water.

5.   Data were taken from audited accounts, contracts, and evaluation reports, supplemented by World Bank file data. A survey of key government and enterprise officials, using a standardized questionnaire and interviews with knowledgeable persons in the country and World Bank, provided further background. See Dyer Cissé (1994) for the sample questionnaire. Although every effort was made to verify the accuracy of the data, in some cases the underlying information systems are weak. However, it seems plausible that errors are not correlated over time and do not greatly affect the trend analysis. Where assets were not revalued by the company, they were revalued using company figures for depreciation and the GDP deflator for inflation. TFP, calculated as the constant value of production over the constant cost of all production factors, was estimated using company volume data to construct company-specific price indices for each factor and output where available; otherwise the relevant country-specific price indices were used. Return on assets was calculated as sales minus cost of goods sold and depreciation over revalued fixed assets.

6.   Exogenous factors seemed important in only two cases—Philippines Electricity and Senegal Telecom. However, the magnitude of these factors was not so large as to rule out the contracts as a significant explanatory factor. The postcontract return on assets of Philippines Electricity was adversely affected by increases in the cost of imported oil, but this cannot explain its poor performance in constant priced TFP. TFP might have been adversely affected by disruptions caused by the Luzon earthquake, plus devastating typhoons in 1989 and 1990; however, observers knowledgeable about the company regard its performance as consistently weak. Moreover, other disasters (the Mt. Pinatubo eruption and Ormoc flood in 1991) did not prevent the firm from recovering its productivity levels. Senegal Telecom may have benefited from the fact that it was split off from the postal service in 1986, the first year of the contract. Although an effort was made to isolate the telecommunications side prior to this split, that may not always have been possible and could cause the period before the contract to look worse than it otherwise would. (The split itself is not exogenous; even though it is not explicitly part of the contract, it was implicitly part of the agreement.)

7.   In fact, the number of nonperforming wells has been increasing since 1992. This increase is partly due to shutdowns of older wells as well as to new drilling.

8.   According to field interviews, monitoring agents are disadvantaged by these changes and their lower status.

9.   Standing boards of directors were replaced by executive boards; government representation on the boards was reduced to two members; only board approval of the budget was required when previously the supervising ministry, the economic planning board, and the cab-

inet also had to approve; responsibility for most personnel decisions was shifted from the supervising ministry to the enterprise; procurement through a centralized office was made voluntary instead of compulsory; all oversight was centered in the contract, with one yearly inspection, compared with the extensive system of controls and inspections used before (in the one year before the contracts, Korea Power had 8 different inspections lasting 108 days); preference was shifted to internal candidates for senior positions (previously over half of all such appointments were from outside the firm) and an explicit merit assessment was introduced (Shirley 1991).

## References

Buchanan, James. 1975. "Microeconomic Theory: Conflict and Contract. A Contractarian Paradigm for Applying Economic Theory." *American Economic Review* LXV(2).

———. 1988. "Contractarian Political Economy and Constitutional Interpretation." *American Economic Review* 78(2).

Dyer Cissé, Nichola. 1994. "The Impact of Performance Contracts on Public Enterprise Performance." Background paper. Policy Research Department, World Bank, Washington, D.C.

Jones, Leroy. 1975. *Public Enterprise and Economic Development: The Korean Case.* Seoul: Korea Development Institute.

———. 1981. "Towards a Performance Evaluation Methodology for Public Enterprises: With Special Reference to Pakistan." Paper presented at the International Symposium on Economic Performance of Public Enterprises, Islamabad.

———. 1985. "Public Enterprise for Whom? Perverse Distributional Consequences of Public Operational Decisions." *Economic Development and Cultural Changes* 33(2):333–47.

Laffont, Jean-Jacques, and Jean Tirole. 1986. "Using Cost Observation to Regulate Firms." *Journal of Political Economy* 94 (Part 1):614–41.

Nellis, John. 1989. "Contract Plans and Public Enterprise Performance." Policy, Planning, and Research Working Paper No. 118. World Bank, Washington, D.C.

North, Douglass C. 1990. *Institutions, Institutional Change, and Economic Performance.* New York: Cambridge University Press.

Ross, S. 1991. "The Economic Theory of Agency: The Principal's Problem." In Robert Kuenne, ed., *Macroeconomics: Theoretical and Applied.* International Library of Critical Writings in Economics 2(11). Aldershot, U.K. and Brookfield, Vt.: Elgar.

Sappington, David E. M. 1991. "Incentives in Principal-Agent Relationships." *Journal of Economic Perspectives* 5(2):45–66.

———, and Joseph E. Stiglitz. 1987. "Privatization, Information, and Incentives." National Bureau of Economic Research (NBER). Working Paper 2196. Harvard University, Cambridge, Mass.

Shirley, Mary. 1989. "Evaluating the Performance of Public Enterprises in Pakistan." Policy, Planning, and Research Working Paper 160. World Bank, Washington, D.C.

———. 1991. "Improving Public Enterprise Performance: Lessons from South Korea." *Annales de l'economie publique sociale et coopérative* 62(1). De Boech Université, Brussels.

State Enterprise Commission (SEC). 1991. *SOE Performance Evaluation Report.* Accra, Ghana.

———. 1993. *The SOE Reform Program 1984/1992: Review and Recommendations.* Accra, Ghana.

Stiglitz, Joseph E. 1989. *The Economic Role of the State.* Cambridge, Mass.: Basil Blackwell, Inc.

Trivedi, Prajapati, ed. 1990. *Labor Redundancy in the Transport Sector: The Case of Chile.* Washington, D.C.: World Bank.

Williamson, Oliver. 1975. *Markets and Hierarchies.* New York: Free Press.

———. 1976. "Franchise Bidding for Natural Monopolies—in General and with Respect to CATV." *Bell Journal of Economics* 7(1):73–104.

———. 1985. *The Economic Institutions of Capitalism: Firms, Markets, Relational Contracting.* New York: Free Press.

World Bank. 1995. *Bureaucrats in Business: The Economics and Politics of Government Ownership.* Washington, D.C.: Oxford University Press for the World Bank.

## Comments on "Performance contracts: a tool for improving public services?" by Shirley

*Leroy Jones*

Mary Shirley's study, to my knowledge, is only the second serious evaluation of performance evaluation systems for public enterprises. This fact suggests that, like business people who believe in competition in every market but their own, evaluators believe in evaluating others but not in being evaluated themselves.

Why do I call this a serious study? It is not simply because the study is quantitative. There are a number of studies that deem performance contracting a success on the grounds that a substantial portion of the targets have actually been met. The author, rightly in my view, dismisses such assertions as potentially the result of nothing more than the fact that the targets were soft to begin with. She also looks briefly at profitability, but for a regulated monopoly, profitability is irrelevant. The single most important determinant of profits for public enterprises is the degree to which output prices are allowed to rise relative to input prices. It is thus not an appropriate measure of management reform. Another indicator, labor productivity, usefully ignores the effect of price changes, but less usefully ignores the costs of capital and intermediate inputs. The seriousness of the study therefore follows from its focus on TFP as a measure of performance. If TFP rises faster with performance contracts than it would have without it, then the contracts have accomplished something. Otherwise, whatever the processes or other accomplishments, performance contracts will have done nothing useful for an economist. The fact that Shirley finds no significant improvement is therefore to be taken seriously.

What does the other serious study say? Song Dae Hee of the Korean Development Institute evaluated 25 enterprises in the Korean system according to the same criteria.[1] Using regression techniques, he compared actual performance with predicted performance and found it to be 5.4 percent higher after the system was introduced. This result was worth about a billion dollars then, or twice that today. Such an amount may be small potatoes to the World Bank, but it presumably passes Shirley's test that the benefits should more than cover the transaction costs of the effort.

Song also did a survey of 750 enterprise employees, stratified by rank and enterprise, and found the following responses to the question of how much "overall management improvement" followed from the reforms: significant (more than "substantial"), 19; substantial, 45; so-so (moderate), 28; few, 5; none, 3. Allowing for some ambiguity in the translation of Korean into English, this survey would seem to enforce the notion of positive consequences.

What are we to conclude when the two competing studies give completely opposite results? We might conjecture that everything works in Korea and that at least this technology is not exportable. However, the discrepancy in results cannot be due solely to differing samples, since two firms are in both studies: Korea Electric Power and Korea Telecom. The Korea study finds significant increases in productivity, but Shirley's study finds none. If this disconnect makes me a little nervous about accepting either study, it would be relatively cheap to replicate both sets of results and ascertain whether the difference is due to methodology, data errors, assumptions, or something else. Such an analysis might also provide a useful example of evaluating the evaluators.

Until this test is conducted, what must the objective observer do? Suspend judgment. I, however, am somewhat biased on this issue and would agree that casual empiricism supports Shirley's formal empiricism and that there is undoubtedly some truth to her conclusion. I doubt that performance contracting has been the unmitigated disaster she finds it to be, while I think it fair to say that it has been considerably less successful than many of us would have expected based on the agency theory she so ably expounds at the beginning of her paper.

I therefore want to turn to her analysis of what went wrong. Here I am very much in agreement with her list of problems and how they might be solved but would like to add a little emphasis. In my view, the most important source of problems is the criteria chosen. These are uniformly multiple, including such things as improving capacity utilization, output, and labor productivity. As an illustration, assume that these three items constitute the entire list and are equally weighted. These are all good things, so who could object? I can, and so will you after you think about it. Assume that I conducted a *project* evaluation of a fertilizer project by counting the benefits as the output at the world market price multiplied by three and the costs as those of labor. The end. You would fire me, first, for ignoring capital and intermediate input costs, and second, for viewing a dollar of increased output as worth three times as much as a dollar of cost reduction. However, when exactly the same thing is done in *performance* evaluations, World Bank employees affirm conditionalities as being met and reward consultants for a job well done. Why are these performance and project examples the same? The problems with the tripartite evaluation examples are first, that capital and other intermediate costs enter into none of the criteria and so are ignored; and second, that an increase in output increases all three indicators while a decrease in labor costs reduces only one, resulting in the former being weighted three times as heavily as the latter.

In this sort of system, it is not surprising that TFP has not increased, because it will almost always be the case that decreasing TFP can harm performance. And it will often be the case that it is easier to earn rewards by reducing TFP than by increasing it. Under these conditions, another of Shirley's problems may not be a problem but a blessing. She notes that all too often there are no effective incentives in these schemes and therefore no reason for managers or workers to make the effort to change traditional ways of operating. Given the criteria actually chosen, this lack of incentives is probably a good thing, but if the technical problems are overcome, it will become a binding constraint.

To summarize:

- The paper is to be applauded as a seminal empirical work on an important topic. Privatization is not happening overnight; thus improving the performance of the remaining large and critical SOEs matters a great deal.

- I would have greater confidence in the results were it not for the conflicting evidence on the Korean case. Nonetheless, it is safe to say that performance evaluation programs have been considerably less successful than many of us expected.

- To improve the performance of performance evaluation, we should first apply technical standards comparable to those widely accepted in project evaluation. The World Bank has a role to play here.

### Note

1. Song Dae Hee, "New Public Enterprise Policy and Efficiency Improvement." Korea Development Institute Working Paper No. 8811, forthcoming 1998. For the record, he actually estimated the inverse of TFP

## Comments on "Performance contracts: a tool for improving public services?" by Shirley

*Tawfiq E. Chowdhury*

Mary Shirley has made an interesting analysis and evaluation of cross-country experiences regarding performance contracts as tools for improving public services in SOEs. The findings do not give us confidence in the usefulness of these contracts. The paper speculates on why such contracts fail to achieve the desired objectives and suggests some modifications that might give them a better chance of success. While I agree with the overall findings of the paper (except the recommendations at the end), I would like to share some general observations based largely on my three decades of experience as a public servant.

It is extremely difficult to promote islands of efficiency in selected public enterprises while leaving the rest of public sector management unchanged. Wasteful expenditures, self-perpetuating bureaucracies, and vested interests plague governments and limit efficiency, productivity, and the quality of public services. In developing countries in particular, inadequate incentive packages, lack of appropriate rewards and punishments, and poor accountability in general are some of the hallmarks of public sector management. Thus, for example, an incentive structure that sets things "right" in one sector may destabilize other areas, offset their gains, and throw into doubt the net gains for the government as a whole. Adequate incentives for power utility workers may lead to resentment among state-owned bank employees or tax collectors. How can a government explain such discriminatory practices? Creating such a structure for one set of employees may set off claims from others that ultimately lead to higher public expenditures without any meaningful gains.

Commitment is also a difficult concept to operationalize. One reason performance contracts are designed at arms' length is to differentiate among the responsibilities and rewards of the contracting parties. This strategy may not be very desirable. (Private business encourages teamwork in place of a patron-client framework; "alliancing" among industries is an example of how contracting parties aim for a better convergence of goals.) Discussions and negotiations in developing performance contracts might encourage better understanding between patron and clients, as some would like to believe. But it also risks promoting adversarial relationships among the groups and could lead to unintended and adverse results.

Lack of "objectivity" (coupled with what the author defines as asymmetric positions between government negotiators and SOE managers) could result in contracts that are not only flawed but devoid of real ownership. Moreover, these could translate into routine work lacking the special effort underlying the contract. Both parties may engage in a ritual that neither has any particular interest in. Finally, after some years government attention "fatigue" may lead to their de facto demise. In Bangladesh, even a special law to promote the efficiency and accountability of SOEs (which were governed by other laws) turned out to be ineffective. A cabinet committee showed some initial enthusiasm but then became so fatigued that even meetings became infrequent. Information asymmetry and lack of incentive and commitment all contributed in varying degrees to this process.

The failure to manage SOEs effectively is one more good reason why the state should not be doing any business. Performance contracts were conceived at a time when the domain of the state was not as clearly understood and agreed upon as it is today. There are some "empiricists" who would still look for "evidence" to argue for continued state presence in business. Any argument for a better "performance contract" would give this school a new lease on life. On the contrary, I argue for writing a final epitaph so that governments can get down to concentrating on those responsibilities that remain theirs for now.

Governments should try to find an overall framework for improving efficiency and productivity in core operations. They should be driven by client or customer satisfaction and should try to mimic competitive markets. Funding and provision of public services should be separated. Provision of public services can be outsourced through competition where public sector managers are allowed to compete. Government involvement in utilities, such as power and telecommunications, should be devoted to unbundling the industries, introducing competition wherever possible—there are always niche markets to start—and moving toward corporatization and commercialization of the industries. Along with this process, a proper regulatory framework should be set up to oversee the interests of all parties.

Since a fixed time horizon determined by tenure places a special limitation on political governments, government management attention should be focused on time-bound results rather than on open-ended reform programs unrelated to a political time frame. Finally, I would like to reemphasize that governments should get out of doing business as quickly as possible. The earlier we end the debate on how to improve the performance of SOEs, the better. Government would better serve the people (customers) if it concentrated on efficiency, productivity, and value for money for its core operations. It should also continuously review the domain and nature of its responsibilities. Nothing is sacrosanct.

**Floor discussion on
"Performance contracts: a tool for improving public services?"**

The chair noted the competing views of the discussants, one of whom (Chowdhury) would like to bury performance contracts and the other (Jones) to rescue them.

The first questioner wondered why incentives work in a private environment and not in the public sector and asked whether governments can learn from the experience with regulating private monopolies. Robert Klitgaard noted that the issue should be analyzed in the light of institutional economics. Performance contracts work poorly if the measures are poor, and the conclusions should not be overgeneralized without looking at the degree to which things go wrong. The problems come in different varieties. The question is how to identify the circumstances under which performance contracts work.

Brian Wall of the Irish Aid Development Division wanted to know how aid projects can take the limitations of institutional capacity into account. Irish Aid has found it has to consider three aspects in designing incentive systems in its projects: capacity, motivation, and criteria. He asked for views on incentives and wanted to know whether the World Bank has a policy. A fourth questioner wanted to know whether performance contracts are more likely to be demanded from managers or whether they are state imposed.

Mary Shirley responded that she has a lot of sympathy for the notion of burying performance contracts but had tried in this particular paper to address the question of the circumstances under which performance contracts work, especially in public agencies where privatization and competition are not an option. One critical factor is politics. The Bank's Quality Assurance Group is trying to develop some indicators to show when a country is politically ready to reform. In looking at state enterprise reform, it was found possible to predict whether a country was ready to reform based on three political measures: political feasibility, political desirability, and credibility. In most of the cases examined, it seemed clear that if a country met all three conditions, it would not only be able to do contracts well, it would be able to privatize well. It would also be able to do a lot of other reforms well.

Why not use pricing regulations for public companies that provide the same incentives as, for example, price cap regulation does for private monopolies. A very good question. Why don't we ever see that? Again, it appears to relate to the political problems. She said Chile is the one country she knows that has introduced anything comparable. They used benchmark pricing arrangements for their monopolies (setting prices so that a hypothetical, efficient firm would earn a reasonable return) before they privatized their state-owned companies. Then they privatized them to lock in the efficiency gain, to prevent politically motivated pricing from being reintroduced in the future.

Roger Douglas stressed the idea of locking in the efficiency gain in New Zealand. Even if a public company works well using the same kind of regulatory framework as a private company, how can we keep the politicians' hands off? In New Zealand, even though the companies were performing well, they had to be privatized to lock in the gains. The Chileans also privatized companies that had begun working well, because the reforms had to be protected from political interference.

Were these contracts demand-driven by the SOE employees? Not at all. Private sector managers can walk away from a contract if they don't think the government is committed. But state-owned managers have to sign. They are not given a choice. And, interestingly, none of these contracts were bid. Why not? Competitive bidding provides more information; as Joe Stiglitz noted earlier during the conference, competitive bidding has a lot of beneficial features. But unfortunately, the appointment of managers in all the cases the group looked at was politically driven. There was no competition. Politics ultimately seems to explain a lot about those findings.

Finally, many development agencies grapple with the question of whether providing incentive pay to public servants is a good idea. There are many kinds of incentives, and monitoring them is only part of the picture. Certainly it is necessary to raise the compensation of people whose pay is so low that they cannot survive without collecting some kind of bribe or graft. Beyond that, offering such things as bonuses and share contracts is a good idea, but there are other conditions that have to be right for incentives to work to improve management. For example, managers must be hired and fired on the basis of merit rather than occupying political sinecures. And they must have enough control over operations to be able to improve performance. In most of the cases where civil service pay has been topped up, increases have probably had perverse effects.

The discussants responded briefly. Chowdhury said he felt there was not much left worth trying in performance contracts and that the focus should be on industry restructuring. Jones pointed out that the privatization and regulation of public monopolies have been shown to work in countries where the per capita income is over $3,000. But he said that outside middle-income countries such as Chile and Mexico, whether monopolies perform better when run by the private sector than by the government is still an open question. More research is needed.

# 8. Reforming budgetary institutions in Latin America: the case for a national fiscal council

Barry Eichengreen, Ricardo Hausmann, and Jürgen von Hagen

*The authors advocate the creation of independent national fiscal councils to address specific problems that arise in the Latin American context. Such an independent authority would combine responsibility for fiscal monitoring and evaluation with jurisdictional oversight of public debt ceilings.*

The economies of Latin America have made tremendous strides in recent years. Economic growth has resumed, and inflation has been brought under control. Trade has been liberalized, and access to international capital markets has for the most part been restored. Yet problems remain on the fiscal front. First, a deficit bias exists. It is reflected in a stock of debt that is large relative to the government's capacity to service it. Second, fiscal outcomes are excessively volatile. Third, fiscal responses are procyclical, especially during downturns. Thus, fiscal policy has amplified, not dampened, the volatility of Latin American economies. This problem is related to the precarious creditworthiness of the governments, which have limited capacity to borrow, especially in bad years. Finally, adjustment to negative shocks is often delayed, creating instability and increasing the size of the adjustment that is ultimately required.

In this paper, we argue that institutional reform of the fiscal decisionmaking process can overcome these problems. We propose the creation of an independent national fiscal council (NFC) to carry out this task in individual countries. The NFC would set a binding ceiling on the deficit and force budget negotiators to recognize trade-offs among programs. The NFC's independence would allow it to adopt a long-term perspective on fiscal policy. However, the NFC would not take the power over fiscal policy away from the executive and legislative branches of government. It would be accountable to the congress. Furthermore, decisions about the total size of the public sector and the distribution of spending and taxes would remain under the government's authority. The NFC's role would be to improve the quality of the fiscal policy decisions of congress and the executive branch.

Our proposal is an extension of recent literature showing that certain budgetary procedures—those that invest in agenda-setting, monitoring, and enforcement powers with the finance minister, for example—yield superior fiscal policy outcomes. Empirical evidence for both European countries (von Hagen and Harden 1994) and Latin America (Alesina and others 1995; Hausmann and Stein 1996) strongly supports this argument. Taking this approach to its logical consequence, we propose to vest the independent NFC with analogous powers.

## The commons problem

Government revenue can be thought of as an inadequately priced common resource subject to overutilization.[1] Concentrated interests tend to internalize the benefits of particular spending programs but not their full budgetary costs. Each group lobbies for spending on programs from which it benefits but which are paid for by society as a whole. Absent a mechanism to coordinate these actions, this lobbying will result in excessive spending and, given a reluctance to raise taxes, excessive deficits.[2]

Empirical evidence suggests the prevalence of excessive deficits in Latin American countries. Between 1970 and 1994, countries in the region had an average deficit-to-GDP ratio of 3.9 percent. While this average is similar to that of the countries of the Organization for Economic Cooperation and Development (OECD), which had an average deficit ratio of 3.8 percent during the same period, deficit-to-GDP ratios are deceptive, because they neglect the much lower capacity to tax and the lack of financial depth in the Latin American economies. Thus, the average ratio of deficits to government revenues was 21 percent in Latin America (25 percent without Brazil) compared with 14 percent in the OECD, indicating larger deficits relative to the size of government. The ratio of government deficits to broad money (M2) was 14.2 (compared with 5.1 in the OECD), indicating large deficits relative to the capacity to finance them. In sum, a close look reveals that deficits in Latin America are on average dangerously large.

Associated with the commons problem is an intertemporal distortion that leads governments to squander the benefits of economic booms. When the terms of trade improve or access to foreign capital is restored, it is efficient to spread increased consumption over time. But if different groups fear that others will grab the resources, they have an incentive to do so themselves. The difficulty of ensuring that resources will be carried over leads to their immediate dissipation. Hence, when Latin American economies boom, the additional resources tend to be consumed immediately rather than carried over through public saving.[3] The welfare loss is especially pronounced in Latin America, because the macroeconomic environment there is volatile and shocks are large.

Indeed, there is strong evidence suggesting that fiscal policy in Latin America suffers from procyclicality. Gavin and others (1996) show that, on average, OECD countries let their deficit-to-GDP ratios increase by 33 basis points for each 1 percent decline in GDP. In contrast, Latin American countries, on average, manage to increase their deficit ratios by an insignificant amount. This finding suggests that the stabilizing function of fiscal policy is relatively weak in Latin America. The effects are asymmetric over the business cycle. In the OECD, the stabilizing function of the deficit is about four times stronger in recessions than in upswings. In contrast, deficits in Latin American countries on average show a procyclical response to recessions; the stabilizing function operates only during expansions.

Another problem is the strategic use of fiscal policy by self-interested governments. A government anxious about its reelection may be inclined to tailor fiscal policy to the electoral cycle in an effort to maximize its share of the vote. The classic Nordhaus

(1975) model of political business cycles assumes that deficit spending determines unemployment and that unemployment governs the incumbent administration's reelection prospects. Modern variants add another layer: the electorate may be unsure whether the preelection boom is the result of deficit spending or the government's economic competence. But either way, an approaching election may prompt an inefficient increase in deficit spending.

One consequence of these incentives to engage in strategic behavior is that governments may manipulate revenue estimates and expenditure forecasts to increase their leverage in the fiscal debate. Aizenman and Hausmann (1995) provide evidence of such behavior in Latin America. These authors study budget forecast errors and find that as inflation and the volatility of economic activity rise, so does the systematic underestimation of the budget. They explain this observation as an outcome of the interaction between the finance and spending ministers. Spending ministers, who know more than the finance minister about the true cost of government programs, will tell the finance minister only about cost-increasing shocks and ask for additional funds. They will keep the windfall profits of cost-reducing shocks. Anticipating their action, the finance minister has an incentive to underestimate initial budget allocations, a tendency that increases when volatility rises.

### Delayed adjustment to shocks

If the permanent income of a commodity-exporting country drops because of a fall in world prices, the decline should be accompanied by a reduction in public spending. But each interest group in the affected country will resist cuts to its favored programs. Absent a mechanism to coordinate competing demands, adjustment can lead to excessive deficits and macroeconomic dislocations in the wake of shocks. Gavin and others (1996) find that much of the contraction in fiscal expenditures during recessions is not the result of fiscal decisions but of an accelerating inflation rate that reduces the real value of spending commitments. This finding indicates that adjustment is carried out not through the budget process but through monetary policy. Practical examples of the dynamic abound. Venezuela, for example, was hit by a major deterioration in its oil tax revenues starting in 1992, but adjustment did not come promptly. Rising interest rates and declining financial confidence first led to a banking crisis in early 1994 that worsened the country's fiscal position, and only later did adjustment to a new sustainable fiscal position take place.

### Rules versus discretion

The traditional discretionary approach to fiscal policy suffers from the problems of commitment and collective action just discussed. But rigid fiscal rules are insufficiently flexible for shock-prone Latin American economies. In principle, reforming budgetary procedures provides a third way of importing the advantages of rules without also importing their inflexibility. The essence of this approach is to overcome the commons problem and the shortsightedness and politicized fiscal policy decisions by implementing decisionmaking procedures that limit the externality involved in the commons problem while promoting a long-term perspective and prompt decisionmaking. While these goals can be achieved in part by strengthening existing institutions, the logical consequence of the approach is the creation of a national fiscal council, a new institutional body whose political independence gives it the capacity to overcome partisanship and develop a credible, long-term fiscal strategy.

But discretion, as we have seen, is subject to abuse. Partisan governments can manipulate policy for their own interests or, in their efforts to commit their successors, bequeath an excessive burden of debt. Policies can be distorted in socially inefficient directions by governments seeking to maximize their chances of reelection. Individuals who fail to internalize the costs of spending may lobby for additional programs to the point where excessive deficits result. Governments who do not commit to future policies may be unable to borrow efficiently.

Rules are a logical alternative. Statutory debt ceilings and balanced budget amendments have been suggested as ways to limit deficit bias and force rapid adjustment. But balanced budget laws can be hard to enforce; they encourage off-budget spending, the creation of semiautonomous government agencies exempt from fiscal ceilings, and other forms of evasion (von Hagen 1992). Furthermore, stringent rules are inflexible; they can prevent fiscal policy from providing automatic stabilization and discourage officials from stabilizing the economy through the use of discretionary policies, hampering adjustment to shocks.[4]

In theory, contingent rules (rules with escape clauses) combine the advantages of the rules- and discretion-based approaches. Unfortunately, it is difficult to satisfy the prerequisites for the operation of contingent rules. If the contingency cannot be observed and verified, politicians will be inclined to invoke it even when it has not occurred. If the contingency can be manipulated, the authorities may provoke it in order to relax the rules-based constraint. Under these circumstances, a contingent rule may be destabilizing (Obstfeld 1993).

## Procedural reform as a solution

Literature on procedural reform inspired us to examine and adapt such reform to the Latin American context. With regard to fiscal policy, procedural reform can involve the following kinds of changes to national budgetary procedures:

- Strengthening the finance minister's budgetary powers over spending agencies

- Restricting the scope for off-budget spending

- Requiring a binding vote on overall spending and the admissible deficit at the beginning of the annual budget round

- Limiting earmarked expenditures

- Empowering the executive branch to cut the budget unilaterally in the event that the annual deficit ceiling is breached

The empirical evidence on the beneficial effects of such procedural reforms is compelling. Von Hagen and Harden (1994) show that cross-country differences in deficits and debt ratios among the members of the European Union are to a large extent explained by differences in budgetary processes. In Latin America, those few countries with coherent budgetary procedures stand out. They are able to conduct anticyclical fiscal policies during recessions, unlike countries with incoherent budgetary procedures. This fact suggests that countries with strong procedures gain access to capital markets even during recessions—that is, markets reward the gain in credibility from credible budgetary institutions. Furthermore, countries with strong budgetary procedures are better able to spread the fiscal adjustment to adverse shocks over a period of years. Fiscal surpluses also tend to dissipate faster in countries with weak budgetary processes. In sum, reforms strengthening the budget process promise not only to reduce the deficit bias but also to improve the efficiency of dynamic adjustment.

## National fiscal councils

Procedural reforms that make the budgetary process more centralized eliminate deficit bias and similar problems. In Latin America, such reforms, effectively applied by a national fiscal council, would have the same effect.

The NFC we propose would be an autonomous body established by law or constitution, independent of the congress and the government. Members would be appointed to staggered and relatively long terms in office, with one member retiring each year to help ensure continuity and minimize partisanship. Their mandate would be to ensure the stability of public finances and advance the general economic strategy of the government and nation. The NFC's central function would be to set the maximum allowable increase in government debt—the debt change limit (DCL)—at the beginning of the annual budget round. The failure of congress and the executive branch to adopt a budget conforming to NFC guidelines would place them in violation of the law.

The council could be expected to adopt a long-term perspective on policy. Annual DCLs, rather than placing fiscal policy in a straitjacket, could take into account the need for appropriate responses to changing conditions. Because the NFC would also be insulated from immediate political pressures, it could credibly ensure that debt accumulation remained sustainable.

How would an NFC eliminate the specific distortions identified above? First, it addresses the commons problem, in which the beneficiaries of public programs fail to internalize their costs, by setting a binding ceiling for the deficit. This action forces budget negotiators to recognize trade-offs among programs and limits the ability of special interest coalitions to win additional and potentially damaging spending for their favored programs.

Second, a deficit ceiling addresses the dynamic commons problem by forcing governments to increase public saving during booms and preventing different political factions from dissipating the additional resources. Neglect of the implications of current spending for future debt burdens can be offset by making members of the council independent of government and appointing them to long terms in office.[5] The NFC's power to mandate a reduction in spending or an increase in taxes speeds adjustment to shocks. The knowledge that such actions will occur after, say, 30 days if no political agreement has been reached should speed up a negotiated solution among interest groups.[6]

Finally, the creation of an NFC would address the problems of commitment. The fact that the NFC would be a permanent entity whose members serve long, overlapping terms (see section below on structure) promises more policy continuity than a government that may be out of office tomorrow can offer. The NFC's independence insulates the budget deficit from strategic manipulation by politicians seeking reelection, moderating the tendency for interest rates to rise and for access to capital markets to become more precarious as elections approach and the survival of the current government is placed in doubt.[7] Finally, the NFC would make it easier to credibly commit to offsetting deficits during recessions with surpluses during expansions, relaxing credit constraints on the government and enhancing its ability to pursue countercyclical policies.

The NFC would not, however, have the authority to determine either the total amount or composition of taxes and expenditures. These competencies would remain in the hands of elected officials in the executive and legislative branches of government. We emphasize this point to make clear that the purpose of the council is not to somehow dictate fiscal policy, but rather to improve the quality of democratic decisionmaking.

*Setting the annual debt-change limit*

As noted, the NFC's central function would be to set the maximum allowable DCL at the beginning of the annual budget round. Any budget adopted by the congress and signed by the executive would have to conform with the DCL. Budget proposals would be costed by the council to determine whether they satisfy this requirement. If the new fiscal year began without the passage of a budget act that satisfied the DCL, the previous year's budget could continue to be used as a basis for public sector functions. To prevent evasion through accounting gimmicks, a core responsibility of the NFC would be to define the relevant measure of the public debt. While a general definition could be included in the statute establishing the NFC, the power to decide what specific public obligations would be counted in its measure should be reserved for the council.

*The need for in-year adjustments*

The volatility of the economic environment in Latin America places flexibility in policymaking at a premium. The fiscal adjustments required of Argentina in the wake of the 1994–95 Mexican crisis, for example, had to be completed in a matter of weeks. For this reason, and in contrast to industrial countries (where an annual DCL may indeed be sufficient), Latin American NFCs should be able to revise the DCL within the fiscal year in response to new information.

A flexibility-credibility trade-off is involved here: if councils can make in-year adjustments, economic actors will perceive that a given DCL may not remain in force and therefore may pay less attention to the importance of the requisite compromises. This problem can be contained by requiring the NFC to justify any revisions it undertakes on the basis of new information. Increases in the DCL would be justifiable only if there were unforeseen revenue shortfalls or clearly exogenous shocks. In this way, an increase in the DCL could never be used to make room for discretionary spending.

One of the main problems with discretion, in practice, is that governments tend to interpret all positive shocks as permanent and all negative shocks as transitory and therefore to abuse the notion of flexibility in policy decisions. The NFC has no incentive to misinterpret shocks in this way. Based on its objective interpretation of events, the NFC could deliver a more appropriate response to permanent and transitory shocks as they arise.

### Advantages of an NFC over partial procedural reforms

Partial approaches to reforming the way fiscal policy is created recommend procedures that concentrate power in the hands of the finance minister or the president. The problem with this approach is that the finance minister is still a member of the executive. As such, he or she is not as thoroughly insulated from adverse political incentives as the members of an NFC. Furthermore, a finance minister attempting to impose discipline on the executive can be removed too easily. In this sense, our proposal is more robust because it builds an institution that is difficult to circumvent.

Other authors have stressed the desirability of establishing an authority independent of both the executive and the congress to construct the assumptions underlying the budget and to forecast nondiscretionary spending. An independent authority promotes budgetary transparency, and the information it provides is a basis for negotiation and compromise. The NFC would serve this function. It would further enhance budgetary transparency by publishing, at the beginning of the annual budget round, staff forecasts of government revenues, expenditures, and general economic conditions. It would generate supplementary forecasts as needed in the course of the fiscal year. Thus, measures to ensure budgetary transparency would be regularized even more effectively than under piecemeal procedural reform.

While an NFC cannot prevent the congress or finance minister from underfunding spending programs, it can identify discrepancies early on and point out their implications for the global budget constraint. If it concludes that expenditures have been underfunded, it can revise upward the government's or parliament's estimate of the deficit. It can add to its estimate of the budget any off-budget items and supplementary appropriations. By publishing independent estimates of projected revenues and outlays, it can ensure that congressional debate over the budget is predicated on realistic assumptions. In particular, by highlighting discrepancies between its revenue and expenditure projections and those of the executive or congress, the NFC can increase the transparency of the budgetary process and shape the fiscal debate in a constructive way. If its warnings about excessive deficits do not lead to revisions in appropriation and tax legislation, passing such bills would provide grounds for declaring the government in violation of the DLC, setting in motion the responses required by law.

### Issues of implementation in the Latin American context

*How should the NFC deal with state and local governments?*

The DCL, as we envisage it, would apply to the central or federal government. But macroeconomic conditions depend on the consolidated public sector deficit, not just on that of the central government. Mechanisms limiting the spending autonomy of state and municipal governments are the simplest solution to this problem but are not consistent with constitutional arrangements in all Latin American countries. Some countries, such as Venezuela, prohibit states from borrowing without the permission of federal authorities. Others, such as Argentina, allow much more autonomy. In the former, imposing borrowing limits at the federal level would be enough. In the latter, however, the NFC's role in restricting the borrowing capacity of state governments is an open question.

The problem here is that expanding the powers of the NFC to cover state governments would intensify political resistance to the formation of such a council. And it is unclear whether an NFC needs to worry about the deficits of state and local governments to the same extent that it worries about those of the federal authorities. State and local deficits are constrained by the relatively limited debt-carrying capacity of these entities. State governments, which cannot print money to backstop the market in their debts, tend to be rationed out of the credit market relatively quickly.[8] The mobility of their tax bases and constitutional limits on their capacity to tax reduce their credibility if they promise to raise taxes in the future to service additional debts.

Still, many state governments acquire debts, and the danger that they will default raises the possibility that the federal government will feel obligated to assume their obligations. The problems of state banks in Brazil illustrate this point. The NFC can take this contingency into account by calculating the likelihood of default and the potential cost to the federal government. This contingent liability would then be figured into the council's calculation of the DCL in the same way as the contingent liabilities of the federal government itself. But expecting the federal government to assume the obligations of a state or municipality in default creates a serious moral hazard problem. In this case, efforts at fiscal control at the federal level may be jeopardized. The argument for statutory or constitutional restrictions on the ability of subnational governments to borrow is strongest under these circumstances.

The question is, then, under what circumstances would the central government tend to assume the liabilities of subcentral governments that are unable to pay their debts? Eichengreen and von Hagen (1995) argue that the risk of a bailout depends on the vertical fiscal structure of the federation. If the subcentral government has scope to raise taxes or cut public spending in order to generate resources to service and retire debts, the federal government can resist pressures for a bailout. But if states have restricted fiscal capacities because they cannot impose taxes and are therefore dependent on federal government transfers, it will be hard to enforce a no-bailout rule. In other words, the greater the dependence of subcentral governments on central government resources, the greater the bailout risk. In the most extreme situations, it may be desirable constitutionally to limit the borrowing capacity of subnational governments. But if the bailout risk is low, the NFC may need only to take the behavior of state and local governments into account in setting the DCL.

*How should the NFC deal with public enterprise debt?*

It may or may not be appropriate to think of public enterprise borrowing as part of overall public sector borrowing. If the government extends an explicit guarantee to public enterprise debt, this debt should be formally recognized as public sector obligations, and any increase should count toward the DCL. However, most guarantees are implicit, and the NFC will have to assess their expected value. Public enterprises that face hard budget constraints entail no liability for the government, and the NFC has no reason to factor these firms' borrowing into its calculations. However, bailout risk is higher in the presence of politically powerful enterprise managers, employers, and customers, when high economic costs result from disruptions to the flow of services the enterprise provides (as with power, water, telecommunications, sanitation, and transportation companies), and when government price caps prevent an enterprise from generating an adequate cash flow.

Clearly, enterprise borrowing can be thought of as a contingent liability for the government, the value of which should be factored into NFC forecasts of outlays. But there is no general argument for empowering the NFC to limit public enterprise borrowing. A contingent liability incurred by the government as a result of borrowing by a public enterprise affects only the composition of public spending. Since the composition of public spending falls in the domain of the congress and executive branch, any measure designed to limit borrowing by public enterprises should be adopted separately, not as part of the statute creating the NFC.

### How should the NFC deal with public investment?

Some countries account separately for current and capital spending by the public sector. They exempt capital spending from budgetary ceilings on the grounds that public investment projects generate revenues that will ultimately offset their costs. Should the DCL similarly exempt spending associated with public investment? Capital budgeting, which is essentially what this procedure implies, presents both conceptual and practical problems. While teachers' salaries are typically included in the ordinary budget, for instance, and the construction of school buildings in the capital budget, it is hard to argue that the second item contributes more than the first to future productivity and therefore has a larger public investment component. There is obvious scope for abusing the distinction between ordinary and capital spending, as well as an incentive for politicians to shift onto the capital budget items with low social returns.

The solution to this problem is for the NFC to apply the DCL to the budget as a whole and, in addition, to monitor the composition of spending. If, for example, the council sees that the share of productive public investment in total spending has increased, it may have grounds for revising its forecasts of economic growth or future tax revenues upward and for tailoring the current year's DCL accordingly. [9]

### How should the NFC treat deferred commitments?

By publishing projections of the revenue- and growth-generating capacity of public investment projects, the NFC can shape the congressional debate over public investment in a constructive way. The council can have the same effects on expenditure programs such as social security that imply spending commitments in the future. Elected officials, who are unlikely to still be in office when the bills come due, tend to put off the adjustments required for sound funding of such commitments. By publishing its estimates of those future spending commitments and explaining how they figure into its decisions of where to set the current DCL, the NFC can encourage—and if necessary, force—speedier adjustments to anticipated future fiscal developments.

*Dealing with arrears*

Budgetary arrears are a widespread problem in Latin America. Governments pass laws that not only authorize public expenditures but also specify permissible issues of public debt. When revenue turns out to be lower than expected or spending turns out to be higher, the gap shows up as arrears. How would an NFC handle them? Theoretically, it is not necessary to take special account of arrears. It is only important that obligations taking the form of arrears be included for accounting purposes in tabulations of public spending and debt. In practice, however, arrears pose a number of problems. First, the NFC must take special steps to ascertain their existence, since it may be in the interest of spending ministries to hide them. In addition, arrears sometimes threaten the stability of banking systems. Banks extend loans to contractors on public projects. When the budgetary outturn is unexpectedly bad and arrears accumulate, these contractors are forced to default on their debts, threatening the stability of intermediaries. This dynamic is likely to place special pressure on the NFC to accommodate the needs of contractors and their creditors.

Given the vulnerability of Latin American banking systems, governments often respond by paying arrears with bonds. This action takes place outside normal budgetary processes.[10] For a DCL to be effective, arrears must be counted as part of the deficit for the year in which they are incurred. In this way, refinancing does not involve an NFC decision, since the arrears have already been counted as part of the debt.

*Should the NFC oversee the composition of taxes and spending?*

The NFC should monitor the composition of taxes and spending and factor into its forecast the impact on such variables as economic growth, unemployment, and tax revenues. Using that forecast, it could tailor the current year's DCL to ensure appropriate adjustment to shocks, provide countercyclical stabilization, and offer tax-smoothing services. Beyond that, however, there is no reason why the NFC needs to be endowed with the power to determine the composition of taxes and spending.

*Should the NFC be responsible for debt management?*

The distinction between setting a ceiling on the overall budget deficit, which falls under the purview of the NFC, and setting the level and composition of taxes and expenditures, which remains in the domain of the congress and the executive branch, applies here as well. Debt service obligations can be thought of as part of the composition and level of public spending. As such, it falls logically within the domain of the executive branch and the congress and does not have to be made the responsibility of the NFC.

Still, even if it lacks the power to mandate debt-management practices, the NFC could offer recommendations. Latin American countries have limited access to multilateral and bilateral lending at relatively long and inexpensive terms. Beyond that, the supply curve of credit becomes steeper, often very significantly. When issuing its forecast of revenues and expenditures and justifying the DCL, the NFC would make explicit its assumptions about the availability of finance. It would need to pay attention to the relatively large impact of additional borrowing on the interest rate, since higher interest rates will raise the cost of servicing not only new but existing short-term debt that must be rolled over.[11]

The NFC will need to take this possibility into account in projecting the impact of current deficits on future debt service obligations. The existence of short-term debt also increases the danger of a Tesors-Bono-style debt run, in which investors refuse to roll over maturing obligations, forcing the government to buy them up to prevent a financial crisis. When large amounts of public debt are short term, the NFC may decide that deficits must be smaller to guard against this contingency. But the NFC need not be empowered to manage debt. Its ability to determine the DCL provides enough leverage to keep public finances sound.

### Credibility, accountability, and legitimacy

There are reasons to think that a congress and its constituency would embrace such a scheme. Countries acknowledge the advantages of delegating authority to independent central banks in the presence of incentive problems, to trade negotiators representing national rather than sectoral interests, and even to base-closing commissions. Such delegation stems from the recognition that political competition may limit cooperative solutions. Why should this principle not carry over to fiscal policy?

The authority of the NFC could be lent legitimacy through provisions similar to those required of independent central banks. Independent central banks are required to publish documents justifying their policy actions. Members of their boards are required to testify before congress. If their governors are found to have pursued agendas that are at variance with the public interest, the governors can be dismissed. The NFC could be similarly required to publish a statement explaining and justifying the DCL for the coming year. It could be required to submit a retrospective commentary of the preceding fiscal year to congress early in the subsequent budgetary round. Members of its board could be required to testify before congress at regular intervals and provide justification for their policy decisions. It is even conceivable that the members of the NFC could be dismissed by the congress as long as the DCL for the year remained in effect.

It is important to reemphasize that the NFC would not control fiscal policy. It would set a ceiling on the size of the deficit, but the level of spending and taxes, and the composition of both, would remain in the control of elected officials. The NFC's influence over fiscal policy would be more limited than an independent central bank's over monetary policy.

Since the basis for the NFC would be provided by simple or constitutional law, the congress would be able, with an appropriate majority, to pass a law abolishing the NFC and the budget process for which it provides. This action is the ultimate sanction that would prevent the NFC from pursuing its own agenda without democratic legitimation. While such an action would call into question the commitment of the executive branch and congress to stable and sound public finances, the history of independent central banks suggests that a congress would not take this decision lightly. The danger of making dismissal too easy is that it would undermine the credibility of the NFC's policy. Further, council members subject to ready dismissal might be reluctant to exercise independent judgment. The threshold for dismissal must be set high enough to avoid undermining the NFC's independence and autonomy, but the congressional requirements (in terms of the number of votes required) for making this decision should be the same as those required to revoke the law establishing the NFC itself. Countries with differing preferences for trading fiscal policy credibility for political accountability will wish to set this threshold at differing levels.

Ultimately, if the NFC demonstrably improves the conduct of fiscal policy, it will gain credibility, legitimacy, and respect. We have emphasized that measures recommended in the European context to buttress credibility may backfire if they are applied too mechanically in Latin America—for example, requiring automatic across-the-board spending cuts when the DCL is violated may entail such high political and economic costs that it undermines credibility. In Latin America, where international organizations have played a prominent role in the process of economic reform, there may be a role for the International Monetary Fund (IMF) in buttressing the credibility of the NFC by supporting its establishment and endorsing its DCL. If the DCL receives the IMF's stamp of approval, the government's precarious access to credit markets will be strengthened even more dramatically than it would be by the simple creation of the NFC. This development will reinforce the advantages of the new fiscal institution and help cultivate political support.

## Conclusion

Rather than recommending budgetary arrangements for Latin America that have worked well in the United States and Western Europe, we have advocated, based on Wildavsky's warning, [12] the creation of a kind of fiscal council that does not exist in the advanced industrial countries. The structure of this NFC is intended to address specific problems that arise in the Latin American context. The council is designed to deal with the consequences for deficit spending of political fragmentation and instability. Where governmental instability creates a bias toward dealing with problems in the short term, it is fashioned to superimpose on the budgetary process a medium-term planning horizon. It is structured to relax financial constraints and enhance access to international credit markets for governments that have difficulty obtaining credit because they are unable to commit to balancing the budget over the credit cycle. The NFC is constructed to encourage adjustment to shocks in a macroeconomic environment that is buffeted by swings in inflationary expectations, international terms of trade, and real interest rates. In other words, the institutional innovations we recommend are expressly designed to take into account important features of the Latin American habitat.

The reform of fiscal institutions, by itself, will not solve all problems of macroeconomic instability in Latin America.[13] The bias toward deficits and slow adjustment fiscal policies display are but two factors contributing to macroeconomic volatility in the region. Monetary stability and a climate of low and stable inflation are also needed to minimize disruptions to economic activity. An exchange rate regime that prevents the need for major adjustments in a climate of crisis would buttress both real and financial stability. Adequate capital requirements and prudential supervision of banks would prevent financial crises from disrupting economic activity. Prudent borrowing on international capital markets would insulate economies from destabilizing capital market shocks. Greater export diversification would help to reduce terms-of-trade risk. And heightened political stability would enhance the credibility of policy commitments and allow governments to formulate economic strategies in light of medium-term targets.

Although the reform of budgetary institutions cannot achieve all of these goals, there are important synergies between fiscal reform and reform in other domains. Improved fiscal policies will strengthen the central bank's capacity to pursue stable monetary policies, just as low inflation will simplify fiscal planning. Stable fiscal policy will prevent swings in government spending from destabilizing the exchange rate, while a realistic exchange rate will avoid disrupting fiscal planning with forced devaluations. Minimizing the increase in public spending when capital flows in will limit the need for fiscal adjustment when capital flows out. Above all, fiscal and political stability have the capacity to create a virtuous circle of economic growth for Latin America.

## Notes

1. For discussion to this effect see Wildavsky, 1986, chapter 2.
2. An analogy is the problem faced by the patron of a restaurant. The menu offers two courses: chicken for $10 and lobster for $50. An individual dining by himself might prefer chicken, feeling that lobster was not worth the $40 premium. But consider now the same individual going to the restaurant with nine companions. If he expects the others to choose chicken, he has the choice of also having chicken for $10 or instead having lobster for $14 ((9x10+50)/10). At this relative price he prefers lobster. If instead the others ask for lobster, he then can choose lobster for $50 or chicken for $46. At this relative price he again prefers lobster. So no matter what his companions prefer, he will order lobster if the decision is made in a collective context, while he would have ordered chicken had he chosen independently. This problem is endemic to public finance, where decisions are made about public goods, the consumption of which is not chosen independently and which cannot be financed through user charges.
3. See Hausmann, Powell, and Rigobon (1993).
4. Eichengreen and Bayoumi (1994) document that U.S. states that are subject to stringent balanced budget restrictions do relatively little fiscal stabilization over the cycle.
5. This approach can be thought of as analogous to appointing independent central bankers and giving them narrow mandates.
6. This can be thought of as analogous to the impact of impending binding arbitration on the conduct of pre-arbitration labor-management negotiations.
7. In Venezuela in 1993 and Ecuador more recently, incumbents were inclined toward policies of fiscal rectitude, but the markets were concerned about the possible inclinations of future presidents. Another example is the traumatic transition in Argentina between Alfonsín and Menem. Our argument is that an NFC would constrain any inclination of incoming governments toward deficits, thereby reducing preelection uncertainty and fiscal jitters.
8. See McKinnon (1995). However, in the Latin American context, states and provinces often possess their own banks, and may be able to create highly liquid liabilities or force the central banks into bailing them out. The argument for separating the central bank from the finance ministry at the national level could justify eliminating state-controlled financial institutions.
9. This situation is especially apt to occur if the deficit is related to investment projects that are likely to generate large additional cash resources in the near future, so that cutting them would reduce fiscal solvency. For example, on completion a bridge will allow the government to collect tolls from users. Meeting the DCL by cutting spending on an almost completed bridge will affect future revenues.

168

10. In practice, contractors typically ask for a loan rollover, and the banks renew and increase the extent of the obligation in expectation of future payment. This can create a spiral of continuously increasing nonperforming loans, which are hidden by rollovers for an extended period of time. Often these pre-existing debts are refinanced at longer terms by issuing government bonds. Contractors receive those bonds and give them to banks, thus canceling bank loans. Typically this refinancing occurs outside the budgetary process, since it takes place in response to arrears developed in previous budgetary rounds. This allows arrears to effectively undermine fiscal ceilings.

11. In addition, the NFC needs to worry about the tendency for international bank loan agreements to feature grace periods. The presence of a grace period means that the cost of debt service is back-loaded, depressing current spending obligations relative to future ones, *ceteris paribus*. The NFC will want to publish its spending forecasts to encourage the congress to take this into account, and reduce the current DCL to build up a surplus to use later for additional debt service obligations.

12. "Before prescribing the budgeting procedures of rich countries for poor ones, it might be well to bear in mind the obstinate waywardness often displayed by institutions when transplanted from their native habitat" (Wildavsky 1986).

13. The policy agenda to reduce volatility is discussed in IDB (1995) and in Hausmann and Reisen (1996).

# References

Aizenman, Joshua, and Ricardo Hausmann. 1995. "Inflation and Budgetary Discipline." National Bureau of Economic Research (NBER). Working Paper No. 5537. Harvard University, Cambridge, Mass.

Alesina, Alberto. 1989. "Politics and Business Cycles in Industrial Democracies," *Economic Policy* 8:55–98.

———, and Allen Drazen. 1991. "Why Are Stabilizations Delayed?" *American Economic Review* 81.

———, and Roberto Perotti. 1994. "Budget Deficits and Budget Institutions." Unpublished manuscript, Harvard University and Columbia University.

———, Ricardo Hausmann, Rudolf Hommes, and Ernesto Stein. 1995. "Budget Institutions and Fiscal Performance in Latin America." OCE Working Paper.

Barro, Robert. 1979. "On the Determination of Public Debt," *Journal of Political Economy* 87:940–71.

Buiter, Willem, Giancarlo Corsetti, and Nouriel Roubini. 1993. "Excessive Deficits: Sense and Nonsense in the Treaty of Maastricht," *Economic Policy* 16:57–100.

Cukierman, Alex, Sebastian Edwards, and Guido Tabellini. 1989. "Seignorage and Political Instability." NBER Working Paper No. 3199. Harvard University, Cambridge, Mass.

Eichengreen, Barry, and Tamim Bayoumi. 1994. "The Political Economy of Fiscal Restrictions: Implications for Europe from the United States," *European Economic Review* 38:781–92.

———, and Jürgen von Hagen. 1995. "Fiscal Restrictions and Monetary Union: Rationales, Reservations, and Reforms," *Empirica* (forthcoming).

———, Jürgen von Hagen, and Ian Harden. 1995. "Hurdles Too High: Improving Budget Procedures is the Best Preparation for EMU," *Financial Times* (28 November):16.

Gavin, Michael K., Ricardo Hausmann, Roberto Perotti, and Ernesto Talvi. 1996. "Fiscal Policy in Latin America: Volatility, Procyclicality, and Limited Creditworthiness." Working Paper, mimeo, Inter-American Development Bank, Washington, D.C.

Goldstein, Morris, and Geoffrey Woglom. 1994. "Market-Based Fiscal Discipline in Monetary Unions: Evidence from the U.S. Municipal Bond Market." In Matthew Canzoneri, Vittorio Grilli, and Paul R. Masson, eds., *Establishing a Central Bank: Issues in Europe and Lessons from the U.S.* Cambridge: Cambridge University Press.

Hausmann, Ricardo, and Michael K. Gavin. 1996. "Securing Stability in a Volatile Region: The Policy Challenge." In Ricardo Hausmann and Helmut Reisen, eds., *Securing Stability and Growth in Latin America.* Paris: OECD-IDB.

———, Andrew Powell, and Roberto Rigobon. 1993. "An Optimal Spending Rule Facing Oil Income Uncertainty." In Eduardo Engel and Patricio Meller, eds., *External Shocks and Stabilization Mechanisms.* Washington, D.C.: Inter-American Development Bank.

———, and Helmut Reisen. 1996. *Securing Stability and Growth in Latin America.* Paris: OECD-IDB.

———, and Ernesto Stein. 1996. "Searching for the Right Budgetary Institutions for a Volatile Region." In Ricardo Hausmann and Helmut Reisen, eds., *Securing Stability and Growth in Latin America.* Paris: OECD-IDB.

Hibbs, Douglas. 1977. "Political Parties and Macroeconomic Policy," *American Political Science Review* 7:1467–87.

Inter-American Development Bank. 1995. *Overcoming Volatility.* 1995 Annual Report, Washington, D.C.

McKinnon, Ronald I. 1995. "Comment: A Fiscally Consistent Proposal for Reforming the European Monetary System." In Peter B. Renen, ed., *Understanding Interdependence: The Macroeconomics of the Open Economy.* Princeton: Princeton University Press.

Muagrave, Richard. 1959. *The Theory of Public Finance.* New York: McGraw Hill.

Nordhaus, William. 1975. "The Political Business Cycle," *Review of Economic Studies* 42:169–90.

Obstfeld, Maurice. 1993. "Destabilizing Effects of Exchange Rate Escape Clauses." NBER Working Paper No. 3603. Harvard University, Cambridge, Mass.

Premchand, A. 1983. *Government Budgeting and Expenditure Controls: Theory and Practice.* Washington, D.C.: International Monetary Fund.

Saint-Paul, Gilles. 1994. "Monetary Policy in Economic Transition: Lessons from the French Post-War Experience," *European Economic Review* 38:891–99.

Tabellini, Guido, and Alberto Alesina. 1990. "Voting on the Budget Deficit," *American Economic Review* 80:37–49.

von Hagen, Jürgen. 1992. "Fiscal Arrangements in a Monetary Union: Evidence from the U.S." In Donald E. Fair and Christian de Boissieu, eds., *Fiscal Policy, Taxation and the Financial System in an Increasingly Integrated Europe.* Kluwer: Dordrecht.

———, and Barry Eichengreen. 1996. "Fiscal Restraints, Federalism and European Monetary Union: Is the Excessive Deficit Procedure Counterproductive?" *American Economic Review* (forthcoming).

———, and Ian J. Harden. 1994. "National Budget Processes and Fiscal Performance," *European Economy Reports and Studies* 3:311–408.

Wildavsky, Aaron. 1986. *Budgeting: A Comparative Theory of Budgetary Processes*. New Brunswick: Transaction Books.

Williamson, John. 1986. *IMF Conditionality*. Washington, D.C.: Institute for International Economics.

## Comments on "Reforming budgetary institutions in Latin America: the case for a national fiscal council," by Eichengreen, Hausmann, and von Hagen

*Juan L. Cariaga*

I would like to begin by congratulating the authors, Ricardo Hausmann and others, on this splendid piece of work, which is the result of lengthy research into the institutional reform of the budget process in Latin America. Their identification of problems is entirely on the mark, and the analysis of Latin America's reality is up to date. The presentation is informative and easy to understand. The proposal itself is very imaginative and, if applied in a constitutional manner, could solve Latin America's problems in the areas of budgetary credibility and stability.

By way of comment I offer the following remarks:

First, as the authors indicate, they are specifically not recommending budgetary arrangements for Latin America that have worked well in the United States or Western Europe. Instead they advocate the creation of a type of NFC that does not exist in industrial countries. This proposal is bound to be very eye catching. It creates the impression that the recommended solution is designed to respond only to the specific problems of Latin American countries, where the traditional methods of budgetary control and execution have presumably not worked. If this impression is correct, in my view it represents a serious weakness of the approach—that is, a focus on a cultural rather than an economic problem. Such a focus begs one question: is Latin America incapable of obeying budgetary discipline in the same way as the United States and the countries of Western Europe?

Second, the authors' proposal raises a legal question and an issue of constitutional principle. Is it constitutionally possible to reduce the powers of congress in budget matters? While this question could lead us into an endless debate on constitutional issues that this commentator neither wishes nor is qualified to launch, we cannot lose sight of the fact that parliaments were established for the main purpose of taking away the monarch's prerogative of levying taxes and deciding how the proceeds were to be spent. The modern history of most Western countries is full of civil and internal struggles and conflicts culminating in the demand that elected representatives in a parliamentary body be given these rights.

The proposal does not abolish this right, since it does not transfer the level or composition of expenditure or taxation to the NFC. It nonetheless involves the establishment of an independent body with supracongressional powers to limit the maximum allowable increase in general government debt and even to increase taxes. To some extent, it curtails the constitutional powers of the elected representatives of the people. One can even argue, at the extreme, that the power to create deficits, which are a form of inflationary tax, is also a prerogative of the congress, among whose most important powers is the right to approve taxes.

As already noted, the issue thus raised is a legal and above all a constitutional one, although laws and constitutions can, of course, always be changed. It is important to remember that an irrefutable constitutional principle holds that no branch of the state can be allowed to trespass on the powers of another branch without affecting the proper balance of power.

By way of illustration, let me briefly mention a case in which the budgetary difficulties Hausmann and others discuss were eased somewhat, without any damage to constitutional precepts. In 1986, while implementing a stabilization program, Bolivia was in the problematic position of trying to administer a budget at a time when government receipts were being seriously affected by external shocks and hyperinflation. In these circumstances, the congress was approving expenditures that the executive had to carry out, despite the fact that it lacked sufficient receipts to do so.

The Bolivian government's solution to the problem was to limit the execution of expenditures to the amount of revenues. However, since under the constitution the executive branch was obligated to execute all the expenditures authorized by congress, the government chose to present to congress for approval an annual expenditure statement that contained both expenditures executed and expenditures not executed. In this way, the executive branch released itself from the obligation to execute all the authorized expenditures when it lacked the necessary receipts to do so.

The lesson learned from Bolivia (and other countries) is that whenever there is a need to apply political economy, institutions are not as important as the political willingness to accomplish the objectives. Nevertheless, I would like to stress that this work by Hausmann and others constitutes a serious, well-considered, and above all rigorous proposal. The authors have spent a great deal of time examining other recommendations made with the same purpose. Their diagnosis of the budgetary situation and problems in Latin America cannot be faulted, and the study deserves to be analyzed and discussed as a significant contribution to the question of the continent's budget problems.

## Comments on "Reforming budgetary institutions in Latin America: the case for a national fiscal council," by Eichengreen, Hausmann, and von Hagen

*Jonathan D. Breul*

The authors present an intriguing proposal for institutional reform of the fiscal decisionmaking process in Latin America. Their "national fiscal council" does not exist in the advanced industrial countries but rather is expressly designed to address problems that arise in the Latin American context.

### The role of the central budget office

The NFC would not control fiscal policy. It would set a ceiling on the size of the deficit, with the level of spending and taxes (and the composition of both) remaining in the control of elected officials. Precisely because of this role, an NFC would have profound implications for the role of the central budget office. Depending on how it is structured, an NFC could compromise the ability of a robust, central budgetary authority to integrate fiscal and control issues with the policymaking process.

#### Central budget process

It is generally accepted that a well-developed central budget process should serve three complementary objectives (see Campos and Pradhan 1996):

- Controlling the totals by assisting in aggregate control (that is, sound fiscal policy)

- Establishing priorities by making allocations between competing functions and activities in accordance with government priorities

- Improving operational performance by seeking efficiency and effectiveness in the implementation of the government's programs

The first of these objectives, achievement of aggregate fiscal control, is the key role of the central budget office and the focus of the paper by Hausmann and others. But a focus on this role alone is insufficient. Fiscal control must be supplemented by a concern with resource allocation and public expenditure management. Effective public sector management depends on all three functions working together in a complementary fashion. And, important for this volume, the second and third objectives should rely heavily on the use of evaluation.

#### Lessons from OECD countries

Of course, there is no absolute answer to the question of whether a particular organizational structure would help or hinder efforts to improve public management. Not only are there significant cultural and political differences among countries, but no single model of reform emerges from experience. Nevertheless, lessons from OECD countries suggest that improved integration of budget and management decision-making is the most productive and effective approach to a better understanding of the relationship between investments and outcomes.

At a March 1996 symposium of the OECD (1997), ministers responsible for public management met to identify common features of successful governance. What became apparent was that efforts to improve public management are likely to fail if management considerations are seen as distinct from (or worse, in opposition to) budgetary policies. Successful countries have seen these efforts as inherently budgetary and worked to coordinate them with policies. This coordination includes controlling the costs of direct government operations, providing financial flexibility to permit resources to be used more effectively, financing essential training, reallocating tasks to the private or voluntary sectors, and assessing performance. Thus, these countries see improved public management not as an end in itself but as one aspect of a government strategy designed to support sound fiscal policy, improve service to the public, rationalize the distribution of tasks between the private and public sectors, and lower the cost of government.

### Institutional arrangements

In the OECD context, it is clear that countries successful in carrying out reforms to improve public management have lodged responsibility in two locations:

- "Centers" of government such as the prime minister's office (or in the case of the United States the executive office of the president, or the White House)

- Central management bodies such a finance ministries

In some cases, new institutions have been set up. In others, new responsibilities have been allocated to existing institutions. Several countries have made reform initiatives shared responsibilities.

Regardless of where they have located these responsibilities, OECD countries seem to be moving in a direction opposite to the one proposed in the paper by Hausmann and his colleagues. These countries do not see "getting the aggregates right" as sufficient. There is a strong sense that they need an integrated, rather than fragmented, approach to central budgeting and management.

### Implications for evaluation

Evaluation has helped us better understand the efficacy of the traditional budgeting tools, such as ex ante specification of the items of expenditure and allocation of the increment. The question, then, is what evaluation can do to help the Bank or borrowing countries develop the "right" institutional approach.

I would suggest that there are a number of institutional questions that merit some attention. For example:

■    What makes for good and bad central budget institutional arrangements?

■    How do these arrangements relate to fiscal performance, program effectiveness, and policy coherence?

■    Under what circumstances, and to what extent, do these three goals work?

■    In practice, how do we keep the three goals from getting in one another's way?

■    Each goal requires different types of information, work orientations, and skills. How do we get all three to work in tandem?

As appealing as an NFC may be, I am uncomfortable fragmenting the central budget process until I know more about what works and what doesn't.

## References

OECD. 1997. Ministerial Symposium on the Future of Public Services. Paris, March 1996.

Campos, José Edgardo, and Sanjay Pradhan. 1996. "Budgetary Institutions and Expenditure Outcomes: Binding Governments to Fiscal Performance." Policy Research Working Paper No. 1646. World Bank, Washington, D.C.

## Floor discussion on "Reforming budgetary institutions in Latin America: the case for a national fiscal council"

Daniel Artana opened the discussion with three questions. First, he wanted to know how enabling legislation will be passed if a country accepts the idea of an NFC. Second, if the necessary legislation is passed, what will keep special interests from coopting the council? In asking this question, he drew a parallel to a tenured supreme court, which can be biased. Third, he asked whether the council should be made a federal body that can enforce budgets at both the national and provincial levels. If the council operates at the federal level only, it will have a limited effect.

Anwar Shah questioned the feasibility of NFCs, given the structural constraints of many governments. If a parliamentary body combines the executive and legislative functions, a country will have a bureaucratic agency with no elected mandate. In such a situation, how can the agency be held accountable? Under an alternate model such as Maastricht, budgetary deficits cannot exceed 60 percent of GDP, so a federal structure may not be the most effective. In fact, the first Australian Loan Council failed because of its federal structure. The findings on the new Australian Loan Council are more encouraging, but its role is consultative—to share information with the private sector. Why not have rules rather than a bureaucratic structure that sets annual limits? Societal norms may offer stronger possibilities for enforcing fiscal discipline.

A participant from the European Commission noted that the European Union does not have fiscal councils that infringe on government credibility. He observed that the Maastricht agreement creates a double commitment. First, it enshrines the European Union's internal institutional constraints; if a country wants to join, it must stick to the agreement. Second, if a country exceeds the target once it is "in the club," it must pay a fine, an arrangement that holds countries to certain limits.

Sanjay Pradhan commented on Jonathan Breul's three levels of budgetary performance (controlling the totals, establishing priorities, and improving operational performance). The last two are important, he noted, because all three levels are interrelated, and the first one may be difficult to put into operations without the other two. A hierarchical structure may help with control, but a lack of collegiality can impede the circulation of information. World Bank and IMF arrangements for cutting spending can also interfere with setting strategic priorities.

Malcolm Holmes, though supportive of Pradhan's three levels of budgetary performance, then posed two questions. First, he suggested that New Zealand's Fiscal Responsibility Act leads to greater predictability. Does the type of relationship common in Latin America between the finance minister and fiscal policy place too much emphasis on one individual—the finance minister? Budget and policy planning should be conducted separately, because bringing them together creates an institutional problem. Second, referring to institutional evaluation, Holmes asked what arrangements have been made to help fiscal councils function as effective tools in improving institutional performance.

Mustafa Nabli noted that creating an executive council "embeds" an advocate for fiscal control. This role differs from that of a ministry of finance, which is responsible for tax structures. In Tunisia, a council has effectively empowered an advocate for fiscal control. But in establishing an NFC, he warned, waiving a balanced budget rule may not be the best idea, since the council will be contentious.

Peter Laws noted that the New Zealand central bank structure is almost the opposite of a council's. The government still sets the objective and thus has an impact. If the government reverses fiscal incentives and the benefits of extra spending appear quickly, fiscal incentives that govern behavior disappear. If targets are changed, there is a price to pay. The New Zealand minister of finance investigated whether the same structure would work for fiscal policy. But he found that there were too many variables to set a rigid target, which would change the time horizon for fiscal policy and make it necessary to publish multiyear projections and explain changes.

In response, Hausmann called the New Zealand Fiscal Responsibility Act "insightful." It takes the discipline function of disclosure to its highest level. But it is not unique in, for instance, trying to ensure the sustainability of fiscal accounts. Independent central banks can discipline monetary policy with floating exchange rates. Countries with central banks lack an independent, autonomous institution like the New Zealand treasury, which is free of outside interference.

On the question of whether he would be happier in a central budget office with a national fiscal council, Hausmann stated that if the political contentiousness of the aggregate were taken away, all that would be left would be the technical sophistication of the budgeting. Removing the issue of volatility from the picture would eliminate the problem that needs to be addressed. Volatility makes setting a target rate unfeasible; stabilizing the budget deficit means stabilizing government spending and tax rates.

On the points made by Juan Cariaga, Hausmann commented that the constitutional parameters must be tackled first. Chile has turned in the best performance, and it has no federal structure. He responded to the question concerning enabling legislation for a fiscal council by asking, in turn, what might make a congress want to vote for it. The participant seemed to be suggesting that the legislative body might not want to take back powers on fiscal matters. On the question of whether special interests might try to coopt a council, Hausmann noted that constitutions exist to protect the minority from the majority. No legislative body can afford to bequeath too much of a debt to the future. He asked what is wrong with moving averages, which require a referee—in this case, the fiscal council. In some countries, disclosure may be enough, but there must be some autonomy and some simple rules.

# 9. Credible regulatory policy: options and evaluation

Brian Levy

*Workable approaches to regulation vary from country to country, depending on a country's underlying institutional capabilities. In particular, the design of regulatory practices must take account of the quality of the judicial system, the checks and balances between the executive and legislative branches, the competence of the civil service and its insulation from political influence, and the restraining influence of civil society.*

Skillfully designed and implemented regulation can help societies overcome market failures and influence market outcomes for public purposes. Regulation can help protect the environment by reducing the pollution and other negative externalities that are a by-product of some private business. It can protect consumers and workers from some of the consequences of information asymmetries. It can foster competition and innovation while constraining the abuse of monopoly power. And, more broadly, it can help win social acceptance of the fairness and legitimacy of market outcomes.

In designing regulatory policy, market failure needs to be balanced by a recognition of the likelihood of government failure. One well-recognized consequence of government failure is that regulation may lead to inefficient patterns of resource allocation. A second consequence—less recognized, but highlighted in this paper—is that government failure can undermine confidence in the regulatory system and hence private investment and private sector development in general.

As the paper will show, since countries differ from one another in the nature and extent of government failure, workable approaches to regulation should also vary from country to country. The key to successful regulatory policy is thus to match a country's regulatory role (what it does and what tools it uses) to its underlying institutional capabilities. Concretely, as the paper will argue:

■ When regulation is desirable, credibility must take precedence over content. Without a credible commitment to pursuing the social objectives specified on paper, regulation will be unworkable and the cleverness of regulatory design irrelevant.

■ Flexible approaches that provide regulators with substantial discretion may be less successful in countries where there are fewer checks and balances to restrain arbitrary decisionmaking. The latter group of countries may be able to make binding commitments to private investors only at the cost of radically constraining their room to respond flexibly to change.

■ In some countries, the institutional basis for regulation anchored in formal rules may simply not be present. Under such circumstances, alternative approaches that give more emphasis to competitive pressures and citizen participation should receive particular attention.

As the final section of this paper will discuss, when the importance of balancing role and capability is brought to center stage, the challenge of distinguishing between good and bad regulatory initiatives—and hence the challenge of evaluation—is a complex one.

## The quest for regulatory credibility

Economists have invested enormous efforts over many decades in devising regulatory schemes that on paper are capable of yielding outcomes with higher social returns than unregulated private markets. In practice, it has often proved difficult to persuade politicians to enact these schemes. Yet even getting formal rules that seem beneficial onto the books does not automatically translate into a regulatory system that is credible to both citizens and private firms. For citizens, credibility implies confidence that desired social objectives are indeed being pursued, not just promulgated into formal law. For private firms, credibility implies confidence in the stability of the system—that having sunk money into irreversible investments, firms will not find themselves suddenly confronted with adverse changes in the regulatory rules of the game. Credibility results when expectations are clear as to what kind of behavior is or is not acceptable and when participants have confidence that these expectations will remain reasonably stable over time. Without credibility, private investment will be low. (For a general discussion of the relation between credibility and private investment, see Borner, Brunetti, and Weder 1995; for a series of applications in the context of regulation, see Levy and Spiller 1996.)

Formal rules need to be precisely specified if they are to provide a credible anchor for a regulatory system. Further, the mechanism for rule making (which could take the form of either legislation or firm-specific, legally binding contracts) needs to be reasonably resilient to pressures for change. And there need to be institutions (generally a judiciary) that credibly enforce both the specific restraints and the restraints on system changes.

Within these broad parameters, a spectrum of options exists that countries can use to develop formal rules to strengthen the credibility and content of their regulatory systems. Countries can choose:

■ To adopt systems of "process regulation" that make little effort to specify desirable outcomes up front, instead specifying formally what process must be followed in reaching decisions

■ To embody in laws or legally binding contracts "content regulation," which specifies in precise detail the terms under which private firms have the right to operate

■ To underpin process or content regulation with extraterritorial mechanisms of conflict resolution, including international arbitration or third-party guarantees, to protect private firms against direct expropriation and other noncommercial risks

These options vary in the extent to which they offer regulators and firms the flexibility to adapt the system to changing circumstances. Other things being equal, more flexibility is preferable to less. In practice, though, the workability of alternative options varies with a country's background and institutions, including:

- The quality of its judicial system

- The extent to which checks and balances are built into its legislative and executive structures

- The administrative capability and insulation from political influence of its technocracy

- The restraining influence of informal norms and social capital

The discussion of utility regulation that follows will show that some countries have background institutions capable of supporting very flexible formal regulatory systems. However, others may have to choose between refraining from actively making and enforcing rules and relying on more rigid options. Indeed, as the example of environmental regulation illustrates, under some circumstances it may be better to focus not on the formal rules themselves, but rather on other ways to alter the incentives confronting private firms.

### Regulating utilities: formal rules as commitment mechanisms

Utilities have certain characteristics that make fostering credibility especially challenging. Utility services have important economies of scale and scope, implying that the number of providers of basic services will be small, with significant accompanying risks of abuse of monopoly power. Utility services typically have a broad range of domestic users, so that utility pricing has a political component. And most utilities' assets are specific and cannot be redeployed to other uses, suggesting that utilities operate willingly as long as they can recover their working costs (even if they cannot recover their sunk investments). For this reason, they are especially vulnerable to administrative expropriation—for example, when regulations set prices at below long-run average costs. A well-designed regulatory system can enable countries to meet these challenges successfully.

New opportunities for competition have emerged in both the telecommunications and power industries. In telecommunications, dozens of countries throughout the Americas, Europe, and Asia (plus a few in Africa, including Ghana and South Africa) have introduced competition into long distance, cellular, and value-added services. A few countries, including Chile and El Salvador, are exploring options for creating competition in local fixed-link networks. Power generation (though not transmission or distribution) is also increasingly viewed as an arena for competition. In China, Indonesia, Malaysia, and the Philippines, private investors are making major additions to generation capacity through independent power projects, thus alleviating acute shortages and enabling private finance to fill the gap resulting from shortfalls in public resources.

Despite the rise of competition, the need for regulation persists, for three reasons. First, regulation can facilitate competition. In competitive telecommunications and power markets, most services are not offered through exclusive networks of single suppliers. Telecommunications signals traverse multiple network segments owned by different operators. Similar problems of interconnection also affect the electricity sector, where generators supply customers through common-carrier transmission lines. Regulation is generally needed to ensure ready interconnection and to prevent incumbents from extracting monopoly rents from new entrants.

Second—and here we come to a country-specific rationale—political realities can inhibit competition and prolong the need for regulation. In many countries, utility prices for selected groups of consumers are set below cost, and the utilities subsidize these losses with profits earned elsewhere in the system. In the Philippines, the response to this dilemma has been to permit only limited entry into the highly profitable long-distance service industry and to require entrants to invest in extending the underdeveloped and unprofitable local fixed-link network.[1] In Jamaica, a single telecommunications provider was awarded a 25-year concession in 1988 to operate the entire system. The provider was required to extend the unprofitable local fixed-link network with revenues from the highly profitable long distance network (Spiller and Sampson 1996). There is continuing debate, though, about whether Jamaica, with its political constraints, could have retained room for competition in some value-added services. Had it been able to, it could have preserved at least a modicum of pressure for innovation and productivity improvements in an era when telecommunications was undergoing rapid global technological changes. Since responses to the dilemmas of cross-subsidization and price rebalancing like those adopted in the Philippines and Jamaica imply continuing restraints on competition, regulation continues to be called for.

A third reason—again country-specific—for continuing regulation is that competition may not eliminate the risks to private investors of administrative expropriation. As long as utility operators are large and their assets cannot be redeployed, the utilities remain potentially vulnerable to punitive price and other regulations. Consequently, countries without a track record of respecting property rights may find it difficult to attract private investors into utilities, regardless of any commitment to competition in utility markets. A well-designed regulatory commitment mechanism can offer the reassurance that potential investors need.

A workable regulatory system for utilities needs to balance the goals of constraining monopoly power, responding flexibly to technological changes, and providing enough assurances against arbitrariness to attract private investors. No single approach will yield the optimal balance for all countries. Where the fit between institutions and regulatory approach has been good, countries have attracted private investment into utilities; where the fit has been bad, attracting investment has been difficult. Getting the fit right has sometimes required countries to depart from textbook prescriptions for regulating utility prices.

A cross-country comparison of telecommunications reform illustrates the range of options between restraint and flexibility from which countries can choose as they put in place regulatory systems capable of attracting private investment. At one extreme are industrial countries such as New Zealand and the United Kingdom. In these countries, institutional checks on regulatory arbitrariness are strong enough to permit experimentation with highly flexible regulatory approaches and still attract substantial private investment. The United Kingdom has experimented with a flexible price-cap approach to reform. Gross fixed capital formation in British Telecom, which had been stable before privatization in 1984, increased over the next six years at a real annual average rate of 16 percent. By the turn of the decade, real annual investment was more than double what it had been before privatization (Galal and others 1994; Spiller and Vogelsang 1996).

Further along the spectrum, Jamaica represents an intermediate case. Its background institutions have enabled the country to put in place regulatory commitment mechanisms capable of attracting sustained private investment, but at the cost of limiting flexibility. Since independence, the country's telecommunications sector has been on a regulatory roller coaster, thriving when the country is willing to forego flexibility, but lagging when the country tilts toward flexibility at the expense of commitment (box 9.1).

Unlike Jamaica, the Philippines has only recently been able to put in place commitment mechanisms capable of credibly signaling that the rules of the game will endure beyond the term of the president in office. Consequently, from the late 1950s until the early 1990s, the country's private telecommunications utility repeatedly followed a political investment cycle. Investment was high immediately following the inauguration of a government aligned with the group controlling the utility. It tailed off in the later years of the regime and stagnated when its relations with the group in power were more distant (Esfahani 1996).

The long-term goal for countries with background institutions incapable of supporting any credible commitment must be to strengthen their domestic institutional arrangements, with improvements in judicial credibility often the first order of business. In the short term, one option to help countries with weak background institutions attract private investment in utilities is to substitute an international mechanism for the missing national foundations. Options here include "take-or-pay" contracts that can be enforced offshore and guarantee programs along the lines of those offered by the World Bank, which protect private investors and lenders against noncommercial risks, including administrative expropriation.

The trade-off between credibility and flexibility can also constrain countries' decisions on choices for regulating utility prices in market segments that are potentially subject to monopoly abuse. Take the choice between rate-of-return (ROR) regulation and price-cap regulation. As implemented in the United States, ROR regulation has long been known to cause inefficient behavior, inducing firms to invest excessively and pay little attention to the efficiency with which they use resources. Price-cap regulation gives utilities an incentive to be efficient and can encourage innovation, but it delegates substantial discretionary power to the regulator. In the United Kingdom, telecommunications and electricity regulators impose an umbrella ceiling on utility prices that is based on the annual rate of price inflation ($RPI$) minus an adjustment factor ($X$), or $RPI$-$X$. The regulators decide on the level of the adjustment factor and can change it at will. The United Kingdom's regulator is constrained by systemic checks and bal-

BOX 9.1: TELECOMMUNICATIONS REGULATION IN JAMAICA

During much of the colonial period and in the years immediately following independence, the terms under which Jamaica's largest telecommunications utility operated were specified in a legally binding, precisely specified 40-year license contract. Then, as now, the ultimate court of appeal for Jamaica's independent, well-functioning judiciary was the Privy Council in the United Kingdom. This system was adequate to ensure steady growth of telecommunications services, and the number of subscribers trebled between 1950 and 1962. Yet newly independent Jamaica chafed under the apparent restrictiveness of a concession arrangement that afforded virtually no opportunity for democratic participation. Consequently, in 1966 the country established the Jamaica Public Utility Commission. Modeled on the U.S. system, the utility commission held regular public hearings and was afforded broad scope to base its regulatory decisions on inputs from a wide variety of stakeholders.

- However, Jamaica lacked the background institutions needed to make a regulatory system based on a utility commission workable. The United States has a variety of constraints on regulatory discretion (including well-developed rules of administrative process and constitutional protections on property). Jamaica had virtually no checks and balances on commission decisions. The result was that price controls became progressively more punitive—to the point that in 1975 Jamaica's largest private telecommunications operator was relieved to sell its assets to the government. In 1987, after a decade of underinvestment, Jamaica reprivatized its telecommunications utility, this time using a precisely specified, legally binding license contract similar to those used prior to 1965. In the 3 subsequent years, average annual investment was more than 3 times what it had been over the previous 15 years.

ances: any decisions that the utility opposes must be cleared by both the country's Monopolies and Mergers Commission and the Secretary of State for Trade and Industry. If countries such as Jamaica (box 9.1) with weaker checks and balances sought to adopt this type of regulation, private investors might reasonably expect the X-factor to increase dramatically at the first-point renewal of the price cap. Consequently, investors would either not invest or require very high rates that ensured a quick payback (Spiller and Vogelsang 1996; Bradley and Price 1988; Littlechild 1983).

The need to ensure credibility partly explains why some countries have adopted approaches to utility regulation that appear, at least superficially, less attractive than *RPI-X*:

- Jamaica incorporated U.S.-style ROR regulation in its successful 1987 telecommunications privatization. Despite the "inferior" efficiency properties of the approach, it provided a transparent, quantitative foundation on which to base legally binding contractual agreements with private investors.

■ In both electricity and telecommunications, Chile has put in place a system of benchmark ROR regulation that bases regulatory decisions on the performance of a notional best-practice firm. Although supportive of efficient behavior by utilities, the Chilean model is exceptionally complex to implement. What has made the system workable is its good fit with the country's judicial and political institutions and Chile's depth of professional capability, which enables the major actors (regulators, judges, and academics) to evaluate complex, competing proposals on their empirical merits (Galal 1996).

■ Contracts for independent power providers in Indonesia and the Philippines have had some highly restrictive take-or-pay provisions. These restrictions have locked the countries into a system that requires paying prespecified prices and procuring fixed quantities of power, regardless of aggregate demand or the price of power from other sources.

Note that an excess of enthusiasm for private participation can lead countries to commit to price terms that consumers may view as exploitative, making it politically impossible to pursue further systemwide reforms. In the Philippines, these potentially high costs have been contained by entering into the initial take-or-pay agreements at high prices and only with small private generation facilities. As credibility improves, subsequent agreements with much larger facilities are concluded at more competitive prices. Other countries have not managed this sequencing as prudently.

The challenge for price regulation is to identify approaches that preclude arbitrary regulatory action yet encourage utilities to improve productivity and enable citizens to share in the benefits. One option is to combine price-cap regulation in which $X$ is fixed with an agreement to share any unexpectedly high profits on the basis of a prespecified formula.

### Regulating pollution: "voice" as a commitment mechanism

The regulation of pollution illustrates, in a very different context, the ways in which countries' institutional capabilities determine whether or not an approach is workable. As with utilities, the core challenge for environmental regulation is to make credible commitments to rules of the game that appropriately modify market outcomes. For utility regulation, meeting this challenge has led to a new emphasis on finding the best way to enforce and limit changes in formal regulatory rules. For environmental regulation, the emerging response is more far-reaching. In a number of countries, citizen participation is becoming a key element of environmental policy. Participation sometimes occurs as a complement to formal rules and sometimes as an alternative approach that promises better real results on the ground, at least in the near term.

Environmental management confronts three special challenges in fostering credibility that go beyond those confronted by utility regulators. First, in utility regulation and ownership, countries have no choice but to make decisions early in the development process, when investment in urban infrastructure first begins. But environmental management is often perceived (albeit wrongly) as a task that can be postponed. Environmental issues typically appear on the policy agenda only once the challenge of meeting basic human needs for food, fuel, shelter, and rudimentary health and education no longer seems so daunting (Dasgupta and others 1995).

Second, environmental regulation often has a diffuse target, unlike utility regulation, whose targets—pricing, competitive access to fixed link networks, and investment—are readily visible to the citizenry. The consequences of noxious fumes, poisoned water, and earsplitting noise are immediate and unmistakable. But the costs of many forms of environmental damage are not concentrated among small groups of people and may be invisible to those near the pollution source, even if they suffer especially adverse consequences over time. Moreover, pollution emissions can be hard to measure. And the environmental consequences of identical emissions can vary with the proximity of human settlements and the ecological characteristics of a region (Rose-Ackerman 1995).

Third, and in part as a consequence of the first two reasons, the political incentives of key community, private sector, and political stakeholders foster ambiguity and negotiated outcomes rather than predictable, consistent implementation. Poor communities daily confront the bleak need to balance immediate survival against long-term environmental consequences. Private firms weigh the predictable but often quite costly certainties of well-defined environmental regulations against the prospect of keeping costs low by taking advantage of inherent uncertainties such as the impact of the firms' actions on the environment and the communities' desires for jobs. And politicians considering an activist regulatory agenda weigh the certainty of conflict with the private sector against the ambivalent response of communities. In doing so, they may often conclude that environmental inaction (perhaps veiled by the appearance of activism) is the politically expedient course. In the resulting "equilibrium," the gap between regulatory form and practice is often enormous (box 9.2; see also Margulis 1996; Margulis and de Gusmão 1996). In contrast to utilities, environmental agencies in many developing countries are often politically weak, implying that this open-endedness need not negatively affect private investment.

The special challenge of winning credibility for environmental regulation suggests that a top-down, technocratically driven approach alone may not yield the intended results. Rather, community and other pressures can provide a powerful springboard for progressively strengthening the credibility and efficacy of environmental regulation (Afsah, Laplante, and Wheeler 1996).

Two recent experiments in Indonesia suggest that transparent, information-intensive initiatives may help mitigate industrial pollution, even in the absence of enforceable formal rules:

■ Compliance with the country's Clean River Program (PROKASIH), which was launched in 1989, is largely voluntary. Even so, by 1994 the total discharges of 100 participating plants had fallen by more than a third. Though most of the gains came from a small number of plants, participants had reduced their pollution intensity (Afsah, Laplante, and Makarim 1996).

■ A voluntary Program for Pollution Control, Evaluation, and Rating (PROPER), announced in mid-1995, rates factories on a five-grade scale according to their environmental performance and makes the results public. In the pilot phase, 187 factories were rated. Within months, 10 of the 121 factories with poor ratings had significantly improved their performance.

---

Box 9.2: Rio's environmental morass

In early 1995, newly appointed managers began to try to turn around the performance of the Brazilian state of Rio de Janeiro's environmental agency, Fun-
dacão Estatual de Engenharia do Meio Ambiente (FEEMA). Once highly
regarded, FEEMA had become progressively bogged down in an administrative and political morass. But in a setting in which environmental issues were
accorded (by many citizens as well as the state government) a lower priority
than concerns for security, health, and education, the reformers repeatedly
found themselves at the losing end of contests for resources and influence:

■ FEEMA had virtually no access to the resources required to run an innovative, performance-oriented environmental agency. By 1996, the average real
salaries of its 1,000 employees had fallen to one-third the levels of the 1970s
and 1980s. The best people had left, it was impossible to hire competent new
staff, and staff morale was at a low ebb. The secretariat of planning was
unwilling to provide additional salary resources in the face of tight overall
budget constraints. The secretariat also authorized only 12 percent of
FEEMA's request for funds for nonpersonnel activities.

■ FEEMA was unable to enforce environmental regulations in the face of
opposition from private industry. Industrial discharge tariffs were promulgated in 1986, but without any credible enforcement mechanism. Five years
later, a proposal for a noncompliance fee reached the legislature; after five
more years in committee, it has not yet been voted on by the legislature as a
whole. Moreover, individual foreign investors were able (through the secretariat for industry and commerce) to win relaxation of state emissions standards—even though in one instance the investment cost of compliance was
less than 0.5 percent of the total investment bill.

■ Relations with the state-owned water and sanitation utility (slated for privatization) were rocky. The utility blocked FEEMA from making information
public about the quality of Rio's water (which is generally very good). For
the past five years, it has failed to transfer funds (for water quality analyses,
water effluent charges, and a percentage of the water effluent charges private
firms paid to the water utility) to which FEEMA is contractually entitled.

After 18 months of trying, the new management concluded it was powerless to
turn around the state's environmental management and resigned.

---

Such programs have obvious limits. Nearly half the firms participating in the Clean
Rivers Program did not reduce the intensity of their polluting activities. As for the
pollution rating program, heavily polluting firms have little incentive to participate.
Clearly, as countries develop, they will need to move toward more institutionalized
approaches that integrate community pressures with formalized mechanisms of
enforcing compliance.

In a pattern seen throughout the world, bottom-up initiatives can set the stage for action at the national level. In the two decades after 1945, Japan rushed headlong into industrialization, with little concern for the environmental impact. This period of neglect ended in 1967 with the landmark Basic Law for Environmental Pollution Control. But well before then, grass-roots initiatives in many localities had set sustained environmental reforms in motion (UNDP and World Bank 1996).

Although citizen participation can help both to win credibility for controls on pollution and to modify them to the needs of specific settings, local solutions are only one step in the evolution of environmental policy. Industrial countries typically have national policies for environmental management and technically specialized environmental agencies that are responsible for most decisionmaking and enforcement. One challenge is to harmonize this technical excellence with the political legitimacy and policy credibility that comes from participation. A variety of approaches have been adopted (Lovei and Weiss 1996):

- France, Germany, and the United Kingdom have taken the view that having elected legislators delegate the task of spelling out the details of policy to an environmental authority is sufficient to secure legitimacy. Though the environmental authority in all three countries routinely consults with affected parties and responds to direct political pressure, none of the countries formally requires this consultation.

- In the United States, the Administrative Procedures Act mandates that rules promulgated by executive agencies (such as the Environmental Protection Agency) are legally binding only if the agencies give public notice of these rules in advance. All interested parties must have an opportunity to comment (typically through public hearings), and a "reasoned opinion" must accompany agency decisions. Additionally, the Freedom of Information Act ensures that all government information is publicly available.

- The Netherlands and Sweden have formal mechanisms for forging consensus on policy formulation and development. In Sweden, these include the routine appointment of study commissions (made up of a broad cross-section of society) to ensure that proposed new policies are widely discussed throughout the country. In addition, proposed legislation is formally reviewed and local referenda are sometimes held. These measures are supported by liberal freedom of information laws. To strengthen the technical capacity of NGOs, the Dutch government provides more than half the funding for 30–40 environmental NGOs and consults with them and other affected parties routinely when preparing new environmental legislation.

Viewed through the narrow lens of economic efficiency, the industrial countries' responsiveness to "voice" is not without cost. Consider the examples of Germany and the United States, two leaders in environmental policy since the late 1960s. Both have been strikingly successful in reducing the emissions of some major pollutants. Yet both countries continue to rely overwhelmingly on command-and-control approaches to environmental regulation, even where market- and incentive-based regulation can achieve similar gains at substantially lower costs (Rose-Ackerman 1996). They do so in part because they want to be seen as responding directly to citizen concerns.

Environmental agencies continue to play a key role in many countries. These agencies often are key repositories of technical excellence, backstopping local initiatives with the technological and scientific information necessary for effective and efficient pollution control. And in a small number of countries, such as the Republic of Korea, Malaysia, and Singapore, committed top-down leadership has made significant progress in controlling pollution, even when the impact of citizens' voice has been muted. Yet the limitations of a centralized technocratic approach have become apparent even in Korea. Since 1986, Korea's environmental administration has repeatedly tried to decentralize its activities to regional offices and local governments but has been frustrated by bureaucratic weaknesses at the local level. One-third of the 92 industrial firms interviewed in 1994 reported that they had been subjected to "community pressure." Statistical analysis reveals that this pressure has resulted in substantial investment in pollution abatement over and above nationally mandated requirements (Aden 1996).

### Evaluating regulation

This paper has argued that skillful regulatory policymaking requires a good understanding of both the economic and institutional dimensions of regulation and that exclusive preoccupation with one dimension can have disastrous consequences. Introducing the institutional dimension explicitly raises some new opportunities—and some new challenges—for the task of evaluating regulation.

The opportunities arise because work on the institutional foundations of regulation is now quite well developed. At least for utilities, there is now a reasonably good conceptual basis for fitting approaches to regulatory rule making and enforcement to the institutional setting (see the typology developed by Levy and Spiller 1994). In many cases—for example, the Jamaican experience between 1966 and 1975—it may be possible to define exactly how a mismatch between a country's institutions and a regulatory approach have undermined performance. Using this information, it may then be possible to draw useful lessons for the future.

The challenge, though, is that once institutions are brought into the picture, the point at which regulation is "good enough" becomes much less clear. One key conclusion of the multifaceted approach is that what is economically optimal in the abstract may be undesirable in specific country settings. So long as one is not looking at a blatant case of failure, it is all too easy to conclude that "what is" was the best achievable under the circumstances. This notion may be true even though the system in place falls well short of best practice (see again Jamaica, this time post-1987).

One way out of this dilemma is for institutionally sensitive evaluations to make explicit what was not achieved in relation to the notional "first best" objectives. For Jamaica, this might include the absence of competition and associated pressures for innovation and cost reduction. The evaluation could then consider some counterfactual benchmarks—that is, incremental improvements that might have been pursued but were not. For each benchmark, the key question to ask is whether it could have been implemented—that is, whether there were any compelling obstacles built into the local institutional environment that kept these notional improvements from being put in place. By requiring a more explicit effort to generate institutionally sensitive alternatives, this approach can strengthen the ability of the evaluation process to yield useful, practical lessons. But it also puts a burden on the evaluators themselves, especially in terms of their professional creativity and judgment.

## Note

1.   Esfahani (1996) highlights the dilemma as of the early 1990s. Since 1994, the government of President Fidel Ramos has permitted entry on the basis described in the paper.

## References

Aden, Jean. 1996. "Industrial Pollution Abatement in the Newly Industrializing Countries: Korea." Asia Technical Department. World Bank, Washington, D.C.

Afsah, Shakeb, Benoit Laplante, and David Wheeler. 1996. "Controlling Industrial Pollution: A New Paradigm." Policy Research Working Paper No. 1672. World Bank, Washington, D.C.

———, Benoit Laplante, and Nabiel Makarim. 1996. "Program-Based Pollution Control Management: The Indonesian PROKASIH Program." Policy Research Working Paper No. 1602. World Bank, Washington, D.C.

Borner, Silvio, Aymo Brunetti, and Beatrice Weder. 1995. *Political Credibility and Economic Development.* New York: St. Martins Press.

Bradley, I., and C. Price. 1988. "The Economic Regulation of Private Industries by Price Constraints." *Journal of Industrial Economics* 37:99–106.

Dasgupta, S., A. Mody, S. Roy, and D. Wheeler. 1995. "Environmental Regulation and Development: A Cross-Country Empirical Analysis." Policy Research Working Paper No. 1448. World Bank, Washington, D.C.

Esfahani, Hadi. 1996. "The Political Economy of the Telecommunications Sector in the Philippines." In Brian Levy and Pablo Spiller, *Regulations, Institutions, and Commitment: Comparative Studies of Telecommunications.* New York: Cambridge University Press.

Galal, Ahmed. 1996. "Chile: Regulatory Specificity, Credibility of Commitment, and Distributional Demands." In Brian Levy and Pablo Spiller, eds., *Regulations, Institutions, and Commitment: Comparative Studies of Telecommunications.* New York: Cambridge University Press.

———, Leroy Jones, Pankaj Tandon, and Ingo Vogelsang. 1994. *Welfare Consequences of Selling Public Enterprises: An Empirical Analysis.* New York: Oxford University Press for the World Bank.

Levy, Brian, and Pablo Spiller. 1994. "The Institutional Foundations of Regulatory Commitment: A Comparative Analysis of Telecommunications Regulation." *Journal of Law, Economics, and Organization* 10(2):201–46.

———, eds. 1996. *Regulations, Institutions, and Commitment: Comparative Studies of Telecommunications.* New York: Cambridge University Press.

Littlechild, S. 1983. *Regulation of British Telecommunications Profitability.* London: Her Majesty's Stationery Office.

## Comments on "Credible regulatory policy: options and evaluation," by Levy

*Daniel Artana*

In this paper, Brian Levy extends the analysis of previous work on the regulation of public utilities to environmental regulation (Levy and Spiller 1994). The paper's basic idea is that "the key to successful regulatory policy is . . . to match a country's regulatory role (what it does, and what tools it uses) to its underlying institutional capability." From this point, he draws three inescapable conclusions: that credible rules are more important than the content of the regulation, that flexible rules are less successful in countries with fewer checks and balances to restrict arbitrary decisions, and that in some countries formal rules may not be possible. In these cases, more emphasis should be placed on competitive pressures and citizen participation.

The regulatory approach to the environment becomes more complicated, because decisions may be postponed and the target of the regulations is diffuse. These two constraints—together with the incentive problems of different lobbies (private firms and politicians)—open the door for more ambiguity and less predictability. I agree with the general conclusion that establishing a system of formal rules based on textbook models does not automatically translate into a credible regulatory system. In other words, institutions matter a lot, and the regulation of utilities and the environment must take into account the weaknesses of each country's institutional framework. But I do not quite agree with some of the pessimistic conclusions that Levy and his colleagues draw from this point. This pessimism appears, for example, in the following comments:

> A key conclusion from a multifaceted approach is that what is economically optimal in the abstract, may be undesirable in specific country settings. So long as one is not looking at blatant cases of failure, *it is all too easy to conclude that "what is" was the best achievable under the circumstances*, even though the system in place falls short of best practice . . . (emphasis added)

> Finally, and perhaps more important, the institutional realities of some countries may be such that resolution of the governance problems constrains the range of regulatory incentive options to *third (or even fourth) best* . . . (Levy and Spiller 1994, 209, emphasis added)

I argue that it is generally possible to find second-best solutions to adapt regulatory frameworks to the institutions of each country. With third- or fourth-best solutions that apparently are a better match with a country's institutions, there are some efficiency costs that are not worth paying.

### Credible decisions and fourth-best instruments

It is clear, as Levy points out, that credible regulations are necessary to attract private investment. Regulations may need to be less flexible in some countries than in others in order to reduce the scope for discretionary decisions. As it is impossible to anticipate all future contingencies in a contract, private parties usually rely on implicit agreements (Klein 1980; Klein, Crawford, and Alchian 1978). These agreements are not always available when the government participates in the deal. It is difficult for the government to make a credible commitment, because the other party to the contract (the private sector) is the one that makes the sunk investment and may also be the one with its reputation at stake.[1] It is therefore necessary to introduce other restrictions on government discretion to raise the cost of an eventual opportunistic decision.

An independent judiciary is important to improve credibility but is not sufficient because it is impossible to specify all contingencies in the contract. There need to be other costs for the government, even in credible countries. Such costs could include potentially negative effects on the investment decisions of utilities (other than those affected by an arbitrary resolution of a conflict) or on other investment decisions in the economy. For less credible countries, they might also involve the potential loss of future government revenues from a sequential privatization program like the one suggested by Levy and Spiller (1994). Or they might encompass increased participation by foreign investment in utilities in a globally integrated world in order to create an interest group that will help reduce the risk of arbitrary government decisions.

As already noted, the suggestion that third- and fourth-best solutions may be the only options in countries with weak governance is overly pessimistic. So is Levy's conclusion that except in blatant cases of failure, it is often easy to conclude that what we observe is probably the best possible outcome. This idea becomes clearer if Levy's conclusion is extended to other areas of government policy. There is no doubt, for example, that a country gains by having a credible tax system able to finance government outlays. In many countries, evasion problems have led governments to use "tax handles" such as export and stamp taxes. This practice cannot be considered a blatant failure in countries with weak tax administrations. But the World Bank has been fostering tax reforms that eliminate or reduce inefficient taxes, and many countries have had success with these reforms, even if other institutions remain unchanged.

The defense of ROR regulation or cross-subsidies as viable instruments in weak institutional settings (Levy and Spiller 1994) also reveals too much pessimism. In the first case, if one believes that ROR and price-cap regulation tend to coincide in practice, then it is not clear that much can be gained by using ROR. But even if one thinks that these methods of regulation differ, there are many opportunities for the regulatory agency to act opportunistically in calculating the rate of return.[2]

Cross-subsidies are also not effective as a means of financing private investment in situations where institutions are weak, because they create problems in the future, as the debate on the rebalancing of telecommunication tariffs in Argentina suggests. There are better alternatives (for example, explicit taxes and subsidies) that have the advantage of being neutral with respect to the development of competition. Moreover, cross-subsidies themselves lack credibility, because skimming off the top undermines the source of financing. In addition, to the extent that the implicit tax is charged on inputs of other sectors (the usual case in cross-subsidies), the potential inefficiencies of the policy are higher than they would be with taxes on final products, because the extra distortion induced in the selection of inputs must be added in. It is always better to finance the subsidies from the budget, as was done in the privatization of the Argentine railways and natural gas industry (both of which activities, according to Levy and Spiller [1994], were carried out in a weak institutional setting).

Accepting fourth-best policies as the only possible solution in countries with weak institutions increases the probability of starting the kind of "vicious circle" that has been pervasive in less-developed economies. In unstable economies, private investment in any activity faces higher risks than it does in more stable countries. Would it then be reasonable to compensate for this additional risk with subsidies and tax breaks to private investors, or would this practice be considered a blatant case of failure? My answer to this question is probably influenced by the huge fiscal cost of industrial policy in Argentina and its negative impact on the productivity both of the economy as a whole and of the firms favored by the policy. Therefore, I think it may sometimes be better to do nothing than to accept a third- or fourth-best policy. Not only could the present value of the welfare losses be very high, but, by creating lobbies that try to maintain a profitable status quo, the policies could also reduce the chances of improving institutions.[3]

I agree with Levy (1997) on the additional difficulties that environmental regulations introduce, most of them related to the high discount rate of politicians and the diffuse nature of environmental regulations:

> Viewed through the narrow lens of economic efficiency, the industrialized countries' responsiveness to voice is not without cost. Consider the examples of Germany and the United States, two leaders in environmental policy since the late 1960s. Both have been strikingly successful in reducing emissions of some major pollutants. Yet, in part because of the need to be seen to respond directly to citizen concerns, both countries continue to rely overwhelmingly on command and control approaches to environmental regulations, even where market-and incentive-based regulation can achieve similar gains at substantially lower cost . . . (17)

However, I have two reservations. First, citizen concerns introduce pressure in other areas as well, but it has not been seen as an excuse for adopting first- or second-best policies. For example, trade liberalization has resisted the attack of lobbies and popular support for "buying local." In environmental issues, people's concern goes in the right direction, although in some cases there may be an overreaction. Second, after a hesitant start, transferable entitlements have gained credence in environmental regulation in the last two decades. If this trend continues, Levy's remark will be valid only as an explanation of a transition toward a better policy. It would also be interesting to review what changes (institutional or others) explain the change itself and the speed of the transition.

### Concluding comments

Levy's paper is a good contribution to the goal of achieving better regulations. Institutions matter a lot, but I am more optimistic about the likelihood of finding second-best policies in countries with weak institutions.

Following are some conclusions extracted from economic reform in Argentina (a country with weak institutions):

■ Initial conditions matter. In a distressed economy such as Argentina's in 1990, it is relatively easy to pass better rules, and the initial expansion in demand that follows a quick reorganization of the economy helps boost investment. These facts may explain the investment boom in telecommunications.[4] However, to the extent that poor initial conditions are not sector specific (as in Argentina in 1990, when the government began privatizing utilities), a general improvement in the economy leads to an important revaluation of privatized assets and increases the likelihood of opportunistic political behavior.

■ Competition should be extended as much as possible, not only for the traditional textbook reasons, but also because of its institutional value. Competitive segments, like electricity generation, attracted massive investment flows in Argentina after privatization. Although competition per se does not eliminate all expropriation risks,[5] it does reduce the scope of government intervention and the likelihood of opportunistic behavior. Moreover, the idea of privatizing a legal monopoly in weak institutional settings to raise more money at the bid also increases the expropriation risk. If the bid is competitive, the winner will sink the present value of the monopoly rent, increasing the risk of a government holdup.

■ As mentioned above, cross-subsidies create problems that undermine confidence on the rules, because sooner or later regulators face the need to rebalance the tariffs. The increase in residential rates that occurred in the course of rebalancing telecommunications tariffs in Argentina was a clear instance of politicization.[6] It is better to avoid unbalanced tariffs at the beginning; this is another area where efficiency and institutions are mutually reinforcing. Moreover, as Levy argues, in weak institutional settings it is better to have more rigid rules, although rigid rules imply that there is less room for fine tuning. Cross-subsidies and ROR regulation demand extensive fine tuning and periodic discussions between the regulatory agency and the regulated firms. This situation creates more chances to hold up private firms.

■ Although institutions matter, they are only one factor in the successful regulation of utilities. Argentina provides another example. The institutions (for example, the judiciary) did not improve during 1992–96, a period during which different approaches to privatization and regulation were tried, with different outcomes that are difficult to explain from an institutional point of view. For example, water and sewage were privatized in 1992, the same year as the distribution of natural gas and electricity. The regulatory frameworks for electricity and natural gas were much better than for water. In fact, the water contract was renegotiated in 1994, two years after the bid was decided, raising the tariffs by 13.5 percent. The increase, which was based on the lowest tariff, was set for five years. But even in the best cases there are differences in performance.[7]

■ Although the general institutions of the country were the same, the degree of "capture" of the regulatory agencies was different. It was more in line with differences in design (for example, the independence of the directors and the sources of financing) and context (for example, the number of firms under the agency's supervision and the visibility of the agency's decisions).

- In terms of the regulatory issues regulators face in countries with private utilities, there seems to be a "contagion effect" from one country to another, regardless of the institutions. The rebalancing of telecommunications tariffs is one example, the problems with the automatic passthrough in natural gas costs another.[8]

- The creation of interest groups with a strong interest in protecting sunk investments can be a partial substitute for weak domestic institutions. The participation of foreign investors on a large scale increases the costs for an opportunistic government, which may face economic retaliation in other areas of the economy.

## Notes

1.   Reputation is defined as the present value of the rents one loses by acting opportunistically, expropriating the sunk investment made by the other party in the contract. The government's reputation is low because the government may be able to disguise such behavior toward private investors, with a resultant cost that may be transferred to future governments.

2.   Agencies in developing countries must determine the relevant opportunity cost of capital for each sector, opening room for some discretion. (In developed countries, which are supposed to have better institutions, the issue is less urgent.) For example, which general rate should be used—the one implicit in Brady bonds that were forced on the holders of public debt? The rate on new issues of debt that currently have a shorter maturity than most investments created by private utilities? How does one define the sector specific rate—using other countries' experiences?

3.   There is much political pressure to find "quick solutions," which itself creates a lot of lobbying that may delay the approval of structural reforms. But the burden of proof as to which route may be less expensive falls on those who advocate the use of third- or fourth-best policies.

4.   Note that the other arguments advanced by Levy and Spiller (1994) to explain this investment are problematic. Levy and Spiller argue that prices were high enough to allow high rates of return and that high dividends were reinvested simply because it was not politically feasible to repatriate them abroad. However, the annual yield of Argentine short-term public bonds in 1990 (when Entel was privatized) was 27 percent net of taxes (39 percent gross of taxes), suggesting that for private investors to have an interest in the privatization they had to get at least that return. Reinvesting dividends has no purpose if the firms think that regulation is weak; it only increases the size of the sunk investment that the government may expropriate in the future.

5.   For example, there were also massive investments in petroleum and natural gas production after the deregulation of the market and the privatization of some large enterprises. One of the reasons for this success was that the federal regulations ensured tax stability, eliminating one easy opening for opportunistic behavior. However, federal rules were not mandatory for provincial governments, which raised the local tax on production from 1 to 2 percent. As Argentina is a "price taker," the burden of the tax falls only on the producers. This ex post change was a clear example of a holdup. Later on, private companies signed agreements with the provinces that established a ceiling on provincial taxes on the production of hydrocarbons, eliminating this risk, and investment boomed again.

6.   Having commited itself during the sale of the residual shares of Telecom in 1992, the government approved the rebalancing in 1991. It was finally passed in 1997. Currently it is under question, and a supreme court ruling will be required to determine the validity of the change.

For an analysis of the rebalancing of telecommunications tariffs in Argentina, see Artana and others (1996).

7.   The differences in performance of some regulatory agencies in Argentina are analyzed in Urbiztondo, Artana, and Navajas (forthcoming), and the problems with the privatization of water and sewage (comparing the cases of Buenos Aires and Corrientes) in Artana, Navajas, and Urbiztondo (1996).

8.   In the case of natural gas, the regulator in the United Kingdom replaced the automatic passthrough with a general cost of gas index. In the United States, about 30 percent of the states have demanded a discussion of the issue in a public hearing. In Argentina, there have been restrictions on the automatic passthrough (see Artana, Navajas, and Urbiztondo 1997). The distribution companies in Argentina claimed that the regulatory agency did not comply with the license when it restricted the automatic passthrough of natural gas costs (they have filed a legal claim in Argentina that may be valid because the license allowed the passthrough). Even in a relatively well-designed regulatory framework, the problem of opportunistic behavior have cropped up, a problem that cannot be attributed to the country's weak institutions, as there have been no similar problems with the pipeline and electricity companies. In the case of the pipelines, the license has fewer loopholes than for the distribution companies, because the passthrough issue does not exist.

## References

Artana, Daniel, R. López Murphy, F. Navajas, and S. Urbiztondo. 1996. "El rebalanceo de tarifas telefónicas." Working Paper No. 48. FIEL Foundation, Buenos Aires.

———, F. Navajas, and S. Urbiztondo. 1996. "Argentina: La regulación económica en las concesiones de agua potable y desagües cloacales en Buenos Aires y Corrientes." FIEL-Red de Centros del BID/BUE, Buenos Aires.

———, F. Navajas, and S. Urbiztondo. 1997. "Una evaluación de las decisiones del regulador del gas natural en la Argentina." FIEL-Red de Centros del BID/BUE, Buenos Aires.

Klein, B. 1980. "Transaction Cost Determinants of 'Unfair' Contractual Arrangements." *American Economic Review* 70 (May):356–62.

———, A. Crawford, and Armen Alchian. 1978. "Vertical Integration, Appropriable Rents and the Competitive Contracting Process." Journal of Law and Economics 21 (October):297–326.

Laffont, J-J., and J. Tirole. 1993. A Theory of Incentives in Procurement and Regulation. Cambridge, Mass.: Massachusetts Institute of Technology Press.

Levy, Brian, and Pablo Spiller. 1994. "The Institutional Foundations of Regulatory Commitment: A Comparative Analysis of Telecommunications Regulation." *Journal of Law, Economics, and Organization* 10(2):201–46.

Tietenberg, T. 1992. "Relevant Experience with Tradable Entitlements." In *Combating Global Warming*. Geneva: UNCTAD-RDB-DFP-1.

Urbiztondo, S., Daniel Artana, and F. Navajas. Forthcoming. "La autonomía de los entes reguladores argentinos." FIEL-Red de Centros del BID/BUE, Buenos Aires.

## Comments on "Credible regulatory policy: options and evaluation," by Levy

*Yingyi Qian*

Using solid case studies, Brian Levy's paper has achieved three objectives. First, it provides some general and important principles of institutional economics. Second, it presents some specific theoretical insights. Third, it draws practical lessons for project evaluation, which is the main concern of this volume. The main purpose of my comments is to crystallize the above three points.

### The "second-best principle" in institutional economics

The literature on regulation has evolved in three stages. The first is the *market-failure* stage, in which the focus is on how a benevolent government can correct so-called market failure. The second stage is the *government-failure* stage. Here, the "capture" theory of regulation is an important example. The third stage, *institutional analysis*, recognizes the potential for government failure—for example, the incentives problem of government (credibility of regulation)—but then goes one step further. It examines how regulatory schemes produce different degrees of failure, comparing rate-of-return (ROR) with price-cap schemes in achieving credible commitment and showing how each scheme fits, or fails to fit, the existing institutional environment.

The paper's comparative case studies of utility regulation in the United Kingdom, Jamaica, and the Philippines offer such an analysis. Regulation nicely illustrates some general principles that new institutional economics (NIE) can offer. The first is that an "optimal" regulation scheme in an ideal institutional environment may perform poorly in a less perfect institutional environment. As the paper says, "What is economically optimal in the abstract may be undesirable in specific country settings." The second principle is that a "less efficient" regulation scheme may work better in an imperfect institutional environment. For example, ROR regulation works better than price-cap regulation in Jamaica in the absence of checks and balances, because the former system results in improved commitment. And third, a second-best scheme may not always work and may still require certain institutional support. It did not work in the Philippines, for example.

The author's perspective of the analysis urges us to think more deeply. In my view, there is a general second-best principle in institutional economics that has a parallel in price theory. Before the introduction of imperfect information and incomplete markets, we considered the problem using the *first-best* as the only benchmark. Later, with the development of the second-best theory, we broadened our perspectives. Similarly, when we first study regulation and contracts, we tend to take the first-best institutions as a given. But we do not in reality, particularly in developing and transition economies. There is no doubt that as a normative recommendation, we need to strive for the best institutions. But as part of positive analysis, we need to recognize that institutional changes take time.

To show that the principle is general and goes beyond the regulation problem this paper studies, I present an example from a completely different context—my own research on China's transition to markets. Many people have been puzzled by the remarkable success in China of enterprises owned and controlled by local governments (township-village enterprises, or TVEs). In standard theory, it is hard to come up with good arguments to explain why TVEs have comparative advantages over private firms in terms of incentives. However, the puzzle can be solved if we make the realistic assumption that the rule of law and institutions that credibly constrain the state from expropriation are missing. In this institutional environment, private ownership suffers from the fear of state predation and thus is less efficient than it would be in an ideal institutional environment. But local government ownership, by integrating government and business activities, may achieve credible commitment in limiting state predation (for details of the mechanism, see Che and Qian 1995, 1996).

## Theoretical insights: credible commitment and the allocation of information and authority

Levy's paper provides specific theoretical insights built upon many recent studies on credibility. The central issue ultimately involves the allocation of information and authority, which determines incentives. In the well-studied problem of utility regulation, we can pin down the trade-off between ROR regulation and price-cap regulation. The idea is that ROR regulation induces higher static incentive distortions for private firms. But as a benefit, it makes achieving credible commitment in the dynamic sense easier. Price-cap regulation has opposite effects. Here we are really talking about the discretionary use of information. Price-cap schemes are sensitive to new information and, for that reason, are more efficient. But they are also prone to the commitment problem if the regulator does not have the proper incentives. With appropriate institutions for checks and balances, price-cap regulation may be an ideal scheme; without these institutions, it may function badly. ROR regulation is less sensitive to new information and, from the dynamic point of view, may result in better commitment. This scheme is better if a good checks and balances mechanism is in place.

In the absence of a solid institutional environment for monitoring and checks and balances, less discretion and less information have beneficial effects in achieving credible commitment. To push the idea further, in extreme cases commitment can be achieved by not observing information at all. We often hear that institutions are created to reduce information asymmetry and transaction costs, but not in this case. Indeed, most of the literature on credible commitment acknowledges that better ex post information or lower transaction costs may reduce the credibility of commitment and thus increase ex ante inefficiency. Therefore, it is efficient to create institutions to increase information asymmetry and transaction costs; the separation of powers and the independence of central banks are two such examples.

My own research on China illustrates the importance of this idea. In the absence of the rule of law, information gives the state the possibility and incentive to expropriate the wealth of its citizens. One way of achieving credible commitment is not to receive such information. We all know that China's household bank savings are very high. Why do Chinese citizens have such confidence in the state banks, given that the state in principle can confiscate a citizen's wealth? The answer is that in China all private savings accounts are anonymous. In fact, China has a "Swiss" banking system. People can make deposits into banks under several fake names, and they do. By not asking for real names, the state credibly commits to not confiscating bank deposits from individuals. Of course, it can still confiscate the wealth of all depositors (say by inflation), but such a move would be very costly. Notice that lack of transparency is essential here. News from China indicated that China is now considering a change in this practice, for two reasons: to tax interest payments (following the practice common in other countries) and to increase transparency, which NIE supposedly emphasizes. Transparency is desirable; it is an important part of the rule of law but must come with credible institutions to constrain the state. When the state is not constrained, the lack of transparency provides an alternative mechanism for achieving credible commitment for incentive purposes.

## Practical implications for project evaluation

This paper suggests that project evaluation needs to be more sophisticated. Making it more sophisticated requires learning more from economic theory and institutional economics. Three lessons can be drawn:

First, project evaluation, if only for the sake of efficiency, should carefully consider the incentive structures and their effects on all players, particularly government bureaucrats. Credibility is one crucial aspect of the incentive structure.

Second, project evaluation should use the first-best outcome obtained under a perfect institutional environment not as the only benchmark, but as one of several. Unfortunately, project evaluation (say, on regulatory initiatives) often implicitly takes an ideal institutional environment as the only benchmark. That benchmark may be relevant in the long run, but for most developing and transition economies, it may not be relevant in the short or medium term.

Third, in order to evaluate a project in a realistic environment, we need to include many other variables in the analysis (especially institutional variables) before making conclusions. Many potential benefits and costs of a project in an imperfect institutional environment are difficult to appreciate and are often missed. This fact presents a real challenge to project evaluation within institutional dimensions.

## References

Che, Jiahua, and Yingyi Qian. 1995. "Institutional Environment, Community Government, and Corporate Governance: Understanding China's Township-Village Enterprises." Department of Economics, Stanford University.

———. 1996. "Insecure Property Rights and Government Ownership of Firms." Department of Economics, Stanford University.

## Floor discussion on "Credible regulatory policy: options and evaluation"

The discussion centered around the idea that evaluation becomes more complex as regulatory standards are adjusted to local conditions. Flexibility and transparency may be appropriate in one situation, while inflexibility and nonparticipatory conventions may work better in another. In such circumstances, it may be difficult to hold regulators to the optimal standards of accountability for investment. Investment itself may become the sanction that leads countries toward best practices in regulation.

Hedy von Metzsch from the Netherlands Ministry of Foreign Affairs (and an evaluator herself) noted that evaluation becomes more complex when institutions and the cultural environment differ. She asked whether it is possible to see things from the stakeholders' point of view. The task of evaluation, she noted, is to point out the most efficient options, but policymakers and politicians must make the solutions legitimate.

In response, Yingyi Qian noted that it is difficult to identify alternative benefits in a counterfactual situation. If there is a price tag, it is possible to see potential benefits in a "rate-of-return" approach. With a "price-cap" approach, it is harder. What Joe Stiglitz described as an opportunity cost may for some public agencies be a good return.

Daniel Artana looked at the distributional aspect and the pricing of basic needs. He pointed out that the issue is how to proceed when, in practice, money is being shifted from organizations to consumers. It is better to use tax policy, with utilities as the vehicle of distribution. With this strategy, however, cross-subsidies cannot be used; a mechanism that causes less distortion is required.

Brian Levy noted the extent to which new information alters the rules and said that he is most comfortable with RPI-2 when profit-sharing is specified up front. If cross-subsidies are imperative and there is no political space to eliminate them, what develops is free entry, which in turn creates an internally contradictory situation. The question is not one of evaluation versus efficiency. Operations people want to know three or four different ways—suboptimal and sequenced—for confronting reality. Levy noted that he looks to institutionally sensitive evaluation as having the potential to produce better results.

Johannes Linn noted that it is the economist's duty to remind everybody of the efficiency losses from second-best solutions. Evaluation may have to become more pragmatic, he added. Levy's approach puts a strong burden on the evaluators' judgments, so that it may become necessary to evaluate the evaluators.

# PART 3: INSTITUTIONAL DEVELOPMENT AND SOCIAL CAPITAL

# 10. Defining social capital: an integrating view[1]

Ismail Serageldin and Christiaan Grootaert

*The paper argues that different, but mutually reinforcing, types of social capital coexist in society. Consequently, an integrating view is needed on the definition and measurement of social capital that bridges the distinctions in the literature between micro- and macroinstitutional social capital, formal and informal institutions, horizontal and vertical associations. The paper also argues that, for a given country at a given time, there exists an "appropriate" level and composition of social capital, based on complementarities with other forms of capital.*

## Social capital and sustainability

Social capital is best studied in the context of the contribution it makes to sustainable development. Building on this view, this paper puts forth two propositions that will hopefully help integrate the widely different definitions of social capital and facilitate the measurement and operational application of the concept. The immediate advantage of seeing social capital in this context is that sustainable development is a widely accepted concept. It appeals to the public at large, conveying a sense of continuity and concern for the environment and for children but does not imply that the economy must stagnate or living standards fall.

The first formal definition saw sustainable development as "[meeting] the needs of the present without compromising the ability of future generations to meet their own needs" (Brundtland Commission 1987, 43). While philosophically attractive and simple, this definition raises difficult operational questions. Given the variations in living standards within and across countries, defining needs in a meaningful and coherent way is virtually impossible. We have therefore tried to operationalize the definition by referring to the *stock of capital* that underlies the generation of income and welfare.

In an earlier paper, Serageldin (1996b) puts forth an especially promising approach that views sustainability as opportunity. This notion leads to a second definition: "Sustainability is to leave future generations as many opportunities as we ourselves have had, if not more" (Serageldin 1996b, 3). This approach views opportunity, in economic terms, as expanding the capital stock. In economics and finance, the idea of depleting capital to create an income stream is simply unacceptable, because income based on capital depletion is unsustainable.[2] Capital and capital growth are the means of providing future generations with the opportunities we have had—provided that capital is defined on a per capita basis to account for the needs of the burgeoning global population. Sustainability as opportunity thus means that future generations must be provided with as much or more capital per capita than the current generation.

The composition of the capital left to the next generation can differ from the composition of the current stock, however. Thus, defining sustainability as opportunity highlights the importance of looking at a stock variable (wealth) as well as a flow variable (income). The approach requires distinguishing among different kinds of capital (produced assets, natural capital, human capital, and social capital) and recognizing that they are both complements and substitutes.

### Key features of "sustainability as opportunity"

Defining sustainability as opportunity requires looking beyond traditional measures of sustainability to existing stocks of wealth, genuine saving rates, and human and social capital. It also posits three levels of sustainability—weak, sensible, and strong.

- *Existing stocks.* Income measures have traditionally focused on flows. But no corporation runs its affairs using only cash flow and income statements, ignoring balance sheets and net worth. Countries need to behave more like corporations and analyze existing stocks.

- *Genuine saving.* Adjusting national accounts for depreciation of all classes of assets has little effect on trends in traditional income measures. However, similar adjustments to gross investment data provide important signals on saving and investment. A measure based solely on gross investment as a percent of GNP can mask major variations in genuine saving. For example, a constant level of gross investment of 15–18 percent of GNP for Latin America translates into a positive genuine savings rate of 7 percent in 1969 but a negative rate of 2–3 percent in 1982 (Pearce and Atkinson 1993).

- *Human and social capital.* "Back of-the envelope" calculations show that in 192 countries (except for a few raw materials exporters), human and social capital equals or exceeds natural capital and produced assets combined (World Bank 1995). (See figure 10.1.) Produced assets, or manmade capital, represents only 16–20 percent of the wealth of most of the countries. Yet most current economic policies focus on this small group of assets. A more recent comparison based on purchasing power parity reduces the gap between rich and poor countries but provides even stronger evidence (World Bank 1997).

- *Level of sustainability.* Sustainability as opportunity has several levels—weak, sensible, and strong—depending on how strictly the concept of maintenance, or nondeclining capital, is applied (Pearce and Atkinson 1993).

  1. Weak sustainability means maintaining current levels of total capital without regard to its composition (natural, manmade, social, or human). This scenario implies that the different kinds of capital are perfect substitutes, at least within the boundaries of current levels of economic activity and resource endowment.

  2. Sensible sustainability means maintaining capital intact but also considering its composition. Thus, oil may be depleted as long as the receipts are invested in another type of capital (human, for instance). Under this sce-

FIGURE 10.1: COMPOSITION OF WORLD WEALTH BY INCOME GROUP (PERCENTAGE OF TOTAL)

### 1995 estimates

**Raw material exporters**

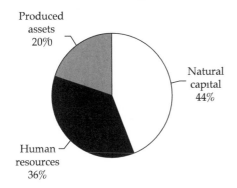

### 1997 estimates

**Raw material exporters**

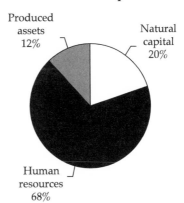

**Other developing countries**

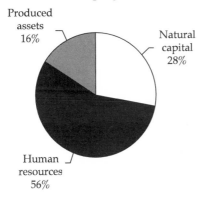

**Other developing countries**

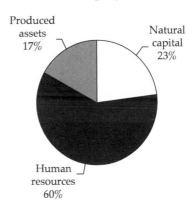

**High-income countries**

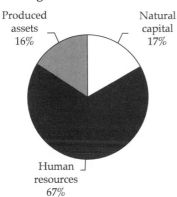

**High-income countries**

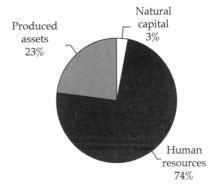

*Source*: World Bank 1995, 1997.

nario, countries seek to set the minimum level of each type of capital that is necessary to allay concerns about substitutability. Monitoring ensures that development does not promote the decimation of one kind of capital in favor of another. This recognizes that manmade and natural capital are to a large extent substitutes but also that they are complements—and that, to function fully, a country requires a mix of all four types.

3. Strong sustainability means maintaining the different kinds of capital separately, keeping the stock of each intact. Thus, receipts from oil (natural capital) are invested in sustainable energy production rather than in another asset. This scenario assumes that natural and manmade capital are not really substitutes but rather complement each other in most production functions. For instance, a sawmill (manmade capital) is worthless without a forest (natural capital). The same logic argues that reductions in one kind of educational investment should be offset by investments in another, not by investments in roads.

### Definitions of social capital

The previous section showed that the sum of human and social capital exceeds that of produced and natural capital in many countries (figure 10.1). But while the concept of human capital is by now well accepted, the concept of social capital is not. A "glue that holds societies together" (Serageldin, 1996a, 196) is generally recognized as necessary to a functioning social order, along with a certain degree of common cultural identification—a sense of "belonging" and shared behavioral norms. This internal coherence helps to define social capital. Without it, society at large will collapse, and there can be no talk of economic growth, environmental sustainability, or human well-being, as Somalia, Yugoslavia, and Rwanda painfully illustrate. More positively, social capital can be identified indirectly in countries where similar stocks of natural, produced, and human capital have turned in very different economic performances. It can also be seen in regions or cities within the same country and even in communities within regions or cities. The examples that follow show how social capital contributes to economic growth.

*East Asia*. Conventional factors such as investments in human and physical capital and technology only partially explain the high growth rates of the East Asian "miracle" economies. These governments have also invested in social capital by creating policies that provide an enabling environment for growth. Institutional arrangements and organizational designs that enhance efficiency, facilitate the exchange of information, and promote cooperation between government and industry characterize this environment (World Bank 1993; Stiglitz 1996).[3]

*Northern Italy*. In a study of Italy, Putnam, Leonardi, and Nanetti (1993) argue that the large number of voluntary associations among people in Northern Italy explains the region's economic success. These associations provide the north with the social capital that the south, where the associations are far less common, does not have.

*Somalia*. After the fall of Somalia's government in 1991, the country was plagued with civil disorder and declining incomes. An exception was the port city of

Boosaaso, where a local warlord supported by local residents organized a security force and a council of clan elders. With this investment in social capital, trade flourished and incomes improved (Buckley 1996).

*India.* In the state of Gujarat, violent confrontations between local people and government officials over forest management led to economic stagnation. But once the communities were mobilized and joint forest management was instituted, conflicts declined and land productivity and village incomes rose (Pathan and others 1993). In this case, the investment in social capital was a joint effort by local governments and communities.

Examples of social capital are easier to provide than one specific definition. The term is used differently according to the field of study, for instance. In the literature of political science, sociology, and anthropology, *social capital* generally refers to the set of norms, networks, and organizations through which people gain access to power and resources and decisionmaking and policy formulation occur.[4] Economists add to this focus the contribution of social capital to economic growth. At the microeconomic level, they view social capital primarily in terms of its ability to improve market functioning. At the macroeconomic level, they consider how institutions, legal frameworks, and the government's role in the organization of production affect macroeconomic performance.

The most famous and in some ways most narrowly defined concept of social capital is Putnam's (Putnam 1993; Putnam, Leonardi, and Nanetti 1993). Putnam views social capital as a set of "horizontal associations" among people that have an effect on the productivity of the community. These associations include "networks of civic engagement" and social norms. Two assumptions underlie this concept: first, that networks and norms are empirically associated; and second, that they have important economic consequences. In this definition, the key feature of social capital is that it facilitates coordination and cooperation for the mutual benefit of the members of the association (Putnam 1993).[5]

Coleman (1988) puts forth a second, broader concept of social capital. Coleman sees social capital as "a variety of different entities, with two elements in common: they all consist of some aspect of social structure, and they facilitate certain actions of actors—whether personal or corporate actors—within the structure" (598). From the outset, this definition broadens the concept to include vertical as well as horizontal associations and the behavior of other entities, such as firms.[6] This wider range of associations covers both negative and positive objectives. Coleman states explicitly that "a given form of social capital that is valuable in facilitating certain actions may be useless or even harmful for others" (598). In fact, this view of social capital captures not only social structures at large but the ensemble of norms governing interpersonal behavior.

A third, still more encompassing view of social capital includes the social and political environment that enables norms to develop and shapes social structure. In addition to the largely informal horizontal relationships included in the first concept and the vertical hierarchical organizations of the second, this view encompasses formalized institutional relationships and structures, such as governments, political regimes, the rule of law, court systems, and civil and political liberties. (See box 10.1.)

---

BOX 10.1: THREE VIEWS ON SOCIAL CAPITAL: COMMON FEATURES

The three views on social capital progressively broaden the concept. The first includes mostly informal and local horizontal associations, while the second adds hierarchical associations. The third interpretation builds on the first two, adding formalized national structures such as government and the rule of law. The three views have several common features:

- All link the economic, social, and political spheres. They share the belief that social relationships affect and are affected by economic outcomes.

- All focus on relationships among economic agents and the ways in which formal and informal organizations of these agents can improve the efficiency of economic activities.

- All imply that desirable social relationships and institutions have positive externalities. Since individuals cannot appropriate these externalities, agents tend to underinvest in social capital, creating a role for public support.

- All recognize not only the potential social relationships created for improving development outcomes but also the possibility that these same relationships can have negative effects. The outcome depends on the nature of the relationship (horizontal versus hierarchical), preexisting norms and values, and the wider legal and political context.

---

The impact of this more broadly defined concept of social capital on macroeconomic outcomes has been investigated by North (1990) and Olson (1982). They argue that differences in per capita incomes across countries cannot be explained by the per capita distribution of productive resources (land and natural resources, human capital, and produced capital, including technology). Institutions and other forms of social capital, along with public policies, determine the returns a country can extract from its other forms of capital. Olson argues that low-income countries, even those with a large resource base, cannot obtain large gains from investment, specialization, and trade. These countries are limited by a lack of institutions that enforce contracts impartially and secure long-term property rights and by misguided economic policies.

### The effects of social capital

There is growing evidence that social capital can have an impact on development outcomes, including growth, equity, and poverty alleviation (Grootaert 1996). Associations and institutions provide an informal framework for sharing information, coordinating activities, and making collective decisions. Bardhan (1995) argues that what makes this informal model work is peer monitoring, a common set of norms, and sanctions at the local level.

*Sharing information*

Formal and informal institutions can help avert market failures related to inadequate or inaccurate information. Economic agents often make inefficient decisions because they lack needed information or because one agent benefits from relaying incorrect information to another. (Credit or employment applications are good examples of the latter.) In other circumstances, optimal decisions may be difficult to make because of uncertainty and the response of other agents to that uncertainty. Institutions can help disseminate adequate, accurate information that allow market players to make appropriate, efficient decisions. Group-based lending schemes are a case in point. These schemes—from *tontine* (informal saving circles) in West Africa to the Grameen Bank in Bangladesh—work because members have better information on each other than banks do.

Information problems can be particularly severe in capital markets. Japan and Korea have responded to such problems by developing "deliberation councils," which manage competition among firms for credit and foreign exchange. The process is transparent, encouraging cooperative behavior and information sharing among firms by removing incentives for rent-seeking behavior (World Bank 1993; Campos and Root 1996). The rule of law and a well-functioning court system (elements of social capital in its broadest definition) also help reduce uncertainty in capital markets by enforcing contracts. The contracting parties thus receive a priori information about the penalties for noncompliance. In the absence of effective courts, many informal associations internalize this policing role for their members. Diamond merchants, who often base deals involving millions of dollars worth of diamonds on a handshake, present a striking example. Failure to deliver on a deal irrevocably leads to expulsion from the group, and all members are aware of this fact. Unfortunately, this mechanism also works for groups pursuing undesirable outcomes, so that mafias function efficiently as well.

*Coordinating activities*

Uncoordinated or opportunistic behavior by economic agents can also lead to market failure. Such behaviors lie behind the failure of many irrigation projects. Because these projects often lack formal or informal (social) means of imposing equitable agreements for sharing the water, some farmers use water needed by others or fail to contribute to maintenance. Effective social capital in the form of water user groups can overcome such problems (Meinzen-Dick and others 1995; Ostrom 1995). These associations reduce opportunistic behavior by creating a framework within which individuals interact repeatedly, enhancing trust among members (Dasgupta 1988).[7]

*Making collective decisions*

Collective decisionmaking is a necessary condition for the provision of public goods and the management of market externalities. It is one of the basic rationales behind the notion of government. But like governments, local and voluntary associations do not always effectively maximize their ability to make collective decisions. The extent to which they do depends not only on how well they address the problems of information sharing but on the degree of equity that prevails. Local institutions are more effective at enforcing common agreements and cooperative action when the assets are relatively equitably distributed and benefits shared equally. On the local level, then, efficiency and equity go together. Sharing provides an incentive for improved coordination in the management of local public goods, increasing productivity for everyone.

This microfocus on markets is only part of the story. Market outcomes are also influenced by the macroeconomic environment and the political economy. The latter can be enabling, enhancing the effects of formal and informal civil associations (as has arguably been the case in the East Asian success stories). But the macro environment can also damage or undo the effects of local-level social capital. Where there are good governance, well-functioning courts, and freedom of expression, local associations thrive and complement the functions of macroinstitutions. But where these are absent or function poorly, local institutions may try to substitute for them, resulting in more stress and fewer economic benefits. Just as it makes little sense to assess an investment project without looking at the sector and relevant macroeconomic policy environment, it makes little sense to consider local associations in isolation. What is needed is a balanced view of the role of the central state and local-level institutions. This point suggests that the three definitions of social capital are not really alternative views but complementary aspects of the same concept.

### Social capital: an integrated view

The distinctions drawn in the literature among the three definitions are largely artificial and unnecessary. We argue that an integrated view of social capital is an important step toward measuring and operationalizing the concept. Such a view is based on the recognition that the four types of capital can coexist and are in fact needed to maximize the impact of social capital on economic and social outcomes. This complementarity applies not only across but within the types of capital. Physical capital provides a good example. The production process depends on different types of physical capital that work together (machines that produce goods, factories that house machines, roads that transport workers to factories and goods to market). Likewise, limited substitution possibilities exist across and within types of capital.

Stone, Levy, and Paredes (1992) illustrate the complementarity between micro- and macrolevel social capital and the limits to substitution in their comparison of the garment industries in Brazil and Chile. Brazil has a complex regulatory system, with laws that are often inconsistent and very expensive courts. Businesses have learned to rely on informal alternatives in their day-to-day transactions with customers and suppliers, especially when credit is involved. Brazilian garment entrepreneurs have worked out an effective informal credit information system that places a premium on an untarnished reputation. Nevertheless, contracts remain insecure and are frequently renegotiated, even up to the moment of delivery. The entrepreneurs have therefore adopted risk-reducing strategies, such as producing only standard items and reducing the size of orders, that ultimately hinder expansion.[8]

In contrast, Chile's relatively simple legal system and consistent enforcement of contracts have made the contracting process more secure, so that few contracts are renegotiated and the default rate on loans has dropped. The comparison suggests that the extent to which informal associations can replace the rule of law and a formal court system is limited, underscoring the importance of the role of macrolevel social capital in making business possible and especially of the government's role in providing an enabling environment that is simple, transparent, and consistent.

Complementarity between micro- and macrolevel social capital not only influences economic outcomes but has a mutually strengthening effect. Macroinstitutions can provide an enabling environment for microinstitutions to develop and flourish. In turn, local associations help sustain regional and national institutions and give them a measure of stability. The key measures of successful interaction between the two levels of institutions are shared values and norms and mutual trust. These can be expressed in the recognition and acceptance, at both levels, of a common entity (which could be the state itself) or a common objective (such as peace or economic progress) (figure 10.2, a). Switzerland, where the cantons joined in a confederation that supported the common objective of creating a sovereign state, offers an example of successful micro and macrolevel interaction—in fact, the modern Swiss state may well be pictured in figure 10.2, b. Local institutions are not initially required to share norms among themselves, other than the norm that is also common to the macro institution. But cohesion is likely to improve (through bonding and overlapping norms at the local level) as institutions work toward a common objective. This mutually reinforcing interaction between the micro and macrolevels increases the stock of social capital.

Sometimes micro- and macrolevel institutions fail to develop shared norms or overcome distrust (figure 10.3, a). Such a situation is likely to be unstable and to deteriorate until all bonds are broken (figure 10.3, b). If the key norm in question relates to basic human respect, the outcome is civil strife or war, as in Yugoslavia. If the distrust is in the economic sphere, the result is economic setback, as in Québec.

Among the factors that determine whether a positive (figure 10.2) or negative (figure 10.3) scenario prevails is the macroscale framework and the extent to which it is both enabling and perceived by the microscale institutions to be legitimate, representative, and fair. The relationship between formal and informal institutions also needs

FIGURE 10.2: POSITIVE INTERACTION BETWEEN MACRO- AND MICROINSTITUTIONS

**(A)**  **(B)**

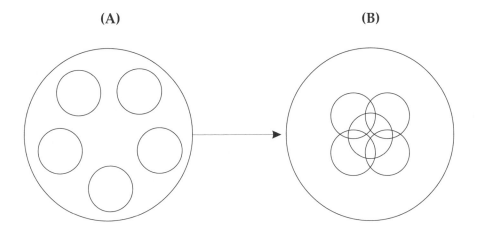

FIGURE 10.3: NEGATIVE INTERACTION BETWEEN MACRO- AND MICROINSTITUTIONS

**(A)**                                                                    **(B)**

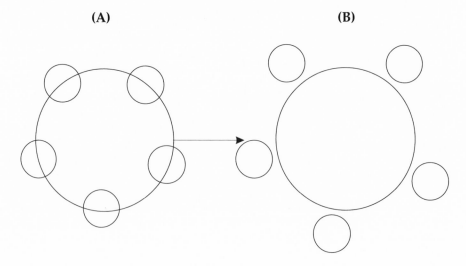

to be considered. At the local level, formal government and other institutions interact with a dense set of informal networks, associative frameworks, and voluntary
associations. These interactions help define the constraints on and the scope of individual, household, and group activities.

The quality of the institutions themselves is also important. The abilities and effectiveness of the institutions at the macro and microlevels (and in the formal and informal spheres) make a difference to outcomes. Institutions need values, but they also
need organizational and management capacity and communication and technical
skills in order to act effectively upon these values. This observation provides an
entry point for donors, at least in the positive scenario portrayed in figure 10.2. Support for capacity building and training can improve institutions and promote social
capital to make the positive interaction more efficient.

The transition economies of Eastern Europe and the former Soviet Union provide a
dramatic instance of the importance of constructive interaction between macro- and
microlevel social capital and the costs of the absence of such interaction. The sudden
disappearance of government from many social and economic functions has eroded
trust, forcing people to rely on local networks and informal associations. Rose
(1995b) creates the "new democracies barometer" to measure this phenomenon. He
notes that people have withdrawn from the "official" economy and begun to rely on
multiple informal economies to satisfy most needs. Informal activities include growing food, repairing houses, and helping friends in return for needed assistance. In a
well-functioning market economy, these activities may be hobbies (and helping out
may reflect friendship), but in the transition economies, this "social economy" has
developed out of necessity. In Ukraine, for example, three-fourths of the households
are involved in such activities (Rose 1995a). In Russia, the transition has led to what
Rose calls an "hourglass society" (Rose 1995c) . At the base is the "rich" social life of
most Russians, consisting of strong informal networks based on trust among friends
and face-to-face interactions. At the top is another "rich" social life and the political

life of the elite, who compete with each other for power and wealth. The links between the base and the top are limited and characterized by a general distrust of the elite. Not even one in three Russians expects fair treatment from the police or their municipal offices (the post office is the most trusted institution). Sustainable development is unlikely in Russia without a change for the better in the linkages between micro- and macrolevel institutions.

The process by which interactions between micro- and macrolevel social capital develop is dynamic. A good example is the gradual replacement, in the course of successful development, of informal associations and networks with formal administrative structures and impersonal market mechanisms. Large anonymous markets are more efficient than networks because the "best" buyer or seller may not be part of a network. If the development path is supported by a solid court system and a mechanism for enforcing contracts, anonymous markets will over time replace the "named" transactions within networks (that is, whereby the number of agents in each network is small and they know each other by name). In this situation, all participating economic agents gain.[9]

We suspect that, in principle, complementarity among different levels and types of social capital can be recognized and readily accepted. Capturing this complementarity empirically is not so straightforward, however. Should the shift from informal to formal networks be registered as declining or increasing social capital, or as a steady total amount, with one-for-one substitution among "units" of social capital? An initial step in measuring social capital could be to aggregate the indicators that have been developed at the micro- and macrolevels in an index that resembles the Human Development and Physical Quality of Life indexes. For microindicators, there are the Putnam-type examples of associational activity used by Narayan and Pritchett (1996). For macroindicators, there are the cross-country analyses of Knack and Keefer (1995, 1996) and Klitgaard and Fedderke (1995) and the macroinstitutional and trust indicators used by Rose (1995a, b, c). Indicators for the same country can in principle always be aggregated (abstracting from the usual issue of weighing component indexes).

Measuring complementarity or the feedback process between social capital at the micro and macrolevels—particularly determining whether the process is additive or multiplicative—is even more difficult. The index suggested in the previous paragraph assumes an additive process. Conceptually, it is not difficult to describe a multiplier or exponent-type process in the context of a production function, and social capital can be factored into the equation in much the same way as technology. In this case, certain types of social capital enter the process additively, but others have multiplier effects. The empirical estimation of such a function is still a distant objective, but a conceptual start can be made by thinking through what mathematical form the function will take. Theoretical conceptualization then guides the empirical investigation, and the results of the empirical research feed back to the theoretical constructs and help validate, reject, or refine them.

### Appropriate social capital

The recognition that all different types of social capital are necessary to produce optimal results (and can in fact be mutually reinforcing) has a further implication—

namely, that an "optimal mix" of types of social capital exists. This paper posits that the optimal mix is defined in terms of an objective function and that the obvious candidate is the maximization of economic outcomes—a process described by the macro production function and constrained by resource endowments.

This proposal is akin to arguing that we can identify an "appropriate technology" for a given country that will maximize returns to the other factors of productions. It takes into account the nature of complementarity and substitution across these factors. A nuclear reactor, for instance, is not appropriate technology in a country that lacks the human capital to manage and maintain it. In practice, appropriate technology is not identified with formal economic models but is based on ad hoc insight and a thorough knowledge of a country. The same is true for appropriate social capital, which also enhances the efficiency of the combination process of the other factors of production. In Putnam's words, "Social capital enhances the benefits of investment in physical and human capital" (1993, 36). In other words, it is not just an input into the production function but, like technology, a shift factor (or exponent) of the entire production function.

The key to determining what constitutes appropriate social capital is data—both on the composition as well as the level of the total stock. This information needs to be assessed in light of the other types of available capital in a country. We think that the most useful way to advance this notion is to undertake case studies in selected countries where a good bit of information on microinstitutions is already available. These case studies would investigate the interaction of the institutions with other organizations and levels of government and determine which economic processes they affect (as well as the levels and types of human, physical, and natural capital involved). However, to be truly useful in the context of this discussion, the case studies must be guided by a methodological framework that facilitates the measurement and analysis of findings and assesses testable hypotheses.

### Summary and conclusions

This paper argues for an improved understanding of social capital by putting forth two propositions. First, it suggests that the distinctions drawn in the literature by competing definitions of social capital are largely artificial and unnecessary. They detract from the fact that different types of social capital coexist and can be mutually reinforcing. We propose an aggregate formulation (if not a single index) of social capital and a continuing investigation into the additive and multiplicative nature of the interactions among the different types of social capital. Second, we argue that there is an appropriate level and composition of social capital for a given country at a given time. This level takes into account complementarities with other types of capital. Its composition is likely to change over time, but the total should increase through accumulation.

We hope that the discussion of the two propositions advances our understanding of how social capital contributes to economic and social outcomes. While these proposals make new demands on both conceptualization and measurement, they also open the door to bringing together data sources and approaches to data collection.

## Notes

1.   This paper draws on earlier work on social capital by the authors. See especially Serageldin (1996a) and Grootaert (1996).
2.   This notion goes to the heart of the definition of income given by Nobel Laureate Sir John Hicks: "The maximum value a person can consume during a week, and still expect to be as well off at the end of the week as at the beginning."
3.   There are dissenting views on the role of social capital in the growth rates of the East Asian economies. Some authors argue that increased mobilization of resources—that is, increases in labor force participation rates, education, and investment in physical capital—explain most or all of the growth (Krugman 1994). Other observers, relying on endogenous growth models, argue that low income inequality (which characterizes the East Asian economies) has been an important stimulus to growth (Birdsall and others 1995). For a recent review and interpretation of the evidence, see Stiglitz (1996).
4.   Coleman (1988) has been attributed with introducing the term "social capital" into the sociological literature. He defines it as a "social structure [which] facilitates certain actions of actors within the structure" (598). Similar to this definition is Etzioni's (1988) concept of "social collectivities," or "major decisionmaking units, often providing the context within which individual decisions are made" (186). In economics, Loury (1977) introduced the concept of social capital in an analysis of racial inequality to describe the social resources of ethnic communities. More generally, economists have argued that aspects of social capital, such as institutions, have always been present in economic analysis.
5.   While this concept of social capital was originally limited to associations having positive effects on development, it has recently been relaxed to include groups that may produce undesirable outcomes, such as rent-seekers (for instance, the Mafia in Southern Italy, and militias).
6.   This concept of social capital is closely related to the treatment of firms and other hierarchical organizations in institutional economics, which sees the organization's purpose as minimizing transaction costs (Williamson 1985, 1993). Vertical associations are characterized by hierarchical relationships and the uneven distribution of power among members.
7.   This *backward-looking* motivation for trust has been discussed in the social psychology literature. Trust can also be *forward looking*, based on the perception of retaliation for untrustworthy behavior.
8.   A study of Peru shows that the sheer complexity of laws and regulations can undermine their effectiveness and provide economic agents with strong disincentives to adhere to formality (de Soto 1989). In Peru, the complexity of the legal framework has led to the shifting of economic transactions to an informal sector that is not protected by formal law but is functional, thanks to informal substitutes.
9.   Under the narrow definition of social capital, this phenomenon registers as a decline in social capital. But using the broader concept, the same phenomenon emerges as the substitution of one form of social capital (the rule of law) for another (horizontal associations).

## References

Bardhan, P. 1995. "Research on Poverty and Development—Twenty Years after Redistribution with Growth." Paper prepared for the Annual Bank Conference on Development Economics, May 1–2, 1995. World Bank, Washington, D.C.

Birdsall, N., D. Ross, and R. Sabot. 1995. "Inequality and Growth Reconsidered: Lessons from East Asia." *World Bank Economic Review* 9(3):477–508.

Brundtland Commission (World Commission on Environment and Development). 1987. *Our Common Future.* New York: Oxford University Press.

Buckley, S. 1996. "No Somali Government? No Problem." *Washington Post.*

Coleman, J. 1988. "Social Capital in the Creation of Human Capital." *American Journal of Sociology* 94(Supplement):S95–S120.

Dasgupta, P. 1988. "Trust as a Commodity." In D. Gambetta, ed., *Trust: Making and Breaking Cooperative Relations.* Oxford: Blackwell Limited.

de Soto, H. 1989. *The Other Path: The Invisible Revolution of the Third World.* New York: Harper and Row.

Etzioni, A. 1988. *The Moral Dimension: Towards A New Economics.* New York: The Free Press.

Galtung, J. 1996. "On the Social Cost of Modernization—Social Disintegration, Atomie/Anomie and Social Development." *Development and Change* 27.

Grootaert, C. 1996. "Social Capital: The Missing Link?" In *Monitoring Environmental Progress—Expanding the Measure of Wealth.* Washington, D.C.: World Bank.

Klitgaard, R., and J. Fedderke. 1995. "Social Integration and Disintegration: An Exploratory Analysis of Cross-Country Data." *World Development* 23(3):357–69.

Knack, S., and P. Keefer. 1995. "Institutions and Economic Performance: Cross-Country Tests Using Alternative Institutional Measures." *Economics and Politics* 7(3):202–27.

———. 1996. "Does Social Capital Have an Economic Payoff? A Cross-Country Investigation." World Bank Policy Research Department, mimeo. World Bank, Washington, D.C.

Krugman, P. 1994. "The Myth of Asia's Miracle." *Foreign Affairs* 73(6):62–78.

Narayan, D., and L. Pritchett. 1996. "Cents and Sociability: Household Income and Social Capital in Rural Tanzania." Environment Department, mimeo. World Bank, Washington, D.C.

North, D. 1990. *Institutions, Institutional Change and Economic Performance.* New York: Cambridge University Press.

Olson, M. 1982. *The Rise and Decline of Nations: Economic Growth, Stagflation, and Social Rigidities.* New Haven: Yale University Press.

Pathan, R., N. Arul, and M. Poffenberger. 1993. "Forest Protection Committees in Gujurat—Joint Management Initiatives." Reference Paper No. 8 prepared for Sustainable Forest Management Conference. Sponsored by the Ford Foundation, Delhi.

Pearce, D., and G. Atkinson. 1993. "Capital Theory and the Measurement of Sustainable Development: An Indicator of Weak Sustainability." *Ecological Economics* 8:99–123.

Putnam, R. 1993. "The Prosperous Community—Social Capital and Public Life." *The American Prospect* 13:35–42.

———, R. Leonardi, and R. Nanetti. 1993. *Making Democracy Work: Civic Traditions in Modern Italy.* Princeton: Princeton University Press.

Rose, R. 1995a. "Adaptation, Resilience and Destitution—Alternative Responses to Transition in Ukraine." *Problems of Post-Communism* (November/December):52–61.

————. 1995b. "New Russia Barometer IV—Survey Results." Studies in Public Policy No. 250. University of Strathclyde, Glasgow.

————. 1995c. "Russia as an Hour-Glass Society: A Constitution Without Citizens." *East European Constitutional Review* 4(3):34–42.

Serageldin, I. 1994. "The Challenge of a Holistic Vision: Culture, Empowerment, and the Development Paradigm." In I. Serageldin and J. Taboroff, eds., *Culture and Development in Africa.* Environmentally Sustainable Development Proceedings Series, No. 1. Washington, D.C.: World Bank.

————. 1996a. "Sustainability as Opportunity and the Problem of Social Capital." *The Brown Journal of World Affairs* 3(2).

————. 1996b. *Sustainability and the Wealth of Nations—First Steps in an Ongoing Journey.* Environmentally Sustainable Development Studies and Monographs Series No. 5. Washington, D.C.: World Bank.

Stiglitz, J. 1996. "Some Lessons from the East Asian Miracle." *World Bank Research Observer* 11(2):151–77.

Stone, A., B. Levy, and R. Paredes. 1992. "Public Institutions and Private Transactions: The Legal and Regulatory Environment for Business Transactions in Brazil and Chile." Policy Research Working Paper No. 891. World Bank, Washington, D.C.

Williamson, O. 1985. *The Economic Institutions of Capitalism—Firms, Markets, Relational Contracting.* New York: The Free Press.

————. 1993. "the Economic Analysis of Institutions and Organizations—In General and with Respect to Country Studies." Economics Department Working Paper No. 133. Organization for Economic Cooperation and Development, Paris.

World Bank. 1993. *The East Asian Miracle.* New York: Oxford University Press.

————. 1995. *Monitoring Environmental Progress—A Report on Work in Progress.* Washington, D.C.

————. 1997. *Expanding the Measure of Wealth—Indicators of Environmentally Sustainable Development.* Washington, D.C.

# 11. An institutional framework for learning from failed states

John R. Eriksson

*In failed states, important formal and informal economizing institutions have broken down or, in some cases, have never fully developed or have been prevented from doing so. Until recently donor agencies have tended to ignore the exclusionary and predatory behaviors that presage state failure. Assisting recovery from state failure is typically a prolonged process and donors must be prepared to accept setbacks and to support institutional innovations.*

*The transition to peace is not primarily the reconstruction of damaged infrastructure, it is the transition from fear and the defensive responses that have become ingrained.*

—Collier and Pradhan 1994, 133

This paper explores some of the lessons development agencies can learn from countries that have experienced state failure or collapse and from attempts to rebuild those countries. The paper draws on selected literature dealing with the new institutional economics (NIE) and the phenomenon of state failure. Another source is the author's own involvement in the international community's evaluation of the international response to the 1994 Rwandan crisis and its aftermath (Joint Evaluation 1996). The paper also draws from a World Bank Operations Evaluation Department study, "The Bank's Experience with Postconflict Reconstruction," being prepared by a team led by Alcira Kreimer. The OED study includes an extensive review of the literature and the Bank's portfolio, plus nine in-depth country case studies, and is scheduled for completion by the end of 1997.

## Significance of the problem

Since 1980, over 50 countries have been involved in major civil conflicts, many of which are still in progress or have only recently ended. Excluding China and India, about one-quarter of all IDA commitments in 1994 went to countries that had undergone or were in the process of emerging from significant periods of civil conflict.

### Definitional issues

The choice of the term *failed state* is deliberate. The alternative term, *collapsed state*, may be defined as a scenario in which the state no longer performs its basic functions. According to Zartman (1995), in this scenario:

As the decisionmaking center of government, the state is paralyzed and inoperative; laws are not made, order is not preserved, and societal cohesion is not enhanced. As a symbol of identity, the state has lost its power of conferring a name on its people and a meaning to their social actions. As a territory, it is no longer assured security and provisionment by a central sovereign organization. As the authoritative political institution, it has lost its legitimacy, which is therefore up for grabs, and so has lost its right to command and conduct public affairs. As a system of socioeconomic organization, its functional balance of inputs and outputs is destroyed . . . . It no longer is even the target of demands, because its people know that it is incapable of providing supplies. No longer functioning, with neither traditional nor charismatic nor institutional sources of legitimacy, it has lost the right to rule. (5)

Although it may seem a distinction without much difference, the term *failed state* appears to convey a wider range of possibilities than *collapsed state*, at least as characterized above. All of the nine countries under review in the OED study have manifested—for varying lengths of time and to varying degrees—some loss of state function. Even in El Salvador and Sri Lanka, the two countries of the nine that least match the characterization of the collapsed state, state functioning failed in certain geographical areas, albeit at some distance from the economic and governmental centers of gravity.[1]

One sad but common characteristic all nine country experiences share is intense violent conflict, often resulting in widespread damage to physical, human, and social capital. A major concern for development agencies is how best to assist countries in their efforts to repair this damage. However, the term *postconflict reconstruction* does not itself adequately capture the reality of the challenge. Some of this reality is suggested by the following passages:

> . . . in many cases the issue is really one of *construction* rather than *reconstruction*, of building rather than rebuilding, politically as well as economically. (Lake 1990, 16)

> . . . civil war removes legitimate authority. Consequently, the restoration of "economic peace" is not the automatic corollary of military victory; it is the reconstruction of systems of legitimacy. (Collier and Pradhan 1994, 119–20)

These passages broaden the concept of reconstruction to include the institutional as well as the physical dimension and acknowledges that *new* construction may be involved as much as reconstruction. These points will be revisited in the following sections, which first discuss some relevant insights from the NIE literature. They then suggest some lessons for development agencies in countries experiencing and attempting to recover from violent conflict and the accompanying manifestations of state failure.

### Some relevant constructs and insights from the new institutional economics

In a literature survey, "Institutional Economics and Development," in the *Handbook of Development Economics,* Lin and Nugent (1995) offer the following definitions of institutions:

> . . . a set of humanly devised behavioral rules that govern and shape the
> interactions of human beings, in part by helping them to form expecta-
> tions of what other people will do . . . . Institutions can consist of both
> formal entities like laws, constitutions, written contracts, market
> exchanges, and organizational by-laws and informal ones like shared
> values, norms, customs, ethics, and ideology. (2,306–07)

A basic function of institutions is to economize—that is, to allow one or more economic agents to improve their welfare without making others worse off or to attain a
higher level of their objectives within their resource constraints. Lin and Nugent
(1995) note that the efficacy of the economizing function of a specific institution will
depend on how well the institution copes with the opportunistic behavior of relevant economic agents and utilizes the existence and strength of auxiliary institutions, whose economizing functions may be indirect. As an example, the authors cite
competitive managerial, labor, and stock markets that mitigate the discretionary or
opportunistic behavior of corporate managers, aided by such nonmarket, informal
institutions as loyalty, team spirit, and morality. In failed states, important formal
and informal economizing institutions have broken down or, in some cases, have
never fully developed or have been prevented from doing so.

### Transaction costs

A major contribution of NIE has been the elaboration and application of the concept
of transaction costs. These may be viewed as the costs of organizing, maintaining,
and enforcing the rules of an institutional arrangement. An institutional arrangement is said to be more efficient than an alternative when it performs a given institutional function (or level of service) for a lower cost (the transaction cost). A basic economic institutional arrangement is the formal or informal contract for the sale or
purchase of final and intermediate goods and services and for factors of production
of goods and services.

### Transaction-cost politics and political transition costs

Two recent extensions of the transaction-costs approach to political processes are relevant to the analysis of failed states. Oliver Williamson coined the term *transaction-
cost economics* for the study of the effects of transaction costs on economic organizations and outcomes. Borrowing from Williamson, Avinash Dixit (1996) coins the
term *transaction-cost politics* as a framework for the study of the "mechanisms by
which political processes and institutions [attempt] to reduce . . . transaction costs or
to minimize their effects." Dixit finds that obstructions to the institutional change
designed to reduce transaction costs affect political processes more severely than
they do economic organizations and outcomes. An example of such an obstruction
might be a common agency with multiple principals (for example, a regulatory
agency that must simultaneously answer to executive branch superiors, the legislative branch, and interest groups). Or there might be substantial information asymmetries among the parties (superior information in the hands of one party or a lack
of transparency or observable behavior by one or more parties).

In the 1992–93 Arusha negotiations, the Rwandan government could be viewed as
an agent faced with multiple principals or representatives of several states, such as

France and the United States, as well as of the invading Rwandan Patriotic Front (RPF). The government, or at least elements of the government, probably had information (about genocide plans) and was supporting unobservable (to the principals) behavior (preparing for genocide). Greater transparency might have led to different behavior by the principals (for example, negative sanctions on the government and greater efforts to include extremist representatives in the negotiations) (Adelman and Suhrke 1996).

In a critique of NIE, Mushtaq Khan (1995) employs the term *transition costs*, which he distinguishes from transaction costs. He defines transition costs as the political costs that potential losers from a proposed institutional change can impose on the proponents of change. He argues that transition costs provide a better explanation than transaction costs for the relatively rapid transition of some countries to institutions facilitating development and sustained economic growth. In particular, he cites the United States and United Kingdom in the 19th century and the contemporary East Asian newly industrialized countries and China, as opposed to Pakistan in the 1960s and the "South Asian democracies." He concludes with the warning that "it is worth remembering that a 'mistake' in the assessment of the transition costs involved in implementing particular programs of institutional change can ultimately result in civil war and large-scale loss of lives" (86).

Khan's analysis suggests that there are junctures in the period prior to state failure, when one or more of the key actors involved with a state on the brink of failure make fateful miscalculations of the cost of transition to new institutions. In the last half of the 1970s, the military governments of El Salvador, which combined both reformist and repressive policies, made such a miscalculation. So too did the parties (including the Western countries represented at the table) to the Arusha Peace Accords for Rwanda in 1992–93.[2]

*The evolving concept of the project and institutional development*

In a recent paper, Robert Picciotto (1995, vi) presents development projects as "instruments of policy reform and institutional change" that aim to overcome market failures. He recognizes that this view of development projects has evolved from the original conception of one-shot efforts involving physical investments and carried out over a limited period of time. Picciotto's new conception of projects draws heavily on the language of institutional and business economics:

> Fundamentally, a [business] project is a set of contracts linking principals and agents, that is, owners, employees, contractors, consultants, and beneficiaries. An overarching contract also links the country and the external development agency in the form of a negotiated agreement that incorporates rewards and penalties . . . . Disbursements may be suspended or project loans canceled if misprocurement takes place or if fundamental provisions embedded in the agreement have been violated. Conversely, effective project performance produces positive spillover effects, for example, with respect to the use of project savings, the provision of implementation support, or the financing of "repeater" projects . . . . Moral hazard is a central preoccupation of development lenders . . . opportunistic behavior must be discouraged. While rela-

tively minor infractions are not penalized, egregious free riding is inhibited by incentives and penalties. (2–3)

The above passage stands in contrast to a recent analysis by Peter Uvin (1996) of two agricultural development projects in the 1970s and 1980s in Rwanda. Uvin notes that the economic rate of return at the close of the first project was either negative or at best marginal and cites an analysis of the social aspects of the first project by René Lemarchand (1982). Lemarchand finds a pattern of opportunistic and discriminatory behavior that presages practices, which, by the early 1990s, had become much more pervasive. Uvin summarizes Lemarchand's conclusions as follows:

> The end result of this project, then, is a great increase in inequality between regions, classes, groups, and people. It is a system in which a small group of people managed to obtain most of the advantages of a multimillion dollar project: jobs in and outside the project; free land to be cultivated by family members, renters, or political clients; or large herds overgrazing at the expense of the original Tutsi and Hima herdsmen. It is no accident that those who benefited were often from the president's region, nor that almost all of them belong to the usual class of *evolués*, that is, those in the loop, those with the right connections. They also received the benefits of cars, motorcycles, foreign training, and 47 new buildings. They, in return, fueled a system of clientelism, through which ordinary Hutu could get access to land, salaried jobs, agricultural inputs, etc. (22)

Notwithstanding these problems, a second project was proposed and approved in 1979, extending the area to be covered and using the same implementing parastatal. The "repeater" project in this case, rather than serving as a reward for good performance, provided an additional free ride for those who continued to extract rents by highjacking project benefits. Uvin argues that these two projects were not isolated, and there is evidence that corruption and lack of accountability became a major concern for a number of development agencies and donors in Rwanda in the late 1980s and early 1990s. During the massive population movements within the country during the early 1990s, which were induced by a combination of invasions from Uganda, state violence against civilians, and serious drought, the highjacking phenomenon also extended to relief assistance.[3]

*Institutional design parameters*

Picciotto (1995) describes three basic institutional design parameters that vary in dominance depending on the nature of the goods to be delivered by a project. This device has the heuristic value of bringing together in one framework a number of the insights and constructs of NIE and their implications for development agencies. The three parameters are hierarchy, or the state sector; the market, or the private sector; and participation, or the voluntary sector.

NIE suggests six different types of project goods:

- *Government goods*, which include the implementation and enforcement of policy and require state agencies for their provision (for example, regulatory agencies, police, and the courts).

- *Toll goods*, which have the characteristic of excludability or control of access but lack the characteristic of subtractability—that is, consumption by one person that does not reduce availability to others, therefore making provision by the market feasible and efficient but necessitating hierarchy in the form of regulation (for example, regulated public utilities).

- *Public goods*, which lack excludability and subtractability and therefore require a combination of hierarchy and participation, or voice, in the form of civil society and legislature for their provision and/or responsiveness and accountability (for example, policy formulation and rural roads).

- *Market goods*, which have both excludability and subtractability and therefore can be provided most efficiently, given an appropriate policy framework, by the market.

- *Civil goods*, which are provided through participation by NGOs and other organizations of civil society as a response to dissatisfaction with the failings of both market and hierarchy (for example, public advocacy, professional standards, civic action).

- *Common pool goods*, which lack excludability but have subtractability and are thus not feasible for market (private sector) provision; they impose high transaction costs for public sector provision through monitoring and enforcement and thus must rely on voluntary cooperation and persuasion (participation) through local organizations (for example, community natural resource management).

According to Picciotto (1995, 10), participation in the above framework, especially as harnessed by NGOs and other entities of civil society to produce civil goods, plays a "vital supporting role by filling gaps in private and government activities, by exhorting, motivating, and restraining the state, and by calling attention to the excesses of free and unrestrained markets." However, a serious problem arises from the fact that civil society organizations do not necessarily produce such civil goods. Picciotto observes:

> To be sure, there is no guarantee that all components of civil society are benign or genuinely concerned with the fate of the downtrodden . . . Thus, some private voluntary organizations are specifically created to advance the interests of narrow and privileged constituencies. Therefore, failing effective self-policing, the civil society must be restrained to work for the common good both by the workings of the market and by the enabling environment of the state. (10)

In addition to being "restrained to work for the common good," civil society organizations must also be nurtured in a hospitable climate of enabling laws and regulations. Such a climate gives them the freedom to work and advocate for the common good without fearing that the state may take arbitrary and repressive actions against them. The deterioration of such a climate is one of the hallmarks of a failing state. Zartman (1995) notes that:

It is the tyrant's destruction of the institutions of civil society that makes the hard state's destruction a matter of collapse rather than one of simple replacement . . .

State collapse involves the breakdown not only of the governmental superstructure but also that of the societal infrastructure . . . [and what distinguishes state collapse] is the inability of civil society to rebound, to fill positions, restore faith, support government, and rally round the successor. (7–8)[4]

### The roles of development agencies in the stages of state failure and recovery

It is possible to distinguish stages or periods that lead up to, take place during, and follow state failure. This section proposes a delineation of such periods and analyzes selected country and donor experiences in each period, drawing on the NIE constructs and insights discussed above.

### The prefailure period[5]

In some respects, this period is the most difficult period to analyze, even ex post (let alone ex ante). What are the signs that the institutions of governance and civil society are about to unravel, resulting in the failure or collapse of one or more state functions? The causal factors typically are multiple and difficult to prioritize. Ethnic fissures have been one obvious factor in Bosnia, Rwanda, and Sri Lanka. In Rwanda and Sri Lanka, ethnic discrimination by the state exacerbated ethnic tensions. It had been practiced by a colonial power that explicitly or tacitly favored the ethnic minority and then by the independent government, which reversed the situation in favor of the majority. At the extreme, in Rwanda, such discrimination took the form of systematic, state-sponsored violations of human rights, including arbitrary arrests, imprisonment, torture, and mass murder. Ideological extremism was a driving causal factor in Cambodia, as it was in El Salvador, albeit in a less virulent form and combined with entrenched socioeconomic discrimination. Predatory government behavior appears as a proximate cause of conflict or state failure in many (but not all) instances, with unabashed predatory behavior appearing as a dominant factor in the state failures of Haiti and Uganda.

An obvious question arises: what can development agencies, including the Bank, do to prevent or avoid the appalling consequences that state failure and collapse often entail? One step would be to assess more systematically—in analytical work, country assistance strategies, and design and supervision missions—such factors as ethnic tension, discrimination, and exclusion; human rights violations; and predatory practices.[6] The analysis of such factors could inject sensitive issues into policy dialogue with the recipient country. Among such issues would be intervention in what many countries regard as sovereign, internal affairs and vulnerability to the charge of inconsistent treatment across countries, especially if withdrawal of assistance is intimated. The mention of withdrawal of aid implies the possibility of predicting that conditions are on the cusp of disaster and state failure. In terms of NIE constructs, the question might then be posed as follows: when do information asymmetries become so great and the resulting opportunistic behavior so egregious that state failure is on the cusp of being inevitable?

The present paper makes no attempt to provide an answer to such a question ex ante. In the specific case of Rwanda, an ex post review of evidence on human rights violations and genocide plans suggests that point was reached by early 1993 (Adelman and Suhrke 1996; Eriksson and others 1996). However, it may also be the case that short of strengthening the UN peacekeeping force in Rwanda (UNAMIR) and broadening its mandate, which was not done until June 1994 (when it was too late), no other action taken by the international community at that point could have prevented the genocide. The point at which a "lesser" option, such as the threat of withdrawing aid, could have had an impact may have been as much as a decade or two earlier, before Hutu extremism became entrenched. But this fact poses a dilemma: while the leverage of the donor community is likely to be greater some time before the cusp of disaster is reached, the evidence of predation and extremism will also likely be weaker then, decreasing international support for interventionist approaches.[7]

### The peak conflict period

In most (but not all) cases, development agencies will have withdrawn during the period of peak conflict, especially if that conflict involves state collapse. When a donor such as the World Bank withdraws from a country during widespread conflict, it continues to monitor the situation in order to be well positioned to reenter when conditions permit. In El Salvador, two events pushed the World Bank into intensive monitoring, dialogue, and engagement while the conflict was still intense. The first, which took place some five years before the peace accords signed in Chapultepec, Mexico, in January 1992, was the San Salvador earthquake of October 1986, which led to an emergency earthquake reconstruction project that in turn initiated a series of periodic country visits by a Bank economist. The second was the election of a reform-minded government headed by President Alfredo Cristiani in 1989. The government subsequently paid the arrears it owed the Bank, an action that was followed by a request for a structural adjustment loan (SAL). The request led to the Bank's intensive reengagement in the country and the approval of SAL I in February 1991.

### The first "benchmark" period

The potential for an end to intense conflict is usually marked by the onset of serious discussions among the belligerent parties that in turn lead to peace negotiations. The term *first benchmark period* conveys the sense of a turning point and the potential for setbacks as well as progress. During this period, development agencies can support the transition from war to peace by helping to prepare a national reconstruction plan. The Bank and other donors played this role in El Salvador during the last half of 1991, before the conclusion of the peace accords of early 1992.

This first benchmark period is not always preceded by successful peace negotiations. In Rwanda, the so-called Arusha Accords negotiations held in Arusha, Tanzania in 1992 and 1993 did not end the massive violence. In fact, the violence escalated on two tracks: first, in the form of state- and militia-sponsored violence against civilians, and second, in the form of renewed attacks by the RPF from the north. In Rwanda, then the first benchmark period began with victory—that is, the establishment of the RPF-backed government at the end of the genocide in mid-July 1994— and can be said to have ended at the time of the first government and United Nations Development Programme (UNDP)-led donor "round table" in January 1995. This six-month period was critical for future construction and reconstruction efforts in Rwanda. With impressive speed, the Bank approved in August 1994 an emergency grant (financed from surplus) for $20 million. The grant, intended to expedite rehabilitation assistance to adversely impacted survivors and returnees, was implemented by four UN agencies (the United Nations Food and Agricutlure Organization, United Nations High Commissioner for Refugees, United Nations Children's Fund, and World Health Organization). The Bank subsequently fielded several assessment and planning missions to the country, convened donor meetings in Paris in September and October, began restructuring $25 million of its previously undisbursed portfolio to better meet the current situation, and designed and negotiated a $50 million Emergency Recovery Credit.

### *The initial construction/reconstruction period*

The process of construction and reconstruction is likely to be long term and to consist of several periods or phases, each separated by a benchmark or watershed. The initial period is the first of those phases.

*El Salvador.* The overriding reference point for the El Salvador construction/reconstruction process is the peace accords. Most observers judge country and donor performance by this benchmark. The basic thrust of a recent volume of essays sponsored by UNDP (Boyce 1996) is that international donors, and the Bretton Woods institutions in particular, did not direct enough assistance or push policy dialogue with the government strongly enough in explicit support of the peace accords. What Boyce terms "peace conditionality" was not pursued.

Boyce and other observers are suggesting that growth in El Salvador has been concentrated in the financial and commercial sectors and that investment and thus growth in agriculture and industry have lagged.[8] Poverty amelioration, especially in rural areas, has been spotty. Visible improvement might be virtually nil were it not for the substantial remittances from the million or so Salvadoran refugee-immigrants living in the United States. Reliable statistics are hard to come by, but unemployment is believed to be extremely high, and there is a universal perception of high and increasing personal crime. Two key components of the peace accords, the program of land transfers to former combatants and the creation of a new civilian police force, have encountered difficulties and setbacks.

Boyce and others recognize that the Bank and other donors face legal constraints in providing support in some of these areas, such as law enforcement and land transfers. However, they argue that the Bretton Woods institutions, in particular, could have pursued other issues more aggressively with the government. They suggest that the government could have been encouraged to emphasize domestic resource mobilization and the equity of mobilization, as well as the composition of public expenditures. The latter, for example, could have been shifted away from defense-military expenditures in favor of areas such as health, education, and governance (see also Segovia 1996).

Nevertheless, the second SAL to El Salvador in September 1993 in effect provided timely, fungible resources for the government to allocate to programs mandated by the peace accords.[9] The Bank also funded, under its Social Sector Rehabilitation project (approved in June 1991), an innovative and risky pilot approach to basic education that other donors were not prepared to support. This approach, which was modeled on a spontaneous institutional innovation by some communities during the civil war, provides funding to local parent associations. The associations have considerable autonomy, including the ability to hire and fire teachers. Based on the success of this Educación con Participación de la Comunidad (EDUCO) pilot, the Bank and the Inter-American Development Bank have cofinanced a broader Basic Education Modernization project (approved September 1995) that supports the extension of the EDUCO approach to all rural areas and, in a modified form, to urban areas. These efforts should have a substantial, long-term positive impact on sustainable development in El Salvador. The 1996 Land Administration Project, which involves establishing the country's first nationwide land registration and titling system, could have a similar impact.

Donor coordination is particularly critical at the early stages of postconflict reconstruction. In NIE terms, donor coordination can be viewed as an institutional arrangement intended to reduce the transaction costs of providing assistance. Some aspects of coordination in El Salvador during the peace negotiations, namely between the United Nations and the Bretton Woods institutions, have been widely criticized. But Bank-led donor coordination through the consultative group process has received high marks for encouraging support from bilateral donors and reinforcing the positions of moderate elements on both sides of the conflict (Belt and de Palomo 1994).

*Rwanda.* The main development assistance issue during the initial construction/ reconstruction period was the development agencies' approach to a new government struggling to cope without the institutions of governance. A high proportion of former civil servants either had been killed or had fled the country. Office furnishings, equipment, and files had been looted or trashed, and new arrivals to the country filled many key positions. In the latter case, the problem was confounded by the fact that many of the new arrivals had no previous experience with governance and lacked even basic knowledge of a country they had not visited in decades, if at all.

Development agencies were largely unprepared for this situation, leading to significant vacillations and delays in committing and disbursing development assistance, especially the relatively fast-disbursing, flexible assistance for augmenting capacity that the new government needed. Several donors had doubts about the new government's legitimacy, exacerbating the situation. In normal circumstances, disbursement of 50 percent of project funds by the end of the first year would be considered a good record. However, in view of the government's need for fast-disbursing assistance, the development assistance disbursement record has been criticized by both the government and outside observers. The 1996 *Joint Evaluation* concludes that a major factor in this lag has been "the inability to achieve a mutual understanding between donors and the new government over their respective requirements and constraints" (Eriksson and others 1996). It also observes that to provide fast-disbursing aid (program or budget support), donors need assurance about the transparency and accountability of the government's budget preparation and execution processes (Kumar and others 1996).

The *Joint Evaluation* goes on to recommend that donors pursue some institutional innovation of their own by developing guidelines. Such guidelines would provide rapid and flexible procedures for disbursing recovery funds, much like procedures for emergency assistance. They would also discuss ways of meeting basic donor accountability requirements for providing fast-disbursing and untied recovery funds without reintroducing protracted processes and requirements that recovering countries cannot meet (Eriksson and others 1996). The intent of such measures would be to offset possible donor concerns about the legitimacy of postconflict governments.

Another issue anticipated during the initial recovery period is that of property rights. With the return of over a million refugees from Burundi, Tanzania, and Zaire, this issue is assuming special urgency. The *Joint Evaluation* calls for development agencies to support the government in identifying clear procedures and institutions for settling disputes over property rights. Such measures would also include strengthening land tenure and property rights legislation, especially to allow women to inherit and own land (Eriksson and others 1996; Kumar and others 1996).

### *The second benchmark period and beyond*

Since El Salvador and Rwanda have just entered this stage, an analysis would be largely an exercise in trying to predict the future. A number of major challenges lie ahead for each country and for development agencies. The experiences of El Salvador and Rwanda, and the author's more cursory knowledge of other failed and near-failed states, suggest that these countries' attempts at recovery are likely to extend through several successive benchmark and construction/reconstruction periods. Recovery, especially of private investment, will be slow. The findings of Collier and Pradhan (1994) on Uganda and other sub-Saharan African countries reinforce this notion. If development agencies are to be relevant to the needs of these countries, they must be prepared to stay actively engaged through each period and for the long term.

### The institutional dimension: some concluding thoughts

This paper emphasizes the importance of the institutional dimension to understanding the causes and consequences of failed states. But as important as it is in postconflict as well as in other settings, the institutional dimension is just one of several dimensions that development evaluation needs to assess. Other evaluative criteria, such as relevance, efficacy or impact, efficiency or cost-effectiveness, financial and environmental sustainability, and donor and recipient performance, remain pertinent and important.

### Notes

1.   Classifying El Salvador and Sri Lanka is problematic, because the authority of both governments in most of their state territories, including the capitals, was never in serious question. This remained the case, notwithstanding the penetration of the Faribundo Martí Liberación Nacional (FMLN) forces into parts of San Salvador in November 1989 and terrorist incidents that have erupted from time to time in southern Sri Lanka, including Colombo. The other country experiences being reviewed in the OED study are those of Bosnia, Cambodia, Eritrea, Haiti, Lebanon, Rwanda, and Uganda. These choices reflect deliberate diversification, taking into consideration the region, the timing of the Bank's involvement in reconstruction, and factors contributing broadly to conflict.

2.    For an analysis of the Arusha Accords suggesting such an interpretation, see Adelman and Suhrke (1996). The reform attempts of El Salvadoran governments, including a rather sweeping agrarian reform promulgated on March 1980, the same month that Archbishop Oscar Romero was assassinated, are chronicled in Boyce (1996, 28). With the killing by the military of scores of mourners at Romero's funeral, by the end of 1980, "virtually all avenues for peaceful opposition to the government had been closed."

3.    There is evidence that a substantial portion of food aid was being diverted by mid-1993, apparently with the involvement of senior government officials (Borton, Brusset, and Hallam 1996). For a further discussion of the corruption and lack of accountability in Rwanda in the early 1990s that ultimately led several donors to withdraw, see Sellström and Wohlgemuth (1996); Adelman and Suhrke (1996).

4.    In a subsequent passage, Picciotto (1995, 16) observes, "the emergence of a strong voluntary sector depends on a host of cultural and historical factors. In some countries (Bangladesh, Chile, Colombia, India, Kenya, Mexico, Zimbabwe) voluntary agencies have mushroomed. In others, they have not and remain very dependent on official sponsorship and support. Pressures to coopt NGOs are ever present and must be resisted."

5.    The author has changed the title of this section from *the precrisis period* to *the prefailure period* in response to the observation of William Zartman (in his comments included in this volume) that crisis and conflict are as often the consequences of state failure as they are proximate causes.

6.    Uvin (1996) finds that donor analyses of Rwanda in the 1980s and early 1990s (he cites several by the World Bank) contain little or no mention or analyses of these factors.

7.    In view of the many issues surrounding the use of conditionality, the *Joint Evaluation* (1996) recommended undertaking a systematic analysis, including an in-depth study of Rwanda, that covers the timing, nature, and effects of both positive and negative conditionality (Eriksson and others 1996; see also Adelman and Suhrke 1996; Sellström and Wohlgemuth 1996).

8.    In Uganda, one reason given for the lags in these sectors is the need for private investors to have confidence that they will not be subject to arbitrary government actions, such as confiscation. They also need to know that they will be protected against crime when making investments in relatively nontradable and immovable assets, such as buildings and heavy equipment. The fact that until the slowdown in 1996 the most rapidly growing segment of manufacturing in El Salvador was the so-called *maquila* enterprises in the free-trade zones is consistent with this observation. So is the fact that the rehabilitation of tea estates in Rwanda has lagged, as it has in Uganda (see Collier and Pradhan 1994).

9.    Boyce (1996) also recognizes this linkage and further suggests that it prompted Germany's decision to provide cofinancing for this loan.

## References

Adelman, Howard, and Astri Suhrke. 1996. "Early Warning and Conflict Management." *The International Response to Conflict and Genocide: Lessons from the Rwanda Experience*. Joint Evaluation of Emergency Assistance to Rwanda, Study 2. London: Overseas Development Institute.

Belt, Juan A. B., and Anabella Lardé de Palomo. 1994. "El Salvador: Transition Towards Peace and Participatory Development." Paper presented to a Seminar of the Organization for Economic Cooperation and Development in Paris, November 21, 1994. San Salvador: USAID/El Salvador.

Borton, John, Emery Brusset, and Alistair Hallam. 1996. "Humanitarian Aid and Effects." *The International Response to Conflict and Genocide: Lessons from the Rwanda Experience*. Joint Evaluation of Emergency Assistance to Rwanda, Study 3. London: Overseas Development Institute.

Boyce, James K., ed. 1996. *Economic Policy for Building Peace: The Lessons of El Salvador*. Boulder and London: Lynne Rienner Publishers, Inc.

Collier, Paul, and Sanjay Pradhan. 1994. "Economic Aspects of the Ugandan Transition to Peace." In Jean-Paul Azam, David Bevan, Paul Collier, Stefan Dercon, Jan Gunning, and Sanjay Pradhan, eds., *Some Economic Consequences of the Transition from Civil War to Peace*. Policy Research Working Paper No. 1392. Washington, D.C.: World Bank.

Dixit, Avinash. 1996. *The Making of Economic Policy: A Transaction-Cost Politics Perspective*. Cambridge, Mass. and London, U.K.: Massachusetts Institute of Technology Press.

Eriksson, John, and others. 1996. "Synthesis." *The International Response to Conflict and Genocide: Lessons from the Rwanda Experience*. Joint Evaluation of Emergency Assistance to Rwanda. London: Overseas Development Institute.

Joint Evaluation of Emergency Assistance to Rwanda. 1996. *The International Response to Conflict and Genocide: Lessons from the Rwanda Experience*. London: Overseas Development Institute.

Khan, Mushtaq. 1995. "State Failure in Weak States: A Critique of New Institutionalist Explanations." In John Harris, Janet Hunter, and Colin M. Lewis, eds., *The New Institutional Economics and Third World Development*. London and New York: Routledge.

Kumar, Krishna, David Tardiff-Douglin, Kim Maynard, Peter Manikas, Annette Sheckler, and Carolyn Knapp. 1996. "Rebuilding Post-War Rwanda." *The International Response to Conflict and Genocide: Lessons from the Rwanda Experience*. Joint Evaluation of Emergency Assistance to Rwanda, Study 4. London: Overseas Development Institute.

Lake, Anthony, ed. 1990. *After the Wars: Reconstruction in Afghanistan, Indochina, Central America, Southern Africa, and the Horn of Africa*. New Brunswick, U.S., and Oxford, U.K.: Transaction Publishers for the Overseas Development Council.

Lemarchand, René. 1982. *The World Bank in Rwanda. The Case of the Office de Valorisation Agricole et Pastorale de Mutara (OVAPAM)*. Bloomington: University of Indiana, African Studies Program.

Lin, Justin Yifu, and Jeffrey B. Nugent. 1995. "Institutional Economics and Development." In J. Behrman and T. N. Srinivasan, eds., *Handbook of Development Economics* Vol. 3. Amsterdam and New York: Elsevier Science B.V.

Picciotto, Robert. 1995. *Putting Institutional Economics to Work: From Participation to Governance*. World Bank Discussion Paper No. 304. Washington, D.C.: World Bank.

Segovia, Alexander. 1996. "Domestic Resource Mobilization." In James K. Boyce, ed., *Economic Policy for Building Peace: The Lessons of El Salvador*. Boulder and London: Lynne Rienner Publishers, Inc.

Sellström, Tor, and Lennart Wohlgemuth. 1996. "Historical Perspective: Some Explanatory Factors." *The International Response to Conflict and Genocide: Lessons from the Rwanda Experience*. Joint Evaluation of Emergency Assistance to Rwanda, Study 1. London: Overseas Development Institute.

Uvin, Peter. 1996. *Development, Aid, and Conflict: Reflections from the Case of Rwanda. Research for Action 24*. Helsinki: World Institute for Development Economics Research and United Nations University.

Zartman, I. William, ed. 1995. *Collapsed States: The Disintegration and Restoration of Legitimate Authority*. Boulder and London: Lynne Rienner Publishers, Inc.

## Comments on "An institutional framework for learning from failed states," by Eriksson

*Harris Mule*

John Eriksson's paper undertakes a formidable task: an analysis of the phenomenon of the failed state. He draws lessons for development agencies from case studies of recent evaluations, showing how the new institutional economics (NIE) can shed light on the phenomenon, help to arrest failure, and begin moving the country toward reconstruction. My perspective is that of someone who has been involved in development matters, policy formulation, and implementation in a developing country but is not very familiar with NIE. This lack of familiarity with NIE means my comments will be very broad.

Eriksson defines a failed state as one that has not quite reached the stage of collapse—a very useful definition. We have also been given a useful, all-encompassing definition of institutions as the way society does things, formally and informally. But when a definition is so broad, it can also become operationally difficult to apply.

The phenomenon of failed states is of immediate concern to aid agencies and of even greater concern to us in developing countries, especially in Africa, where the phenomenon is quite common. It would thus have been useful if the paper had taken the discussion a step further, addressing the following questions: What are the natures, respectively, of a failed and collapsed state? More important, what are the causes of state failure and collapse? Once a state collapses, how does it recover?

The causes and nature of state failure or collapse are multidimensional and cannot be answered by NIE or economics alone. In fact economics, including new institutional economics, may not be the most important explanatory factor in state failure. In some states, economic failure did not cause collapse—for example, Tanzania between 1970 and 1985. Hypothetically, in fact, successful economic performance may in some cases cause state failure. Thus, we must take into account the lessons of history, political economy, and social science, in particular, the history of a country just prior to and during failure.

While an interdisciplinary approach is important to understanding state failure, understanding institutions is also key. One of the important failures in Africa is that state institutions have not been fully taken into account in development planning and implementation. In some cases, state failure resulted from the rising tensions created when new institutions were imposed on a country's traditional institutions. Another critical and often ignored factor in state failure is the role of leaders, who can either cause or ameliorate state failure.

What does the interdisciplinary approach mean for evaluation? It means we need to undertake case studies of countries that have gone through state failure and reconstruction to reach some level of stability. The countries studied should have had significant international assistance. Such a sample will identify the extent to which intervention by development agencies has either abated or exacerbated the conditions leading to state failure. More important, it will show the extent to which interventions by development agencies have assisted countries in reconstruction. This approach would carry Eriksson's effort a step further by addressing the questions his paper raises.

Finally, Eriksson's treatment of the new project cycle that incorporates NIE is particularly useful. It allows us to understand the nature of projects and how they can be designed to be more effective and participatory. To the extent that good projects can stop state failure, this approach is interesting but needs to be explored further.

## Comments on "An institutional framework for learning from failed states," by Eriksson

### *I. William Zartman*

The paper presents a fine summary of conceptual developments in dealing with problems posed by state failure and collapse and wrestles well with the problem of remedial measures and appropriate responses. The problem it addresses is what to do to prevent and overcome state failure and collapse. Beyond the conceptual distinctions of the new institutional economics (NIE), the paper focuses usefully on policy requirements of the different stages of state failure and collapse.

But there is a problem within the problem. The question concerns not only what to do but also how to do it. NIE conceptualists bemoan the "limitations" of social science knowledge and the "failures" of social scientists to unite general theory with the specific institutional structures of developing countries. But the problem seems to be more one of conceptual labels than of pragmatic policy. Whether the following discussion falls under the concept of institutions or not depends above all on their definition. Building on the paper, I will argue that the problems and nature of state failure and collapse are first and foremost political; there are clear indications of what to do, and the inhibitions to doing it have to do with sovereignty and leverage rather than with developmental institutions and philosophies. I will note in conclusion that this has implications for World Bank (and other international philosopher king—IPK) programs.

For economy of argument, my comments follow the "periodization" of the paper despite its conceptual problems. Periodization refers to a specific conflict or crisis scenario, whereas state failure and collapse are not peaked but plateaued processes, with long periods of debilitating policies and behaviors. In these processes, the sharp identification of a crisis is absent or incidental; early warning is a common condition that may or may not lead to eventual failure or collapse; and even violent conflict may be absent. (Its absence is often a notable feature of state failure and collapse, and, in many cases, such as Bosnia, Haiti, Somalia, and Zaire, it is present only as the consequence, not the cause, of state failure or collapse.)

### The precrisis period

The precrisis period encapsulates the problem in its name: there is no crisis (yet), and so the problems are considered to be minor, sectoral, technical, or institutional. The reason for the institutional inadequacy (and not its consequence) is found in political behaviors and values. Ethnic discrimination and favoritism, violence toward citizens and human rights violations, predatory government actions, time-at-the-trough ethos and privatization of political goods, and political unaccountability are accepted if not actually legitimate, and go unpunished. There is no doubt that such behaviors and the values behind them are absolute obstacles to effective governance and efficient development. It does not take ex post inferences to see the inherent incompatibility between predatory status and national economic growth.

Such economically inefficient (not to speak of socially repugnant) behaviors and values also relate to specific moments where, arguably, a precrisis turning point could have been effected in failed/collapsed states:[1]

- November 1962: In Eritrea federal status could have been strengthened rather than abolished.

- February 1976: In Lebanon the announced constitutional document could have been modified and reinforced.

- 1979: In Sri Lanka local development councils could have been created and funded.

- 1979: In Zaire the activities of the Blumenthal Mission could have been reinforced.

- 1979-89: In Rwanda equal treatment and opportunity in rural development programs could have been enforced, or 10 years later an equitable economic recovery program could have been provided.

- October 1985: In Liberia the fraudulent elections could have been decertified.

- 1986: In Haiti a controlled transition with protected elections could have been provided.

- October 1988: In Somalia a cease-fire and leadership transition could have been monitored.

Prior to any institutional modification, these were the kinds of measures needed to put the state back on the track to effective governance and efficient development. Without them, the political system blocked any meaningful development measures. Such actions for the most part were indicated well before the "cusp of disaster," a point at which they would have been too late to be preventive measures. They highlight correctable behaviors that stood as an obstacle to reform: massive discrimination and inequalities, electoral fraud, ethnic repression and violence, privatization of public finances. Clear and indefensible ills, these practices constitute a category of behaviors whose correction can be considered a necessary precondition for development assistance. Thus, early identification and punishment of specific correctable behaviors, rather than the use of a heavy stick (such as donor withdrawal once states have actually collapsed), is a more effective way of dealing with the contributors to state failure and collapse.

## Peak conflict period

Once potential successors start fighting over the collapsed or failed state, international financial institutions can do little but monitor the situation for the moment to return. At this stage, the measures required to deal with collapse and failure involve massive penetration of a state's political space and infringement on state sovereignty. Even in the case of correctable behaviors, most of the kinds of measures mentioned above involve intense diplomatic intervention and pressure beyond the will of most states and the capability of multilateral agencies. Indeed, in the case of the 1979 "receivership" of Zairian finances, the Blumenthal mission withdrew over its own ineffectiveness; its restoration would have required a major (if justified) exercise of interference in the affairs of a sovereign state. In cases where state collapse has already occurred, the withdrawal of the World Bank probably has had much less effect on the target state's behavior than the collapse itself. Withdrawal in such cases has been more a consequence of the Bank's inability to operate under conditions of state collapse than a means of pressure on the defective entity.

## The first benchmark of a postcollapse period

The moment of return is of great importance, since it represents a window of opportunity for policy reform. Entrenched groups that formerly opposed reform are destroyed or at least unbalanced by the conflict and collapse, and the barriers of sovereignty are at their lowest. There is more leverage for reform inherent in the situation, and that leverage takes the form of carrots (promises and predictions) rather than sticks (threats and warnings), a situation more propitious for cooperation. Two major obstacles counterbalance that leverage: the new regime's sensitivity over sovereignty (by the very fact of its fragility), and the additional burdens of (re)construction posed by the collapse and conflict itself. At the same time, this is the very moment when norms about correctable behaviors need to be enforced from the very beginning. The danger inherent in the moment of return and reform is that the new opportunity to induce policy changes favoring development may well overwhelm attention to basic behavioral and value problems. The latter are less easily handled later and are guaranteed to return, bringing state failure and collapse with them, as they did the last time.

In sum, the problem of dealing with state failure and collapse is less a matter of knowing what to do than figuring out how to do it, given the barriers of sovereignty and the limitations on leverage. There are major political causes of state failure and collapse that need correction before the lesser, more technical, and even institutional aspects of policy can be addressed. Such correctable behaviors can best be addressed early in the process of collapse, well before the process has reached its completion, when it is simply too late.

> There is little that donors can do, directly, to impose tolerance among parties, constructive cooperation among separated powers of government, or [attitudes of] ethnic tolerance. But some specific conditions of electoral transparency and human rights can be improved, and it might be well to think in the same vein of useful pressure points for fostering better interagency cooperation within governments (Zartman 1995).

Finally, on a matter within but beyond the lessons addressed in the paper, such measures to deal with specific correctable behaviors cannot be ad hoc or self-justifying; they must be announced beforehand, self-committingly, as standards. More broadly, the notion of sovereignty as responsibility rather than license and protection needs to be propagated (Deng and others 1996). It is a natural corollary of the idea that states are responsible for the economic welfare and development of their population to hold that states are equally responsible for the security and political welfare of their population. Other states and multistate agencies have a responsibility to help them when they are unable or unwilling to exercise that responsibility.

> Suggestions have come from various quarters that the Organization of African Unity (OAU), and subregional organizations could both play an important role and refurbish their own images by adopting norms and codes of conduct for a number of state practices, notably the conduct of elections. The preliminary Conference on Security, Stability, Development, and Cooperation in Africa (CSSDCA), Africa's putative Helsinki process, has already outlined such norms. Such efforts would be strengthened by a parallel call, if not condition, by the World Bank and other donors. It should be in the interest of economic performance (Zartman 1995).

## Note

1.   Some of these points draw from my current study, "Preventing State Collapse," supported by the Carnegie Corporation and the Carnegie Commission for the Prevention of Deadly Conflicts.

## References

Deng, Francis, Sadikiel Kimaro, Terrence Lyons, Donald Rothchild, and I. William Zartman. 1996. *Sovereignty as Responsibility: Conflict Management in Africa.* Washington, D.C.: Brookings Institution.

Zartman, I. William. 1995. "Governance and Development in West Africa." Report on a mission for the World Bank.

**Floor discussion on "An institutional framework for learning from failed states"**

The first participant, Yves Albouy, asked whether enough of a distinction had been made between humanitarian and development assistance, since humanitarian assistance must be offered quickly in an emergency. Another participant, Robert Klitgaard, underscored the question by asking whether humanitarian strategies can help repair fractured institutions. Steve Holtzman then noted that societal collapse and state collapse are closely connected. When either threatens, development agencies should be willing to reintroduce external interventions. But they should also feel confident that they can offer help without being held responsible for state failure. Some societies have been living without functional states for 20 years or more, and development agencies that may be able to help sustain such societies cannot remain aloof.

In this regard, Holtzman noted, it may be that there is no line between humanitarian relief and development aid. Afghanistan, which has been without a state for some time, is no longer a "conflict emergency." The same can be said for parts of Liberia, Zaire, and other countries. In such situations, reforms are not just long-term measures but can also help with short-term transitions. In Angola, in a period of 4,000 percent annual inflation, a transition to fiscal health would have been impossible without short-term assistance. Such examples show the positive side of certain reforms. On the negative side, there may be costs involved in reinforcing peace that are incompatible with reform. For that reason, reforms should be undertaken carefully. In some cases, using reforms to promote development initiatives is an opportunistic response to fragile regimes that are not in a position to assert their own best interests.

John Eriksson began his response by addressing Harris Mule's comments, expanding on the distinction between a collapsed and a failed state. The latter can be brought about by failings in state functioning that fall short of collapse. The crises and conflicts arising from functional failings may not even develop to the point of state collapse, yet the mere fact that they can happen amounts, in a sense, to state failure. He illustrated this point with the experiences of Sri Lanka and El Salvador, the two countries examined in the OED study. Their failings may not meet William Zartman's rigorous test of state collapse, but they could still have serious consequences that retard development. Zartman, drawing on Mule's comments, had noted that the institutional dimension is not only very important but requires a multidimensional approach—that is, the insights of disciplines other than economics or new institutional economics. Eriksson agreed that there is a need for intensive country case studies and cited the possibilities arising from his own current work with OED, even though the relative emphasis is on postconflict rather than prevention.

In response to Holtzman, Eriksson referred to Zartman's examples of historical entry points, when there might have been more international leverage than was used. But there are also times when external intervention can cause rather than prevent failure. Concerned actors must include not just development agencies but other member states. In response to Holtzman's point that state collapse implies the collapse of society, he referred to Zartman's recent book on collapsed states. The introductory chapter describes the interaction that takes place between state and civil society in a collapsing state as a vicious circle.

Eriksson acknowledged the need to think about the short-term reforms that are essential to a transition phase as well as to long-term development, drawing a parallel to one paradigm of the Bretton Woods institutions—the need to bring about a measure of macroeconomic stability at a very early stage in the reform process. Some early reforms, however, need close scrutiny in the context of the particular country, since they could be constrained by the fragility of private sector investment. In the case of Uganda, one expert has argued that the Bretton Woods institutions pushed too soon and too aggressively on tax reform. But humanitarian assistance and development assistance form a seamless web. In certain complex emergencies, such as Rwanda, the international community responded to humanitarian need without addressing the political issues surrounding it.

Mule found the distinction between state collapse and "stateless" societies useful, because so many donor agencies lack the instruments to intervene in the latter. NGOs can often help in such societies, but donor agencies must find ways to act in any arena, including a collapsed state, where society has not collapsed. External interventions can in fact cause state collapse, particularly in Africa, where institutions are weak. Donor intervention takes over the development agenda, replacing the government and even the country. In these cases, donors tend to hinder the formation of an effective and democratic society, leading to state collapse. Similarly, rapid changes in donor assistance governed by the domestic agendas of donor countries can also cause state failure by putting too much stress on institutions in recipient countries. The lesson is that donors should give serious attention to institutional capacities in recipient countries.

Elizabeth McAllister noted that Mule's comments ring true in the context of the Rwandan government's perspective on development assistance in postcrisis Rwanda. Donors "played to the cameras while filling the stores with cookies" and not to the real needs of the Rwandan government. In response, Zartman acknowledged that he had not taken humanitarian assistance sufficiently into account in his remarks. He suggested that humanitarian assistance can make use of institutions to help in the process of rebuilding a state by, for instance, developing local channels for food distribution.

State collapse and failure, he noted, are two different things. Failure is much broader than state collapse. Sri Lanka is a particularly good example of this distinction, as the state failed in one important function but did not collapse. Failure should not be used to signify collapse, because collapse is a "core phenomenon" in which the state disappears. National society also collapses then, because its ability to rebound and fill the political vacuum the dying state creates has been destroyed in the same process. But society continues at the local level. People make do and continue to run their lives in some way, as they do in Somalia. But this condition is not comfortable: Afghanistan and Somalia are not comfortable. Of course there are stateless societies, and anthropologists love to talk about "prestate" societies. But today too many things cannot be done without a state. The state is not a dispensable item, so rebuilding states, or institutionalization, is important.

# 12. Learning from early childcare and education programs

Mary Young, Jacques van der Gaag, and David de Ferranti

*Development projects depend heavily on a complex network of local, regional, and national institutions, on formal and nonformal organizations, and on organizing principles that constitute the social fabric of society. This paper shows the importance of such institutional support for early childcare and education projects in different settings.*

"Institutions" include all the formal and nonformal organizations and organizing principles that constitute the social fabric of society. The families, social groups, and civil organizations, as well as the attitudes and values they embrace, all contribute to a society's economic and social development.

Operational experience attests to the importance of including social dimensions in the design of development projects. Social conditions need to be properly analyzed and stakeholders consulted. Failure to take into account how implementing institutions actually work and how communities can participate is a common cause of failure in development projects. Understanding who will gain and who is likely to lose when instituting new policies is critical when making a policy change (World Bank 1996).

Supportive institutional frameworks are particularly important for sustaining large-scale early childcare and education (ECCE) programs, which typically consist of thousands of small locally managed projects, each serving 15–20 children. To succeed, these small (micro) projects must have support from parents, communities, health clinics, nongovernmental organizations, and other local institutions. As part of broader national programs, they also require national support from societal institutions for training, information sharing, quality control, and evaluation.

This paper describes examples of sustainable ECCE programs that combine these important ingredients of local and national support. In each case, monitoring and evaluation were critical to improving the quality of the intervention. The first section reviews the history of two ECCE programs that have been successful in the United States: Head Start and the Special Supplemental Nutrition Program for Women, Infants, and Children (WIC). Section two describes the development of Colombia's national community-based early childcare and education service. The third section highlights Kenya's nationwide preschool program. A concluding section summarizes the lessons learned from these efforts.

## ECCE in the United States

The two major ECCE programs in the United States are Head Start and WIC. Both programs are federally funded and were launched as part of the War on Poverty during the mid-1960s and early 1970s.

### *Head Start: ingredients of success*

The Head Start program has enjoyed continued support through successive administrations. Political will and financial support, the right timing, and the enthusiastic participation of central, local, and community-based institutions have been key to the program's sustainability. However, Head Start's emphasis on only one aspect of program outcome—cognitive development—and its failure to consider other outcome indicators created many undeserved obstacles during the program's early years. Many people still associate Head Start with a failure to "raise the IQs" of poor children.

*Background.* With the Economic Opportunity Act of 1964, the U.S. Congress opened the War on Poverty on several fronts: the Job Corps, to provide education and training for employment; the Community Action Program (CAP), to mobilize poor people in the fight against poverty; and Volunteers in Service to America (VISTA), a domestic Peace Corps to revitalize poor communities through volunteer support. Head Start, a program dedicated to preparing poor children for first grade by helping them overcome their fears about school, began as an eight-week program during the summer of 1965.

*Political will and the right timing.* Head Start owes its existence to the disappointing early record of CAP, which focused on organizing and employing poor adults. An analysis of the distribution of poverty in the United States showed that nearly half of the nation's 30 million poor people were children, most of them under 12. Sargent Shriver, director of the Office of Equal Opportunity and President Johnson's chief advocate in the War on Poverty, underscored this when he said, "It was clear that it was foolish to talk about a 'total war against poverty' if you were doing nothing about children" (Zigler and Muenchow 1992). Faced with the possibility of a federal budget surplus, government officials created Head Start. Establishing a nationwide Head Start program also seemed to be a worthwhile way of allocating unused CAP funds. Federal financial support came in the form of matching funds, strengthening ownership at the grassroots level.

The Head Start planning committee Shriver convened in 1964 charted new territory by acknowledging that children's physical and emotional needs must be met in order for children to take full advantage of educational experiences. The original committee consisted of educators, physicians, a professor of nursing, a social worker, a clinical psychologist, and a research psychologist.

*National support.* Head Start garnered the support of everyone from the president to grassroots educators and community leaders. President Lyndon Johnson particularly liked Shriver's vision of Head Start. Compared with other components of the War on Poverty, such as the Job Corps (which dealt with unemployed inner-city adults), this program for poor preschool children was likely to be widely accepted by the public. No one could argue that preschool children were not the "deserving poor." Without President Johnson's early and enthusiastic support, Head Start would never have become the program it is today, but his interest in the program also made Head Start a political entity. The nation's widespread belief in education as the key factor in eradicating poverty also played a role in promoting the program.

Lady Bird Johnson also was enthusiastic about Head Start, saying that "the Head Start idea has such hope and challenge." She accepted the invitation to serve as honorary chairperson of Project Head Start and, noting that first ladies "don't chair small pilot projects," decided to hold a White House tea to launch the program (Zigler and Muenchow 1992). The entire country joined in the excitement. Head Start began not as a pilot project but on a grand scale. Within a few months, the program was reaching 500,000 poor children, providing services that many of them had not experienced before, including basic medical and dental care and two nutritious meals a day (Zigler and Muenchow 1992). Nationwide implementation made Head Start highly visible and created grassroots political support for it in every congressional district. This support protected the program later when questions arose about its effectiveness.

*Local variations.* Rapid expansion, however, had a price—the sacrificing of consistent quality. Head Start depended on the support of an available, local institutional framework; no new facilities were built. Public support was offered by everyone from policymakers, mayors, and state legislators to Kiwanis and Lions clubs, local chambers of commerce, the National Farmers Union, the National Council of Negro Women, and the YMCA. The requirement that communities provide matching funds was an essential feature in promoting community participation. Such funding could take the form of in-kind contributions, and the national organization developed a sliding scale to give communities credit for the value of the labor they contributed. Different hourly rates were established for typists, physicians, and other personnel. Volunteers did not benefit financially themselves but gained the satisfaction of knowing that they were contributing to a percentage of their community's matching resources.

Head Start solicited hundreds of universities to provide training to meet the shortage of trained preschool teachers. More than 200 colleges and universities offered six-day orientation programs. By the first summer of Head Start, more than 44,000 teachers had received basic training through university-sponsored programs (Zigler and Muenchow 1992).

*Accomplishments.* Over the past 30 years, Head Start has served some 14.6 million children and their families. It has also aided families by providing health, social, and educational services and by linking families with services available in the community. Finally, a range of institutions—educational, economic, health care, social service, and others—have been influenced by Head Start staff and parents to provide benefits to both Head Start and non-Head Start families in their communities (McKey and others 1985).

*Evaluation.* The creators of Head Start recognized that evaluation was important, but lack of clarity about what to measure almost destroyed the program. Ignoring the fact that Head Start was a comprehensive ECCE program that provided educational, health, and social services to low-income children and their families, evaluators focused solely on cognitive outcomes. A study conducted in 1969 by Westinghouse administered standardized tests of cognitive measures to first, second, and third graders who had attended Head Start. The investigators found that summer-program participants showed no benefits, whereas full-year participants showed cognitive and language gains in the first grade that faded out by the second or third grade. From these findings, the authors concluded that the positive gains were not worth the program effort.

In addition to focusing on only one outcome measure, the evaluation depended on a sample size that was far too ambitious. It was designed to cover every participant using a one-size-fits-all approach. Evaluation data gathered after Head Start's first summer of operation provided information on the teachers' backgrounds, the economic status of the families served, and the recruitment of children. These unwieldy data suggested that the evaluation component should be more decentralized and tailored to local conditions. Head Start subsequently established 14 regional research and evaluation centers, some of which eventually provided longitudinal findings that showed the long-term, positive effects of this early childhood intervention.

*Challenges.* Head Start's two greatest challenges have been the inconsistent quality of the program and the tendency for preschoolers' gains on achievement scores to fade by the time the children reach third grade. But the children maintain other gains, including improved school attendance and reduced grade retention rates. Because of the broad flexibility Head Start affords local program, along with the diversity of participants, the program is difficult to assess in a large study. It cannot be regarded as a uniform "treatment" and must be assessed in relation to multiple goals and multiple outcomes (Collins 1990). Future Head Start evaluations will focus on identifying the most effective program elements and the conditions surrounding them. Such evaluations will depend heavily on local capacity and institutional support.

### Women, infants, and children program

Unlike Head Start, which has multiple goals, WIC has one clear goal—to improve the health of children. Like Head Start, WIC relies on local institutions, including the private sector, but it has clear, well-defined eligibility criteria and specific target groups.

*Background.* WIC was first authorized in 1972. It provides supplemental food, nutrition, education, and health care services as well as breastfeeding counseling to nutritionally at-risk, low-income pregnant and postpartum women and their infants and children up to age five.

*National support.* WIC was originally developed in response to the 1969 White House Conference on Food, Nutrition, and Health. A federal program administered by the U.S. Department of Agriculture, it provides funds to the states in support of local WIC clinics. Unlike Head Start, WIC does not require local matching resources.

*Local implementation.* As with Head Start, WIC clinics rely on the institutional framework provided by local private and public health and human service agencies. Participating groups (hospitals, community health centers, and private nonprofit health clinics) provide health care and nutrition practitioners. Where public transport is not well developed, mobile vans are used for service delivery. Supplemental food prescribed by a WIC clinic is provided through redeemable vouchers that can be used at local participating grocery stores. The state reimburses these vendors for the WIC vouchers.

To qualify for WIC, recipients must meet both low-income and nutritional-need criteria. States where the program is implemented set income criteria no higher than 185 percent of the federal poverty line (Jones and Richardson 1995), and local WIC clinics must certify that participants are nutritionally at risk. Evaluation of participants' nutritional status includes height and blood hemoglobin measures. In addition to these eligibility criteria, and because of funding limitations, WIC gives different priority to different target groups. Pregnant women and infants at nutritional risk are given first priority, followed by children at nutritional risk and postpartum women at nutritional risk.

*Evaluation.* Like Head Start, WIC has been evaluated extensively. In contrast to Head Start's evaluation, however, WIC's evaluation has been more direct and less unwieldy, partly because WIC benefits are limited to specific health outcomes and not the broad range of health, nutrition, and education benefits expected of Head Start. In 1994 alone, WIC served 6.47 million individuals (Jones and Richardson 1995). It has been one of the most effective programs for improving the health of children in the United States (GAO 1992). WIC decreases the incidence of very low birthweight by 44 percent (GAO 1992) and lowers the incidence of late fetal deaths by up to one-third (Rush and others 1988). It has proven to be cost-effective: every dollar spent on a pregnant woman in the WIC program saves $1.92–$4.21 in Medicaid costs.

### Lessons from Head Start and WIC

These U.S. efforts in early childcare and education convey two messages: that large-scale, locally implemented programs require strong national commitment and support, and that well-conceived monitoring and evaluation (M&E) approaches must be included in the initial program design.

Both Head Start and WIC were embedded in (and constituted only a small part of) the many new programs that made up the U.S. government's antipoverty program. Both WIC and Head Start benefited from this national institutional framework. They had ample resources, federal support for local institutions, nationwide information sharing, a conducive policy environment, and complementary services such as health care and skills training.

WIC demonstrates the strength of an intersectoral, collaborative effort involving the agriculture, health, and private sectors. Because the food vouchers can be redeemed in local grocery stores in the private sector, the program does not require a separate or parallel food distribution system. This efficient system stands in direct contrast to the Colombian example discussed in the next section. In Colombia, the food supplement (known as *bienestarina*) is manufactured and distributed by the government, as part of Colombia's ECCE program. WIC also illustrates the importance of communicating with the target group. Nutrition counseling is part of the service package provided to pregnant women. Pregnant women are taught about the types of food the body requires during pregnancy and are given food vouchers to obtain the supplemental food they need. Improving women's knowledge of appropriate dietary practices and providing food supplements are mutually reinforcing ingredients of the program.

Both programs included M&E from the beginning. But the long, controversial history of evaluating Head Start points to one important lesson: the need to carefully design an evaluation approach that utilizes a manageable sample size and makes ample use of the available knowledge of and varying circumstances in local situations.

Head Start and WIC clearly demonstrate the importance of broad-based local and national institutional support for ECCE programs. This support has made both of these programs sustainable and effective. Constant M&E has improved the quality of both programs, and this improvement in turn has broadened the base of domestic political support for early childcare and education

## ECCE in Colombia

Institutionally supported early childhood education has also evolved in Colombia to address the needs of infants and preschool-age children living in poverty. Evaluations of earlier pilot projects have led to the development of three major ECCE programs. The first is an initial government effort in early childhood education, the Centros de Atención Integral al Pre-Escolar (or preschool childcare centers). The second is an alternative, low-cost option for reaching children in low-income families, the Programa para el Mejoramiento de la Educación, la Salud, y el Ambiente (PROMESA, or program for the improvement of education, health, and environment). The third, which builds on the success of PROMESA, is a nationwide expansion of the Hogares de Bienestar Infantil (HBI, or homes for children's well-being).

### Initial efforts

The Colombian government created the Instituto Colombiano de Bienestar Familiar (ICBF, the Colombian Institute for Family Welfare) in 1968 under the chairmanship of Colombia's first lady. Its main purpose was to improve family welfare by supporting school feeding programs; day care, including feeding; legal assistance; and other community development activities. The aim was to provide direct services and programs in concert with other agencies for more than 2 million infants and children, with emphasis on preschool children up to seven years old (World Bank 1994).

The ICBF first became a provider of day care during 1972–74, when it established more than 100 centers for children under seven years old. Law 27 of 1994 granted the ICBF the proceeds of a 2 percent tax on the wage bill of all formal sector enterprises and institutions, thus earmarking funds for Colombia's first large, nationwide program of child assistance. The program's center-based care is provided in well-equipped preschool childcare centers by trained personnel (health workers, nutritionists, and educators). Services are mainly free of charge. Today, the ICBF supports about 1,100 centers serving about 280,000 children (World Bank 1994).

*Evaluation.* Criticism of the program emerged in the late 1970s. The centers were costly, provided services largely for middle-income rather than low-income clientele, and did not foster significant community involvement. These findings led to widespread experimentation with new models of day care and nutrition programs that would serve poor families in urban slums more directly. The United Nations Children's Fund (UNICEF) and foundations such as the Bernard van Leer Foundation and Save the Children assisted in these endeavors, which also promoted community participation and the deinstitutionalization of services. Experiments with home-based programs were conducted in several locations in the search for low-cost approaches that could be replicated nationwide.

### Pilot program of a home-based approach

PROMESA is a well-known Colombian program that adopted the home-based approach. It is administered by the Fundación Centro International de Educación y Desarrollo Humano (International Center for Education and Human Development), a Colombian nongovernmental organization supported by, among others, the Bernard van Leer Foundation. PROMESA was designed as an alternative approach to meeting the needs for health care, early childcare, and education. PROMESA began in 1978 with 100 families in four small farming and fishing villages. It now serves approximately 2,000 families along the coast and in the interior regions of Choco, Colombia. Other parts of the country are also implementing variations on its approach (Nimnicht, Arango, and Hearn 1990).

*Client participation (addressing clients' needs).* PROMESA trains mothers to be parent-educators and community leaders. Initial program activities included encouraging mothers, under the leadership of "promoters" (community leaders who are also local mothers), to stimulate the physical and intellectual development of their preschool children by playing games with them at home. Over time, the mothers started to identify related problems pertaining to health, nutrition, environmental sanitation, vocational training, income generation, and cultural identity. As the mothers gained confidence and developed a greater understanding of their overall needs, PROMESA expanded into an integrated community development program, with entire communities participating in one or more aspects of the program. The expanded program includes sociointellectual, physical, productive, and sociocultural components.

The sociointellectual development component involves teaching adults (parents of children 0–9 years) how to improve their quality of life and family interactions, using workshops, self-study groups, and follow-up activities. The topics covered in the training include providing a healthy environment for young children, vocational training for the mothers, and education for leaders. The program also involves developing sets of educational toys and games to improve interaction between parents and their children and to encourage logical thinking. The communities organize and operate preschool and nutrition centers with the support of local institutions.

The physical component of the expanded program addresses health, nutrition, and environmental sanitation. The productive component involves organizing groups interested in improving their income-generating, organizational, and administrative capacities and establishing revolving funds and activities to improve the quality of work and the marketing of products. Finally, the sociocultural component fosters activities to strengthen cultural identity by having the groups recover and review important aspects of their history and culture. Community groups organize cultural activities such as plays, musical events, and games and study indigenous myths, legends, and medical practices.

*Evaluation.* PROMESA's success has been influenced by four key features. First, it identifies community leaders, many of them mothers, to serve as the main educators in the program. Second, it limits the external agent's involvement with the community to educating community leaders, facilitating the development process, and forging links with other institutions. Third, it emphasizes coordination among local and regional institutions. And fourth, it focuses on educational and organizational aspects, despite the poor socioeconomic status of the geographic areas. Evaluation of this program shows that participating children stay in school longer and learn more than nonparticipating children and that participating mothers have more self-confidence and influence and feel they have greater control of life events than mothers who do not participate. The success of PROMESA, demonstrated by evaluation, has influenced policy decisions favoring use of home-based interventions nationwide.

## Going to scale

In 1987, the ICBF launched HBI programs on a large scale as a creative response to several poverty issues. Building on the success of PROMESA, HBI combines feeding and community-managed day care for preschool children aged three to six in low-income urban neighborhoods. HBI programs, which are established in marginal urban neighborhoods, are specifically designed to meet a community's interests and needs. The Instituto Colombiano uses criteria based on income, population, and local service standards to identify target clientele, giving priority to the poorest neighborhoods. Participation in the program is self-selective.

*Program organization.* In communities with HBI programs, groups of interested parents choose a "community mother" to care for 15 children in her home. The community mothers do not need to meet any special qualifications. The ICBF provides initial training in nutrition, childcare, and protection; the suitability of the women selected is confirmed through the training process. The institute pays community mothers a small monthly stipend and arranges loans through the Low-Income Housing Credit Institute to help mothers upgrade their homes to meet minimum standards for day care (for example, to install or extend roofs, put in wooden or concrete floors, and install toilets).

The ICBF manufactures and provides *bienestarina*, a nutritional supplement, for poor individuals at nutritional risk, including infants, preschool- and school-age children, and pregnant and nursing women). In most locations, the ICBF also helps community leaders purchase fresh foods at wholesale prices by contracting with a network of community suppliers.

HBI programs are administered through a three-tiered community structure, as follows: first, a parents' association formed by parents of children enrolled in 10–15 centers; second, a local assembly of representatives (three from each center) elected by the parents; and third, a board of directors comprising five parent representatives elected by the local assembly. The parents' associations manage the ICBF funds and the nominal contributions from parents that are used to pay community mothers' stipends and to purchase food. A wide range of private and public agencies (including universities, secondary schools, government agencies, and NGOs) contribute services on an ad hoc basis, assisting community mothers or providing technical and managerial skills training related to HBI services.

*Evaluation.* An evaluation of the overall program in 1989 confirmed the viability of HBI as a low-cost mechanism for reaching children in the poorest neighborhoods, especially in urban areas. The early success of HBI led the ICBF to expand the program to reach the estimated one million or more children aged two to six in the lowest income groups in Colombia. Law 89 of 1988 increased the wage tax to 3 percent of the wage bill, which enabled HBI to expand to every department and major city in the country.

HBI is now the ICBF's fastest-growing program. Because the program has expanded in a short time, difficulties related to mass coverage continue to plague it, and quality may be sacrificed for quantity. For example, because there are few checks on accuracy in program administration, the number of children attending daily is likely to be overreported. Two incentives contribute to this problem. First, community mothers' stipends are reduced when attendance drops. Second, community associations receive a smaller payment when fewer than 15 children attend a center. The supervisory staff who visit each program once every three months are reluctant to report such deficiencies. The lower coverage estimated in an independent survey conducted by Colombia's national department of statistics seems to reflect program attendance more accurately.

Evaluations of the benefits of ICBF programs are few. A major study undertaken by UNICEF for the ICBF suffered from serious design flaws. It compared the development of children who had been in HBI programs for one to two months with those who had participated for more than six months, but it lacked both a control group and a longitudinal perspective. Despite these flaws, the authors concluded that extended program participation does benefit child development (World Bank 1994).

The data do not support this conclusion, however. Despite substantial spending on nutrition assistance, for instance, no improvement in nutritional status was noted among the children. This lack of improved nutritional status may reflect families' decisions to divert food from children who participate in HBI to other family members because they assume that the HBI program is meeting all the children's nutritional needs.

No comparative, longitudinal evaluations of HBI have been conducted, and medium- to long-term benefits or costs have not been estimated systematically. The importance of institutional support also may not have been appreciated sufficiently when the ICBF made the decision to expand the program. The pilot program was "hands on" and labor intensive, utilizing well-trained staff and motivated parents and communities. The availability of local institutional support in every community was not self-evident when the program expanded. The importance and difficulty of developing national institutional support for a nationwide intervention were also underestimated. Still, the program has been influential and has achieved some positive effects. Today the HBI symbol is recognized widely, even in the toughest periurban neighborhoods.

## ECCE in Kenya

The messages regarding the need for broad institutional support and for M&E at all stages have been heard and practiced in Kenya. Kenya's preschool program expanded countrywide after President Kenyatta's call for *harambee* (self-help) in 1963. Kenya now has a substantial network of community-supported preschool facilities, with about 18,400 centers caring for approximately one million children age three to six. Most important, Kenya places great emphasis on using local culture and language in its curriculum development.

### National and local cooperation

Communities have organized themselves to establish the preschools that make up the network of facilities. The communities provide the facilities, pay caregivers, organize children's food programs, and supply materials for learning and play. The national government funds training for preschool teacher trainers and designs the preschool curriculum. District governments train teachers and inspect and evaluate programs. Local governments and NGOs, such as the Bernard van Leer and Aga Khan Foundations, provide financial and supervisory support to some centers. The Bernard van Leer Foundation, in particular, deserves much credit for its long history of involvement in Kenya's ECCE activities.

The Ministry of Education, in cooperation with the Bernard van Leer Foundation, has been supporting a ten-year pilot study, the Preschool Education Project. Included in this project is the development of training modules for children, teachers, and trainers. With financial support from external partners (the Aga Khan Foundation, the Bernard van Leer Foundation, and UNICEF), the National Center for Early Childhood Education and the network of district centers are now training ECCE teachers using these modules (Kenya 1992; Kabiru 1993). Most important, their approach to curriculum development emphasizes the strength of Kenya's culture. Stories, poems, riddles, and games are translated into more than 20 local languages, enabling parents and teachers to appreciate their cultures and the resources available in their own surroundings.

### Shortfalls in funding

Kenya's program faces continual budget shortages. It has not been blessed with the level of funding committed to U.S. or Colombian programs. With these shortages—and despite long-term efforts to develop a cadre of trained educators—only a limited number of staff have been trained. The program needs more systematic in-service training for a larger number of teachers to ensure that quality services are provided. The funding shortages also affect the ability of national and district centers to fulfill their respective roles. With adequate funding, these roles could be expanded or strengthened to include developing standards, monitoring performance, and disseminating training more broadly.

### International collaboration

Fully appreciating the strengths and weaknesses of Kenya's Preschool Education Project, the government is initiating a complementary project with financing from the World Bank. This project is one example of how international funding organizations can support and strengthen ECCE efforts throughout the world. Scheduled to begin in 1997, the program will utilize existing local institutional frameworks to improve the overall quality of the nationwide program. Specific activities will include testing ways to improve the quality of services; increasing access for poor children; strengthening communities' capacities to organize, manage, and finance programs; and developing and testing broader packages of services. To measure the success of the Preschool Education Project, the government will monitor poor children's access to the program, children's health profiles on entering primary school (average age, height, weight, and immunization status), and dropout and repetition rates in the early grades (Young 1996).

The project will support the training of 15,000 preschool teachers and 5,000 community representatives to operate and monitor enriched childcare programs. To improve preschoolers' health and nutrition, project staff will monitor growth and offer immunizations and supplements (food and micronutrients). Pilot preschools will employ staff capable of diagnosing and treating common ailments, deworming children, and referring severe cases for higher levels of care. Parents' committees trained in organizing, managing, and monitoring early child services will continue to manage the centers. An operations manual will outline targeting, disbursement, accounting, and auditing methods, and communities will receive grants to improve services. NGOs will help oversee the management of childcare centers.

The project will introduce new ways of mobilizing community financing for teachers' salaries, subsidize fees for the poorest children, purchase school supplies, provide health and education materials, and improve facilities. In some cases, poor children will receive direct grants for attending preschool. The project will also test a primary school curriculum that continues the preschool teaching methods.

## Conclusions

The ECCE programs discussed in this paper, like other such programs throughout the world, have a number of characteristics that make them uniquely dependent on a complex network of local, regional, and national institutions for financial, managerial, and implementation support. From the bottom up, these programs consist of thousands of microprojects that each provide services to 15–20 children. The microunits often use semivolunteer labor and depend heavily on parental participation. Groups of 10–20 microunits form neighborhood clusters that depend on parent associations for organizational support that ranges from helping to establish contracts with local health care providers to networking with NGOs and other voluntary organizations. In general, the parents work to improve the environment in which these units operate (for example, by lobbying local authorities for improvements in the water supply or public transportation systems). These neighborhood clusters, in turn, depend on a citywide support system to procure and distribute food, train caretakers, and conduct public information campaigns and M&E.

These local networks all aim to strengthen the basic unit of society: the family. Indeed, some have argued that improving the ways families function is the greatest benefit of ECCE programs. Parents focused on improving the environment in which

their children grow up are especially effective in creating social capital. Parent organizations, neighborhood groups, and other voluntary institutions have long-term
development benefits that go well beyond individual health and education.

From the top down, these programs need strong, broad political support, stable and
sustainable financing, and intensive supervision for quality control. They make
heavy demands on the technical capacity of the relevant national institutions in the
areas of health, nutrition, and the cognitive development needs of young children.
The need to target these services to heterogeneous groups of disadvantaged children
and to tailor the intervention to local needs and conditions complicates the programs. ECCE programs require comprehensive, integrated networks that combine
the support of local, regional, and national institutions.

*Lessons learned*

Perhaps the major lesson learned from the examples presented in this paper is that
strong national institutions need to complement but cannot substitute for local capacity and commitment. For instance, the nationally supported Head Start program
made mistakes when it failed to take local conditions into account during implementation and evaluation. Conversely, in the early stages of the expansion of HBI projects
in Colombia—which had enjoyed strong local support—the program suffered from
lack of quality control, supervision, and M&E capacity at the national level.

Second, ECCE programs need strong national support in order to become financially
sustainable. Financing may be used to strengthen the institutions vital to the programs' success, but it can also weaken them. Federal financial support to local
projects in the form of a mixture of block and matching grants strengthens local
ownership. Complete reliance on national funds provides little in the way of incentives to increase local efforts. Furthermore, vouchers or other direct payment mechanisms for procuring food or other supplies from local private providers raises the
number of stakeholders. Conversely, the use of earmarked taxes, as in Colombia,
and the production and distribution of program-specific food supplements keeps
political constituencies relatively small.

Third, the cases described in this paper underscore the importance of M&E. Rapid
expansion of the Head Start program without the benefit of an initial pilot project
constrained overall program quality and compromised early evaluation efforts. Subsequent evaluations showing long-term beneficial effects proved vital to maintaining broad political support for the program. Early experience with the program in
Colombia identified deficiencies in reaching poor neighborhoods with cost-effective
interventions. This awareness led to local-level experiments with alternative service
delivery models, which subsequently found their way into the national program.

Bolivia is now applying the lessons learned in Colombia. Supported by the World
Bank, the United States Agency for International Development (USAID), and public
and private donors, Bolivia's Integrated Child Development Project targets poor
households in urban and semiurban areas. This project includes a built-in system for
evaluating the project's impact through an integrated household survey that compares outcomes for participants and nonparticipants and for randomly selecting
home daycare centers for evaluation. Because national ECCE programs require

extensive resources, it also gives special attention to the program's efficiency in reaching its targets.

### *How the Bank can make a difference*

For many years, the World Bank has invested in physical and human capital but is increasingly acknowledging the need to invest in social capital (Coleman 1990). This type of investment supports the relationships, organizations, attitudes, and values that contribute to economic and social development. To this end, the Bank is increasing its expenditures on capacity-building and community-driven initiatives. The ECCE project in Kenya is one example.

The Bank is also incorporating social assessments into its projects to provide an integrated and participatory framework for gathering data, prioritizing social concerns, and enhancing stakeholders' involvement (World Bank 1996). More M&E components are built into projects. Listening to the concerns of individuals participating in projects has stimulated appreciation for qualitative approaches to assess outcomes (Salmen 1987). As we have tried to show in this paper, these new approaches to development are especially important in projects that depend heavily on local, regional, and national institutional capacity, such as ECCE interventions. The Bank will continue to support improvements to the capacity of these vital institutions. Careful M&E will be needed to guarantee that these programs reach the intended target groups and that the interventions are cost-effective.

### References

Coleman, J. S. 1990. *Foundation of Social Theory*. Cambridge, Mass.: Harvard University Press.

Collins, R. C. 1990. *Head Start Research and Evaluation: A Blueprint for the Future*. Recommendations for the Advisory Panel for Head Start Evaluation Design Project. Vienna, Va.: Collins Management Consulting, Inc.

Jones, J. Y., and J. Richardson. 1995. *Child Nutrition Programs: Facts and Issues.* Report for Congress by Congressional Research Service (CRS). Washington, D.C.: Congressional Research Service.

Kabiru, M. 1993. *Early Childhood Care and Development: A Kenyan Experience.* National Institute of Education. National Center for Early Childhood Education. Nairobi: United Nations Children's Fund.

McKey, R. H., L. Condelli, H. Ganson, B. J. Barrett, C. McKonkey, and M. C. Plantz. 1985. *The Impact of Head Start on Children, Families and Communities.* Final Report of the Head Start Evaluation, Synthesis, and Utilization Project. Washington, D.C.: CRS.

National Institute of Education. 1992. *Early Childhood Care and Education in Kenya: A Report of an Evaluation of UNICEF-Sponsored Districts.* Nairobi: National Institute of Education. National Center for Early Childhood Education.

Nimnicht, G. P., M. M. Arango, and L. A. Hearn. 1990. *Highlights of an Evaluation of Project PROMESA.* Paper Presented at the International Conference on Children and Youth At Risk, Washington, D.C.

Rush, D., D. G. Horvitz, W. B. Seaver, J. M. Alvir, G. C. Garbowski, J. Leighton, N. L. Sloan, S. S. Johnson, R. A. Kulka, and D. S. Shanklin. 1988. "The National WIC Evaluation: Evaluation of the Special Supplemental Food Program for Women, Infants, and Children." *American Journal of Clinical Nutrition* 48 (2 Supplement):389–93.

Salmen, L., 1987. *Listen to the People: Participants Observations.* Evaluation of Development Projects. New York: Oxford University Press.

U.S. General Accounting Office (GAO). 1992. *Early Intervention: Federal Investments Like WIC Can Produce Savings.* GAO/HRD-92-18. Washington, D.C.: GAO.

World Bank. 1994. *Poverty in Colombia.* A World Bank Country Study. Washington, D.C.

———. 1996. *Social Development and Results on the Ground.* World Bank Task Group Report. Washington, D.C.

Young, M. 1996. *Early Child Development: Investing in the Future.* Washington, D.C.: World Bank.

Zigler, E., and S. Muenchow. 1992. *Head Start: The Inside Story of America's Most Successful Educational Experiment.* New York: Harper Collins Publishers.

## Comments on "Learning from early childcare and education programs," by Young, van der Gaag, and de Ferranti

*Willem H. van der Eyken*

The authors of this paper—Mary Young, Jacques van der Gaag, and David de Ferranti—have really posed three questions. First, what works? Second, what is sustainable? And third, what makes a difference? All of these are good, solid evaluation questions.

In addressing these questions, however, the authors have left out one outcome of Head Start that is known internationally—the Perry Preschool Project in Ypsilanti, Michigan, whose graduates have been tracked into middle age. The sample size of the project cohort was very modest (58 in the experimental group and 65 controls) and almost certainly too small to bear the statistical analyses that were subsequently conducted. But the Perry School project produced such dramatic developmental outcomes that they have stimulated debate for a decade: better educational achievement, less delinquency, better employment prospects, less criminal involvement, and more stable family lives than their non-Head Start counterparts. So dramatic are the outcomes that some observers have felt rather skeptical. Nevertheless, the data are there.

No studies anywhere in the world have been able to replicate the dramatic outcomes of the Perry Project. Few have had the necessary baseline data or the resources to conduct longitudinal inquiries over a sufficiently long period. In any case, no one study can tell us what works in early childcare and education. We need to look for trends in different settings in a number of countries. One study I worked on that did have the resources of the Perry Project (Osborn and Milbank 1987) focused not on 58 children, but on an entire national cohort—16,000 English children, all born in one week in April 1970.

We had birth data and preschool data at age five. When we looked at these children again at age ten, we asked a simple question: "Did preschool experience, of itself, make a difference in terms of subsequent school attainment?" The answer was yes. Despite all the intervening variables of class, race, gender, type of preschool experience, size of family, geography, economics, housing, social status, and employment—all of which have a bearing on outcomes—a small residual "preschool" effect remained at age ten. This effect resulted in better scores on measures of both language and mathematics performance. These results at least hinted at the subsequent dramatic outcomes the Perry Project found among its 58 black, sorely disadvantaged, poor, low IQ-scoring experimental group. Developmental outcomes are incremental. As well as reflecting more profound attitudinal changes, small but significant differences at age ten may very well signal subsequent developments in a child's educational profile.

Because no single scientific study can provide a complete picture, we have to build that picture up from a series of experiments, each of which is likely to be flawed in some respects. I sympathize with my former colleagues Glen Nimnicht, Marta Arango, and Lydia Hearn, quoted in the substantive paper, who did heroic work in Choco, Colombia, over many years. Together we tried to deal with the problems of missing or invalid baseline data and of many intervening variables. But try as we would, in the end we had to admit that, as the paper indicates, we could not prove what we all knew to be true: that they had made a difference in the lives of many Colombian families.

But elsewhere around the world, we have been more fortunate. Two longitudinal studies arose from, an ECCE program supported by the Bernard van Leer Foundation. The first, which comes from Australia (Bochner and Philp 1993), involved 144 children in a variety of preschool programs. Followed up through secondary school and beyond, they appeared to experience not only better conceptual development at school but better subsequent social outcomes (longer schooling, better behavior, and particularly for girls, more employment opportunities) than those who had not participated in ECCE.

The Rutland Street Project (Kellaghan and Greaney 1993), a very different study from Dublin, Ireland, found much the same outcomes, although in very different circumstances and with a small cohort of 83 "experimental" children. And again, girls benefited more than boys. Girls' achievements at school at age eight were superior, and a greater proportion of girls than boys stayed on at school and sat for public examinations. Of the eight who actually sat for the leaving certificate, only one was a boy.

In addition to these studies from the industrial countries, there is evidence from the developing world. Robert Myers (1992) conducted a massive survey of preschool programs in developing countries. While Myers' work cannot take us into longitudinal evaluation outcomes, the pattern of development is much the same.

What do all these studies tell us about ECCE and development? They tell us the following:

- ECCE "makes a difference," not necessarily in cognitive terms but in achievements, and has incremental long-term effects.

- The effects are particularly striking for girls. In 1990 the World Bank, together with the United Nations Development Programme, United Nations Children's Fund, and Educational, Scientific, and Cultural Organization, sponsored the World Conference "Education for All" in Jomtien, Thailand. The conference's declaration stressed the need to focus on the education of girls. ECCE may provide a key to realizing this aim.

- Evaluation initiated at the start of ECCE projects is essential. Moreover, that evaluation must look beyond the project. We all know of the famous evaluation that concluded "the operation was a great success; unfortunately, the patient died." Similarly, we could coin the phrase "the project was a great success; unfortunately, the country collapsed."

- Programs must be bottom up, not top down.

- Appropriate infrastructure, especially educational, must be in place for projects to prosper. The case of Belize is relevant here as an example (van der Eyken 1996).

- Continued support from regional and national administrations is essential.

- Outcomes are generational and depend on social stability and institutional support. Many of the papers at this conference are addressing a difficult question: "What are the characteristics of states that produce long-term developmental outcomes?" (See Chibbber, Chapter 3 of this volume.)

Evaluation must develop anthropological and ethnocentric approaches if it is to appreciate cultural differences and recognize important local factors affecting outcomes (van der Eyken and others 1995).

### References

Bochner, Sandra, and Hugh Philp. 1993. "Report on the Mt. Druitt Follow-On Study." Macquarie University, New South Wales, Australia.

Kellaghan, Thomas, and Betty Jane Greaney. 1993. "The Educational Development of Students Following Participation in a Preschool Programme in a Disadvantaged Area in Ireland." Studies and Evaluation Papers No. 12. Bernard van Leer Foundation, The Hague, The Netherlands.

Myers, Robert. 1992. *The Twelve Who Survive: Strengthening Programmes of Early Childhood Development in the Third World*. London: Routledge.

Osborn, A. F., and J. E Milbank. 1987. *The Effects of Early Education*. Oxford: Oxford University Press.

Van der Eyken, W., D. Goulden, and M. Crossley. 1995. "Evaluating Educational Reform in a Small State: A Case Study of Belize, Central America." *Evaluation* 1(1):33–44.

## Comments on "Learning from early childcare and education programs," by Young, van der Gaag, and de Ferranti

*Nohra Rey de Marulanda*

This paper examines a number of early child care and education programs that are linked by certain broad common characteristics. There are good reasons to look at them, as David de Ferranti mentioned. These programs combine important ingredients of local, national, public, and private support for critically important projects in the social sectors and have fought to evaluate the impact on the poor. These comments reflect what we at the Inter-American Development Bank's (IDB) Inter-American Institute for Social Development (INDES) have learned in the four years of working with the people who actually have to make these programs work.

The cases examined offer several important lessons. First, formal and informal institutions that participate in early childhood education are the key to success. Nobody would disagree with that notion, but what is particularly crucial is to stress the importance of informal institutions, because they often tend to be forgotten and thus are not supported. Yet the characteristics of these institutions and the profile of their support frequently determine the continuity and the effectiveness of the programs themselves.

Second, evaluations of early childhood programs should focus on identifying program elements and institutional constructs that have contributed positively or negatively to overall effectiveness. I include, among other things, the impact of multiple objectives. A good example is the U.S. Head Start program, which has multiple objectives and seems akin to the sort of programs we are managing in these areas.

Third, de Ferranti and others bring out the importance of institutions in producing the expected results and show that monitoring and evaluation is an essential tool in understanding and redefining objectives and correcting problems early on. It also shows that M&E should be a circular, interactive process that begins with the original design. Program managers should be prepared to change what is required to make the programs work, even if doing so means changing the original design. This lesson is one that development institutions are learning painfully, as are the agencies designing policies at national levels. Programs developed in Washington or in national capitals sometimes have to be adapted to work in the trenches, but it is not easy to document the changes.

Overall, there is not enough documentation of the factors and conditions needed to boost the success of social programs. As we have learned during four years of teaching people from social ministries and nongovernmental organizations, the number of case studies for the Latin American region is strikingly small. In part, the lack of information results from the difficulty of demonstrating needs or results, particularly in referring to things like institutional constructs. There is simply not enough information or research.

Fortunately, we have learned that institutions and organizations matter. Unfortunately, we do not know how best to promote sound institutional and organizational constructs. Learning how is our most daunting challenge right now. Papers like this one by Young, van der Gaag, and de Ferranti help clarify not only what tends to work and what does not, but also the overwhelming importance of elements that not so long ago were not even considered when analyzing the results of a given program.

The need to understand the interactions that ultimately break or make a policy or program is indeed a general problem affecting early childhood programs. The delivery of services in general and of social services in particular needs to be tackled using the same central questions. How can governments improve the delivery of these services? How do other agents in society participate? How can they participate? How do we evaluate efficiency, effectiveness, and equity in the delivery of these services?

In Latin America, countries spend an average of 30–40 percent of their annual budgets on the social sectors—an enormous amount of money. IDB estimates for 1990 or 1991 found that the amount governments in the region spent on the delivery of basic social services—education, health, and social security—equaled around $100 billion. World Bank and IDB expenditures in the region for programs of this type are minute compared with what the countries themselves are spending. So our challenge is not only to make our programs work better but to make them leverage the much larger investments and expenditures of the countries themselves. The latter—much more than our specific projects, which touch on only a small part—are what will really make the difference to alleviating poverty and inequality in the region. These programs are a crucial part of the second generation of reforms the region is facing.

Not so long ago, it was thought that the poor quality of program design was a major difficulty for governments of developing countries that needed to improve such things as macroeconomic indicators or the delivery of social services. Once the political will existed at the top, the problem of enhancing development was seen as primarily technocratic. Put good, technically trained people in the policymaking institutions, and they would design policies that would promote and enhance development through the institutions themselves.

We have painfully learned that life is not that simple. Countries have not always experienced this sequence of events. There are numerous examples of policies, apparently impeccably designed technically, that have not produced the expected results. We are now understanding that enhancing development is not just a technocratic problem of design. Design is certainly part of the problem, but the challenge of producing results goes beyond design. It requires that the many institutions—formal, informal, national, local, private, and public—empowered to implement policies or programs actually do so in ways that reach the final beneficiaries. In other words, the impact of the policies and programs are what really counts. The solution involves institutions. It involves politics. It involves consensus building.

By analyzing specific programs, as de Ferranti and others do, we learn that certain components seem to accompany successful programs. These components include the following: the participation of different actors in civil society (to guarantee ownership); trust, credibility, the flexibility to adapt the program to local conditions (and community development to the program), and M&E from the beginning of the process.

But the larger question remains: how can we turn the lessons learned at the project or the program level into systemic components of broad national policies? How can we take successful programs to a larger scale? In other words, how can governments learn something from which they can generalize from programs that, however good, are very limited? How can they apply that knowledge more widely to reduce inequality and poverty among a significant proportion of the population—not just use it to support specific programs? In my view, these questions are what the issue is all about.

Many papers in this volume have touched on aspects of this question that seem relevant to my concern. How can governments promote linkages at both the macrolevel (among ministries of health and education and institutions of social security, for instance) and at the microlevels (among families, associations, and schools)? What sort of market incentives and regulations are needed to make these linkages happen? How much can be generalized, and how much is still only at the level of cases? These are the questions we need to include in our research agenda.

I would like to try briefly to apply these questions in the context of Latin America. This is a region that, after much hard-won reform, continues to face social conditions that challenge the very sustainability of those reforms. This situation belies the common belief that at the bottom of social inequity and widespread poverty in the region is the fact that governments do not invest enough resources in human capital. A careful examination of the figures shows, however, that most of the region's countries in fact devote a substantial share of resources to education and health.

Failure to obtain results, or equitable results, is not connected only to the amount of resources spent in those areas. It has more to do with the way in which institutions that deliver services and their systems of operation actually work, and with the incentives that are in place. I present two examples. First, ministries of education and health in Latin America are enormous, given the size of the countries (and relative to countries of similar size and income levels in other areas of the world). The ministries of education in Brazil, Colombia, Guatemala, Mexico, and Venezuela are the biggest enterprises (and employers) that exist in these countries. They employ several thousands of people, while a large-scale private sector enterprise may employ one thousand people.

Second, the institutions are highly centralized. A ministry of education in a capital will sometimes decide the color of the walls of a school in a tiny village hundreds of miles away. How do you change that? What incentives are needed? The recent trend has been to decentralize, because decentralization brings the government closer to the people being governed. But decentralization doesn't necessarily bring with it the solutions to these problems. Decentralization may simply move centralized control from the capital of a country to the capital of a state, but not necessarily down to the microelements. If the correct incentives and market structures are not in place, resources may in fact be transferred from poor populations in the center to rich populations at the local levels. So decentralization by itself, although it offers enormous potential, has enormous risks.

The end of the 1980s and the beginning of the 1990s in Latin America were years of major structural reform. The reforms were necessary to encourage growth but clearly were not enough to ensure the reduction of inequity and poverty. What we have learned in recent years by acknowledging the importance of institutions and their impact on developmental outcomes shows that the task before us is reforming these institutions. But the task of achieving deep institutional change is going to be a challenge.

**Floor discussion on "Learning from early childcare and education programs"**

In introducing the discussants, Jan Piercy quoted from Gautam Kaji's presentation, noting that addressing early childhood development is essential to poverty alleviation. She added that the Bank's previous president, Lew Preston, believed that if the Bank could simply accelerate its support for female education, the catalytic effect would be enormous.

She kicked off the questions with three of her own. How do we take the lessons from experience and translate them into systemic components of broad national policy? How do we develop institutions that not only carry out these national policies effectively but do so in a style that is closer to direct service delivery? How do we know when to generalize from case studies and use what we learn in international policy?

The first participant from the floor, representing USAID, addressed the challenges from Nohra del Rey Marulanda by proposing a return to the topic of evaluation. She cited a proposed evaluation for strengthening NGOs that might go further than most evaluations, which simply tell USAID if the grantee did what it was supposed to do. She suggested that it might be possible to build a common vision of what NGOs can do for a nation and what future foreign assistance can do when USAID is gone. This objective concerns operations, but she noted that some U.S. programs are harnessing the power and capacity of local citizen committees for program monitoring, oversight, and evaluation. These methods, which could be replicated in development programs, have the potential to strengthen the social capital needed to make these programs work. A participant from the Canadian International Development Agency noted that the presentations and especially this suggestion about NGO evaluations challenges us to redefine what a successful project is.

Another participant from USAID commented on the success of early intervention with girls. He noted that if the citizens of any country do not get that early training, they are unlikely to be able to catch up. He agreed with the need for an anthropological approach that would scrutinize the micro issues pertinent to replicating results. He also asked how developing countries can produce a broad array of educated people who will not then leave the country, an issue that became a focus for much of the discussion.

In his response, David de Ferranti said that he does not have the answer to the exodus of talent from developing countries. But he added that he knows the problem well from years of wrestling with it, particularly in small African countries that train people and then lose them. He noted, however, that a time may come when the Bank's goal is to "educate the world" and that the movement of people from one place to another is not a deterrent to this objective.

Piercy pointed out that the Bank has recently begun to do some work with this diaspora. She observed that the migrations can be looked at from another point of view. Sometimes the foreign exchange they generate (the currency sent home by citizens living abroad) is a significant element in the economies of developing countries.

Willem van der Eyken noted that he had recently worked on a project in a Central American country that was essentially educating people for unemployment. The education system could be improved, but the job opportunities simply were not there. He asked what can be done with a well-educated, unemployed work force and suggested that the answer is to look beyond the project, as others had said earlier.

In closing, van der Eyken returned to evaluation, which he sees as a virtuous spiral—not a circle, because it does not come back to the same point. If evaluation is an integral part of project design, it will inform both the process and those involved. "Ownership" of evaluation can create problems, however, and evaluations conducted independently of sponsors and communities are sometimes required. We are increasingly asking questions about who owns even this type of evaluation, because at the end of the day, who is going to use it? Who is going to accept the findings and act on them? It is not going to be the sponsor. It is going to be the people.

# 13. Institutional structure and social security systems: lessons from the Chilean experience

Jorge Desormeaux

*Chile's 1980 pension reform is the first to create a fully funded mandatory savings system with private provision. Such a system insulates benefits from the political process and the state of public finances. It also protects the budget from shocks to the pension system itself and is better suited to manage the transition from demographic shock. These benefits come at a price, however, since the administrative costs of a privatized system are higher than those of efficiently run government-managed programs.*

The first significant pension systems in Chile after its independence from Spain were established by the army and the navy in the 1820s. The government established a pension system for public servants at the end of the 19th century. The state-owned railroad company created its own separate pension system at the beginning of the 20th century, an example many private companies followed.

### A historical perspective of mandatory social security in Chile

The first mandatory pension system in Chile was created in 1924 during a brief period of military rule. It had separate social security systems for blue- and white-collar workers, separate retirement ages, and separate contribution rates. Blue-collar workers could retire at 55, 60, or 65, white-collar workers after 30 or 35 years of work, regardless of age. Blue-collar workers contributed 5 percent of their salaries, white-collar workers 10 percent (rates for white-collar workers were raised in 1937 to cover health care and severance pay). Although the system was designed to be fully funded, investment performance was dismal. Controls on interest rates led to negative real rates of return on financial instruments, particularly after the Great Depression of the 1930s. The problem was compounded by rent controls and a substantial reduction in the rates of return of agricultural estates (the result of the import substitution strategy followed since the 1930s). Investment income represented only 8.7 percent of total income in the civilian social security system between 1947 and 1952 (Diamond and Valdés-Prieto 1993) and a little over 2 percent in 1977 (Piñera 1991).

Initially, the pension system created a surplus. Much of this amount was transferred back to recipients in the form of free health services (for blue-collar workers) and family allowances (for white-collar workers).

*The reform of 1952*

A drastic reform of the pension system was introduced in 1952. The reform was based on the recommendations of the Beveridge Report, which had served as the basis for redesigning the pension system in the United Kingdom. Chile's pension system was unified and redefined on a pay-as-you-go basis, and health insurance was separated from the pension system itself.

Because the initial surpluses had been used to finance permanent expenditure programs, contribution rates were substantially increased to avoid a financial crunch. The retirement age for blue-collar workers was unified at age 65. The tax on formal labor increased from 9 to 32 percent of taxable wages. Pensions were defined as equivalent to 100 percent of the average monthly salary of the last five years, after adjusting the first two years for inflation measured by the consumer price index (CPI). This arrangement caused a significant volatility in real pensions. Subsequent adjustments to pensions were legislated to occur whenever the accumulated rate of inflation since the last adjustment surpassed 10 percent.

## Experience after the 1952 reform

The 1952 reforms did not solve the systems' fundamental problems. The legislature continued to mandate benefit increases, with no concern for their financial soundness.[1] The result was opportunism and rent-seeking that led to substantial inequities. Early retirement programs were enacted that favored special interest groups. The public was not aware that these programs would have to be paid for by the community at large and particularly by future generations. The discrepancies in retirement ages for blue- and white-collar workers constituted one of the system's most distinctive inequities. Blue-collar workers were eligible for pensions only at age 65, while white-collar private sector workers were eligible for retirement after 35 years of work, regardless of age, and public sector white-collar workers after only 30 years. Most privileged of all were the drafters of these laws, namely congressmen, who could retire after just 15 years of service.

Government actions also created other inequities. These actions included the decision to offer interest-free loans and rent-free housing to certain affiliates out of social security assets, and above all the decision to suppress the cost-of-living adjustment of mortgages in 1971, a period of hyperinflation. Still another inequity was related to cost-of-living adjustments. By the late 1970s, approximately 40 percent of social security expenditures were explained by *perseguidora* pensions, which only a few high-income workers received and which were fully indexed to wage levels. For most workers, however, pension adjustment in response to the CPI required special legislation.

Clearly, the old system had a number of fundamental problems. For most workers, pensions were low. Close to 70 percent were minimum pensions (Piñera 1991). The real value of pensions was also extremely variable (Wagner 1991), and contribution rates rose dramatically in the absence of significant investment income.[2]

In 1968, President Eduardo Frei Montalva described the state of the system:

There are 2,000 laws on social security in Chile. Think of what this means. Two thousand laws, plus bylaws, the regulations of the SSI, a monstrosity that is increasing. Forty-six new provisions on social security were introduced in the cost of living adjustment law of 1966, 44 in 1967, and 1,234 in 1968. In other words, in only 3 years we have added 1,300 new provisions to the existing 2,000 laws. Nevertheless, the executive branch has no means of stopping this monstrosity. In every social security institution, there are laws that benefit particular individuals. You know that perfectly well, since you are experiencing politics. . . .What is worse, we are spending 18.1 percent of GDP in pensions. . . .The management of the pension system represents 13 percent of the cost of providing social security, more than we spend managing the national health system.

Some of the risks President Frei describes were limited by the constitutional reform of 1970, which restricted to the executive branch the right to initiate social security laws. Still, most of the inequities and distortions of the old system remained in place. Worse, the country was not prepared to deal with the imminent demographic transition that would take place between 1990 and 2030, when falling birth rates and increased life expectancy would drive the system into insolvency. In Piñera's view, responsibility for these shortcomings was certainly related to demagoguery on the part of politicians. But the main problem was related to a fundamental flaw in the existing institutions: the lack of links between contributions and benefits and between rights and duties. The absence of these links encouraged opportunism and rent-seeking on the part of workers and populist management on the part of the executive (Piñera 1991).

### The reform of the pension system

Various proposals for reform were made from the late 1950s onward. Early reform proposals were made by the 1962 Prat Commission, which emphasized the need to reduce the system's inequities and the negative impact of high contribution rates on labor costs. But these recommendations went unheeded. In 1968, the Frei government proposed creating a new funded system out of additional contributions but failed to obtain congressional support. Finally, a third proposal was made in 1973 in a document familiarly known as "The Brick" because of the size it attained. Drafted by a group of free-market economists,[3] it would become influential during the subsequent military regime. The drafters focused on the excessive contribution rates, the injustices in the distribution of benefits, and the high administrative costs of the existing pension system. Key elements in their proposal were separating income redistribution and insurance functions, allowing beneficiaries to make lump-sum withdrawals and purchase annuities, and creating private funds that invested in the capital market. Providers would be freely selected.

*Preliminary reforms*

Between 1974 and 1979, the government prepared for the far-reaching reforms outlined in The Brick. An early evaluation by a government team determined that the transition from a pay-as you-go system to a fully funded one would create a substantial budget deficit. Thus, the reforms required that a budget surplus be built up to finance the transition in order to avoid debt financing. The rate of growth of current expenditure would have to be contained over a long period, compromising the government's social agenda. The economic team, after a careful evaluation of alternatives, decided to start building up the surplus before the reforms, a task that was facilitated by the boom in economic activity that began in 1976. Two reforms were particularly controversial: the introduction of uniform indexation rules for all pensions and the elimination of the *perseguidora* clauses[4] that tied pensions to the wages of active workers. Finally, uniform pensioning ages of 65 for men and 60 for women were introduced in the civilian system. This standardization eliminated white-collar workers' right to obtain a pension based on years of service alone and, after a short transitional period, generated a cash surplus.

### *The pension reform of 1980*

The introduction of the 1980 reform was not an easy task (Piñera 1991). From the start, the reform faced systematic challenges from various groups: sectors that had profited under the old system, social security "experts" from various universities, pension institution managers,[5] trade unions and politicians that opposed the military government, and even prominent civilians that backed the government. However, the most formidable adversary was General Augusto Pinochet's advisory committee, which was composed exclusively of high-ranking military officers. This group claimed that the reforms had no precedent, that they reduced the government's power, and that they presented a monumental political risk. Another complication was the fact that current workers had a constitutional right to their entitlements under the old system and could not be forced to switch.

Nevertheless, the civilian ministers within the military government—their power enhanced by the successful performance of the economy—considered the new system one of the most significant institutional reforms the country would have to face in its road toward prosperity. They pressed the military junta, obtaining key endorsements from the navy and air force chiefs. Against all odds, and emboldened by the success of the government in the constitutional referendum of September 1980, Minister Piñera finally managed to have the law enacted on November 1980.

The most significant aspect of the new system was the introduction of a privatized, fully funded mandatory savings system that would be managed on a competitive basis. Early proposals considered that the new system would not require specialized institutions, since life insurance companies could offer annuities to retiring workers, as in most voluntary private pension schemes in the United States. However, after a careful evaluation, the government team in charge of devising the new system decided on the defined-contribution rather than the defined-benefit scheme implicit in life insurance, because the management risks are lower. Lower management risks made the defined-contribution system better suited to a country with inexperienced financial operators and recurrent external shocks.[6] The decision tilted the balance in favor of specialized institutions and a whole new regulatory body.

In essence, the new system contained two radical reforms: full funding and privatization of provision. Pensions awarded by the new system are directly proportional to contributions, insulating benefits from the political process. Workers in the formal sector are required to pay 10 percent of their monthly earnings into an individual account held by the pension management company (AFP) of the worker's choice. In addition, workers pay the AFPs a commission to cover disability and survivors' insurance, plus a competitively determined management fee. The total mandatory contribution rate in 1997 is approximately 13 percent. AFPs provide fund management services, purchase group insurance policies for disability and death, perform collection and payments functions, and provide information to affiliates. This system is complemented by institutions to redistribute income to the poor elderly, including means-testing. Minimum pensions are available to the poor irrespective of contributions.

The most controversial aspect of the reform was the privatization of provision. Thus, a substantial effort was devoted to limiting the risks of fraud. Pension funds were defined as legal entities separate from AFPs, diversification guidelines were introduced, and a strong regulatory body was created. Because of the government's limited regulatory experience, the law initially did not allow investment in equities or foreign investment. Investment in corporate bonds was also limited to nonholding companies.

To guarantee a sufficient degree of competition among providers, the law established moderate capital requirements for fund management companies, and the government enticed unions and employer associations to create their own AFPs. The low capital requirement was an added reason for tight supervision and strict diversification rules. The decision to favor low capital requirements and tight supervision seems to have been the right one and to have been based on an adequate evaluation at the time of the reform. The result was a competitive market with a low degree of risk.

Widespread concern about the efficiency of the banking supervisory structure led the government to initiate reforms modernizing financial regulations. These reforms strengthened the prudential regulation of banking in 1980. In February 1981, months before the start of the new system, a new law was passed that prevented banks from becoming providers of the new system. In August 1981, another law established a schedule to reduce bank loans to affiliated parties. It is not surprising that concern about the solvency of banks started after the reforms were approved, as a sizable portion of the pension funds was initially invested in bank debt.

A crucial test for the reforms was whether workers would choose the new voluntary system. The government applied the lower contribution rates of the new system to the workers that switched, giving rise to a 6 percent increase in disposable income. In the first month of operation, 500,000 workers (approximately 25 percent of the labor force) opted for the new system. At the end of 1981, after eight months of operation, 1.6 million workers, or 80 percent of the labor force, had moved to the new system (Piñera 1991). Only the armed forces were not allowed to switch, an exception that remains to this day.[7]

Retirees under the old system continued receiving their pensions under that system's rules. Workers who had contributed to the old system for at least 12 months and then switched to the new system were issued a "recognition bond" for their contributions to the old system. Thus, workers who switched to the new system would have their benefits insulated from the political process. This bond matures when the worker reaches pension age and yields a 4 percent real interest rate between the date of the shift and maturity.

*Later reforms*

Three areas have been revisited since the enactment of the 1980 pension reform but have not changed the system's basic structure. These areas are investment regulations, disability and survivors' insurance, and early pensioning.

In the investment area, the main reform granted authorization to invest in domestic equities in 1985 and in foreign instruments after 1992. A reform enacted in 1988 made adjustments for disability and survivors' insurance. In the event of a policyholder's disability or death, the insurance company hired by the AFP must deposit the full amount of the policy in the individual's account. An individual affiliate or survivor may then purchase a real annuity. A second reform introduced in March 1990 extended coverage to partially disabled workers. All disability pensions cover a period of three years and are reviewed at that point. Early pensioning conditions were relaxed in 1988, waiving the age requirement for affiliates holding funds that are sufficient to purchase a real annuity equivalent to 50 percent of their last income.

*Fiscal impact of the transition*

The fiscal impact of the transition—defined as the difference between contributions and pensions of the old system, plus the value of the recognition bonds that become due each year—reached 4.8 percent of actual GDP in 1987. This impact is positively related to overall economic activity and is projected to remain below 4 percent of GDP in the future. The projected deficit decreases rapidly as a proportion of GDP after the year 2000 and virtually disappears after 2015 (Ortúzar 1988).

The government financed this deficit from four sources:

- An increase in general revenues and a reduction in government expenditure that led to a budget surplus of approximately 5.5 percent of GDP by 1980

- A certain degree of domestic borrowing, apart from the issue of recognition bonds

- The sale of assets, including state enterprises, part of whose shares were purchased by pension funds

- An increase in pensioning ages (to 65 years for men and 60 for women) that delayed payments under the old system and generated a slight surplus

The main source of increased revenue was the value-added tax on consumption, which in effect financed the reduction in taxes on formal labor. Thus, a secondary purpose of the transition was to change the financing mix and the associated fiscal deficit.

*Economic implications of the transition*

International evidence suggests that the introduction of a pay-as-you-go system reduces national savings during its maturity phase. Diamond and Hausmann (1984) have determined that savings are reduced by 25–40 percent of the flow of pensions.

In the absence of government intervention, the replacement of a pay-as-you-go system with a fully funded system has an uncertain effect on private savings. The outcome depends on the degree to which the young are prepared to support the generation left without a pension. If the voluntary support provided by the young is smaller than the foregone pensions, the switch has a positive effect on private savings (Valdés-Prieto and Cifuentes 1990).

However, the final effect of replacing a pay-as-you-go system with a fully funded system depends on the behavior of fiscal policy. If the government provides support to those pensioned under the old system using 100 percent debt financing, the final effect is a reduction in national savings, because neither the young nor the old have an incentive to compress their consumption levels. Thus, in order to increase national savings, the government must reduce payments to those pensioned under the old system, use public debt to finance the transition (by increasing taxes or reducing expenditure), or a combination of both.[8]

These conditions were met during the Chilean transition, as the government conservatively built a budget surplus of 5.5 percent of GDP with the aim of financing the transition. The reform of the pension system represented an increase both in taxes on current generations and in the physical capital stock and real wages of future generations. In the long-run, then, the stock of savings must have increased.[9]

In a country like Chile, with imperfect capital controls and incomplete integration in international capital markets, external savings are not a perfect substitute for national savings. Investment is closely related to the country's national saving effort. We conclude, then, that the shift to a fully funded system must have had a positive effect on both savings and investment and therefore on economic growth.

### Administrative costs of a funded system with private provision

The administrative costs of the new system include those of both the AFPs that manage mandatory savings and of insurance companies that supply disability insurance, life insurance, and annuities. Valdés-Prieto (1993) determined that average costs per contributor amounted to $89.10 per year: $51.60 per year for collection and account and fund management, $30.80 per year for annuities, and $6.70 per year for disability and survivor's insurance. These costs are 42 percent lower than those of the old system and are comparable to those in other privately managed pension systems. However, Chilean costs compare unfavorably with the reported administrative costs of well-run government-managed systems such as those in Malaysia and Singapore. In Malaysia, for example, the state-run system costs working contributors $10 per year for services. As a share of covered earnings, the costs figures are 0.32 percent and 1.70 percent for Malaysia and Chile, respectively. Chilean costs are closer to those of expensive government-managed systems, like the Zambia Provident Fund, which costs $46.80 per year. As a share of covered earnings, these costs are 2.34 percent and 1.70 percent for Zambia and Chile, respectively. Chilean costs are also close to those of privately run systems in the United States and the United Kingdom.

The choice of private providers offered by the Chilean system has yielded benefits in terms of insulation from the political process but has become costly in terms of commission charges. Competition among providers should push costs down in the future while holding returns on the risk return frontier. Valdés-Prieto(1997) argues that the high administration costs are related to a provision that requires pension companies to charge the same commission to all contributors. The object was to prevent price discrimination, but the effect has been to encourage the hiring of sales agents in order to recruit the most attractive contributors from competing companies.[10] This is clearly a form of rent-seeking that resulted from an erroneous government evaluation. The government determined that price discrimination could give pension companies too much negotiating power, which they could eventually use against the poor. In fact, because of the low administrative costs involved, organized workers could benefit the most by negotiating a collective contract with pension companies.

### The political economy of pension systems

As mentioned earlier, a key element in the long-run effects of a change to a funded social security system is the impact of the reform on the rest of the government budget. The question of whether the transition will be financed by taxes or debt is particularly important, as are the effects on the political incentives faced by fiscal authorities. Chile's reform appears to have had important effects on political incentives as a result of the way in which the budget is reported. As budget deficits are not well received by the public and foreign investors, switching to a funded system that increases the reported deficit creates a strong incentive to improve the budget balance. Between 1980 and 1996, the reported budget surplus in Chile fell by between 4 and 5 percent of GDP, and the government claims it had a slight surplus. The primary surplus, excluding pensions in 1996, is virtually the same primary balance built up between 1977 and 1980 in preparation for the reform. Thus, 15 years after the creation of the new system, half of which has been put in place under democratic regimes, the Chilean government seems to have locked in the primary surplus that was built at the outset of the reform. This is unquestionably one of the primary reasons for the high national saving rate Chile exhibited in the 1990s, in clear contrast to other nations in Latin America.

Another important consequence of the transition to a funded system of the defined-contribution variety is a change in the incentives to use the pension system as a mechanism for redistribution. Redistribution is usually intermingled with benefit design in conventional pension systems, but contribution-based systems tend to isolate and make the redistribution explicit. Assets must be transferred to the accounts of older workers and retired people, requiring the identification of financing sources. With a benefit-based system, redistribution is more implicit, as it is achieved by applying a benefit formula to the people with the smallest contributions, while financing is left in the background and usually shifted to future generations.

Since 1981, Chile has seen a number of legislated increases in pensions from the old system, means-tested assistance, and minimum pensions. But as the budgetary process requires an explicit evaluation of the fiscal cost of each initiative, and full financing from general revenues must be available, governments have been forced to be conservative. Politicians and trade union leaders have adapted to this new setting, shifting their attention to other policies as pension policy has ceased to be rewarding.

These systems also differ in the incentives they provide to manage a demographic transition. Under a benefit-based system operated on the pay-as-you-go principle, substantial foresight is required to change contribution rates, increase retirement ages, or introduce partial funding 20 or more years in advance. With a contribution-based system, the adjustment to a demographic shock is automatic, as workers accumulate for their own retirement.

In the new system, pensions are paid by private companies, insulating benefits from the political process. In the early years of the reform, few believed that the system could survive independent of political influence. However, as experience has accumulated, workers have begun making voluntary contributions to their individual accounts, suggesting that the perceived value of contributions has increased.

In a benefit-based system, it is hard to isolate pensions from the state of the government budget. It is also hard to isolate fiscal policy from the state of the social security budget. If the pension system suffers a shock, taxes will have to be increased or benefits adjusted in line with available income. In a contribution-based system, it is much easier to insulate pension benefits from the budgetary process. Thus, if the fiscal balance suffers a negative shock, pensions are shielded from it; likewise, if the pension system suffers a shock, the budget is also better protected.

Diamond and Valdés-Prieto (1993) claim that it is socially desirable to isolate the pension system from the ups and downs of the government budget, as pensioners have little opportunity for intertemporal substitution, particularly if they have limited access to credit markets. The typical government-run pension system in the setting of Latin American politics cannot achieve this isolation. But the privatized social security system introduced in Chile can. The authors conclude that "if a privatized system is expensive to run, then from the perspective of workers, the question becomes one of describing the benefit-cost calculation of political insulation relative to administrative costs."

### The impact of the 1980 pension reform on capital markets

The transition from a government-run pay-as-you-go pension system to a fully funded system with private provision has a significant impact on the financial system. In its initial growth phase, the new system demands an important volume of financial assets that was not present in the old system, when the link between contributions and pensions was in the form of an intergenerational transfer. Mesa-Lago (1990) and Arellano (1986) point out that the Achilles' heel of capitalization systems in developing countries is the fact that massive amounts of funds must be trusted to small and underdeveloped financial markets. Thus, one of the key elements in the success and credibility of the new system was the safeguards adopted to limit the risk of fraud. The authorities' initial strategy was to establish strict guidelines for portfolio diversification, limiting investment to widely traded instruments. However, the need to increase the number of eligible instruments led the supervisory bodies to move in two directions. On the one hand, they relaxed investment limits on existing instruments; on the other, they introduced new and updated instruments to increase the selection. These innovations helped to increase the efficiency of the financial system, creating a higher level of output and raising welfare.

Table 13.1 summarizes the evolution of the Chilean capital market between 1980 and 1995. Since 1986, after the economy recovered from the financial crisis of 1981–83, the Chilean capital market has grown substantially. Stock transactions have grown faster than GDP, and bond transactions and financial intermediation (commercial paper and other short-term transactions) have grown substantially. This remarkable expansion—asset values grew at an average rate of about 60.3 percent per year between 1985 and 1995—is related to two developments: the growing volume of funds managed by institutional investors (mainly pension funds and insurance companies) and foreign capital inflows.

It is estimated that when the pension system enters the steady state, the accumulated funds will approximate the size of GDP. Insurance company reserves will also benefit by the fact that most workers purchase annuities when they retire, using the funds accumulated in their individual capitalization accounts. Because pension fund and life insurance investments favor long-term instruments, these institutional investors are generating an important demand for this type of financial asset. Other favorable indicators of financial depth, including mutual funds, foreign investments, corporate bonds, and the M7–M1, lead Arrau (1996) to conclude that the Chilean capital market is today the most developed in Latin America and perhaps among all developing countries. The private pension system has been at the root of this important transformation, which has greatly benefited the rest of the financial system as well. The Chilean banking system, for example, has grown at unparalleled rates since 1986, with a very low share of risky assets. The three stock markets—Bolsa de Comercio de Santiago (the largest in the country), Bolsa de Corredores de Valparaíso (which trades an insignificant fraction of total operations), and the new Bolsa Electrónica—have all grown at spectacular rates since 1986.

### The 1980 pension reform and the creation of social institutional capital

The evolution of the Chilean financial system since the mid-1980s has gone hand in hand with the process of continuous innovation generated by the new pension system. Valdés-Prieto and Cifuentes (1990) interpret this evolation of a particular type of capital, namely social institutional capital. This capital is governed by the set of laws and bylaws that regulate interactions among different agents within the financial system. Institutional capital can also be seen as an input in production that has the characteristics of a public good, since its use by one agent does not prevent others from using it.

An increase in the stock of institutional capital has at least three positive effects on the users of financial markets:

- It reduces transaction costs in the financial markets, making better use of transitory cash flows and reducing the need for working capital.

- It increases the choice of liquidity, risk, and profitability for the liabilities of any company, thereby increasing its market value and offering a better service to the public.

- It increases competition among intermediaries, thereby improving market transparency and reducing the time and effort devoted to socially unproductive rent-seeking activities.

TABLE 13.1: STRUCTURE AND DEVELOPMENT OF THE CAPITAL MARKET IN CHILE, 1980-95

| | Annual turnover | | | | Institutional investors | | | | | |
| | Stocks | Bonds | Financial intermediation | Stock market asset valuation | Insurance company reserves | Pension funds | Mutual funds | Foreign investment funds | Corporate bonds | M7-M1 |
| | (1) | (2) | (3) | (4) | (5) | (6) | (7) | (8) | (9) | (10) |
|---|---|---|---|---|---|---|---|---|---|---|
| 1980 | 2.41 | 0.25 | 3.27 | 41.87 | 2.02 | — | 2.68 | — | 0.19 | n.a. |
| 1981 | 1.39 | 0.35 | 5.54 | 26.58 | 1.91 | 1.16 | 2.62 | — | 0.37 | 27.72 |
| 1982 | 0.56 | 3.29 | 10.42 | 21.55 | 2.32 | 3.50 | 2.44 | — | 1.66 | 32.22 |
| 1983 | 0.31 | 5.74 | 3.24 | 13.08 | 2.59 | 6.43 | 0.55 | — | 1.51 | 31.06 |
| 1984 | 0.21 | 4.42 | 2.90 | 11.41 | 2.91 | 7.58 | 0.49 | — | 1.37 | 31.05 |
| 1985 | 0.32 | 10.61 | 9.23 | 13.08 | 3.41 | 10.63 | 0.76 | — | 1.53 | 37.94 |
| 1986 | 1.67 | 24.26 | 16.54 | 22.90 | 3.89 | 12.67 | 1.21 | — | 0.85 | 39.62 |
| 1987 | 2.43 | 26.24 | 24.64 | 25.43 | 4.44 | 14.20 | 1.43 | — | 1.37 | 43.03 |
| 1988 | 2.54 | 34.13 | 40.14 | 27.47 | 4.39 | 14.97 | 1.39 | — | 2.01 | 42.08 |
| 1989 | 2.98 | 42.48 | 32.64 | 33.16 | 5.15 | 17.65 | 1.29 | 0.38 | 3.37 | 49.52 |
| 1990 | 2.53 | 45.50 | 17.28 | 43.73 | 6.71 | 24.21 | 1.58 | 1.65 | 4.57 | 58.94 |
| 1991 | 5.52 | 35.15 | 27.09 | 81.64 | 7.89 | 31.37 | 2.64 | 2.97 | 5.59 | 61.23 |
| 1992 | 4.75 | 53.17 | 39.19 | 69.60 | 8.22 | 30.56 | 2.32 | 2.69 | 4.87 | 61.74 |
| 1993 | 6.13 | 55.86 | 61.30 | 73.15 | 9.65 | 37.02 | 2.86 | 3.63 | 4.80 | 62.62 |
| 1994 | 10.06 | 89.02 | 63.26 | 124.78 | 8.65 | 40.99 | 3.86 | 3.85 | 4.52 | 62.64 |
| 1995 | 16.45 | 120.36 | 89.37 | 108.53 | 9.88 | 40.06 | 3.88 | 2.97 | 3.67 | 63.40 |

*Note:* n.a.=not available.
*Source:* Arrau 1996.

What explains the accumulation of institutional capital in the Chilean financial system? The general orientation of economic policy in Chile since 1973 has clearly had an impact on the accumulation of social institutional capital. But the single most important element behind the decision to invest in institutional capital in Chile was the reform of the pension system in 1980. The reform of the banking law of 1981 was also influenced by the initiation of the new pension system, which relied on the solvency of the banking system for its own success. The rapid growth of the pension funds generates continuous pressure for new instruments and investment alternatives, creating the need to invest in social institutional capital. This factor will remain a positive influence in the accumulation of institutional capital for at least the next 30 years, so it can be considered a permanent effect for the current generation.

The managers of pension funds and insurance companies have also shown a deep interest in creating new instruments and markets to ensure attractive investment alternatives for their clients. Institutional investors are not able to capture the full benefit of the innovation, since other investors may copy it. But Bodie (1989) shows that the development of new markets for stock and debt instruments, as well as the instruments derived from them (options, futures, and asset securitization, among others) have all been promoted by pension funds during the last 20 years. In Chile, we already have an example of financial innovation promoted by pension funds—the creation of mortgage securities. The necessary legislation resulted from research conducted at Catholic University of Chile at the request of an insurance company.

*External effects of social institutional capital*

Institutional capital in the financial system generates at least three externalities:

■ All institutions within the capital market benefit from regulations that reduce fraud risk and improve the liquidity of pension funds. More clients are thus attracted to the financial industry, which enjoys economies of scale and generates further cost reductions. This externality prevails.

■ Other sectors of the economy benefit from the accumulation of institutional capital within the financial sector, learning how to deal with risk and manage time more efficiently.

■ A third type of externality develops when an innovation, regulation, or procedure introduced by the government can be applied in other areas, public or private, that derive a benefit from it. In Chile, for example, risk classification was initially developed for the pension fund system at a centralized level. When the market grew sufficiently to justify the existence of private risk evaluation firms, a new regulation allowed the operation of such entities. Thus, most of the financial innovations that have taken place in Chile in the last 15 years have been generated by the accumulation of pension funds. The resulting interest of fund managers in developing new instruments and markets has generated attractive investment alternatives for their clients. These effects would not have been available in the absence of pension fund accumulation and a relatively free capital market.

## Conclusions

Chile's 1980 pension reform is the first to create a funded pension system with private provision. The main virtue of such a system is the fact that it insulates benefits from the political process and the state of public finances. This has a significant impact on the well-being of pension beneficiaries, particularly if they have limited access to credit markets. In a contribution-based system, the budget is also protected from shocks to the pension system itself. A contribution-based system is also much better suited to manage the transition to a demographic shock. These benefits, however, come at a cost, since the administrative costs of a privatized system are higher than those of efficiently run government-managed programs. But it is doubtful that a government-run system can be adequately insulated from the political process in the setting of Latin American politics. Thus, the Chilean system offers an interesting alternative to workers willing to pay higher administrative costs for the guarantee of insulation from the political process and demographic shocks.

The transition from an unfunded system to a fully funded system has important fiscal and macroeconomic implications. In the Chilean case, the financial costs of the transition amounted to approximately 4 percent of GDP and were financed by a budget surplus of 5.5 percent of GDP built up by the government in anticipation of the reform. This approach ensured that national savings increased as a result of the reform and had a positive effect on investment and economic growth.

However, the benefits of a funded system with private provision are not limited to insulation from political and demographic shocks and a favorable impact on the national savings rate. The Chilean case shows that a shift toward a funded system with private provision also has a significant impact on domestic capital markets. The Chilean capital markets have developed at a spectacular rate and have given rise to a significant degree of financial innovation. As a result, today the Chilean capital market is the most developed in Latin America and perhaps among all developing countries.

The evolution of the financial system and the process of continuous innovation observed in the Chilean case can be interpreted as a direct result of the accumulation of social institutional capital. In the last 15 years, this process has been promoted primarily by regulators and fund managers interested in developing new instruments and markets to accommodate the spectacular growth of pension funds. These effects would not have taken place in the absence of pension fund accumulation and a relatively free capital market.

Finally, the success of a bold and unprecedented reform like that of the Chilean pension system would not have been possible if a careful evaluation process had not taken place at all stages. The reform was thus not only adequately designed but successfully implemented, overcoming the dangers of an underdeveloped financial market and inexperienced regulators. A recent business editorial labeled it "the most important idea ever exported from Latin America to the rest of the world."

# Notes

1. By the early 1950s, the rate had increased to 23 percent of taxable wages for pension purposes alone. For blue-collar workers, the contribution rate had increased to between 7 and 9 percent, depending on the region. (The government contributed an additional 1.7–2.7 percent.)

2. In 1975, blue-collar workers contributed 7.3 percent of their salary, while employers added an extra 44.1 percent, for a total contribution of 51.4 percent. For white-collar workers, total contributions were 64.7 percent.

3. The so-called Chicago boys, who had done their graduate studies in economics at the University of Chicago. Prominent within this group were Emilio Sanuentes and Sergio de Castro.

4. These pensions originated while Chile had a military government, when a large number of retired army, navy, and air force officers were among those favored by indexation rules.

5. Many were retired officers from the armed forces, with close ties to the government.

6. Hernán Büchi, one of the drafters of the pension reform, relayed to me that an evaluation of the performance of life insurance companies in the United States at that time showed that these institutions had escaped bankruptcy on various occasions with the help of inflation, which eroded the real value of benefits that were defined in nominal terms. Since Chile's pensions would have to be defined in real terms, the risk of bankruptcy with a defined-benefit system was judged to be too high.

7. This compromise was one that had to be made to get the reform enacted. Two explanations have been offered for this omission: that officers feared fraud by private providers, and that the military were not prepared to overhaul their complex compensation system, as was required to switch to the new system.

8. Valdés-Prieto (1993) used a simulation model to find out what happens if public debt rises by less then 40 percent of GNP during the transition and the rest is financed by taxes. He found that the steady state poor are better off when a redistributive but unfunded system is replaced by a neutral funded system, even if no targeted transfer/progressive tax system remains in the long run. This outcome is the result of the higher steady state capital stock that arises from the shift to a funded system, which increases GNP per capita, raises real wages, and reduces real interest rates.

9. Nevertheless, the decision to reduce contribution rates from close to 22 percent to approximately 14 percent in 1981 had short-term macroeconomic implications in the opposite direction that seem to have prevailed over the long-run effects at the time.

10. The AFPs are seeking high-income affiliates (contributors), as the industry has opted to raise income largely through a proportional commission on contributions, which yields a much higher return in the case of high-income affiliates. Pension companies are reluctant to charge a fixed commission that adequately reflects fixed costs, because of its negative distributional impact.

# References

Arrau, P. 1996. "Desarrollo del Mercado de Capitales: Lecciones de la Experiencia Chilena." Unpublished.

Arellano, J. P. 1986. "El Efecto de la Seguridad Social en el Ahorro y en el Desarrollo." In C. Mesa-Lago, ed., *La Crisis de la Seguridad Social y la Atención de Salud*. Mexico: Fondo de Cultura Económica.

Bodie, Z. 1989. "Pension Funds and Financial Innovation." National Bureau of Economic Research. Working Paper 3101. Harvard University, Cambridge, Mass.

Diamond, P., and J. Hausmann. 1984. "Individual Retirement and Savings Behavior." *Journal of Public Economics* 23:81–115.

————, P., and S. Valdés-Prieto. 1993. "Social Security Reforms in Chile." Documento de Trabajo No. 161. Pontificia Universidad Católica de Chile, Instituto de Economía, October.

Mesa-Lago, J. P. 1990. *Ascent to Bankruptcy: Financing Social Security in Latin America.* Pittsburgh: University of Pittsburgh Press.

Ortúzar, P. 1988. "El Déficit Previsional: Recuento y Proyecciones." In S. Baeza and R. Manubens, eds., *Sistema Privado de Pensiones en Chile.* Santiago: Centro de Estudios Públicos.

Piñera, J. 1991. *El Cascabel al Gato: La Batalla por la Reforma Previsional.* Santiago: Zig-Zag.

The Brick. 1992. *El Ladrillo: Bases de la Política Económia del Gobierno Militar Chileno.* Santiago: Centro de Estudios Públicos.

Valdés-Prieto, S. 1993. "Administrative Cost in the Chilean Pension System: Evidence from an International Comparison." Working Paper, World Bank, Washington, D.C.

————. 1997. "Comisiones de AFPs: Más Libertad, Menos Regulación." *Economía y Sociedad* 81 (January-March):24–26.

————, and R. Cifuentes. 1990. "Previsión Obligatoria para la Vejez y Crecimiento Económico." Documento de Trabajo No. 131. Pontificia Universidad Católica de Chile, Instituto de Economía, November.

Wagner G. 1991. "La Seguridad Social y el Programa de Pensión Mínima Garantizada." *Estudios de Economía* 18 (June):35–91.

## Comments on "Institutional structure and social security systems: lessons from the Chilean experience," by Desormeaux

*Elmar Kleiner*

Jorge Desormeaux's paper provides a very impressive account of the reform of the pension system in Chile, starting with the historical perspective and the macroeconomic implications of the transition. The paper covers administrative costs of the political economy of the Chilean pension system and the system's impact on capital markets. The paper finishes with an assessment of the institutional capital the reform has created.

My perspective comes from a completely different region—Central and Eastern Europe, including Russia. I suggest that this perspective is indeed a contrasting one in many ways: historically, demographically, macroeconomically, fiscally, and politically—and last but not least, institutionally. To elaborate on this idea in light of the lessons from the Chilean experience, let me start with the last sentence of Desormeaux's paper, which is a quotation from a business editorial that claims the reform of the Chilean pension system is "the most important idea ever exported from Latin America to the rest of the world."

We can assume two things about this remark: first, that there are many other excellent ideas to be exported from Latin America to the rest of the world; and second, that we accept the Chilean experience as unique and specific. For me, this comment highlights one of the most difficult problems of new institutional economics—namely the generalizability and applicability of specific experience to other cases. If the situation in Central and Eastern Europe is so different from that in Chile, what can these countries learn from Chile, and more important, how can we find out what they can learn?

Around 100 years ago, the dominant school of economic thought in Germany was the so-called historical school of Gustav Schmoller. This school can be seen from today's perspective as one of the most important predecessors of new institutional economics, but it is completely forgotten. Why? It was attacked vehemently by the Vienna school of economics, within which lie the beginnings of the neoclassical school of thought. The Vienna school's main argument was that the historical school was "unscientific" because it concentrated on case studies and avoided building generalizations. There is a scope for this kind of reasoning even today, and any specific case study should keep that in mind. My suggestion for an answer to the question of how we can find out what other countries can learn from a specific case is to integrate new institutional economics and political science more systematically into the considerations.

All reform countries in Central and Eastern Europe require a rapid and comprehensive restructuring of their pension systems, for economic and political reasons. These countries inherited comprehensive, unfunded pension systems from an era of central planning. Pension expenditures as a percentage of GDP increased rapidly during the initial years of transition, reaching 10 percent and above in most countries. Initial but ineffectual reforms were geared toward streamlining the unfunded schemes, reducing the many distortions and making the systems financially sound. Many transition economies have recently initiated reform plans, including new laws, that will initiate at least a partial shift from unfunded to funded retirement provisions. But two central questions remain unanswered: first, how will the transition be financed (and what are the minimum financial sector requirements)? And second, how will the transition be achieved politically?

If the initial reform plans had been implemented, they would have put the unfunded schemes on a sound financial footing in the short and medium term. But none of the countries implemented these reforms, instead making frequent minor adjustments and discretionary changes to avoid increasing the social security fund's deficit too much. Some parliaments voted to increase the retirement age, but implementation was suspended afterwards. Other countries increased payments to the elderly at the beginning of economic reform and democratization, so that social security expenditures as a share of GDP continued to increase. As expenditures increased, the discretionary measures were implemented, including flat rate indexation of benefits and even the suspension of benefits. The reason for the lack of progress in pension reform is, of course, political. All these countries are new democracies; parliamentary support for the fledgling governments is often fragile, and mechanisms for developing a consensus among social groups are often lacking. The conditions from which these countries are starting out are such that any traditional reform necessarily means cutbacks for large segments of the population. Thus, neither consensus nor majority solutions have been achieved.

This lack of progress in traditional pension reforms—that is, adjustments—may be one major reason for the success of more drastic proposals for the funded scheme. Moving to a private and funded contribution-based scheme may in fact prove the most credible approach, because future benefits will then depend on individual contributions rather than on the political considerations involved in distributions. A private, funded plan ultimately promises higher benefits for lower contributions. This thinking has certainly been fostered by the World Bank report of 1994, the positive assessment of the Chilean experience (and ensuing reforms in Latin America), and the positive externalities such a reform is expected to have on savings and capital formation, financial market developments, and labor market performance.

But there are still many loose ends to tie up. Against the background of the Chilean experience, administrative costs are always a major concern. Moreover, all the proposals still leave many issues undecided, in particular transitional issues such as recognizing past contributions, voluntary versus mandatory participation, and financing deficits. In this context, knowing that the Chilean transition was financed by a budget surplus the government built up before 1980 in anticipation of the reform does not help much unless we also know the political conditions that enabled this experience. We also need to understand the institutional and political conditions on which implementation and the careful evaluation process that took place at all stages of the reform depended.

Since political systems in Central and Eastern Europe are still very fragile and democratic decisionmaking processes very unsettled, it is hard to see what the Chilean example can show these countries. Moreover, institutions for designing and implementing reforms in the region are still very weak and, in some cases, nonexistent. The countries in Central and Eastern Europe need more information on the political conditions for institution building in Chile. New institutional economics relies very much on case studies, but practitioners also need some kind of methodology to apply the lessons to other cases. The best way to accomplish this end is to give a full picture of the case, including its political dimensions.

Comments on "Institutional structure and social security systems: lessons from the Chilean experience," by Desormeaux

*Gabriel Martínez*

After the reform of 1980, Chile's pension system became the center of attention for governments whose social security systems entail high fiscal costs and often produce questionable results in terms of equity. Jorge Desormeaux states that pension reforms have done more than just contribute to a more fair and time-consistent system.[1] In effect, the reforms have resulted in guaranteed income for workers. They have also promoted the accumulation of social institutional capital, or the laws and bylaws that regulate interactions among agents within the financial system.

Two issues relate closely to the institutional dimension of the evaluation of economic development. The first concerns the actual development of a social security system under decentralized principles, while the second relates to the ways in which decentralized systems promote more competitive financial systems.

## A decentralized pension system

Social security is one of the most ubiquitous public policies of 20th-century states. All industrial countries base their social policies on social security (mainly for old age, disability, health, and, in recent decades, also for child care). All Latin American countries have had social security systems for several decades, and for most countries these systems are also the main social programs.

Before Chile's reforms, social security was taken for granted, and the services it provides were almost always integrated under centralized organizations. Friedman (1962) was an exception in seeing this arrangement as desirable. His main concern was with the obligation it imposed on a wide class of people to acquire an unspecified annuity. He asked why people should buy annuities from government monopolies and questioned the often capricious way social security systems redistribute income.

Social security systems are funded by payroll taxes. Ideally, governments are able to guarantee income to the elderly, the permanently disabled (including those affected by work-related injuries or illnesses), people with temporary disabilities (without the loss of employment), and expectant and new mothers. Additionally, the government provides these groups with health insurance and achieves a certain redistribution of income. Such a government would be hard to find, however. In most cases, governments are not capable of defining consistently the groups to be covered, the levels of benefits, and the rules or even general criteria that will be used to redistribute income.

Desormeaux notes that Chile's reform featured the "introduction of a privatized mandatory savings system of the fully funded type, which would be privately managed on a competitive basis." This statement reflects a number of significant and far from trivial decisions. Most important, the system is a savings system, so it keeps the forced savings provision Friedman does not like. But it gets rid of the rule that requires contributors to deal with a single public supplier.

A main concern of the Chilean reformers was to foster competition. Thus, they avoided imposing high capital requirements for fund management companies and kept banks out of the game, presumably to prevent a banking cartel from using the pension funds to recycle low-grade paper. This aspect of the reform is well understood: the system needs to allow for the maximum return on reserves, and competition is probably the best means of ensuring this result. Desormeaux points also to a feature of the system that is not always widely noticed but that is key to the success of Chile's system—namely, that the reserve is in the hands of workers. This arrangement substantially enhances the credibility of the overall economic policy, because it allows for disclosure of liabilities even if the reserve is fully invested in government bonds.

For disability and death insurance, the Chilean system mandates that pension fund management companies buy insurance for their clients. But this arrangement raises a question about the effectiveness of the Chilean system. If insurance rates are determined by demographic or other characteristics (such as lifestyle), then the rates will differ across groups of workers. Regulations can prohibit fund management companies and insurers from refusing applications by requiring that all applicants be admitted at the same premium. However, as is common in the service (and particularly financial) industries, it is not difficult for providers to discriminate by offering different levels of service or by targeting certain groups. This topic is one that has not been researched for the Chilean social security system. While it is known that there are significant differences in premiums across providers, there is none on the effects of these variations on different groups of workers. Similarly, little is known about the effects of different systems for workers' compensation. Knieser and Leeth (1995) have argued that the systems differ significantly in efficiency, but no one has studied the impact of the reform on health and safety in the workplace.

Finally, Desormeaux notes that the Chilean social security system is not run by low-cost organizations. He proposes that the "nonrefusal" regulation, obligating all providers to sell at the same price, increases costs because it induces competition on a nonprice basis. While this view may be correct, allowing pension fund management companies to refuse to deal with or to select individuals on the basis of price may not be the best solution. A certain equality of opportunity is of the essence in this case, and people who want social security must accept these egalitarian goals. Without them, the program is based on forced savings and insurance and on the assumption of a paternalistic but not egalitarian state. It assumes that forced financial savings and insurance will improve the lot of workers under an inefficient financial system that otherwise is not attractive for them. The result will be that voluntary financial savings from a large part of the population will not be forthcoming.

Social security systems must recognize the high cost of managing individual insurance policies and savings accounts. The results described in the literature are well known, and the regulations should try to accommodate them. For example, the Chilean and other more recent systems regulate commissions extensively but allow competition in interest rates. It would be more appropriate to get rid of the regulations on commissions and allow plain competition in interest rates. And in the case of disability, it would be easier to keep the insurance function in the hands of a government corporation to avoid the cost of breaking up the risk pool and to manage reserves and the annuity itself in a competitive market.

### Decentralizing financial decisions

Desormeaux aptly summarizes the following policy effects of the reforms. New liabilities incurred by social security have an immediate impact on the national deficit because they are explicit. Attempts to tamper with the system in order to benefit special interest groups are more difficult. And the real value of pensions is more predictable for workers because benefits are insulated from the yearly budgetary process.

These results are required for financial competition. When it is not possible to define the amount of benefits, to determine whether resources will be forthcoming to pay for the liabilities, or even to know who will have the benefits a few years down the road, it is certainly unworkable to think about recycling the resources of the system to productive uses through financial channels. But it is also apparent that the Chilean reforms were in part the result of concern about the thinness of the financial market. Could instruments be developed in which the pension fund managers would invest? Could banks use the pension management funds to discharge bad portfolios?

Desormeaux describes the actions taken to face these issues. The results so far are encouraging, because the market has grown substantially, producing high returns for workers. Desormeaux's hypothesis is that the reform accelerated the creation of financial regulations that promote competition. The size of the pension funds is such that the effects are transmitted to the whole economy, and there are overall gains in liquidity, safety, and information to consumers and firms. A number of countries have pursued other strategies to develop financial markets, including "development banks," which have become common in other countries but are not used in Chile.

Behind Friedman's original statement, Chile's reform—and much of the discussion on health regulation that has mushroomed in recent years—is the possibility of developing egalitarian social security policies in a decentralized operation. Social security functions are being unbundled. Perhaps this development will improve operations by the state and other social agents and enhance performance in reaching egalitarian goals.

### Note

1. In this context, time consistency means that the government is willing, at any date, to fulfill the promises it made to workers about the real value of the pensions to be paid.

### References

Friedman, Milton. 1962. *Capitalism and Freedom*. Chicago: Chicago University Press.

Kniesner, Thomas J., and John D. Leeth. 1995. *Simulating Workplace Safety Policy. Studies in Risk and Uncertainty*. Boston and Dordrecht: Kluwer Academic Publishers.

**Floor discussion on "Institutional structure and social security systems: lessons from the Chilean experience"**

Opening the discussion, a participant from Finland referred to the recent calamity in Albania, where private financial institutions had the task of accepting funds destined for pension-related investments. He asked how Chile, where a prime concern has been the security of such funds, would handle this situation.

The second participant, from the European Commission, noted that foreign direct investment in Chile is the same as it is for Russia ($2 billion per annum; Jorge Desormeaux noted in his response that it has now increased in Chile to $5 billion). He asked whether Chile's pension reforms have been an important factor in establishing reliable capital markets and what other factors, if any, have played a part.

The third participant noted that in Germany, social memory encompasses two monetary reforms and all manner of written pension systems that were never funded. He suggested that there may be a problem with credibility in Germany.

Desormeaux agreed that Chile is a special case and that transplanting its system to other countries will require some care. The most important question is how to manage the process of developing a consensus for change. But despite the difficulties, the possibility of transferring such a system should not be discarded. Chile's system was unique at one time but has since transferred well to Argentina, Bolivia, Mexico, Peru, and even Uruguay, each of which has applied the system in its own way. In Bolivia, one of the poorest countries in Latin America, pension reform and the privatization of state companies have been combined, so that past pension contributions can be tied to the ownership of shares in state-owned companies.

On the fiscal question, Desormeaux said that while Chile may be an extreme example, setting up such a system does not require a titanic effort. Simulations indicate that a good part of the deficit of existing systems can be financed by issuing bonds to the new pension funds. Ideally, debt finance should be kept below 40 percent of the deficit so that the savings rate during the transition will not fall. Governments do need to make a fiscal effort. In Chile, for instance, no more than 2.5 percent of the deficit (4 percent of GDP) needed to be financed by an increase in the budget surplus. Chile's deficit ultimately reached 5 percent of GDP, but a country wanting to increase its savings rate will need a higher fiscal effort.

The conditions and therefore benefits of such a system differ across countries, Desormeaux continued. In a country where a large proportion of the population is young, the transition will be much cheaper to finance. This situation does not apply in Europe. The Europeans, with their aging populations, will have to decide whether a transition might simply become too expensive. Not every country can follow Chile's example, and each will have to find out for itself if it is likely to experience any benefits. Countries that already have deep, sophisticated capital markets, for instance, will not enjoy the benefit of seeing such markets emerge, while countries with weak capital markets will.

Desormeaux noted that administrative costs are one of the "missing steps" in the Chilean system. But very prestigious academics have made proposals that would reduce them through competition. Costs have been decreasing over time, and management companies are still focusing on high-income customers because of the structure of commissions. That tendency has to be eliminated and competition introduced.

Risk, too, is an important concern in Chile. The rules are very strict, and because they were well designed from the beginning have undergone minimal changes. A pension fund management company cannot reserve the best business for itself and leave the rest for the fund it manages. So the Albanian disaster will not happen in Chile; it is also unlikely in Argentina, Bolivia, Mexico, and Uruguay.

Responding to the question of whether capital markets in Chile owe their expansion to foreign direct investment or to pension funds, Desormeaux pointed out that the pension funds started in 1981. But important capital inflows to Chile started with the transition to democracy in 1990. Capital markets expanded long before 1990, largely because of the savings rate, which by 1995 had reached 27 percent of GDP. That level is about 10 points higher than in any other Latin American country and represents the most significant effect of the pension reform.

Most Chileans had no reason early on to believe that the new system would be any better than the existing one. Even today, people do not realize exactly how good the system is. Macroeconomists are much more aware of the benefits but have expressed concern that the huge funds that are accumulating could become the target of politicians. The risk today seems lower. People are increasingly aware that the system is working well, and the authorities understand that they now have the possibility of financing projects such as new infrastructure through the pension funds.

Gabriel Martínez noted that reforming social security requires a wide variety of systems that do not necessarily converge. To find better bases for reform, the components have to be looked at separately. In the Chilean system, the savings component is strong and provides a solid basis for the social security system overall. The health reforms have not been that successful and are being reconsidered. But the message of the Chilean pension system is that some components experience significant gains from decentralization. In the end, the question of whether the system is old or new or the population aging or young will not matter.

# PART 4: THE IMPLICATIONS OF NEOINSTITUTIONAL ECONOMICS FOR EVALUATION

# 14. Evaluation as an incentive investment

Joseph Stiglitz

*The themes of institutions and evaluation are naturally linked, first because evaluation is itself an important institution and second because the role of institutions is gaining increasing attention in development thinking, posing particularly difficult challenges of design and methodology for evaluation.*

This volume deals with two very important themes that are receiving increasing attention: first, the role of institutions in our economy and society and their role in economic development; and second, the growing importance of evaluation. There is a natural interplay between the two themes of institutions and evaluation. I would like to focus on two aspects of this relationship.

First, evaluation itself is an important institution. Evaluation is crucial to the process of learning and decisionmaking, especially in a context such as that of the World Bank, in which profit is not the bottom line. (Even when profit is the bottom line, things are not always simple: profits may go up not because the right decision was made, but because of other external events.) In the context of development, which involves a fundamental transformation of society, evaluating performance is extremely complex and cannot be done simply by measuring GDP growth. Hence the need for evaluation.

Second, the Bank is becoming increasingly involved in trying to establish, strengthen, and support institutions in developing countries. The challenges of evaluating these efforts are even more difficult than those facing the evaluation of conventional investment projects. Over the years we have developed certain methods for evaluating physical infrastructure schemes such as dams, highways, and the like. But how do we evaluate an institutional innovation, such as the creation of a stock market? How do we determine what pricing policies ought to be? Even more demanding, how do we assess the efficiency of governance structures to determine those pricing policies?

### Evaluation design: avoiding distortions

Because evaluation, including ex post evaluation, provides an important contribution to accountability, it affects our incentives and influences behavior. Hence, inappropriately designed evaluations can have significant distortionary effects, just as well-designed evaluations can have very positive effects.

One of the reasons we need good, timely evaluation is that we want to make decisions that will lead to better outcomes. This is not just an academic exercise. We want an evaluation methodology that will affect our behavior and the behavior of our partners toward improved development effectiveness. The design of appropriate evaluation is extraordinarily difficult, however. And, if we put into place the wrong kind of evaluation benchmarks, we can actually make things worse rather than better. I would like to give an example as a cautionary tale.

One essential question in all retrospective evaluations is the counterfactual: what would have happened if a project had not been undertaken? For example, would the project have been undertaken by the private sector? We may lend money, and a project may be carried out, but would it have been done better by the private sector? Would it have been carried out more rapidly and efficiently? If it turns out that a government project displaced a project by the private sector, we have, according to the counterfactual, a negative contribution to development—even if the project yielded an acceptable financial return.

Such strategic questions are especially important as we reexamine the role of the state in society. What should the government do? What should the private sector do? What is it that other parts of civil society should do? It is imperative that we have a clear view of the difference a particular project, or a particular institution, makes. Did creating a securities market facilitate the flow of private capital from abroad, or would this have happened anyway?

In many cases, it is very difficult to measure outcomes. Not only is it difficult to measure the counterfactual, but it is difficult even to measure what actually happened. This has led to the use of a number of surrogates for actually measuring outputs. I would like to urge extreme caution, because surrogates that are inappropriately chosen may actually be counterproductive and can lead to a worsening of overall performance.

Let me give one example. Sometimes, performance is measured relative to stated goals. A project is measured according to what was expected to happen. If it falls short of these goals, it is considered a failure. But we must put this relative performance in context. Typically, the private sector measures the profitability of a project by establishing a threshold expected rate of return, usually between 15 and 20 percent. If the "expected" return falls below this, the project is not undertaken. Some companies have even higher expected returns. However, the average return on investments in the private sector as a whole is 7 percent, and in manufacturing it is probably under 10 percent. Does this mean that the private sector of our economy is a failure? I don't believe so.

What inferences can we make from this? A number of us have worked on statistical models that try to explain how people make judgments about expected returns. Those of you who are familiar with the literature may recall a phenomenon in the bidding world called "the winner's curse." Those companies with the most optimistic information about a project make the highest bids. Bidders recognize that if they win a bid, their information was likely more optimistic than anyone else's. Recognizing this allows companies to adjust their bids to more realistic levels. Company managers may not have studied statistical models, but they intuitively recognize these issues.

There is a danger in judging projects based on what they are "expected" to produce, because expectations can simply be reduced. In the end, a project may look better relative to the stated goals, but total output and performance relative to real outcomes may not be any better.

Another example of why we must think very carefully about these issues is that there is sometimes a tendency to measure the outputs that are easiest to measure, but which may not be the most important. For example, in the education sector we have good performance measures for basic skills but not for creative thinking skills. Because schools want to obtain high performance measurements, they focus on basic skills, diverting resources away from measuring skills in critical thinking. The lesson here is that we must try not to be distracted from what is imperfect by what is measurable. Evaluation schemes affect incentives, and we must take this into account in our design schemes.

A third example: sometimes, performance is measured not according to outcomes but according to processes, such as whether people show up for meetings. In some contexts, we know that certain processes help lead to better outcomes, even if we can't measure those outcomes. If we measure and focus on the process, we can indirectly enhance the likelihood of achieving good results. This approach has its own risks. There is the danger that resources will be used to satisfy process criteria with little or no impact on outcomes. This is what red tape is all about. Too much emphasis on process can lead to bureaucracies, in which people get credit for performing according to processes that may no longer be relevant and may even turn out to interfere with intended outcomes.

One area in which process can be measured is participation. We know that participation in decisionmaking is good in many fields, but it can also be counterproductive. The U.S. Environmental Protection Agency (EPA), for example, carried out a study of perceptions of various risks, such as the risks associated with water and air pollution, the ozone layer, and industrial contamination. The EPA surveyed the scientific community and the public separately, and the results were completely different. I assume that scientists have a more scientific basis for assessing risks. But if participatory decisions are made about allocating resources, a society could end up with less health protection than if it relies on the experts to decide which factors have a larger impact.

This does not mean we should not have participation. It means that we must have a process to educate people so that they are better informed. We must have participatory outcomes, but we must be aware of circumstances in which participation may not be effective. For example, the Bank last year released a set of performance monitoring indicators for agricultural extension, most of which were not closely linked to outcome measures. Some of these indicators encouraged short visits with farmers, with little attention to content.

As the Bank reinvents itself as a knowledge institution, it is especially important that the evaluation process be taken very seriously. Knowledge is an international public good, and the World Bank has a special role in the development and dissemination of information related to development and development projects. It is imperative that the Bank design projects in ways that enhance what can be learned and that it explicitly include an evaluation strategy in the design of its projects. Experimental design should be part of innovative projects.

### Integrating design and evaluation

We should think about how to design projects that give us information we can apply in designing new projects. In other words, we must integrate project design and evaluation. A research project I have been carrying out at the department of Development Economics and Chief Economist illustrates this concept. The project evaluates two types of interventions: school-based management reforms in El Salvador and Nicaragua, and the use of NGOs to reach underserved segments of the population in Colombia, Pakistan, and Nicaragua. The researchers established baseline surveys to monitor the impact of the interventions over time. This evaluation is part of the projects themselves. The cost of the evaluation is approximately 1 percent of the entire operation, but it is essential if we are to become a knowledge Bank.

Some points concerning this evaluation are worth noting. First, the baseline conditions can be established not just for the project as a whole but for separate components, including particularly innovative portions. Second, incorporating the evaluation as part of the operation imposes a certain discipline on project design, since the designers must think about the project's value added and the indicators they must use. Third, building evaluation into the lending operation emphasizes to the client the need to learn from the investment and to build local capacity for evaluation and data management. Fourth, since evaluations are part of institutional change, they can observe and document the process and the changes in the process, as well as the outcome. And finally, the very fact that the reforms are innovative makes it difficult to rely on experience or on historical relationships between inputs and outputs. Impact evaluation may be the only way of evaluating these interventions.

Some results from this research are already emerging. In Nicaragua, school autonomy reform is having a positive effect on the way local stakeholders—such as directors, teachers, and parents—perceive the quality of education. A second round of surveys will assess whether there has been a concomitant improvement in school enrollment and learning. In Pakistan, greater community involvement by parents and NGOs has led to higher enrollments of girls in participating areas relative to control areas.

In these examples, we can actually answer the counterfactual question, because we set up a control context from which we could determine if the reforms actually worked. And this made the difference. To me, this approach seems critical if we are going to be able to go about the process of evaluation.

In conclusion, let me reiterate the importance of evaluation. It is precisely because it is so important that we must be extremely careful about how well it is done. As we strive to change the development process itself and the institutions of society, the challenge of developing appropriate evaluation methodologies will grow. We must enter this process with a certain degree of humility and with the willingness to subject our evaluation methodologies to a constant process of evaluation.

# 15. Implications for evaluation

Panelist comments

*Eleanor Chelimsky*

The proposition, as I understand it, is that unimproved institutions constitute obstacles to reaching larger goals like reducing poverty and hunger, protecting the environment, or stimulating economic growth and development. Such a proposition signifies that once institutions have been improved and their improvement measured in some way, it will still be necessary to show that improving them has brought about increased effectiveness in achieving the larger goals. That is, improving institutions, in this context, is an instrumental objective, not an impact or outcome goal.

The panel was asked to consider several questions, based on the papers presented. Although the papers are all clearly economic in their assumptions and orientation, the remarks I intend to present are made from an evaluative rather than an economic viewpoint. By an "evaluative viewpoint" I mean four things: first, a concern about what evaluation's role should be in the brave new institutional world; that is, if the economic assumptions are right and effectiveness is improved by concentrating on institutions, how will we know? What tools will we need to measure effectiveness, and what comparisons will we be able to make? Second, a perspective that is more skeptical than that shown in the papers about what is said to be known versus what is actually known. Third, a willingness to admit that all evaluative questions cannot be answered by rate-of-return or cross-sectional analysis, and a corresponding interest in more relevant, appropriate, and sensitive methods. And fourth, a much stronger emphasis, in Galileo's terms, on understanding how the heavens go, than on understanding how to go to heaven. Mark Twain once said that thunder is impressive, but it's lightning that does the work. To an evaluator like me, theory is good, theory is wonderful, but it's the methods and the data that tell us if the theory is right.

In what follows I will address the questions posed to the panel.

■ *Since "institutions matter," what can evaluation do to help the Bank and borrowing countries develop the "right" institutional capacity?*

Looking across the conference papers, I would note first that it would be hard to base an evaluation argument on the discussions presented here. I found a lot of attention being focused on explanations of what is meant by the term "institutions," on attempts to show that strong institutions engender good developmental outcomes, and on a great many proposals for institutional change to achieve these outcomes. I did not find a whole lot of attention focused on the role of evaluation. With only a few exceptions, not much thought seems to have been given in these papers to the use of evaluation as a way to test at least some of the theoretical formulations about institutions.

This seems somewhat surprising in that many of the key questions needing to be answered about institutions in the development context are also key questions for evaluation. Finding out what works is evaluation's stock in trade, and we are concerned here, as Jeffrey Nugent put it very well in his paper, with determining not just whether institutions matter, but which ones matter most, and how, and why. Whether the question is, "Does it work?" or whether the question is "If it works, does it work everywhere or only in one place?" these questions lie at the heart of institutional development issues, and they explain both why evaluation is needed and the role evaluation should play in the production of information.

For example, do we *know* that specific institutional changes will, in fact, produce favorable developmental outcomes? The evidence presented in some of the papers is suggestive, perhaps, but it is certainly not persuasive, based as it is on cross-sectional designs and one-shot surveys. The problem here is that these designs always allow many competing interpretations of the results to be made, no matter how sophisticated the statistical analysis superimposed on those designs. Evaluation can help here by supplying more appropriate designs. It can also help by examining the generalizability of favorable outcomes, once they are found. However, at this point, I think the first evaluation priority should go to bringing evidence that can support or disestablish the link postulated between institutional quality and beneficial outcomes. Deciding what is the "right" institutional capacity should occur after the link has been shown.

Another important role for evaluation, in my judgment, lies in carefully questioning the assumptions that planners, theorists, and policymakers have made. For example, as many of the conference papers state, it is certainly likely that institutions matter, but so do a lot of other factors. Do we know that institutions matter more than, say, religious, cultural, or political factors (like anti-Western bias, or antimarket sentiments, or concern for national traditions) in achieving or impeding the Bank's developmental goals? Of course we don't know. What we do know is that institutions, however they are defined, not only matter to some degree but also can, at least in some cases, be affected and changed by policy design, whereas the other factors just mentioned are mostly not amenable to a policy fix. The cautionary point here is that although institutions may matter, and may permit policy fixes, they may not matter most, and therefore efforts to change them, although probably not wasted, may not achieve the level of positive results in the larger goals that is currently expected. Evaluation can help here again by developing reasonable objectives for these efforts, based on responses actually observed, rather than postulated, in borrowing countries' institutions.

Similarly, the assumption clearly exists in many of the conference papers that a particular policy fix attempted in the past (whether regulation, or decentralization, or something else) was the "right" one and hence, the job we have before us is to find out where the institutions went wrong. But what if the institutions were right and the policy fix was inappropriate? The role of evaluation here is what it has always been: to look dispassionately at the assumptions that were made, at the process and context in which they were carried out, and at the outcomes that resulted. More of

this kind of information will go a long way toward helping the Bank and the borrowing countries to change institutions in useful and sustainable ways.

■   *How should evaluation evolve to become more effective in acquiring the knowledge*
    *needed to deal with institutional development issues?*

Based on the questions implied or stated in the conference papers, it seems to me
that evaluation has no immediate need to evolve, although it could conceivably
have to do so eventually. What *is* needed immediately is to spell out the kinds of
questions that evaluation will be asked to address. Only then can it be determined
what evolution and what new methods may be needed to answer them.

In speaking about "kinds" of evaluation questions, I do not refer to subject-area
questions such as constitutional provisions, or political checks and balances, or market impediments, and whether or not they are often treated by evaluation. This is a
moot point because one of the great advances of evaluation in the 1980s has been to
show that evaluation could address almost any topic, depending on the kind of
information that is sought. By "kind" of information or question, I refer to whether it
is necessary to establish a cause-and-effect relation, provide rigorous comparisons,
or merely produce descriptive observations.

Do we want to show whether some policy intervention (in whatever subject area)
has been effective, has changed things in specific ways? If so, that is a cause-and-
effect question requiring both the measurement of change and the ability to attribute
any change observed to the effects of the policy intervention. Do we want to find out
what officials from borrowing countries think about some newly initiated reporting
system? Or to understand how the implementation of a program or policy differs
across organizations, or sectors, or nations? These last two questions are descriptive,
not cause-and-effect, and they require methods to answer them that differ from
those needed for cause-and-effect questions because they emphasize the richness
and validity of observation, rather than rigor of comparison.

The kind of question being posed is thus extremely important since it determines
both whether evaluation can answer it (or instead needs to evolve before it can do
so) *and* which methods are appropriate for doing so. Let us imagine that the Bank is
trying to address an accountability (cause-and-effect) kind of question from one of
its donors. For example, did an agricultural program involving increased crop yields
(or a change in institutional mechanisms allowing programs to focus better on target
populations as opposed to rent-seekers) contribute to a decrease in poverty or a
reduction in hunger among the most disadvantaged groups in, say, an African
nation? We know immediately that evaluation can bring credible answers to this
kind of question, and we have a good idea of which methods will need to be
employed.

The point here is that—whether the subject is a change in institutional rules, or
health care delivery, or germplasm, or teaching methods, or defense policy—neither
cause-and-effect nor descriptive questions require evaluation to evolve. The needed
methods are already there. Moreover, these kinds of questions are likely to be posed
over and over again, as is shown by Eduardo Wiesner's paper in which evaluation is
simply asked to do its traditional thing: establish the effects of an implemented pol-

icy in terms of both performance and results, and conduct "strategic evaluation of specific reform experiments under different institutional arrangements."

I am not, of course, arguing that because the kinds of evaluation questions that are likely to be posed about institutional change are much the same as they are in other subject areas, this makes them easy to answer. On the contrary, cause-and-effect linkages are always hard to make and are rarely as conclusive as we would like (although we can certainly do better than relying on cross-sectional data to make attributions). Evaluation has developed a whole panoply of methods drawn from all the relevant disciplines, and evaluators have been using them separately *and* in concert since the early seventies. These methods move from experiments and quasi experiments, through cumulatively designed multiple-case evaluations and replicated (not one-shot) surveys, to meta-analysis and research synthesis. All these methods allow cause-and-effect linkages to be made, albeit with greater or lesser conclusiveness. So it seems somewhat surprising, in this context, to hear calls for new methods to estimate the counterfactual when, in fact, evaluators have been doing that successfully for many years, using interrupted time-series and autoregressive integrated moving averages (ARIMA) or other models. A more routine procedure for estimating the counterfactual would be better constructed data bases and more relevant data collected regularly over time.

Measurement issues also are difficult, especially with regard to intangibles. "Quality," for example, has always been difficult to document, even though considerable progress has been made recently in, say, measuring the quality of health care services. But problems remain: How, for example, can we measure institutional quality in a credible, defensible way? What measurement criteria can we use to qualify institutions as "strong" or "weak"? And which among these criteria can be globally applicable?

The overall point I want to make here is that, although the methodological challenges posed by institutional development issues are real, they are certainly not new. Indeed, they are precisely the same challenges that evaluation has confronted routinely, and often very successfully, over the years.

■   *How should development interventions be designed to build in systematic evaluation of institutional factors?*

This question returns us to the issue of what it is we want to learn. It goes almost without saying that those institutional factors that are to be systematically evaluated must be systematically included in the design of the development intervention. But how systematic can we currently be? Looking across the conference papers, we see many different definitions of what is meant by "institutions," but many of these definitions are too vague and general to be useful in evaluation. Similarly, the institutional changes that authors would like to see undertaken are not always well articulated. Yet a first requirement for the strong design of an intervention is an explicit statement of exactly what the treatment is. Does the effort intend to improve regulatory credibility? To increase citizen participation? To put in place better checks and balances? To establish a more independent judiciary? To create a competent bureaucracy? Do we want to decrease corruption and the power of rent-seekers? Are we trying to ensure control of opportunistic behavior among government officials? Is our goal to maximize the spread of information? For any and all of these undertakings, the design of the intervention needs to specify exactly and explicitly which activities are calculated to achieve the beneficial outcomes, as well as how and why.

The point here is not that the list of policy fixes given in the various papers is too long or too varied; on the contrary, the number and diversity of the suggestions merely reflects that the concept of institutions as a factor in development outcomes is ambitious, comprehensive, and multifaceted. But to be effective and credible, one cannot systematically evaluate everything. A successful evaluation design requires, first, that we focus on answering no more than two or three questions at a time; second, that we spell out those questions very clearly and define them operationally so that measurement can take place; third, that we understand what the project is (1) trying to accomplish, and (2) doing to accomplish it; and fourth, that we lay out an evaluation strategy and methodology that are adequate to answer the questions posed as cost-effectively as possible.

If institutional factors are to be systematically evaluated, then the designers of development interventions need to bear in mind the requirements of evaluation designs. In particular, the project or policy interventions must be laid out with specificity, their purpose explained, and the reasons given as to why and how it is expected that the proposed activities will achieve these purposes. Given that kind of clarity, the evaluations can then ensure that the major institutional factors involved are systematically assessed.

In conclusion, I believe evaluation can be very helpful in answering a number of important questions posed about institutions and how they work. It can do that simply by being itself: that is, by producing the data needed, and by stating unblinkingly what they show. But evaluation can also help in developing institutions, as the recent performance measurement efforts in the Australia, United Kingdom, and the United States have shown. Indeed the match between the needs of institutional development and the capabilities of evaluation is so remarkable that, as Wiesner (Chapter 6 of this volume) notes, it is something of a mystery why neoinstitutional economics, with all its emphasis on microanalytics, has not focused more on the potential that evaluations have to enhance public sector reform and to ensure a more efficient use of resources.

Panelist comments

*Joseph Wood*

My comments address mainly the question of what evaluation of institutions means for operational work, because most of my career has been spent in operations. I only recently moved into the field of evaluation, and I have to say the last few days have been a sobering experience.

What did I learn from the papers I reviewed and the sessions I attended? I didn't learn that institutions are important. I knew that before. Nor was it new to me that the track record of efforts to improve institutions has been very mixed, as the euphemism goes.

The question that engaged me was how development practitioners can become more effective. In particular, what role can evaluation play in helping us to become more effective?

My thoughts on the topic focus on three areas, the first of which is the intellectual framework. The conference presented a bewildering set of methodological discussions on the definition of institutions. As an operator, I came away impressed with the discussions on the framework that focused on rules and restraints, voice in partnership, and competitive pressures, which was broken down according to whether the framework applied to policymaking or service delivery.

As an operator I can identify with that framework and could find it useful. But since I gather it is not all that new, I ask myself why it hasn't appeared more frequently in day-to-day operational work. Partly, the problem is the inevitable lag. But equally, I believe the majority of operational staff do not yet view it as a tool to solve an urgent problem. And that is not, let me emphasize, because operational staff feel that institutions are not important.

Over the last few years, I have found operational staff to be very responsive to a particular aspect of institutional dynamics—namely, the role of participation. So when an institutional insight can be shown to have a practical impact, it gets absorbed and embedded in daily work. Thus, while the framework is useful and intellectually engaging, it needs to begin delivering some results for it to become an integral part of daily operational work.

My second comment concerns the difficulty of applying intellectual frameworks to the complex array of problems faced in operational work. Here, I was very taken by the observation that the goal of the work on institutions is not to define an optimum result. That objective is probably impossible to achieve and certainly not desirable in the near term. What I found striking in that observation is that if the goal is changed from trying to find an optimum result to one of finding a seemingly sensible balance in the tension between flexibility and restraint, then one can at least identify the directions of change, the areas where one would like to see movement, without having to determine what an ideal position is. Indeed, the very definition of the problem in terms of the balance between restraint and flexibility suggests that there is no generalizable ideal. It all depends on the conditions one finds in a particular place where one has worked.

That brings me to my third comment. Operational people are not very interested in theoretical descriptions of ideal outcomes or even just pragmatic goals. They are really interested in what people have to tell them about "how to": how to get there, how to get from here to there, and, even more important, how to advise our clients on the appropriate way to get from here to there.

Here again, I was struck by the variety of circumstances in which institutional economics is applied, and the incredible importance of the dynamics of local situations in answering the question of "how to." There doesn't seem to be a standard approach. It all has to be tailored to the particulars of the local situation.

Now in part that simply confirms something that is already largely absorbed in the daily work of operational people. The term "ownership" is part of our standard vocabulary. But the significance of ownership is not just that it's politically correct but that it offers an intimate knowledge of the local scene, which is crucial to designing an appropriate "how to." There isn't a "how to" that's independent of the local scene, and there is no way an outsider is going to be better informed about the local scene than through the local authorities themselves.

This does not mean we simply turn over responsibility for design to local authorities. Indeed, one of the topics I found most interesting in the conference was on the beginning attempts to assess whether preconditions exist for effective institutional change. These assessments look at the local institutional incentive structure to see whether changes that seem desirable in principle are likely to be sustainable in practice, given the local institutional framework.

There is room for much productive work here. We can do a great deal to define practically the techniques for looking at the institutional incentive framework and judging the ripeness of the local situation for effective institutional change. This reminds me somewhat of the debate (now quite advanced) on how to judge the probability of a successful outcome from project lending.

We have increasingly come to understand that there are plausible ways of judging whether circumstances are conducive for getting effective results. By analogy there must be similar sets of conditions for judging the probability of success in different types of institutional change. The same kind of risk-to-return framework that we have come to apply in judging the appropriateness of project lending can be applied to institutional change.

Finally, what might evaluation contribute? I have come to see that evaluation is unlikely to provide answers to challenges that are fully robust in methodological terms. To me the key is not in how precise the answer is, but in whether we are looking for answers in the right domain, and whether we are focusing on the right kind of questions. Two areas seem to be of particular importance: describing the enabling conditions for successful institutional change—what are they and what can evaluation tell us about them? And, second, how we can make better use of the local knowledge, of local capacity, in defining the "how to," without foregoing the benefits of international experience.

Panelist comments

*Charles F. Sabel*

Like the first speaker, I was struck by how little was actually said in the papers and session about evaluation and the World Bank's own activities. I was also struck by how little was said—in fact, nothing—about how the private actors in the economy you are trying to encourage evaluate themselves. It is as though it were just obvious that they already evaluate themselves effectively, when it is not obvious at all. I believe there is a reason for the omission, which is (paradoxically) the particular way institutions are defined and linked to evaluation.

Given the narrow way institutions have been defined, it is easy to see not only that the definition is open to question but that there is an alternative, which connects innovations in the evaluation of private firms to reconsideration of the evaluation of public sector institutions. Let me show you how I think you got there, why it is possible to do better, and what some of the implications of switching the focus might be.

I believe that the operative definition behind most of what you have been discussing is the following: institutions are arrangements through which potential collaborators achieve the benefits of cooperation while minimizing the risk of opportunism. This interpretation, I claim, is narrow and misleading but completely understandable. The path that leads to it in the academic literature, and from there to amalgamation in your own discussions, goes like this:

In the 1930s, Ronald Coase made the brilliant observation that markets cannot be the most efficient form of solving all coordination problems. If they were, there would be no large organizations called firms that replace markets for a certain domain of cooperation. The existence of firms, in other words, marks the domain in which organizations are more efficient than markets.

The next step is Oliver Williamson's definition of this domain as the one in which the potential for cooperation may go unrealized as long as it depends on the use of project- or asset-specific resources that are under the control of separate owners. The background picture is familiar. Suppose I have a capacity (to dig a coal mine in a particular place) that can be used only in a project in conjunction with a like capacity of yours (the ability to build a coal-burning power station in the locale where I might eventually mine). In this situation the "holdup" problem arises. I fear that if I invest first, you will wait, knowing that my assets are now dedicated to your purposes, and you will delay your coinvestment until you have renegotiated the terms of our agreement to your benefit. The parallel logic applies on both sides, and there will be no project and hence no gains from cooperation.

The most direct of several closely related solutions is vertical integration, with one potential cooperator buying the assets of the other. Since there is now one operator and investor with a single, integral interest, the formerly joint effort goes forward under one sovereign owner. It is a short step from the understanding that institutions can be used to solve the problem of holdups in the private economy to asking what implications that realization might have for the provision of public service. That question generates the series of extremely interesting and provocative papers delivered at this conference, which carry forward, with extreme consequence and real insight, that basic program.

Eduardo Wiesner presents the possible microfoundations of the holdup problem in the public sector and shows how a specific type of public actor, such as teachers' unions, emerges to expropriate others under conditions unique to the public sector. Here is a theoretical underpinning for applying the Williamsonian idea in the public sector.

Ricardo Hausmann proposes an ingenious remedy to public sector holdups through something called a national fiscal council. The basic idea is to create a counterinstitution to public sector rent-seeking by forcing people to accept a constitutional limit on themselves. Knowing that normal democratic institutions operating under parliamentary authority invite holdups, citizens authorize an extraparliamentary council to impose limits on the changes in the debt levels a parliament can contract to finance extortionate deals.

A second proposed remedy, found in Brian Levy's paper, supposes that we cannot solve the fundamental problem of rent-seeking in the public sector of the developing world and therefore should not seek to apply first-best design standards in contemplating improvements. Rather, we should acknowledge that we live in a second-best world and try to determine what, in context, is the best acceptable situation. I believe that this prudence in fact frames the practical work, insofar as it judges that institutions can be part of a solution rather than a source or symptom of a problem.

But given this sensible and practical diagnosis, evaluation can only be an afterthought. It can only help, essentially, in the last, frankly second-best situation. And there, in passing from the first- to the second-best world, one loses the ability to define criteria by which to evaluate the evaluation.

It is not a big surprise, then, that when institutions are linked to evaluation in this way, suddenly evaluation disappears, and the issue is back to property rights in the private sector and hard choices that skirt the boundaries of democracy in managing public affairs. But this narrow view of institutions, as I said, is theoretically questionable and empirically implausible, for reasons that Coase himself anticipated. Coase was (as is often the case with originators) more broad minded and inquiring than his followers. His central theme was that under some conditions organizations can be more efficient than markets. He did not posit as a central issue a "short list" of institutional types that, under a correspondingly short list of circumstances, outperform arms-length exchange. He looked forward to the question of vertical integration and quite explicitly disavowed what became the Williamsonian interpretation.

Coase said quite clearly in his early article in the 1930s (and then in his Nobel lecture) that there are many ways to solve the holdup problem that do not involve vertical integration, and he remained agnostic on the best among them. His argument against the centrality and certainly the inevitability of vertical integration, and implicitly for the multiplicity of possible solutions, was empirical. He visited the factory of A. O. Smith, then and now an independent supplier of auto frames to General Motors in Milwaukee. If A. O. Smith could remain independent (acting essentially as an exclusive supplier to General Motors of some products while producing other products for other car makers) the vertical integration argument and its close relatives hardly looked compelling. Call this the hyperacademic objection to the narrow definition of institutions.

Now let me add a hyperpractical objection. Japanese firms and production methods work by intensifying collaboration among independent units. That is, they work by increasing mutual dependence among potential collaborators without using property as a means of solving the holdup problem. They are thus, if you like, Coaseian but not Williamsonian. For a long time people thought the Japanese could operate this way because they had a culture of trust that made them resist opportunism among themselves and those adopted into their business family. The assumption was that the Japanese system could be used only in Japan, or at least among notional Japanese. It is now generally accepted, however, that the least Japanese people on earth, namely the Americans, are quite good at adapting these methods, and there are good data sets to show that.

So something else is going on. What is it? Part of the answer is that the very organization of production in this new system forces people to collaborate so intensely that, as they are exchanging information about what they do by way of solving joint problems, they are also constantly able to monitor each other. If parts are produced one at a time (the case in just-in-time production), then a defect is noticed immediately (there is no inventory from which to draw a reserve), and the source of the defect must be identified and corrected before production proceeds (otherwise the problem recurs). Having suppliers and customers codesign parts produces analogous effects. Such discussion, together with some straightforward sharing rules (for example, suppliers keep an agreed share, for a set time, of the proceeds from efficiency gains beyond those anticipated at the start of a project), provides just the kind of information about capacities and intention that is needed for monitoring without recourse to control through property rights. Because there is no gap between contract and performance, the familiar problems of opportunism are no longer menacing in their familiar form.

Thus a class of institutions has emerged that learns by constantly evaluating itself and pooling information garnered in applying means to ends—and then redefining the ends in the light of what has been learned. The new institutions may not amount to a full-fledged model of the new corporation. Important questions remain open, especially the relation among day-to-day design, error detection, and project selection based on the new forms of decentralized coordination among insiders (including suppliers and employees). The large, strategic choices regarding lines of business, mergers, acquisitions, and the like are still based on centralized boards of directors (representing outside shareholders) that continue to play a crucial role in these traditional matters of corporate governance. But the methodologies for designing, making, and calculating returns on products in the new way are all well developed. Indeed, notice of the breakthrough in institutions that cooperate by mutual self-evaluation is available in your local newspaper. Yet the subject is left at the margins of a discussion that proposes to advance our understanding of the connection between institutions and evaluation.

What are the implications of this class of institutions for the World Bank? First, many of the firms the Bank now intentionally or unintentionally helps through its actual operating programs at the country level are trying to adopt these methods. I know as much from my association with a Bank program in Mexico, where the money spent to help adopt these methods is booked, in effect, as "money not fraudulently deployed." Even a cursory review of current writings on economic development reveals the accelerating diffusion of the Japanese-inspired organizational methods. Intentionally or not, the Bank will wind up financing systems that are building firms of this kind.

In theory, this fact should make the Bank's job easier. When the aim is having firms learn to evaluate themselves, the Bank can easily evaluate firms by examining the quality of their methods of error detection and proposing systems for improving these. It can also easily evaluate the people it sends to teach the firms to do these kinds of things by reviewing their reviews of error-detection methods. Put another way, as firms strive to diagnose their own problems by comparing their current performance with the performance of more capable competitors (benchmarking), the Bank in fact can learn whether their efforts are effective by observing whether performance improves according to the measures used for comparison. Developing benchmarking and related instruments that small, unsophisticated firms can apply (with qualified help) poses just the kinds of problems of collective action and market failure the Bank should be trying to solve. So does pooling enough data to be informative (without polluting databases with spurious entries). And so does fostering the creation of institutions that can provide assistance in benchmarking and the use of the performance deficits it reveals. The evaluation problem is becoming easier because of the very nature of the production system the Bank is trying to foster at the micro level.

What about the macro level? Here I offer two points to arouse your curiosity and indicate the architecture of the larger argument that informs these remarks. The first starts with Hausmann's paper, which, I said, gave exactly the right theoretical answer to the question of what we should do to eliminate public sector rent-seeking. The assumption is that only cohesive (self-interested and correspondingly self limited) owners can avoid holdups. Jonathan Breul's criticism of this paper goes right to its primary limitations. Efforts to reduce the cost of the public sector will fail unless they are linked to efforts to increase its efficiency. Further, using external discipline to impose debt ceilings (the extra-parliamentary council) obstructs just the kind of information exchange within the public sector, and between it and private actors, necessary for efficiency gains.

To put this point in the language used here: tension exists between the (putatively) ideal ownership structure (getting the people to exercise control over the government that they, in their dispassionate moments, would want to exercise) and the demands of efficient collaboration (producing public services of the right kind at the best possible price). Breul says that doing the second is better than worrying about the first. Arguments about the possibilities of intensified collaboration without recourse to traditional notions of ownership provide a theoretical backdrop for understanding how this intuition, which is born of practical experience, could be correct. The further and pressing question is how the public sector might look if the new principles of collaboration emerging in firms and the correlate types of (self) evaluation were applied to it.

This question brings me to my second point. One way to begin imagining this extensive, profound reorganization of the public sector and the reconceptualization of democracy that it entails is to learn from public sector efforts to provide benchmarking and related services to firms striving to master the new disciplines of cooperation. These micro developments are no substitute for macro solutions, but they may in part prefigure those solutions and suggest elements of the new institutional framework that can be provided only at the national or macro level.

If the foregoing is right, the Bank's understandings of theory are narrowing its possibilities, just as practical activity in the economy is expanding them. There is a new kind of institution that is easier to build than familiar ones precisely because of the way it joins evaluation and learning. The availability of this institution should help in fostering improvements in the public sector at both the micro and macro levels. The Bank needs better reasons than those presented so far for not considering the possibilities.

## Panelist comments

*Lyn Squire*

We have been asked to discuss the implications of institutional economics for the theory and practice of evaluation. Unlike my fellow panelists, I am neither an institutional economist nor an evaluation expert, so I feel well qualified to speak with a certain degree of freedom.

That said, I have read the papers presented at this conference. So I thought I would set out the two lessons that I took away from them as they apply in the specific context of the Bank's evaluation activities. In particular, I want to focus my remarks on how one evaluates changes in the state's ability to deliver services through changes in the structure of institutional rules and regulations, both formal and informal.

The two lessons, which I will illustrate with examples, are the following:

- If we believe that it is the set of formal and informal rules that determine the behavior of public servants, then when attempting institutional reform, we need to identify which rules to change and why we believe the reforms will improve performance. This should be the basis for the design of the interventions. I'll draw on Mary Shirley's paper (Chapter 7 in this volume) on performance contracts to elaborate this point, and on research by Beth King to illustrate the implications for evaluation.

- When measuring institutional performance, we may often have to rely on subjective assessments of various kinds. Here I'll draw on the paper by Ajay Chhibber (Chapter 3 in this volume) and the background work that was done for the *1997 World Development Report*, which illustrates how subjective assessments can be used to measure overall government performance. I'll then use background research done by Lant Pritchett, Deepa Narayan, and colleagues for an earlier WDR to illustrate how the same idea can be used to evaluate institutional interventions at the project level.

### Incentives

The key point in Shirley's paper is that contracts did not change behavior because the real rules and regulations governing behavior were not changed. Indeed, some of the contracts simply reflected actual behavior, and where the contracts differed from actual behavior, no mechanisms were in place to bring about real change. Thus, in the design of Bank interventions, we should be focusing on measures that will genuinely change behavior. In the specific case of public enterprises, we could focus on:

- More competition, either in the market or for the market

- Rewards and penalties based on performance

- An enforcement mechanism to ensure that contracts, implicit or explicit, have credibility

Such measures should be identified and made explicit in the design of projects aimed at improving institutions. But, of course, we cannot know with certainty that any of these interventions will have the desired outcome. That is why we need evaluation. And if we are to learn from such interventions, we will need to ensure that evaluation specifies the counterfactual, as Joe Stiglitz emphasized in his opening remarks.

The research project managed by Beth King deals explicitly with the counterfactual. It examines five innovative World Bank education projects that involve different degrees of decentralized decisionmaking over such matters as the selection of teachers and the allocation of school budgets. The research project built into these efforts control groups and other mechanisms to get the best possible measure of impact. With these mechanisms it is possible to learn the effects of the different institutional arrangements.

The research illustrates a general point. The World Bank, through its projects, is engaged in a range of genuine social experiments—poverty projects, environmental projects, and privatization projects, to name a few, most of which have a major institutional dimension. And in each case we are innovating.

Evaluating innovations and sharing the results with other countries is an international public good. Each country by itself will tend to underinvest in this activity because the benefits accrue to other countries. There is therefore a strong rationale for international agencies to engage in this activity. Yet too little has been done. David de Ferranti and others (Chapter 12 in this volume), for example, note that evaluations of the benefits of early childcare programs are few. The Bank has a tremendous opportunity to step in and use the networks and the Operations Evaluation Department to implement a program to evaluate innovative projects in each sector. This would provide truly valuable information that could form the foundation of the Knowledge Bank.

### Perceptions

Let me now turn to the use of subjective assessments in evaluating institutional performance. As Chhibber explained, the *1997 World Development Report—The State in a Changing World*—conducted a survey of over 3,700 enterprises in 69 countries. The questions were on predictability of rule making, concerns about crime, prevalence of corruption, and so on.

In each case the survey asked for the entrepreneur's perception of performance. Together, the responses provided a composite view of how the business sector assessed government performance. Of course, there is no reason why the views of business people should form the only (or even the most important) basis for assessing government performance. But the exercise did make it possible to develop quantitative indices from which to conduct more rigorous statistical tests.

Chhibber's paper showed that the assessment appeared to be an important predictor of both economic and social progress. This in turn suggests that appropriate use of such surveys over time could be a means of tracking government performance and gauging the impact of changes in the structure of incentives influencing government behavior. The essential characteristics of this exercise—subjective assessments translated into quantitative indices for use in statistical analysis—can be a valuable tool for evaluation at the project level. Recent research by Pritchett and colleagues illustrates the point.

The researchers used subjective measures to examine the effect of various degrees of participation in rural water supply projects on project outcomes. Participation was measured on a continuum—from information sharing, to more in-depth consultation, to shared decisionmaking, to control over decisionmaking—at three points in the project cycle: design, construction, and operation.

Using a quantitative index based on these subjective assessments, they were able to use regression analysis to provide some of the most compelling evidence to date that different institutional arrangements involving increasing degrees of participation are positively related to project success.

## Conclusion

To conclude let me just draw the two points together. Where we have a really innovative project, we should be willing to invest the resources to build into the design an evaluation technique, such as a control group, to arrive at a true measure of impact. And where we have many examples of a new institutional approach, we should be willing to use subjective measures of institutional change so that we can draw on standard statistical techniques to measure impact. Both suggestions are attempts to ensure that we have systematic and rigorous evaluation of projects involving institutional change.

Panelist comments

*Sharon Capeling-Alakija*

The mantra of the meeting has been "institutions matter, but we must get the incentives right." This is fine as long as we remember Voltaire's dictum that the best is the enemy of the good or, to paraphrase Machiavelli, that if we focus too much on what should be rather than on what is, we may never get to what is possible.

This poses a dilemma that has been implicit throughout much of the discussions in the conference and was considered most explicitly in Brian Levy's paper. The options are whether it is better to focus on "first best" development policies that have worked in already developed societies and risk accomplishing little or nothing in societies that are not ready for them, or whether it is better to adapt development policies to local capacity and risk running out of benchmarks for measuring their effectiveness.

It's a fine line, and in my comments I am going to focus on some of the methodological challenges to evaluation that have emerged from our discussions. But first a few words about incentives themselves and their implications for methodology.

If evaluations create incentives, then evaluators must think more strategically about the purpose of an evaluation, for whom the evaluation is being conducted, and what the process will be for absorbing the evaluation findings. This seminar has raised a number of very real methodological questions about incentives for which answers are not easily found. They include such questions as these: How do we set up the "right" kind of incentives in evaluation? How do we apply incentives? Is there an incentive structure that really will encourage service in the public interest and, if so, how do we document it in the context of evaluation? How do we detect the "real" incentives that are at work?

When we touch on the "real" rather than the "official" incentive structure, we are, in fact, mapping power. We are looking not at organograms but at sociograms—the "eminence grise," the "kitchen cabinet," and so forth—that never find their way onto the organization chart. To be operational, this kind of evaluation requires methodologies drawn from political science, sociology, anthropology, and even psychology—not just economics. The very nature of these issues, which touch the political core of institutions and organizations, entails risk. An examination of the institutional environment of the evaluation function itself is required. And this inevitably touches upon the issue of independence of evaluation, which in my view, comes down to four words: access, choice, clout, protection. Let me elaborate on what these four words mean for evaluators:

1.  *Access* means access to the boss for a reciprocal exchange of information and authority; to the governance body for a mutual understanding of goals; to

senior managers to disseminate awareness of the criteria for developing and evaluating projects; to information for common ground for mutual understanding; and to resources (time, human, financial) with the authority to manage them and set priorities.

2. *Choice* means choice of subjects for evaluation and of evaluators.

3. *Clout* means authority and freedom to establish evaluation policy, to develop guidelines and procedures, to oversee compliance and report on it frankly and transparently, and to influence enforcement.

4. *Protection* means protection of careers of evaluation staff from political and personal interference and from conflict of interest.

Other methodological concerns emanating from neoinstitutional economics include how to assess policies and programs that don't have a "bottom line"; how to measure the role of culture; how to assess institutional capacity; and how to judge intangibles such as commitment, flexibility, esprit de corps, and adaptability.

Speakers over the last two days have underscored the need to get evaluation incorporated during program design and the need to deliver evaluative information in a timely manner if we expect it to be used as a tool for management. At the same time, it is worth remembering that in public institutions we are functioning in a political economy, not a market economy, and the obstacles are not easily overcome.

We need to understand the limitations on outsiders and realize that using coercion, upsetting the equilibrium, exploiting uncertainty, and engaging in a trickery will jeopardize the sustainability of our efforts.

In this era of evaluation primacy, some modesty is also in order. Since we are in Washington it might be wise to ponder the citation from the Greeks made by Dick Morris after his recent fall from grace: "Those whom the gods would destroy they first make mad with power."

Panelist comments

*Ray C. Rist*

The theme of this volume raises issues for evaluation that have not been part of the conventional evaluation discourse. Indeed, there is little discussion of institutions in the evaluation literature, which tends to focus on projects, programs, and policies. How much less, then, has the focus been on how to evaluate the role of institutions in development. Thus the conference breaks new ground, albeit not in a neatly patterned fashion. The theme of the conference forces the evaluation community to consider a new frame of reference, the institution. This new concept presents the further challenge to the evaluation community of understanding the relation of institutions to development.

The comments that follow raise four issues that evaluators would need to clarify if this new frame of reference is to find its way into the "what and how" of evaluation studies. The "what" refers to the focus, which here is institutions (instead of, or in addition to, projects, programs, and policies), and the "how" refers to the implications for the evaluator's methodological tools if new ones are needed to study institutions. It is by no means clear what this new frame of reference (institutions) means for the evaluation community, and it would be premature to assume that the concept will be included immediately in the evaluator's toolbox. The scope and conceptual imprecision of what is meant by an "institution" suggests that evaluators will be wary of this new concept for a long time. But the dialogue has to start somewhere, and so here we go.

## Evaluation of institutions versus evaluation of organizations

First, evaluators must know precisely what is meant by institutions when they talk about evaluating them. The evaluation community has some conceptual agreement, largely sociological, on the notion of an "organization." For example, organizations can be formal or informal, large or small, permanent or transitory. But whatever their specific characteristics, organizations are identifiable social units that establish rules, norms, procedures, criteria for admission, rewards and sanctions, and most often have hierarchies. In this context, organizations can be schools, prisons, day care centers, juvenile gangs, or factories, to name five.

These organizations can be described and analyzed in terms of the characteristics noted above as well as an array of variables familiar to evaluators, patterns of interaction, achievement of goals, fiscal costs, formal versus informal patterns of communication, and so forth. The organizations are likely to have within them activities that can be evaluated, an after school tutoring program, a day care center that mainstreams children with disabilities into regular activities, a hospital that undertakes an AIDS prevention program, and so forth. These are rather discrete, bounded, and definable projects or programs, as are the organizations within which they are housed. An organizational evaluation would be largely then an aggregation of the evaluations of the various units, programs, and activities within them.

309

But how are we to evaluate institutions when they are defined, for example by North (1990) and cited in Nugent's paper, as society's rules of the game, which cannot be seen, felt, or even measured? (Others at this conference have referred to institutions as a combination of ethics, values, and cultural norms.) Evaluators generally try to stay out of theological discussions when thinking about measurement of performance or impacts. But defining institutions as ethics and values, or as combinations of factors that cannot be seen, felt, or measured, seems to have about as much precision as giving guidance on how to count angels on the head of a pin. It also suggests that the conventional evaluation concern with outcomes or impacts may be largely misplaced if not entirely inappropriate.

This characterization may overstate the case, but there currently appears to be little common conceptual ground between evaluators and new institutional economists. Much work needs to be done and ideas debated before the two disciplines can find mutual areas of conceptual agreement. This conference has provided an opportunity for the economists to share their views with the evaluation community. This is all to the good. But the reciprocal dialogue also needs to take place.

## How do we measure institutional reform?

The need for institutional reform, if countries are to achieve their development objectives, has been a recurring theme in this conference. Countries are admonished to "get the institutions right." As hard as it is to know what it means to get the institutional arrangements "right" when they cannot be seen, felt, or measured, it is fair to ask how one will know when an institution has reached that point. Are there indicators of the outputs one might use as a proxy measure? What about a set of indicators for outcomes or impacts? Admonitions for change are less than helpful if there is no way to know specifically what is intended or how success will be revealed. An evaluator might ask: How does one set up a monitoring system for tracking the reform of institutional arrangements?

Indicators might be a good starting point for developing a discussion between evaluators and neoinstitutional economists. If they can reach agreement on what dimensions of institutional reform are subject to even the lightest measurement, a common understanding on how to measure such reform may emerge. The indicators can be of any nature as long as they are defined and agreed on as ways to track and monitor institutional reform. At present, evaluators have some strategies to assess whether an organization is or is not getting it right, both at the procedural and substantive levels. Moving into the domain of institutions presents new challenges, first to understand what it means for an institution to get it right vis-à-vis reform and, second, to document whether or not the reform has happened.

## What works and when in institutional reform?

Woven through the papers are suggestions on how to bring about institutional reform—whether via legislation, fiscal councils, performance contracts, or privatization. These and other policy tools are presumed to be in the toolkit of policy reformers. The gist of the papers is that policymakers should select the appropriate tool or tools and then use them to effect the desired reform.

But the papers do not take the analysis far enough. They should go two steps further and suggest, first, how to determine whether the appropriate tool was chosen in the first place. It is easy to imagine an inappropriately chosen tool influencing the direction and intensity of reform efforts. The comparative domain is missing. For example, when do we privatize instead of legislate? Or when do we use fiscal councils instead of regulation? There are no answers here. We are given little guidance in this collection of papers on when to pick which policy instrument to achieve which reform objective.

The second step would be to analyze the effect of the selected policy tool on reform. Each policy tool has its own strengths and weaknesses, and institutional reformers may want to know which tools are the more robust and which the weaker for particular reform objectives. The evaluation community knows something of the tradeoffs among tools at the micro level—for example, when incarceration is more or less effective than juvenile diversion programs for particular target groups of juveniles, or when crop rotation is more or less effective than additional fertilizers for soil replenishment. But when one moves to the macro level of institutional reform, the evaluation community falls silent. So, too, do the neoinstitutional economists, if the current set of papers are any indication.

The end result suggests a cautionary stance: we need to be careful of the prescription to use one or more tools to achieve reform objectives when we do not know how well one tool or cluster of tools works in comparison with others. Picking particular tools for particular institutional reform objectives ought to be based on more than random chance, which argues for designed interventions where different policy instruments can be evaluated against agreed on reform criteria.

## Political climate and institutional reform, what is the relation?

The papers are largely silent on the issue of power, and thus there is little articulation of a relation between power and reform or between politics and reform. Consequently, they are silent on when, how, and whether one can get the institutions right in the absence of the political power to do so. Further, there is no discussion on where that power needs to reside administratively or organizationally if the reform efforts are to succeed. Finally, there is no discussion on which individual roles are pivotal to institutional reform. There are persons in powerful roles in any society. Which of these persons needs to be aligned with reform efforts for there to be a chance of success?

These papers seem to avoid dealing with the messy business of political compromise, concessions, and corruption as realities to be recognized and addressed in any effort to engineer change. Because they are not mentioned does not mean they do not exist. They also do not go away because they are not mentioned. Save for the paper by Eduardo Wiesner, little attempt is made to answer the brute question of what it takes for those with power to want to support reform. When and how does one create the arrangements so that institutional reform coincides with the self-interests of the powerful? And if these interests do not coincide, what are the implications for reform? The answers are not in these papers.

The evaluation community may not have perfect answers to these issues, but it does recognize the reality of political power and how such power shapes policies, programs, and projects. Evaluators are constantly encouraged to talk to all relevant stakeholders, including the powerful. That there will be contending political agendas is taken for granted. These agendas should then be factored into the study as a matter of course. Sensitivity to political power is one contribution the evaluation community can make in the discussions with the neoinstitutional economists on the preconditions for successful reform.

## Postscript

Social-science-based project, program, and policy evaluation gives its practitioners a different perspective for studying change from that of practitioners of new institutional economics. The differences are both conceptual and methodological, and it will not be known for sometime whether these differences are insurmountable.

# Postscript: the institutional dimension of evaluation

Robert Picciotto

Inevitably, like blind people groping the elephant, each participant got something different out of the conference. To me the papers included in this volume highlight some specific challenges for the evaluation profession. These challenges are not new. They involve generic questions with which we grapple with everyday as evaluators. But as the profile of our business rises these questions are being asked with ever greater urgency.

Within tight resource constraints and given the inevitable trade-offs between accuracy and timeliness, how should evaluation allocate its efforts—inputs, processes, outcomes, or impacts? Given data limitations, how can the counterfactual be simulated? Do objectives matter in judging outcomes? If not, what is the implication for accountability? How are evaluation benchmarks set and who should be involved in the evaluation process? It is precisely because such questions cannot elicit simple and standard answers that evaluation professionals are needed. Yet, evaluators seem unable to persuade practitioners and researchers that they have reasonable ways of dealing with these basic methodological dilemmas.

In fact, as a profession, evaluation has made considerable headway in inculcating more rigor to its work while improving the relevance of the topics it is addressing. Yet, even more progress is needed in living up to the high-quality standards our clients are expecting. At the same time, evaluators need to do a better job in disseminating and explaining the good work we are already doing.

Development evaluators have established considerable credibility in the assessment of investment projects and adjustment policies. But they lack basic concepts and instruments insofar as institutional development is concerned. This is not a trivial challenge considering that capacity building is now widely perceived as the centerpiece of development assistance.

## Development and institutions

The paradigm shift triggered by recent advances in institutional economics will have profound implications for development evaluation. This is because, as suggested by Jeffrey Nugent, we may be witnessing the birth of a "new development economics" that will concentrate on explaining the linkages between institutions, organizations, and human welfare. As this vision materializes, the new development economics will be neoinstitutional. Its grand theme will be the interaction between the enabling envi-

313

ronment (the rules of the game) and the "players" (that is, the individuals and organizations which are both the agents and the beneficiaries of development). This does not mean that neoclassicism is dead. Instead, the constraints imposed by its tenets will be relaxed to reflect neoinstitutionalist findings. Just as the end of World War II triggered a historic crusade to comprehend and encourage the processes of growth in poor countries, the end of the cold war has induced a resurgence of interest in the bewildering changes taking place in developing countries. So, to paraphrase Mark Twain, reports of the death of development economics may well be exaggerated. Developing countries have become the engine of the global economy. And they are where the bulk of the world's population lives. Therefore, more than ever, economists are probing what Adam Smith called the "natural progress of opulence."

By now, the notion that "institutions matter" has become solidly rooted in development experience. Following a brief euphoria in the early 1980s, it became evident that the neoclassical model fails to explain adequately the highly differentiated economic performance of developing and transition economies. The contrast between the East Asian miracle and the disappointments associated with development programs in sub-Saharan Africa—as well as the travails of the formerly socialist economies—have brought to the fore the role of enabling institutions in promoting and sustaining policy reform.

The central role of institutions in development has been illustrated in concrete terms throughout the conference. Thus, Ajay Chhibber highlighted the fundamental role of the state for efficient markets, for productive investment, and for equitable access to development opportunity. Specifically, he provided concrete evidence to show that institutions matter for economic growth, private investment, quality of life, and economic rates of return for development projects.

Conversely, John Eriksson traced the appalling human costs associated with extreme dysfunctions in governance to imbalances in the production of various types of goods, especially public goods, government goods, and civil goods. Concentrating on the budgetary processes of Latin America, Ricardo Hausmann observed that chronic fiscal deficits are equivalent to a "tragedy of the commons" characterized by free riding, overexploitation of a scarce resource, opportunistic manipulation of data to achieve electoral ends, cyclical resort to conservative fiscal measures to achieve credibility in financial markets, and so on.

Seeking to understand the systemic causes of failure in the crucial arena of "externalities," Eduardo Wiesner pinpointed public sector rent-seeking as the main obstacle to development. Thus, he challenged the "immaculate conception" theory of governance and explained government failure in terms of the deliberate capture of state institutions by rent-seekers and the unwitting complicity of the public in the process.

A corollary of Wiesner's thesis is that the veil of ignorance under which rent-seekers operate needs to be torn, and this implies an enhanced role for independent evaluation in the monitoring of public goods contracts as well as in the oversight of the collective action mechanisms that oversee the design and implementation of such contracts. In other words, Wiesner postulates a growing role for evaluation in the new development economics, both as a meta-discipline focusing on the efficacy of institutions and as a distinct development institution in its own right.

## Evaluation of institutions

A fine example of the kind of evaluation needed to illuminate institutional design was provided by Mary Shirley. She highlighted the difficulties that stand in the way of inducing accountability and transparency through intra-state contracting systems (even for market-oriented public enterprises). She showed that performance contracts had little impact on profitability or productivity for one or more of the following reasons: incoherent policy goals, poorly designed contracts, information asymmetry and lack of competition, weak managerial incentives, and absence of credible commitment to accurately monitor and enforce the contracts.

In the same vein, Brian Levy noted that the risk of government failure must be explicitly addressed in the search for workable approaches to regulation. Not only is credibility critical but its achievement requires matching the regulatory framework to the capacity to regulate. In particular, the design of regulatory practices must take explicit account of the quality of the judicial system; the checks and balances between the executive and the legislative branches; the influence, competence, and independence of the civil service; and the restraining influence of civil society.

Thus, the task of evaluating a regulatory framework emerges as a highly complex endeavor combining the skills of the economist, the political scientist, the sociologist, the sectoral specialist, and the policy analyst. Ultimately, for Brian Levy, the search for useful institutional lessons "puts a burden on the evaluators themselves, especially in terms of their professional creativity and judgment."

Reexamination of the respective roles of various levels of government raises similarly complex issues for evaluators. This is a high priority for evaluation since, according to Anwar Shah, the demise of centrally planned economic systems, globalization, and the information revolution favors a jurisdictional alignment involving greater decentralization. This is especially true in developing countries that lack the advanced information gathering, transmission networks, and reliable civil servants needed for effective centralized systems.

However, the design, monitoring, and evaluation of decentralized fiscal and administrative systems must be guided by a deep understanding of political and cultural factors, systematic institutional analyses, and effective matching of internal reform initiatives and external support. Thus, Shah highlighted the complementarity of three kinds of institutional changes—improved judicial accountability, financial management strengthening, and evaluation capacity development both at the federal and local levels.

Conference participants reached a broad consensus regarding the priorities for further work with respect to the evaluation of institutions. First, as a follow up to the promising analytics of the *World Development Report* more rigorous cross-country data collection and interpretation were proposed with respect to alternative measures of institutional capital and their impact on development outcomes. Second, Robert Klitgaard argued that we need more case studies of development programs and projects guided by a neoinstitutionalist perspective. Third, Joseph Stiglitz suggested that systematic social experimentation be built into development interventions. Evaluation research should proceed on all three fronts.

## The institutional role of evaluation

For many conference participants, evaluation is an integral part of the institutional framework needed to achieve equitable and sustainable development. According to Jorge Desormeaux, "the success of a bold and unprecedented reform like that of the Chilean pension system would not have been possible if a careful evaluation process had not taken place at all stages" of the reform.

Similarly, David de Ferranti underscored the role of monitoring and evaluation in shaping cost-effective, well-targeted early childcare and education programs. In this context, he and his colleagues stress the value of a piloting phase with clear objectives at the outset of a major program, the need for random impact evaluations and benchmark surveys to ensure objective program evaluation as well as the role of performance-based evaluations in sustaining broad-based political support.

The case for a national fiscal council was articulated by Ricardo Hausmann based on the notion that objective and independent gathering and evaluation of economic and accounting information are as important for fiscal management as they are for monetary policy—hence the proposal for an independent authority combining responsibility for fiscal monitoring and evaluation with jurisdictional oversight of public debt ceilings.

Finally, according to Sanjay Pradhan, reinvigorating institutions in countries characterized by a past record of arbitrary and dysfunctional rule will occur only through restoration of the credibility and accountability of the state. In turn, this requires greater contestability and transparency in policymaking, the exercise of more voice from the public, the use of independent watchdogs, and tailor-made arrangements of checks and balances among the executive and legislative branches and the civil society. This suggests a pluralistic, participatory approach to evaluation capacity development.

## Evaluation as an institution

More generally, the clear implication of the conference deliberations is that evaluation capacity should be strengthened in developing countries, since without it the quality of public expenditures management is unlikely to improve. Empirically, we know that evaluation is part and parcel of the new public management movement that is sweeping the industrial democracies. There is no reason why it should not be promoted in the developing countries. Without evaluation the immune system of the state will remain weak and development governance will not be what it should be.

This proposition is consistent with a neoinstitutional approach to the role of evaluation. As an institution, evaluation provides an effective way to overcome information asymmetry between the people as principal and the state as agent. It is a useful complement to the accountability instruments provided by improved auditing standards and more effective financial management. Thus, it can help improve the incentives framework facing public sector managers. Where it is independent of the line ministries, it strengthens the credibility of government commitment to improve fiscal management.

From a neoinstitutionalist perspective, evaluation is part of the framework of rules and regulations within which public sectors operate. To "get the institutions right," it is necessary to combat government failure and collective action dilemmas. And this means finding the right mix among three kinds of evaluation doctrines.

First is independent evaluation—accountability to a central body. It focuses on accountability for results. It is well adapted to situations (for example, Indonesia, Tunisia) where finance or planning ministries have the clout to address a wide range of government failures. It implies substantial delegation to evaluators rather than formula-based evaluation standards that can readily be delegated.

The second stresses self-evaluation—the use of evaluation as an aid to public sector managers operating within a decentralized public sector (for example, Brazil, China, Colombia). This approach responds to a public sector reform strategy based on incentives. It concentrates on quick feedback processes. In this kind of environment, independent evaluation is still needed, but its role is supportive and normative so as to ensure quality and consistency in evaluation standards.

Third is participatory evaluation. It reflects the rise of the voluntary sector and the advent of nongovernmental organizations as full partners in development. It concentrates on the activation of voice mechanisms. It thrives on contestability, advocacy, and transparency. It is evaluation "from the outside in." It can be methodologically messy, and it may lead to perverse results, but it can also be a powerful agent of positive change by facilitating socially sustainable solutions to tough development problems.

Over the long run, these three doctrines are complementary, even synergistic. But at any point in time, trade-offs may be necessary, a judicious balance must be struck. Hence, appropriate sequencing strategies must be designed in evaluation capacity development. The proper mix of participatory, independent, and self-evaluation must be weighed case-by-case in light of initial institutional conditions and opportunities to induce change.

Strengthening of evaluation at only one level may be dysfunctional, especially where rent-seekers can capture the function—either at the center or at the periphery. Generally, evaluation considered as an institution can be conceived in terms of the policy models sketched by Thráinn Eggertsson. In this context, if evaluation is to influence policy, its focus has to shift from one approach to the other as various players adapt their strategies to changing circumstances.

Thus, evaluation managers may have to emphasize one or the other evaluation doctrine as the situation requires. This is akin to the "sailing against the wind" model of reform sketched by Albert Hirschman. Through tacking and triangulation—emphasizing exit, voice, or loyalty as circumstances dictate—evaluation can move forward, even in difficult institutional environments. Thus, while the tactics of evaluation have to adapt to changing circumstances, its strategic objectives are always the same: a win-win outcome for the entire development enterprise.

# List of authors and discussants

**Masood Ahmed:** Director, International Economics Department, World Bank

**Lee J. Alston:** Professor of Economics, University of Illinois, Champaign

**Daniel Artana:** Director, FIEL, Argentina

**Jonathan D. Breul:** Senior Advisor to the Deputy Director for Management, Executive Office of the President, OMB

**Sharon Capeling-Alakija:** Director, Office of Evaluation and Strategic Planning, UNDP

**Juan L. Cariaga:** Executive Director, World Bank; former Minister of Finance, Bolivia

**Eleanor Chelimsky:** President, American Evaluation Association, former Assistant Comptroller-General, United States General Accounting Office

**Ajay Chhibber:** Staff Director, WDR 1997, World Bank

**Tawfiq E. Chowdhury:** Secretary, Ministry of Energy and Mineral Resources, Bangladesh

**Christopher Clague:** Professor of Economics, University of Maryland

**Jorge Desormeaux:** Professor of Economics, Catholic University of Chile

**Thráinn Eggertsson:** Professor of Economics, University of Iceland

**Peter Eigen:** Chairman, Transparency International

**John R. Eriksson:** Former Director, Center for Development Information and Evaluation, USAID

**David de Ferranti:** Director, World Bank

**Jean-Daniel Gerber:** Executive Director, World Bank

**Leonard Good:** Executive Director, World Bank

**Ricardo Hausmann:** Chief Economist, Inter-American Development Bank

**Ishrat Husain:** Principal Adviser, Poverty, Gender, and Public Sector Department, World Bank

**Ruth Jacoby:** Chairman, World Bank Committee on Development Effectiveness

**Leroy Jones:** Professor of Economics, Boston University

**Gautam S. Kaji:** Managing Director, World Bank

**Elmar Kleiner:** Chief, Central and Eastern Europe, Transition Programs, GTZ, Germany

**Robert Klitgaard:** Professor of Economics, University of Natal, South Africa

**Laura Kullenberg:** United Nations Capital Development Fund

**Brian Levy:** Principal Economist, World Bank

**Johannes Linn:** Vice President, World Bank

**Ronald MacLean-Abaroa:** Former Mayor of La Paz, Bolivia

**Gabriel Martinez:** Director of Finance, Social Security Institute, Mexico

**Elizabeth McAllister:** Director, Operations Evaluation Department, World Bank, former Director-General, Performance Review Division, CIDA

**Hedy von Metzsch:** Director, Operations Review Unit, International Cooperation Ministry of Foreign Affairs, Netherlands

**Harris Mule:** Chair, Working Party on Partnership for Capacity Building in Africa, Kenya

**Mustapha K. Nabli:** Former Minister of Finance, Tunisia

**Peter Nicholl:** Executive Director, World Bank

**Jeffrey Nugent:** Professor of Economics, University of Southern California

**Wallace Oates:** Professor of Economics, University of Maryland

**Mancur Olson, Jr.:** Professor of Economics, University of Maryland

**Robert Picciotto:** Director General, Operations Evaluation, World Bank

**Jan Piercy:** Executive Director, World Bank

**Sanjay Pradhan:** Principal Economist, World Bank

**Yingyi Qian:** Assistant Professor of Economics, Stanford University

**Jean Quesnel:** Director, Office of Evaluation, Inter-American Development Bank

**Nohra Rey de Marulanda:** Manager of Integration and Regional Programs, Inter-American Development Bank

**Rudolf Richter:** Professor Emeritus, University of Saarlandes, Germany; co-editor of *Journal of Institutional and Theoretical Economics*

**Ray C. Rist:** Evaluation Adviser, Economic Development Institute, World Bank

**Charles F. Sabel:** Professor of Law and Social Science, Columbia University

**Ismail Serageldin:** Vice President, World Bank

**Anwar Shah:** Principal Evaluation Officer, World Bank

**Mary Shirley:** Chief, Finance and Private Sector Division Policy Research Department, World Bank

**Lyn Squire:** Director, Policy Research Department, World Bank

**Joseph Stiglitz:** Senior Vice President and Chief Economist, World Bank

**William H. van der Eyken:** Committee Member of BBC Children in Need

**Eduardo Wiesner:** Former Minister of Finance, Colombia, and former Executive Director, World Bank

**James D. Wolfensohn:** President, The World Bank Group

**Joseph Wood:** Senior Adviser to the President, World Bank

**William Zartman:** Professor of International Organizations and Conflict Resolution, SAIS, Johns Hopkins University